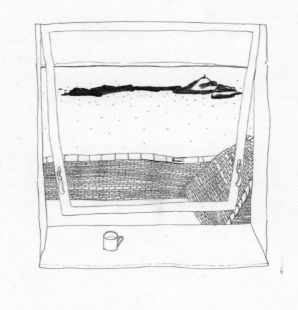

The Fish Store

Lindsey Bareham

MICHAEL JOSEPH
an imprint of
PENGUIN BOOKS

For Ben, Zach and Henry with love

MICHAEL JOSEPH

Published by the Penguin Group
Penguin Books Ltd, 80 Strand, London WC2R 0RL, England
Penguin Group (USA) Inc., 375 Hudson Street, New York, New York 10014, USA
Penguin Group (Canada), 90 Eglinton Avenue East, Suite 700, Toronto, Ontario,
Canada M4P 2Y3 (a division of Pearson Penguin Canada Inc.)
Penguin Ireland, 25 St Stephen's Green, Dublin 2, Ireland (a division of Penguin Books Ltd)
Penguin Group (Australia), 250 Camberwell Road, Camberwell, Victoria 3124, Australia
(a division of Pearson Australia Group Pty Ltd)
Penguin Books India Pvt Ltd, 11 Community Centre, Panchsheel Park,
New Delhi – 110 017, India
Penguin Group (NZ), cnr Airborne and Rosedale Roads, Albany, Auckland 1310,
New Zealand (a division of Pearson New Zealand Ltd)
Penguin Books (South Africa) (Pty) Ltd, 24 Sturdee Avenue, Rosebank,
Johannesburg 2196, South Africa

Penguin Books Ltd, Registered Offices: 80 Strand, London WC2R 0RL, England

www.penguin.com

First published 2006
2

Copyright © Lindsey Bareham, 2006

Set in Meta
Book design by Janette Revill
Printed in Great Britain by Clays Ltd, St Ives plc

A CIP catalogue record for this book is available from the British Library

ISBN-13: 978–0–718–14809–6
ISBN-10: 0–718–14809–6

Contents

An Introduction to the Fish Store

When my sons inherited their father's childhood home, a converted pilchard factory in a small Cornish fishing village, I thought it would be a good idea to record some of the recipes and memories associated with this unusual place. It started as a notebook for their eyes only but soon turned into a journal of stories and anecdotes about the comings and goings at the Fish Store and the changing life of Mousehole, an unspoilt fishing village just three miles west of Penzance in Mount's Bay, near the tip of Cornwall in West Penwith.

Ben John, Zach and Henry's father, was four when the family arrived from France to set up home in 'Mowzal', as the village name is pronounced, and he told colourful childhood stories of growing up in a small fishing village. In those days Mousehole was a working village, with cobblers, carpenters, masons, net- and crab-pot-makers, a butcher and baker, and the harbour was full of big fishing boats. The war years and rationing imposed limitations, but Betty, my sons' paternal grandmother, taught herself to cook from the markets of Paris and knew how to make much out of little and bring variety to the abundance of fresh fish and crabs at her disposal. Then, as now, there were sorrel, wild watercress and blackberries for free and basic vegetables available from nearby inland farms.

There are photographs of the boys' great-grandfather, the notorious bohemian early twentieth-century painter Augustus John, in the harbour. Ben has vivid memories of dreading the command to sit for a painting and then escaping to the rocks for a crab picnic and swim at Dicky Daniel's Cove. Another branch of the John family also lived in Mousehole during the late forties and early fifties and returned years later when Zach and Henry were toddlers. I wanted to record the story of their great-uncle Caspar, when he was an admiral, steaming into the bay on an aircraft carrier, accompanied by a flotilla.

By the time Zach was born in 1978, the charms of the Fish Store and village life had entered my blood. Over the years I developed my own way of dealing with the generous supplies of seafood that came our way from local fisherman and began to introduce my own cooking style into the house. As our two sons grew up, we would spend at least a month in the summer at the Fish Store and often visit for Easter and Christmas, sometimes with family and friends.

One of the most enduring people to affect our visits is Royden Paynter. Royden has made lobster pots in the 'garage' below the house since Henry was born in 1981, but his day job at Newlyn Fish Market sometimes results in the gift of a coolbox full of fish. He grows vegetables in an allotment on a south-facing slope overlooking the sea at the top of Raginnis Hill behind the Fish Store. These plots are notoriously prodigious and his gluts have been my good fortune, forcing me into experimentation and cooking with the seasons. In summer there are tomatoes that taste like tomatoes, wonderful new potatoes and a proliferation of runner beans, broad beans and peas. Beetroot, thanks to Royden, has become a favourite at the Fish Store, particularly for chilled summer borsch or turned into a salad with garlicky yoghurt and freshly chopped coriander.

These days, the Fish Store is one big open-plan living space with three large windows looking out to sea. We watch the fishing boats chugging past as the transforming light plays tricks with the view. On sunny days the magical light turns the sea into shimmering gold and in the winter, when the storm winds howl across the bay, the dark, angry sea is covered with white horses.

I love the place whatever the weather and whatever the time of year, but when the sun streams through the open front door and there is the promise of a crab picnic and fresh fish for supper, there is nowhere I would rather be.

Christmas is a special time in Mousehole. The harbour is filled with floating lights and a Celtic cross twinkles from St Clement's Isle – a small rocky island where once an ancient hermit was said to live – which lies a few hundred yards from the shore. The night before Christmas Eve is celebrated as Tom Bawcock's Eve in the pub, when a humungous

Stargazy Pie, the legendary Mousehole fish pie with pilchards poking through the top, is served to patrons of the Ship Inn on the quayside (see page 53). With the Fish Store windows open wide, we can hear the open-air carol service in the harbour as we sit by the fire and look out to sea with delicious cooking smells whirling round the barn-like room.

Christmas at the Fish Store wouldn't be complete without sea bass, usually caught by Jake Freethy, skipper of *Go For It*, a state-of-the-art fishing boat jointly owned by Ben. We like this elegant fish cooked Chinese-style with ginger and spring onions, or with balsamic vinegar and a mound of home-made game chips cooked in olive oil and tossed with chives. New Year's Eve is usually quiet in Mousehole, so after a particularly luscious fish pie, made extra special with chunks of hard-boiled egg and masses of chopped parsley in a sauce enriched with clotted cream, we might head off to St Ives for the traditional fancy-dress street party.

Mousehole has plenty of its own traditions. One used to be all the children walking over the fields to Lamorna on Easter Sunday. We prefer the daffodil-strewn coastal path which winds past Mousehole Cave – the place where old smugglers hid the contraband goods which they brought over from France in their fishing boats – and ending up at the Wink pub for one of their delicious crab sandwiches.

This book started out as a tribute to the memories of a remarkable house with an interesting background, but took its own momentum, telling the story of my own on–off and on-again relationship with the Fish Store and the village of Mousehole. It is entirely due to my friend Tessa de Mestre, who listened to me talking about past and present Fish Store life and has enjoyed some lovely meals there, that my scribbled jottings turned into a cookbook which spans three generations. Those lists of favourite ways of cooking mackerel, monkfish and sole, and how to make mayonnaise to go with a sink full of crabs waiting to be boiled and picked and then turned into bisque or Betty's crab jambalaya, are here for everyone to enjoy.

Although the recipes are all associated with the Fish Store, it isn't necessary to be by the sea in Cornwall to enjoy cooking them.

Lindsey Bareham, August 2005

Hello, Maid

There is something about Cornwall that gets under the skin and hooks you for life. I'm not sure when the association with St Agnes in north Cornwall started on my father's side of the family. I know they holidayed there when he was a boy and that by the time I was aware of anything very much, his youngest sister, an art mistress in London, had bought the count house of a deserted tin mine on Mithian Downs, just outside the village. When she retired, she moved there and by that time another aunt and her husband had downsized their rare-breed chicken farm in Surrey and bought land near by to augment the chickens with pig farming. Then another uncle followed suit. So it felt as if I'd grown up with strong Cornish connections. It's not true, of course, because the Cornish don't tend to accept someone new as being part of the fabric of a place. I remember one aunt telling me that she'd lived in St Agnes for over thirty years and still felt like a newcomer, or emit, as they call 'visitors' down here.

My father introduced my mother and her family to Cornwall and when my siblings and I came along, we'd holiday *en masse*, with relatives dispatched to different farms and Granny lodged in a B&B above the post office. Somewhere I have a photo of my paternal grandmother on the beach at Chaple Porth wearing a navy blue and white forties-style cotton dress made by her youngest daughter, my Auntie Kitty (or Aunt Kate, as she once announced she would prefer to be called), which I own and which fits me perfectly.

My relationship with St Agnes and Chaple Porth was really only as a holidaymaker. Sure, we got to know the butcher, the greengrocer and the baker and my mum bought eggs and sometimes milk from a farm, but they were holiday relationships. Our friends were people we met on the beach who, like us, came year after year. When I was in my early twenties, I met my future husband there. He had grown up in Cornwall, in a place called Mousehole, somewhere I'd heard of but never visited. His mother, Betty, still lived there, on her own, with a lodger in the 'studio' once used by Ben's father, Edwin, an accomplished water-colourist like his aunt, Gwen John. Ben rarely went to stay. He had transferred his Cornish allegiance, as I was about to do, when he met his first wife, whose family had a holiday home in St Ives.

I can't exactly remember the first time Ben brought me to Mousehole. I do recall the journey, though, and how odd it seemed to be going past the turn-off for St Agnes, which was 'my' part of Cornwall. You get the first promise of Mousehole when you round the corner past the railway station at Penzance and drive along the Promenade towards Newlyn. Newlyn sprawls up and away to the left and peters out along the road which links it to Mousehole. We probably stopped at Jelbert's for an ice cream before swinging past the butcher (now baker) at the bottom of the Coombe on the right and Newlyn's Fish Market and the Tidal Observatory, where Mean Sea Level is calculated daily, on the left. As the road turns up past the pier, you almost turn back on yourself and come parallel with the harbour, where you can see the fishing boats docked up along the quay.

In those days there was a working quarry at Penlee on the road between Newlyn and Mousehole. I remember how white and dusty the road was as we drove past, looking down to the works below on the shoreline. They seemed very Heath Robinson to my inexperienced eye. There was a little railway that ran directly to Newlyn's south pier, taking away the stone and gravel, although the actual quarry was on the Paul side of the road, hidden from view. The quarry closed in the eighties, leaving behind a huge gaping hole from all the dynamiting and a prime piece of real estate by the shore. In the distance you can clearly see St Michael's Mount and beyond that the Lizard peninsula is close enough to see waves crashing on the shore and the shapes of the fields.

Ben pointed out the slipway from the Penlee Lifeboat station. This is where the *Solomon Browne* lived, the lifeboat which, years later, on 19 December 1981, put to sea to assist the coaster *Union Star* and never returned. It was every little boy's dream to grow up to be a member of the lifeboat crew and eight Mousehole men were lost on that fatal occasion. Ben grew up with most of them and, like everyone else in the village, was absolutely devastated when the news was phoned through to us in London. We had already planned to come to Mousehole that Christmas and the misery of the village – no family was untouched – was palpable.

Once past the first sighting of St Clement's Isle, which sits right in front of Mousehole, you come to the Old Coastguard Hotel and moments later the road turns sharply left and immediately to the right, in an awkward dogleg, bringing you face to face with one of the loveliest harbours in Cornwall. I'm ashamed to admit that I can't remember whether the sun was casting a spell over the place, making the sea sparkle and lighting up the granite buildings, or whether I saw Mousehole for the first time without rose-tinted glasses. I know I was impressed by how compact it seemed and how picture-postcard beautiful it looked. You can see virtually the whole village in one sweep of the eyes from this vantage point, past the village clock, the (now gone) Lobster Pot Hotel, right up Raginnis Hill and out of the village. If you know what you're looking for, you can just make out the Fish Store.

At least six people greeted Ben as we drove the short distance to the house. 'You!' someone yelled and 'All right, boy?' said another. I expect they wondered who I was because, looking in my direction, someone said, 'Hello, maid, where you to with Ben banger?' as in 'Hello, female person, where are you going with Ben?' (One of his childhood nicknames was 'Ben banger', because he was always getting into fights.)

Mousehole couldn't have been more different from the Cornwall I knew. This was a proper village centred round a pretty little harbour with fishing boats and seagulls. I was used to beach games on sandy beaches and big waves for body surfing, but there's no beach to speak of here. To be fair, there's been an attempt to rectify that and to a certain extent it works. In the past, lorry-loads of sand have been shipped in from Hayle ('Three miles of golden sand') and elsewhere and emptied at either end of the harbour to make little beaches known locally as the 'old' quay beach, referring to the old quay (originally built in 1393 and extended seawards in the early part of the eighteenth century) at the Fish Store end of the harbour, and the 'new' quay (started in 1837) at the other side. When the tide is in, you can swim in the harbour and jump from the quay into the deep, cold water close to the sea beyond. On the Newlyn side is the so-called 'new beach'. Here the rock is smooth with jagged edges and almost black, with coarse, grey 'sand' reminiscent of the volcanic Canaries. Spurs of rock from the stony beach jutting into the sea make excellent diving boards, but a large, entirely safe natural swimming pool has been built into the rocks and fills with seawater with the tides.

The shoreline on the other, main side of the village is covered with rounded boulders which are collectively known as 'the rocks'. These were repeatedly painted by Ben's father Edwin when he lived here. They have a mesmerizing appeal both for the way they are lodged together and their range of colour through pale grey to tawny and dark brown. Years later, when Zach was four or five, he lost an expensive American trainer while playing on the rocks. It never turned up, but *two* years later someone was fishing in one of the rock pools and – surprise, surprise! – there it was: one nearly new red trainer, instantly recognizable by its distinctive ankle star. The rocks are a child's playground of rock pools and great hiding places for rock hide-and-seek. There's a definite knack to walking with confidence across the rocks at Mousehole. It comes with experience, so lots of visitors never discover the bigger, flatter, more sunbathe-suitable rocks below the Salt Ponds, at the far end of the village. There is one rock arrangement that we love which forms an almost perfect little semi-private sun-trap. I took to the 'flat rock' like a duck to water. Hardly anyone ever goes there and it's next to Dicky Daniel's, a rather lovely cove which is the best ever place to swim.

My strongest memory of coming to Mousehole wasn't the undeniable beauty of the place, it was the relentless screeching of the gulls. There seemed to be no rhyme or reason to it. One bird would start up, gently at first, then build to a crescendo which triggered more and more gulls. If you happened to be close by, it was deafening. In the distance it wasn't too bad, but there was no doubt that the gulls competed with each other to squawk the loudest. I couldn't imagine how anyone got any sleep. I immediately understood why Ben's mother Betty was known as 'Seagull Granny'.

As we made our way along the narrow, twisting road, past the flower-decked, granite fishermen's cottages, and I absorbed the timeless sights and sounds of Mousehole for the first time, I had no inkling what an important part in my life this lovely, typical, small Cornish village was destined to play. I didn't realize it then, but the Fish Store was about to change my understanding of cooking seafood. I would learn how to prepare and cook a munificence of mackerel and monkfish, red mullet and soles, sea bass, squid and scallops and, most memorably, crab.

I can look back now and see that the Fish Store is a treasure trove where some of my most intense memories are locked.

Proper Job

At the far end of the village, past the Methodist chapel, the road forks right up Raginnis Hill or left along St Clement's Terrace. The last building on the left in the terrace is the Fish Store. It stands foursquare on the corner and was built in 1899 for storing and processing pilchards. It had fallen into disuse when, in 1939, my sons' grandparents, Betty and Edwin John, bought it for £300, £600 less than it cost to build forty-odd years before. There are about half a dozen fish stores in varying states of repair dotted around the village and they date back to a time when Mousehole was a thriving fishing port. Other similar buildings were built as net stores, where nets were made, repaired and hung out to dry.

In Cornwall, particularly Mousehole, the local dialect is alive and flourishing. One turn of phrase I particularly like is 'proper job'. It can be applied to anything from a particularly well-made Cornish pasty to a good catch of mackerel. It also refers to a job well done or a clever idea.

It required a huge leap of imagination, I've always thought, to spot the domestic potential of a smelly old fish store. It is a handsome, big, two-storey building made of large granite slabs with no structural internal walls. Only one thick pine pillar seems to support the entire roof, although another is hidden in a wall in what is now the bathroom. It stands at one corner of the inverted roof and appears single-handedly to link into the exposed ceiling beams which support the roof. It's not obvious when you're inside the Fish Store, but when you look down on it from, say, Raginnis Hill, you can see that the roof has a huge inversion in the middle. This was for collecting water for washing the fish. It passed down a central drainpipe hidden in the outside wall of the sitting-room. When it's raining hard, the rainwater splashing through the middle of the house is a reminder of the Fish Store's past life. The floors are made of thick, wide pine boards which slope very slightly across the width of the building towards the sea. Originally, the entrance to the upstairs area where the fish were pressed and packed was through a trapdoor from the store down below and you can clearly see the hole where the floorboards were replaced. The main entrance was on the 'weather wall' of the building, on a sloping road 60 yards from the sea. The store, on the ground floor, or garage, as it's most often known these days, housed twelve 13-foot-square concrete tanks. This is where the pilchards were stored in salt, which drew the liquid out of the fish, for a month before the 15–20 tons of fish came up through the trapdoor to be pressed and packed for export to Italy. The fish were hauled up in baskets and packed in barrels, laid out in traditional fashion like a star. The full barrels were covered with hessian and fitted with a screw-clamp lid, rather like an old-fashioned printing press. The lid was held in place with huge granite loadstones suspended from a pole which slid through special holes in the lid. One of them sits on the wall outside the Fish Store.

Fortunately a builder lived opposite. Curiously, he had the almost identical surname of 'Johns'. Jimmy Johns, whom I can remember and whose son Alan and grandson Duncan have subsequently worked on the house, was instructed to remove a corner of the building. The effect was exactly the same as cutting a corner slice from a square pie, giving street access to the upstairs of the building and a small front yard. Walls were built in line with the structural ceiling beams to divide the loft into a three-bedroom flat with a studio. The tanks down below were filled with rubble. By Mousehole standards, the main living-room – always known as 'the big room' – was huge. Downstairs became an excellent indoor space to have boxing matches and a feisty young Ben aped Edwin's boxing prowess, taking on local boys in a ring they rigged up themselves. Ben had his own pair of boxing gloves and probably fancied himself as the next middleweight champion of England, as Edwin nearly was in the mid-1920s, making it to the last round before being knocked out by Jock McEvoy in a fight which sent his tooth through his lip.

It was his aunt, the painter Gwen John, who persuaded Edwin to give up boxing and become an artist. He had trained at the Royal Academy in Piccadilly and at the time, in early 1936, was living in Paris with his wife Betty and their young son Ben. Later that year, when the threat of war became serious, they left France for England, settling first in Somerset and then in Mousehole a couple of years later. They had chosen Mousehole because Edwin's best friend, George Lambourne, Ben's godfather, was already established as an artist in the village. They had wanted to start up a drawing school in what is now the Cornish Range restaurant, which, coincidentally, was also originally a fish store, but the outbreak of war put a stop to that. Edwin, who was bilingual, volunteered for the Intelligence Service. Being tall and strong, he later joined the Royal Military Police, becoming a Redcap. After the war, he came back to Mousehole and continued his artistic career, capturing the rocks, in particular, the harbour and the timeless countryside in and around Mousehole. In 1939 Edwin's aunt Gwen died and left him her entire estate, including her house at Meudon, just outside Paris, which had remained empty throughout the war. Edwin returned to Paris, signalling the beginning of the end of his marriage. He returned briefly, between 1944 and 1946, and the result was Ben's sister, Sara, born in 1946, when Ben was eleven.

Ben was four years old when they arrived in Mousehole and spoke only French. He became known as 'French Ben'. During the war years the harbour was full of big fishing boats – many had guns mounted forward – and the boys would play cricket and rounders between them at low tide, collecting balls from under the hulls. There were also several Belgium boats belonging to families who had escaped from mainland Europe. The boys all had nicknames – 'Big Boo', 'Shonolly', 'Strom', 'Jinx', 'Wackers', the two 'Nabos' – and Ben became 'Ben banger'.

Farmers would come down to the harbour after a storm to collect seaweed and load it on to a horse and cart. The slippery cargo would be trundled through the village and up Raginnis Hill, to be spread over freshly dug fields. Like horse manure, which was collected regularly, seaweed is a rich fertilizer for the soil of market gardeners. Farmers would also gather up the heads, bones and guts of filleted fish, which provided nourishment for the earth. In those days the fishermen were glad to get rid of the stinking debris, although most of it was dumped at sea. Today's farmers buy their bone meal in dried, sanitized form.

The boys used to collect limpets and cook them on a metal sheet over a fire on the rocks when they weren't fishing for whistlers and bull cats in the rock pools. One November, they weren't allowed to light their bonfire on the rocks because it was thought there was a German sub in the bay and no lights were permitted. At all times the Germans were trying to find and destroy the cable station at Porthcurno. They never succeeded, but they would drop their bombs anyway.

Inflatable lorries were lined up in rows to fake troop activity and the fields were sometimes covered in silver paper, dropped by our side to simulate large aerial build-up on German aircraft radios. All the fields up Raginnis were covered in the stuff: people would see silver fields all around when they went blackberry picking or looking for watercress or to fetch a black-market chicken from one of the farms.

The John family is notably artistic – famously Augustus and Gwen John, but there are other artists, including Sara, Ben's sister; Rebecca, his cousin; and Henry and Tamsin, his children – but Ben's uncle Caspar made a name for himself in the Navy, eventually becoming First Sea Lord. Whenever it was practicable and he was in Mount's Bay, Caspar would visit Mousehole. He would often have supper with Betty at the Fish Store. He was also partial to a Guinness or two (called 'moon milk' by Edwin, Caspar and their brother David, after The Man in the Moon, their local in Chelsea) in the Mousehole pub, the Ship Inn. He was friendly with many of the local fishermen. He would wear a dark navy coat over his uniform, covering up the gold braid on his sleeves. Later, his wife Mary and their three children, Rebecca (who became a close friend when we worked at *Time Out* and introduced me to Ben), Phineas and Caroline, lived in the Salt Ponds, very close to the Fish Store. Mary used to drive an old London taxi. By then, in 1951, Caspar was Rear Admiral, stationed at Plymouth, and Ben was fifteen. On one occasion he steamed into the bay in command of HMS *Vengeance*, an aircraft carrier, accompanied by a flotilla. Caspar had decided to christen his three children on board, by upturning the ship's bell as an impromptu font. A small group of family and friends, including Betty, Ben, four-year-old Sara and Jimmy Madron, who owned the fishing boat *The Renovelle*, were duly taken aboard by liberty boat. After the ceremony, they went to the admiral's quarters, and Caspar, by way of a deprecatory joke, said to his Flag Officer, 'Oh, Flag, I'd like you to meet Jimmy Madron. He owns his own boat.' An overawed Jimmy beamed from ear to ear.

Childhood friends like Barry Cornish, who later became the village postman, remember how unconventional the food and lifestyle were at the Fish Store. The house was always full of actresses and actors, writers and painters.

Betty would grind fresh coffee every day and cook mussels marinière-style as well as other continental, exotic-seeming dishes such as stuffed cabbage and kidneys in red wine. Even sophisticated friends like the artist Rose Hilton, who met Betty when she and her husband Roger came to live in Cornwall in the early sixties, found Betty's cooking impressive. She made her own ice cream, which no one else did, and had shelves of herbs in bottles, which Rose had never seen before. Fishermen were generous with their spoils and would leave fish on the doorstep or give Ben a big crab to take back to Betty. She would make mayonnaise to go with the freshly boiled crab and cook egg custard rather than rely on Bird's instant to go with stewed plums or a fruit crumble. Ben remembers creamy macaroni cheese for tea, and her simple but delicious vegetable soups made with sorrel from the hedgerow and spinach from the farm were appreciated by everyone lucky enough to sit at her table.

Betty didn't cook much when I came to know her in her last years before she needed full-time nursing and moved to a home at St Ives. It was obvious, though, from the way she shopped and organized her kitchen and the pencilled notes in her cookbooks that she was the best kind of inquisitive self-taught cook. She liked things done properly, responding to the seasons and adapting her cooking to what was available and whom she had to feed. This style of cooking and eating, when everyone mucks in and the preparation is just as convivial as the eating, had a huge effect on me and it is the essence of the Fish Store cookbook. Now, that's what I call a proper job.

Looking Out of the Window

Three big windows look out to sea from the Fish Store and they are all in the main living-room. The moment you open the front door, your eyes are drawn out of the window towards St Clement's Isle and beyond. One window lines up very neatly with the polished granite-topped cooking island which stands between the dining-table and the oven. This means that when I'm cooking, I look up to see the sea. The window-ledges are deep enough for a cushion and wide enough to stretch your legs. In fact, I fit this window-ledge perfectly, and sitting here watching and listening to the sea and its constant comings and goings is one of my most favourite things.

Mousehole houses are built in a series of terraces spiralling side-ways and upwards from the harbour, intersected laterally by less than a handful of narrow roads and vertically by a series of alleys and court-yards. When I crane my head to the left from the window on the left, I can see beyond two sides of the harbour wall and right to the end of the village. My view is partially obscured by the slanting roofs and chimney pots of the back of the houses below on the Gurnick. Fortunately for us, the houses directly in front are smaller and lower than those to the left, so our sea view begins above the orange ridge tiles of Morwenna Cottage and Seacrest. Gurnick houses all have yards behind them and some, including those below us, have back extensions or outbuildings which have been built on to the backs of houses in St Clement's Terrace, where we are. This always makes me think of Moroccan riads built round a central courtyard. Sometimes, when it is completely dark and the moon is bright enough to pick out the pale grey of the roof slates, the view can look entirely Arabian.

This mixture of slanting and flat roof-tops with chimney stacks at either end is a favourite resting spot for the gulls. They stand on their spindly legs, shake their black spotted tails and suddenly fan their wings before walking a few paces, pausing and then repeating the whole procedure. They might swivel their heads without moving their bodies to have a good look round before taking a quick peck at the roof and flying off. In the summer there are usually several geeky grey baby gulls plonking around, waiting to be fed. Sometimes a pair of shaggy black birds hop about on a chimney. Unlike the gulls, who point their beady yellow eyes out to sea, the black birds always look inwards towards the land. There is a constant display of aerobatics from the gulls as they swoop down and across in front of the window. Best of all is when they glide in slow motion, freeze-framing every few seconds, and then, whoosh, they're gone. Single gulls fly purposefully to and from the island a few hundred yards away but they often travel in gangs, hovering above the sea as if on an invisible bungee jump, float-ing up and down on a warm thermal. The gulls tramp about on the roof of the Fish Store, shrieking their heads off as they pace up and down. Sometimes they urgently tap and scrape the Velux roof windows with their beaks, as if they've got something important to tell you. Unexpectedly they seem to get bored with all the palaver and then they're up and off, filling the sky, swirling around in different directions before inexplicably arranging themselves in a diamond shape in front of the island. This could mean they've spotted a shoal of fish or, more likely, they're tidying up, so to speak, where an old effluent pipe comes out in the sea. Despite all their noise and carry-on, the gulls add to, rather than detract from, the peace and tranquillity of the village. Occasionally, when they have young to feed, they do wake light sleep-ers during the night. Locals barely notice them and visitors soon adjust.

Cats often slink across the roof-tops in front of our window. Sometimes they mew at the window but most often they're on course, doing their own thing, on patrol, checking out who's been doing what, where and when.

The seagulls love St Clement's Isle and take refuge there in droves. In some lights, when they're roosting towards the end of day, they look like crusty sugar, the sort that sits in little clusters on top of certain cakes and currant buns. Wherever you are in Mousehole, when you look out to sea, the island is right in front of you, following like the *Mona Lisa*'s eyes. Its shape changes slightly as you move. When you come into the village it looks deep and interesting, but from our windows it's long and thin and a bit like a badly flattened croissant. The island isn't much of an attraction these days. No one goes there and there's no reason why anyone would, because it's just a craggy irregular lump of rock inhabited by gulls. It's said that the island was originally one piece of rock but now it's two, divided by a bomb which didn't go off but which had a huge impact. It used to have its own chapel, more probably a monk's cell, but no trace remains. Zach and Henry and their friends, and Ben and his friends before them, used to swim round it and I was once becalmed trying to windsurf round it, but years ago people would row out there for picnics. It was far grassier then, quite lovely in fact, and the nearest place to go for an expedition. Barry Cornish, the postman here for thirty years, remembers how a couple of families would make up a picnic, take ages to get ready, then his father would row them out and land at the little shingle beach on the north side, where you can bring in a small boat. When it was time to come back, his mother would wave a towel towards the harbour and the old man came out in a rowing boat to fetch them back. The island belongs to the Bolitho estate, once one of the biggest landowners in the area. At one time, you could walk from this parish to Land's End without leaving its property. The fishermen call the highest point of the island the Pepperpot and use it as a guide. A few years ago, when a big storm tossed the Pepperpot into the sea, several of them went out and searched for the big piece of granite. They found it lodged on some rocks and used their fishing chains to pull the 300 cwt slab back up into position.

The shape of the island is echoed by the Lizard peninsula beyond, known locally as the eastern land. Its long slim shape is almost always visible but its clarity changes with the weather. On a clear night it's possible to see the lights twinkling in the distance but when the sea mists come down it disappears completely. When the light is fading on a dull sort of day, the distant land, sea and sky all merge into a series of shades of grey, as if someone has taken a giant paintbrush and dipped it into very watery ink. At other times, when the sun goes down leaving big, bold strokes of deep, pink crimson, it looks like a long dark sausage – or lizard – floating in the distance. The mornings can be even more dramatic. The sun rising over the eastern land moves round quickly behind the island, striking the sea at a sharp angle and turning it into shimmering, molten gold.

Sea and sky are constantly changing, often in breathtaking ways, so much so that it can be extremely hard to drag yourself away from the window. The light down here is famously special and it often gives our sea-and-sky view an incredible 3D effect. Stormy weather can be the most amazing. As I write, the sky is split in three distinct parts, with dull grey rising from the distant Lizard giving way to big, sloping, fluffy grey-tinged clouds topped with a dark grey band with changing pockets of the brightest blue. The sea is choppy and moving with gentle undulation, seemingly pulling in several different directions. Every so often, these currents clash into frothy bursts of spray. The colours, too, are changing by the second, alternating through shades of petrol blues and greens. Small, fierce waves are crashing up and over the island and a cluster of seagulls is sheltering in the middle of the green-hued rock. Further still, the sea has a luminescence from the strobes of sun piercing through the clouds. Minutes later I look again. The sky has cleared, the entire sea is bright and covered with small white horses which in the distance look like chips of ice. I glance up again and the sun has disappeared completely and the sea is swelling as it rolls past the island. It looks bleak and beastly. It's a beast all right, but a compelling and beautiful one.

There is some sort of sea-going craft out on the water at most times of day. When Zach was a baby, it was a treat to do the night feeds looking out of the window, watching the green and red lights of the fishing boats as they headed out to sea. If I happened to be there again as the light was coming up and the sun shining on the water, I'd need sunglasses, it was so dazzlingly bright. My favourite boats are the one- or two-man punts, as they call them round here. They look like rowing boats. Alan Johns, whose father carried out the original work to convert the Fish Store, used to have a particularly fine one. It was made of wood, clinker-built, the separate planks clearly visible and highlighted by a clear varnish so there was no doubt that it was a wooden boat. It had a pleasingly old-fashioned look about it. It was kept down at the harbour. From March, when the baulks are lifted to open the harbour to the sea, until November, when they go down, it was tied up afloat, ready to go out to sea. The rest of the time she (boats are always she) lived out of the water on the 'hard', by the side of the beach next to the harbour car park, in front of the house which has shells for sale with a slot in the door for money. Years ago the little table would be set out with empty, spike-free sea urchins, some green, some pink and, best of all, some white, presumably caught by the owner. I have several in my bathroom in London, brought back for me by the boys from childhood holidays. Alan and others like him would finish work at five, have their tea and then go out line-fishing for sea bass. You see the boats drifting downwind with a pole out with its line attached. Line-caught bass fetches a better price than net-caught.

I also like the traditional shape of the inshore fishing boats, dinky little boats they look as they chuff past our window. Their cheerful colours, such as bright yellow or postbox red with chimneys painted a contrasting colour, make them clearly visible from the window. With the help of the binoculars which hang at the ready above one of the windows, it is possible to make out their PZ (for Penzance) registration number. Sometimes it is someone we know. I've come to be quite fond of the look of the bigger boats, the beam trawlers or beamers, so called because they trawl the fish – flat fish and scallops – from the bottom of the sea, disturbing the sea-bed as they go. You see them all lined up in the harbour at Newlyn. The outstretched arms of their derricks or beams which haul the nets from the sea always remind me of giant grasshoppers. It's a bit of a thrill if they come by on this side of the island – which happens when the boat is manned by a Mousehole man – because they are so big and powerful. They're just getting up a head of steam by the time they go past Mousehole from Newlyn and sometimes they stretch their beams like grasshoppers do when they're about to take a leap. In reality they are setting out their beams to calm the roll of the boat. There's usually a flutter of seagulls screeching and diving in their wake, circling overhead, rubbing their metaphorical hands at the possibility of a stray fish coming their way. Some of the boats have kith or kin in Mousehole, so they give a honk on their deep foghorn as they go past. Sometimes, when they're on the way home, it sounds a bit like 'Time to get my tea on'.

In the summer you can check the time by the *Scillonian*, the ferry to and from the Scilly Isles which steams out of Penzance at 9.30 a.m. and returns sometimes close to seven in the evening. I love this ship. It looks like a mini ocean liner with a hint of Art Deco about it and is innately glamorous. Its big creamy-coloured funnel juts out of a glossy white hull with the Cornish flag painted aflutter on both sides. It always lets rip with a deep, throaty roar as it passes the Mousehole harbour. Another, newer, familiar sight in summer is the divers' boat which zips back and forth from Lamorna with people in wetsuits and a cargo of air cylinders, just like something out of a James Bond movie.

It seems strange that the Fish Store never had its own boat. A couple of years ago, egged on by Zach and Henry, now in their twenties and keen sailors, Ben bought a small sailing boat. I'm the only one who can't sail, so I am often left behind. As I watch them zigzagging out towards St Michael's Mount and back across the bay into the wind towards Lamorna, I know that they will come back hungrier than usual.

Up the Crackers

There are three roads in and out of Mousehole. The main one runs along the coast from Newlyn and the other two are at either end of the little village and both involve steep, narrow hills unsuitable for two-way traffic.

Ragginis Hill is at the far end – the Fish Store end – and you can see it winding upwards in the distance from the harbour. It is a killer to walk up and it doesn't get easier, however often you do it. It is worth the effort, though, because Ragginis gives spectacular views back down across this end of the village, past the Fish Store and the island, with eyes inevitably drawn towards the harbour or across the sea to St Michael's Mount. The views get better the higher you go and the more your calves begin to ache. Raginnis is also the beginning of the route to the coast path. The exact whereabouts of this path is the cause of repeated concern to new visitors to Mousehole. Often they miss Raginnis and take the left fork which runs parallel to the sea and which seems the obvious choice. At Merlin Place, just outside the big blue doors to the Fish Store garage, there are two signs. One, painted green with washed-out white writing, has been there for years. The other is smaller and smarter and made of white metal with black trim and writing. It sports a National Trust acorn and is relatively new. The trouble is that the signs point in different directions. Locals are amazingly good-tempered about steering people up the alley past the Johns' house, where the gradient of the hill really begins to bite.

Not very far up Ragginis, you come to the Wild Birds Hospital. I often walk past the back of the hospital, down Love Lane. Here you can see huge wire aviaries where the birds that are well enough to recuperate live. There are usually a few seagulls nestling comfortably on top of the cage, wondering, if they're capable of wondering, what the birds inside are doing.

Love Lane, being higher than Raginnis, is an even better place to 'aerial-view' Mousehole. There are many artists' studios up here, and consequently numerous paintings of the village from this viewpoint. This little lane is also where several of the famous Christmas lights are cunningly positioned to be seen from the other end of the village. This is where a group of reindeer 'run' in the darkness and where a crib scene is hidden in the hedgerow. You can see evidence of the lights and their elaborate wiring all year round, but by the middle of October more equipment and piles of coloured light bulbs appear. These lie heaped in filched red trays from Newlyn Fish Market, semi-hidden at the back of the houses and studios, waiting for the walkie-talkie-wielding task force to swing into action. Our beautiful but bedevilled lurcher Peanut used to love coming up here and he'd disappear in the steep meadows behind the lane on the scent, no doubt, of a rabbit. But Love Lane is a road to nowhere which peters out into a grassy track leading to a painstakingly restored property with keep-out security lights which discourage curiosity.

Off to the right there are two or three muddy tracks between the overgrown vegetation that meander back down to the village. One in particular is used by all the dog walkers and is instantly recognizable by a clump of giant rhubarb on one side and an ancient tangle of thick, sinewy ivy creepers overwhelming a spiky blackthorn on the other. To the right of the track are well-hidden allotments but the left side is edged with coppice. Running alongside the path is a stream which comes from the meadows behind Love Lane. Most of the time it tumbles down the steep slope, but when it's raining hard or there's been a storm the water thunders down the hill behind its stout wall in a hurry to reach the sea. This might well be the very same stream that runs underground past the side of the Fish Store, meeting up, perhaps, with whatever goes on under the gaggle of manholes where South West Water hide meters for the houses nearby. There have been occasions when it has rained so hard that it has been possible to hear water gushing past under the ground as well as on top of it. The force sucks at our water closet, pumping vigorously as though it were being worked by some unseen hand.

On either side of the bird hospital are several grand houses built high above the road with entrances behind a granite wall. Outside one of them, growing out of its overhanging garden wall, are several splendid rosemary brushes. These flourishing plants have informed many dishes cooked at the Fish Store. It's obvious that the plants respond well to our steady pruning.

At the top of the hill, past a couple of picturesque cottages and Royden's netted allotment, which backs on to a network of small terraced fields sloping steeply down to the sea, the road forks round to the right. On the left is a wide gravel track which passes a large, imposing house opposite a few converted farm buildings set back from the track in a semi-private courtyard. This house, its outbuildings and fertile meadows used to be called Asphodel and was a prosperous farm devoted to market gardening. Years ago, Royden's mother Violet used to work there, sorting and boxing the early daffodils, anemones and violets. I've always thought it rather romantic that Lionel, Royden's stepfather, used to pick violets as part of his job as a general land worker. It's not often that you see violets on sale these days, but when you do they are always bundled up in a little posy cloaked by their leaves and laced up the stems with soft twine. I was really touched one Christmas when Royden gave me a bunch he'd picked and done up like this, in the old-fashioned way. To keep them fresh, Lionel told me, violets have to be dipped in cold water twice a day. Treated thus, they should last a week.

When Zach was a baby, Ben and I thought of up selling up in London and moving down to Cornwall. It wasn't a very realistic idea but one of the places we fantasized about was the Ashpodel outbuildings.

This track is the real start of the coastal path to Lamorna and beyond. The stretch from here to the Coastguard's Lookout – probably slightly less than half a mile – is inexplicably known as 'The Crackers'. Past Ashpodel, those once productive meadows which run down to the sea are overgrown with brambles, bracken and ivy. The path along here is incongruously edged with purple and red fuchsia, their lanterns growing profusely on gnarled old trees instead of the more usual 3 or 4 foot shrubs. In the spring the meadows are peppered with wild daffodils, survivors from bulbs chucked out eons ago. Someone told me that during the war the village was banned from growing the famously early flowers and so, to beat the ban, the bulbs were thrown into the hedges and thus not commercially planted. The flowers were duly picked and sent up to London. On Easter Sunday there was a Mousehole tradition of walking to Lamorna and back across the fields to see those surviving early spring flowers.

Along the coast path, the track passes a broken-down, derelict cottage set in a dark and particularly ivy-clad and overgrown patch which rarely sees sunlight. It has a very spooky aura. I hurry past this spot and on beyond The Lookout, now empty and boarded up but which was manned in poor weather until the sixties. Henry would like to convert it into a studio because it has the most amazing view of the entire bay. The path is thick with bright yellow furze bushes and in spring and summer a panoply of pink and white flowers flourish next to tall orange montbretia. Just a little further along the track a well-used wooden bench gives that same superb view. To the right, looking down as the track winds through the steep abandoned meadows and probably halfway to Lamorna, a patch of tall, dark fir trees marks Pellen Point and the start of Kemyal Crease Nature Reserve. This cool, gently sloping glade smells dank and earthy and is in sharp contrast to the little path through the meadows which is what locals are referring to when they say they are 'going up the Crackers'.

Seagull Granny

I have always regretted that I didn't spend more time with Ben's mother, Betty. She was quite old when I came into her life but still a headstrong, determined woman. When she married Edwin, she was disowned by her upper-crust family, who didn't consider the art student turned professional boxer much of a catch. The fact that Edwin's father was society artist Augustus John was not in his favour because Augustus was as celebrated for his bohemian lifestyle as he was for his paintings. As it turned it, Betty effectively brought up two children on her own and more or less separately, because Ben was eleven and away at school when Sara was born. Impressively, she educated Ben 'on a tiara' and wasn't too proud to buy his uniform from end-of-term 'outgrown' sales.

My time spent with Betty was in concentrated spurts when we holidayed at the Fish Store. Occasionally she would stay with us in London. Betty's social life in Mousehole revolved around the pub and she had her own stool there. She would wander down at lunch-time and again in the evening for a couple of gins before supper. In those days, the Ship was the focal point of the village and if you wanted to see someone, you'd be sure to find them in the pub at some point or other. Somewhere among the surviving photographs on the pub walls, of happy faces enjoying a sing-song with the Mousehole Male Voice Choir or dressed up after guise (pronounced 'geez': 'Mowzal' for disguise) dancing in the street, there is one of Betty.

Before Zach and Henry were born, Ben and I fell into a routine of collecting Tamsin, Jasper and Jessica, Ben's children from his first marriage, from their holiday with their mother in St Ives and bringing them over to Mousehole to stay with Seagull Granny at the Fish Store. We'd spend the days swimming and sunbathing off the flat rocks, coming back for a crab lunch with Betty. Sometimes we'd take picnics of pasties and sandwiches made with fresh crusty bread and ham from the Mousehole shop with a big bag of tomatoes and fruit, and head off for Sennen beach. After a sun-baked day on the beach, it was bliss to come back to the cool of the Fish Store and eat saffron cake slathered with clotted cream and Betty's home-made bramble jam. After supper, when sleepy children were tucked up in bed, Ben and I would amble down to the pub and end up in The Legion, drinking staggering amounts but bonding with all Ben's old childhood friends. Many of the men were fishermen, working two weeks out at sea and two weeks on terra firma. Hardly a day went by without the gift of fish or a crab coming our way. The only appropriate way I could think of paying people back was by picking blackberries and making a blackberry pie. I began to feel really at home in the village.

By the time Zach and Henry came along, Betty's health had deteriorated severely and she was living in a nursing home in St Ives. I was in charge of letting the Fish Store to cover its expenses, although a tenant continued to live in the studio. Various people kept boats, cars and fishing tackle in the garage below, so the comforting noise of the big wooden sliding door could be heard at random times.

Zach was born in June 1978 and it was a wonderful summer. We drove down to the Fish Store via Caspar's house in Devon, where we stopped to show him the new baby.

'Why couldn't you have had a girl?' was his grumpy response. 'Girls are so much nicer and there are too many boys already.'

We sat in the garden and ate one of his delicious lentil soups with bacon and scraps of lemon zest. It was a baking-hot summer and we spent the early weeks of Zach's life in a lazy haze. I had bought two long but flimsy white cotton nightdresses specially and have clear memories of the feel of the soft cotton as I sat in the armchair in front of my favourite window looking out across the night and early morning sea as I fed my new baby. I would walk him round the village in his carrycot and later across the rocks so that I could enjoy the sun and swim off the flat rock while he slept in the shade. It was a lovely time.

Soon after Zach was born, Caspar and Mary moved back to Mousehole, to a house at the other end of the village. By then Caspar, who'd been suffering from furred arteries which stopped the blood flow to his legs, had had first one and then the other leg removed. For a tall, independent man, used, by then, to living a quiet lone retirement, it was very frustrating. A special lift was installed in the house so that Caspar could go upstairs and he used to drive round the village in a smart motorized wheelchair, sometimes sitting little Zach on his lap.

There is a lovely photo of Christmas with Caspar and Mary when I was heavily pregnant with Henry. Mary cooked roast goose for Christmas dinner but forgot to turn the oven on, so everyone drank too much and three weeks later Henry was born two months early. Fortunately we were in London and although it was a dramatic and potentially fatal birth, Henry survived a month in an incubator, only to be back in hospital a week later for a stomach operation common to premature male babies.

Henry quickly recovered and was nicknamed 'Limpet' because he loved physical contact, particularly with his mum. One of my most treasured photos is of me lying on my back on the rocks at the bottom of the steps to the sea below the Fish Store with Henry fast asleep on my tummy as if he was still inside.

Zach was much more independent and very inquisitive. When he was quite a young toddler, he would let himself out of the sleeping Fish Store and visit Eia at Gurnick House, a large granite house overlooking the sea on the Gurnick down below the Fish Store. I don't exactly remember the first time I saw Eia von der Flur, but the image of her sitting in her little garden or wafting across the narrow Gurnick road to her house is imprinted on my mind as if it were yesterday. She was an exotic creature by any standards who wore long dresses in bright colours with peasant embroidery. I thought they were probably Mexican. She wore her black hair in a long, loose style and it cascaded in thick waves over her shoulders down her back. Her bohemian husband wore black, which offset his thick white hair, and their children had unusual names like Ru. Eia's children looked like blond fairies and wore old-fashioned clothes and played with home-made toys. I particularly remember a Victorian toy pram abandoned in the road outside the house.

A beautiful brass sun was nailed into the granite next to the always open door which gave on to a little portico and a second door into the house. In summer the couple would eat their meals overlooking the sea in the little garden across the road from the house. They ate from hand-painted rustic Mexican pottery and each plate told a story. The hare was the messenger from the moon, the humming bird a bringer of joy and the mermaid plate, sadly now broken and awaiting repair, symbolized allurement. Zach, like Eia's children and, later, her grandchildren, loved this one best because it came with the story of the Zennor mermaid. You can see her famous carved bench at the church in Zennor, near St Ives. Check out the Wayside Folk Museum and Tinners Arms while you're at it.

One summer, Zach turned up as usual to make breakfast bread rolls with Eia and a tall man answered the door.

'What are you doing in Eia's house?' asked the indignant child, only to be told that it was now the tall man's house. Eia had moved to a house opposite what was the butcher and still lives there, surrounded by her lovely, fascinating things. There is a scented garden and a bird-bath for her beloved birds, and the Mexican pottery I remember from when Zach was a baby is still in use.

Eia was one of a stream of visitors who would pop in to say hello to Betty when Ben collected her from the nursing home and brought her back for lunch at her beloved Fish Store. There are lovely photos of Zach and Henry sitting on Betty's frail lap, but much as she obviously enjoyed seeing this new crop of grandchildren, Betty's eyes really lit up when Ben handed her a glass of Chablis and she saw that there was crab for lunch and Jelbert's ice cream for pudding.

Another constant figure in life at the Fish Store is Royden Paynter. He was born in the village and by his own confession was filling time before he could leave school, which he did at fifteen, to go to sea at eighteen. After school he'd go crabbing, mackereling and long-lining for conger in his own little boat. Then, as now, fish landed for sale had to be taken to Newlyn Fish Market. In those days it was all pretty casual but now the market is a twenty-four-hour operation and it's necessary to register to sell through a dealer – say, Stevenson, traditionally the big boy, or Harveys for shellfish.

By the time Zach was born, Royden was fishing full-time and kept a small boat in the garage or store, as he calls it, during the winter months. In his spare time he made crab and lobster pots to order while

building up to 300 pots of his own. That's where I first remember seeing Royden: in the bay every day, checking pots in *Pandora*, which was
painted a bright yellow. *Pandora* was the boat that towed me in when I
got stuck beyond the island on my windsurfer with rock-hard lactating
breasts and a baby waiting to be fed. These days, Royden's Berthing
Master at the market and still makes pots in the 'store'.

All Right, My Robin?

Cracks started to appear in my marriage soon after Henry was born. Ben had sold his design group and enrolled at the Lycée in South Kensington to brush up his French. The long-term plan was for us to move to France. This coincided with me recovering my health after the birth of Henry and going back to work full-time on *Time Out*'s relaunch following a strike which had involved some nasty sit-ins and lasted all through my maternity leave. I felt trapped by the idea of France and gradually our paths began to diverge and we grew apart. In the mid-eighties our marriage faded completely and with it went my relationship with the Fish Store and Mousehole. I put Cornwall on the back burner and discovered new places. Ben continued with the annual August holiday and I would hear news from the boys of new friendships, barbecues on the rocks, jumps off the pier at high tide and crab suppers. I felt a pang when they moaned about having to eat crab every day and 'making do' with a pasty for lunch. Before I knew it, six years had gone by without me visiting Cornwall.

During that time one of my aunts, who lived thirty-odd miles up-country at St Agnes, died and left my brothers and sister and myself her house. This was my original Cornish connection and I rushed back, anxious to reignite the flame of my abandoned love. In my mind I relived the nostalgic holidays my sister and I had had before we were married, staying on the Beacon camping site, between Chaple Porth and St Agnes. We felt very much at home there. It was on one of these holidays that I ate just-caught mackerel for the first time. There was a fisherman called Snowy who would grill them over a makeshift barbecue on the rocks at St Agnes and we'd eat them sandwiched between thick slices of white bread without butter. When I gathered mussels from the beach and attempted to cook them in the French style, it was just as well that they were wholeheartedly refused because later I discovered that they grew next to the sewage outlet pipe and we'd almost certainly have been poisoned. I had brought boyfriends to this part of Cornwall, introducing them to Cornish beers and the delights of pasties and clotted cream. I had imagined I'd be coming back with my own children. My sister, who had settled in Sydney some years before, and I talked of buying out our brothers and joint-owning Liberty House but neither of us had the heart for it. In the end the best possible outcome was that my younger brother Adam made his life there, running the place as an upmarket B&B.

Life settled down again and then fate took a hand. Out of the blue, someone I'd known for years, who ran a food public relations company and who'd lately got together with one of my best foodie friends, rang to invite me on a trip to Cornwall. His client, it turned out, was smoking fish out of Newlyn Fish Market and marketing it throughout the country. Would I like to fly down to Newquay, stay overnight in a local hotel, then, after a visit to the processing plant, go early to the fish market, have breakfast in the café opposite and go out on a fishing boat?

Well, what could I say? The invitation filled me with trepidation but I knew there was only one answer.

That is how, one beautiful early morning at the start of the summer of 1992, I found myself in Newlyn Fish Market face to face with Royden.

'All right,' he said, tipping his head slightly as he always does when he greets someone, as if he'd last seen me the day before instead of several years past.

Later, after our greasy-spoon breakfast among the fishermen at the café opposite the market, we trooped on to the *Ajax*, a local fishing boat. Ushering us aboard was Adam Torrie, who lives a stone's throw from the Fish Store and is part of one of Mousehole's legendary seafaring families. He was also a one-time suitor of my stepdaughter Tamsin. Again I was greeted as if we saw each other on a regular basis. He hadn't changed a bit, still the wiry, lean lad that I remembered, so I was quite taken aback when he said he was married with four children.

Once out of Newlyn harbour, it doesn't take a boat like the *Ajax* much more than ten minutes before it's steaming past the old lifeboat slipway on the Newlyn–Mousehole road and bearing down on the island which rests outside the imposing walls of the picturesque, almost circular, little harbour of Mousehole. We were close enough for me to make out the gold sign outside the Ship Inn and I could clearly see the distinctive overhanging windows of the (now gone) Lobster Pot Hotel dining-room glinting in the sun. I felt a sudden rush of emotion. Tears pricked my eyes as I pointed out the steps down from the Gurnick to the rocks where eighteen-month-old Henry once fell asleep lying on top of me as I sunbathed. I just had time to identify the windows of the Fish Store sitting-room and run my eyes along the Salt Ponds, the row of whitewashed granite houses which denote the end of Mousehole.

It felt as if my life was flashing before me as we sailed past the tumble of smooth rocks and boulders so often painted by Edwin, Ben's father, and then on to the flat rock at Dicky Daniel's Cove, where I've carried and eaten more crab picnics than is decent to recall. I relived the Lamorna cliff walk, smelling the dank woody undergrowth at Kemyal Crease with its tall, dark fir trees and remembering the relief at emerging into the sunshine, then running past the sheer drop of the land's edge above the huge cave known locally as 'the mouse hole' and thought by many to have given the village its name. In my mind, I lay for a moment on the grassy knoll where I always stopped for a sit down because I liked its springy grass so much. I remembered walking across the stupendous big, flat rocks on the shoreline, then climbing back on to the track, ready for the long slog up the hill to the incredible view of tiny Lamorna Cove.

Coming back like this, I couldn't have been more overwhelmed by the sheer beauty of the place. Rose-tinted glasses perhaps, but on that bright summer day with the sun sparkling on the water, turning it into liquid gold, Mousehole seemed more beautiful than anywhere I could think of. I went back to London feeling as if I'd confronted a demon. I could now put this part of my past to rest. I didn't expect to be coming back and hearing the once familiar greeting, 'Hello, my robin.'

The Return

As the boys got older, they continued their holidays in Mousehole and built up a hard core of friends who either lived in the village or like them had the luxury of a seaside holiday home. Although they were on holiday, visiting for a few weeks every year, they acted, or so I'm told, as though they owned the place, like real Mousehole boys. Nevertheless, they used to take their schoolfriends down to Cornwall and I would get postcards from The Old Fish Door, as they both used to think it was called, telling me about various antics. Ben allowed them to run wild as he had done as a child in Mousehole and they'd be out all day on the rocks down below, often forgetting about food or, if they were hungry, catching up with Ben in the pub, coming in through the back door (Harry's door, named after Harry Drew, who always used it) for some change to buy a pasty. During this period various people lived at the Fish Store, renting it for eleven months of the year and vacating it for the annual August holiday. Someone cut out a newspaper headline that reads 'August is the cruellest month' in big letters. This harrowing message has weathered the years remarkably well. These days, the torn and faded cutting has pride of place above the fireplace, stuck to one of Henry's squares of primed board, the type he used for a series of bold face paintings for his final show at the Ruskin School of Art in Oxford. It hangs like a fine piece of art.

Relations between Ben and me over the years since our split were terrible. Our only communication was through solicitors, so it is curious that, when I really needed support over schooling problems with Henry, I rang him up. In retrospect, that was the first step towards us becoming friends again and me being able to return to the Fish Store.

I was staying with my brother Adam at Liberty House when the invitation came to go to the Fish Store for lunch. We arrived with Zach's dog Sam one hot but overcast August day in 1999. The Fish Store took my breath away with its new kitchen-cum-dining-room at the studio/front-door end of the building. There was a shiny granite-topped island with wooden cupboards underneath and shelves running along the wall above a double butler's sink. The cottagey windows had been replaced with big sheets of glass which swung out towards the sea on special frames, giving uninterrupted views. The house smelled of roast peppers and there on the worktop was a big pile of freshly picked crab on a familiar dark-brown Bernard Leach dish and a bowl of home-made mayonnaise. Everyone was very nervous and the boys, who had grown up with each parent separately, were confused about seeing us together. It was surreal but bearable and quite good fun in an odd sort of way.

Unknown to me, Ben was becoming increasingly anxious that the current Fish Store tenant saw himself as a sitting tenant and might prove difficult to remove. So when, two years later, I was at a major crossroads in my life and suggested almost as a joke that I should take on the tenancy, effectively turning the Fish Store back into a family home, it was the perfect solution.

In September 2001, Zach and I hired a van and moved furniture from our London home down to the Fish Store and kitted it out with new beds. Telling no one of my new arrangement, I began bringing clothes and kitchen equipment to my old holiday home. It was all very curious because in so many ways everything was the same but it patently wasn't. The Fish Store smelled the same but was physically different. A new shower had been installed in what had been Ben's bedroom. The bathroom had been opened into the 'studio' and turned into a kitchen-cum-dining-room. What had been the kitchen was now a huge master bedroom, while the two other bedrooms remained exactly as they had always been. Only one picture which I remembered – George Lambourne's painting of Mousehole harbour – and a couple of etchings by Sara were still hanging on the walls.

I spent a lot of time at the house, initially by myself, just enjoying being there. Sometimes Zach or Henry or some of their friends would come with me or a close girlfriend would arrive by train for a weekend. Mostly I was by myself with my dog Peanut. It was during this time, after a couple of consecutive Christmas and New Year visits when the house filled with Zach and Henry's friends, that the germ of an idea for the book took root.

Royden and Jake kept me supplied with fish and crabs and as the weather improved I spent more and more time at the Fish Store cooking, talking to locals and making notes. In the summer of 2002 I overlapped with Ben's August visit, actually staying under the same roof – unimaginable during all those acrimonious years – with Henry. We all did our own thing during the day but in the evening we were very social, entertaining on a grand scale virtually every night. It was an opportunity for me to cook some of the dishes we'd once enjoyed together regularly. Old favourites such as smoky aubergine dip on garlic toast, Vichysoisse made with just-dug new potatoes, poached sea bass with tomato vinaigrette, and treacle tart with Jelbert's ice cream. I introduced Ben to coriander-and-chilli-flecked crab bruschetta and roast haddock with tomatoes and borlotti beans, and he made his new signature dish of roast peaches with Amaretti. It was a good time for everyone and, without meaning to sound schmaltzy, brought the family together on a different level. Several more overlaps occurred with both boys and more old and new friends and a new, hitherto unimaginable, phase in our relationship began. The boys, of course, were delighted but a lot of people are still, several years later, scratching their heads.

All the grief and animosity that Ben and I went through in our different ways in the years following our separation and divorce has been put behind us. I wouldn't say the 'war zone' has been forgotten, but at least we are now able to be friends and friendly with each other's new partners.

It is the Fish Store that has made this possible.

In the middle of 2004, my daily recipe column for the London *Evening Standard* came to an end and I could no longer afford to run two homes. By then, Ben had gifted the house to the boys and I'd begun to feel increasingly uncomfortable with paying rent to my sons. After an emotional family powwow, it was decided to return to the old arrangement of letting the Fish Store to friends and friends of friends as a holiday let. The house was duly decorated and Zach, a graphic artist and designer, produced a lovely brochure. Whenever the place isn't let and it fits in with the rest of our lives, both Ben and I, separately and sometimes together, hurry back to the Fish Store.

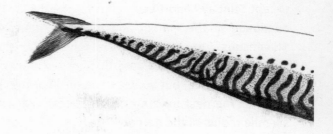

Fish

When I first came to Mousehole in the early seventies, most of the working menfolk earned their living from fish, either as fishermen or in a trade related to it. We were always being given fish and when we wanted crab or something particular we'd drive into Newlyn, which is home to the second largest fishing fleet in the country. Each morning except Sundays and bank holidays, the fish landed at the harbour is auctioned at the market and many of the big companies, such as Stevensons, Turners and Harveys, run a trade counter from their wholesaling business. These places change very little with the years and offer a no-frills service, but you can be sure that the fish is truly fresh from the sea. The best buys are the seasonal inshore fish caught within a six-mile radius of the harbour.

These days, though, Ben has a share in an inshore fishing boat – *Go For It* – and if I need six sea bass, say, or a few red mullet, and it fits in with Jake's fishing pattern, I can sidestep the shop and arrange a home delivery.

Jake Freethy is a Newlyn boy who bought a house in Mousehole and ended up living at the Fish Store. He met Ben in the pub in the early nineties during one of the famous lock-ins, when Tracey and Michael Madern were running the Ship. In true pub-talk style, they came up with the idea of Ben helping Jake buy a state-of-the-art fishing boat. The idea survived the night, was refined over a period of time and they decided to 'go for it'. Jake put his house up for sale, Ben dug deep in his pockets and at the end of 1990 a boatbuilder was commissioned to build a Kingfisher 24. On 9 September 2003, the boat was christened *Go For It* and launched to the sound of Jake serenading his girlfriend Tracey with a wedding proposal. PZ 903 is moored up in Newlyn harbour next to the new Penlee lifeboat, the *Ivan Ellen*, which cost a cool £1.8 million and makes *Go For It* look like a pretty toy. To an inshore fisherman like Jake, who has fished all his life, it is a dream come true.

Go For It has a chart plotter, autopilot, a fish finder, radar, two VHS radios and a GPS (global positioning system), a winch and automatic net hauler which coils the nets into net bins ready for shooting over the stern. It is useful having such a close connection with a fisherman working out of such a busy market. Just before Christmas one year, I was tipped off about sea bass being sold at £2 a kilo. Another time, I was given a big bucketful of unwanted crab claws, and when it is pilchard-driving time, the catch is so enormous that I have only to ask.

Pilchards, herring and mackerel are the fish notably associated with Cornwall and Nick Howell is trying to improve their image, particularly bony little pilchards.

Until the winter of 2005 he ran the Pilchard Works in Newlyn, the only surviving working pilchard-curing factory in the country, which he called a heritage working museum. It gave a glimpse of what life must have been like at our Fish Store and between Easter and the end of October it was possible to watch the traditional salt fish processing in full swing. Seventy-year-old screw presses were used to pack the fish into wooden boxes for export to Italy, where they have been sent since 1905. It was a fascinating place and Cornish salt pilchards, cured and canned or bottled, are still available. One aspect of Nick's upgrade entails canning the pilchards, sardine-style, in traditional flat tins decorated with paintings by Walter Langley of the Newyln School of painters. They are called Cornish pilchards on the cans, but why not claim them as Cornish sardines? After all, pilchards are nothing more than large sardines.

For details of Newlyn Fish Market, visit www.penwith.gov.uk and for information about local and mail order seafood, see LOCAL SHOPS AND SUPPLIERS, page 393.

Oily Fish

To prepare pilchards, herring and mackerel
To fillet pilchards, herring and mackerel
To butterfly-fillet pilchards, herring and mackerel

Grilled Herring Fillets with Dijon Mustard
Grilled or Barbecued Pilchards
Marinaters
Escabeche
River Café Roast Sardines
Stuffed Pilchards
Grilled Pilchards with Tomato and Rocket
Oatmeal Herrings with Bacon
Snotched Herring or Mackerel
Soft Herring Roes on Toast
Stargazy Pie
Marinated Mackerel Sushi
Devilled Mackerel with Beetroot, Tomato and Spinach Salad
Cumin Mackerel with Gooseberry Couscous
Butterflied Mackerel with Smoked Paprika and Garlic
Mackerel with Peas in Wine and Tomato

Mackerel, Herring and Pilchards

Mackerel, herring and pilchards (or Cornish sardines, as Nick Howell, who used to run The Pilchard Works, a heritage museum in Newlyn, would have us call them) are rich in omega-3 fatty acids – which help reduce cholesterol levels – and extremely good for us. These undervalued fish suit being cooked simply, usually whole, under the grill or on the barbecue, but they are also quick and easy to fillet and their robust and interesting flavour suits some surprising seasonings. The fillets can be stuffed and rolled or used to sandwich all manner of ingredients, such as spinach and mushrooms with garlic and lemon zest. They look impressive butterfly-filleted. People are put off these wonderful fish, particularly herring and pilchards, because of their whiskery bones, but they are easy enough to remove. During their season, in the summer and in the winter months, Cornish waters teem with mackerel, herring and pilchards. They can be picked up for next to nothing and are virtually given away by local fishermen. They swim in shoals in mid-water and are easy to catch with hook and line. This is a common sport down here and appeals as much to children as it does to old salty sea dogs. The 'line' has about twenty hooks on either side and success relies on 'wiffing'. The idea is to tickle the water with the line, pulling it in and letting it out, and when there is a bit of a tug, you know you've got a bite. What you're after, obviously, is a full line, and because mackerel swim in a shoal, there is a good chance of succeeding. The line is whipped out of the water and if you're lucky there will be thirty-odd fish wiggling about on the one line. The trick is quickly to flick the fish off the line on to the boat. You have to wear gloves to do it, to protect your hands from the hooks. On a good catch, an inshore fisherman like Jake can catch several tons of mackerel, herring or pilchards, or a mixture of all three. For big catches like this, he uses a ring netter which shoots in a circle, leaving the nets overnight. Then, usually at about 4.30 a.m., the purse rope is pulled tight so that the fish are caught in a bowl of water. The net is hauled to the stern, lifted with a winch and packed on crushed ice in the big red plastic trays which are familiar all over Mousehole for all manner of uses, none of them connected with fish.

Mackerel is the largest and most striking of these three oily fish, followed by herring and then pilchards. The taste and texture of their flesh are quite different, although many recipes are interchangeable, and so too is their preparation. One November day, thanks to a particularly good catch by Jake, I had all three types of fish and a couple of sea bass in the sink at the same time and was able to have a good look at them together.

Mackerel always strikes me as a masculine fish. It's a fit, body-beautiful kind of male; firm and smooth, lean yet well covered, and appears to have no scales, the fish equivalent of body hair. When you look closely, you can see that mackerel is covered with hundreds of tiny scales, but they rub off quickly and easily in the water. Watch out, though, for the sharp fin on its back. Mackerel is clearly a peacock and a modern one at that. Its look is bold and colourful. Distinctive black squiggly stripes radiate from its backbone and overlay a petrol-blue, green and beige 'wash' on its creamy, silvery-white belly. It's a beautiful fish. It has dense, creamy-coloured yet meaty flesh which can be dry when overcooked. It has big bones which are easy to see, but there are quite a lot of them.

Herring, by comparison, is sleek and feminine and lightly covered with thin, flaky scales. Its predominantly grey 'back' has heathery undertones of purple-blue with a close, cross-hatch pattern which resembles fine netting. Female fish sometimes contain creamy plump roes that are delicious when dusted with flour and fried to a crisp. The flesh is slightly darker than mackerel but the texture is silkier and the flavour more interesting.

Pilchards are really mature sardines and resemble a somewhat shambolic herring. The *Sardina pilchardus* caught in Cornish waters were probably spawned in Namibia or South Africa. The millions of little sardines which streak through Italian waters are bigger by the time they get to Cornwall and so become pilchards or Cornish sardines. They are usually smaller and slightly more compact than the smallest herring and are altogether shaggier-looking, with a mottled blue, grey and black 'back'. This pattern is hidden under a dense coating of thick, overlapped scales with the texture of plastic. Once removed, the colouring is noticeably brighter. When it has been scaled, the fish is soft and quite floppy. Its flesh is the darkest of the three and has lots of annoying little bones. These healthy little fish, so highly regarded in Portugal, Spain and Italy, and once the mainstay of the local economy, are largely passed over these days in Cornwall. Fourteen tons were landed one week just before Christmas and they were impossible to buy at Trelawney Fish, one of the wholesalers-cum-shops opposite the fish market in Newlyn. Snooping the local supermarket shelves for locally grown canned fish reveals that Glenryck source their pilchards young in South Africa and the Co-op's canned mackerel comes from Denmark. Many local fishmongers and some delicatessens sell Newlyn Pilchard Works canned Cornish pilchard fillets, available smoked in sunflower oil or salt-cured (known as 'fermaid' in these parts) in extra virgin olive oil. The little flat tins are instantly recognizable by the Walter Langley paintings which decorate them and although they cost twice the price of regular sardines, the taste is superb.

To prepare pilchards, herring and mackerel

All these fish are quick and easy to clean up and prepare for cooking. I usually scale them first by holding the fish by its head and rubbing the blunt edge of a knife vigorously up and down the fish, taking care not to snag the flesh. Rinse away the scales under cold running water as you go, continuing until the fish feels floppier and all the scales are removed. Next, get rid of the guts by slicing up the length of the soft belly towards the head until you meet bone and can go no further. Pull out the guts with your fingers. To remove the head, lay the fish on its back and slice firmly at a slight slant under the gills. Rinse thoroughly under cold running water to remove any blood and the fish is ready to fillet or cook. Some people trim away the fins, but it's not crucial.

To fillet pilchards, herring and mackerel

Use a very sharp thin-bladed knife, preferably a filleting knife.

Lay the fish on its side with its tail towards you and its backbone to your right (unless you are left-handed). Cut across the top of the fish below the head to release the top of the fillet. Turn the knife and slice close to the backbone, cutting all the way down to the tail in one swoop but gently stroking the flat of the knife across the rib cage towards the belly as you slice. It helps to lift the fillet with your left hand as you move down the fish so that you can see what you're doing. Turn the fish over and repeat on the other side. I find it easier to run the knife from tail to head on this side. Use tweezers to remove the stray little bones, using your finger to locate them. This is known as pin-boning.

A perk from the female herring is the roe. These are plump and white and come in sets of two. Soft and hard are both equally good but on balance the soft roes are favourites. Rinse thoroughly before use. They freeze successfully.

To butterfly-fillet pilchards, herring and mackerel

Trim and scale the fish as above, then remove the head (the fish look nicer with the tail intact) and completely cut along the length of the belly. Open out the fish, turn so that it's skin-side up and press all along the backbone with the base of your palm. Turn and pull out the spine from the head end, bringing most of the small bones with it. Tidy up by scraping stray bones away with the knife.

Turn into two neat fillets by slicing down the middle. Pin-bone (see above) as necessary. If buying from a fishmonger, he may be per-suaded to do this for you.

GRILLED HERRING FILLETS WITH DIJON MUSTARD
Serves 1–infinity

On a visit to Nick Howell's Pilchard Works, located a stone's throw from the fish market in Newlyn, I fell in love with his fish-filleting machine. Fish are piled on a circular bed of ice in the middle of a revolving wheel and – bang! – seconds later, the head and tail, guts and bones end up in a container down below, and two neat little fillets come out of the other end. It can fillet 250 fish a minute, getting rid of all those fiddly little bones that put people off eating sardines, pilchards and herrings.

> 2 herring fillets per person
> smooth Dijon mustard

This way of cooking the fillets is more of a tip than a recipe and works for as few or as many fillets as you like. Simply smear the flesh side of the prepared fillets with smooth Dijon mustard, lay out on foil and cook for a couple of minutes under a hot grill. No need to turn the fish. Eat them on or with buttered wholemeal bread or with boiled potatoes and a green salad which includes a few slices of crisp apple tossed in lemon juice.

GRILLED OR BARBECUED PILCHARDS
Allow 3 or 4 fish per person

Roll the gutted but unscaled whole fish in coarse sea salt and place under a hot grill or on a barbecue when the coals are covered with white ash. Turn when the skin begins to blacken and cook the other side. Serve whole; the skin and scales come off together and the fish will fall off the bones.

MARINATERS
Serves 12–14

Sometimes, usually late at night, as you walk a Mousehole backstreet, you may catch a strong whiff of spiced vinegar. It could be someone enjoying a late-night chip supper but it is far more likely that a catch or gift of pilchards is being 'marinated'.

Back in the day, when villagers were dependent on pilchards and herring to see them through lean times, every home would have a supply of pickled or soused fish, known locally as 'marinaters' or marinated fish. The fish are quickly prepared by removing their guts and heads, then layered up head to tail in a suitable dish with bay leaves (conveniently abundant in many Mousehole gardens), pickling spice and a little salt, then drowned in malt vinegar. The fish need to be covered with a sheet of waxed paper or tinfoil to avoid evaporation and they are then cooked very slowly overnight in the oven. Big dishes would be carried down to the bakehouse – in those days behind the Ship Inn, with a bakery next door – to cook overnight.

Several people gave me their imprecise recipes (and offered a supply of fresh bay leaves) but my first attempt with 32 pilchards freshly landed that day was pretty traditional. Only Peno Barnes, a very old friend of Betty's who moved to the village before her, told me to add a little dark brown sugar and that's what I did. Ben remembers Betty adding sliced onion, which was eaten with the fish, but he might be thinking of escabeche (recipe follows) or rollmops. The same recipe also works for herring and mackerel, and the flavours can be altered by using white wine or cider vinegar and isolating particular spices and dried herbs. I am a recent convert to marinaters and am delighted to report that the curing process also softens the little bones. In fact, the bones, including the backbone, should entirely disintegrate and be soft enough to eat. It was Lionel Wallis who told me the Mousehole name of marinaters. In St Ives they call them 'malio' or 'maliose'. The fish can be preserved indefinitely if kept covered in their pickling liquid and are always eaten cold, usually with bread and butter. They are also very good, Scandinavian style, with a bowl of cream beaten with a squeeze of lemon, salt and pepper and flavoured with chives, and black rye bread. Shots of chilled vodka are what you serve with this. Soused or marinated pilchards make an excellent impromptu snack or starter and are a lovely gift. Some people, though, and Henry is one of them, find the vinegar a bit overpowering. He likes them with boiled potatoes and a crunchy salad. If you have more or less fish, just adjust the recipe accordingly.

32 fresh pilchards, heads off and gutted
40g pickling spice
sea salt
about 20 fresh bay leaves
1½ litres malt vinegar
1 tbsp dark brown sugar

Any non-reactive, ovenproof dish is suitable.

If you have to prepare the pilchards yourself, scale them (see above) and cut off the head just below the gills. Slit the belly and remove the guts. Rinse the fish and shake dry. Arrange the fish snugly together (think canned sardines), season lightly with salt, lay a few bay leaves on top and sprinkle with pickling spices, continuing thus making layers until all the fish is used up. Pour over the vinegar and trickle the sugar down the sides. Cover with a sheet of greaseproof paper or foil and tuck it up the sides to avoid evaporation. Cook overnight in a very, very low oven, the lowest possible. Allow to cool naturally. Store covered with pickling liquid.

ESCABECHE
Serves 4

A European version of marinaters in which the fish are fried, sandwiched between a highly seasoned onion stew and left to marinate for three days. A favourite with Picasso, who is much admired at the Fish Store. Serve as a starter with crusty bread and butter.

> approx. 150ml olive oil
> 8 pilchards or 12 sardines, heads off and butterfly-filleted
> 2 large onions
> 1 small red chilli pepper
> 1 small red pepper
> 2 small carrots
> 2 bay leaves
> 1 tsp tomato paste
> 2 generous sprigs thyme
> 4 big garlic cloves, unpeeled
> 250ml white wine vinegar
> 250ml leftover white wine
> salt and pepper

Heat about 5 tablespoons of oil in a frying pan and, when very hot, fry the sardines in batches for 2–3 minutes on each side until golden. Transfer to kitchen paper to drain as you go, leaving them to cool.

Peel, halve and finely slice the onions. Heat the remaining oil in a spacious frying pan and gently cook the onions until soft and slippery. Meanwhile, trim and split the chilli, scrape away the seeds, slice into

skinny strips and then into tiny dice. Cut the pepper into 1cm dice, discarding the seeds and white membrane. Trim and scrape the carrots
and slice finely. Stir the chilli and red pepper into the onions and cook
for 5 minutes before adding the carrot, bay leaves, tomato paste,
thyme, unpeeled garlic, vinegar and white wine. Bring to the boil,
reduce the heat slightly so that everything simmers steadily, season
and cook for 20 minutes, stirring occasionally.

Spoon one third of the onion mixture into a gratin-style dish and
arrange half the fish on top. Cover with a second third of the onions.
Arrange the remaining sardines on top and cover with the last of the
onions. Cool, cover and leave to marinate in the fridge for at least 2
days, preferably 3, before serving.

RIVER CAFÉ ROAST SARDINES
Serves 4

This recipe comes from the *River Café Cook Book Easy* by Rose Gray
and Ruth Rogers, though we use local pilchards, which are interchangeable with Italian sardines but slightly larger. It's a great no-fuss
dish for loads of people, so we just double or treble the quantities
accordingly. All you need with it is plenty of crusty bread to mop up the
copious juices. You will also need paper napkins: it's hands-on food.
Another good point is that everything cooks in one dish.

    500g cherry tomatoes
    5 tbsp extra virgin olive oil
    salt and black pepper
    50g black olives
    24 small pilchards or sardines
    4 large lemons

Pre-heat the oven to 400°F/200°C/gas mark 6. Place the tomatoes in
an ovenproof frying pan or small metal oven dish and toss with 2 tablespoons of olive oil. Pierce each one with a fork or the point of a small,
sharp knife and season with salt and pepper. Cook in the oven for 15
minutes.

Meanwhile, smack the olives with something hard to crack the flesh
and loosen the stones. Remove and discard the stones. Choose an

ovenproof dish large enough to hold the fish in one layer, and drizzle with olive oil. Place the fish, side by side, in the dish and season. Grate the zest from 2 lemons directly over the top. Scatter over the olives and the tomatoes and their juices. Drizzle the last of the olive oil over the top and bake for 10 minutes or until the sardines are just cooked through.

Halve the lemons and pop them into the oven for the last 5 minutes of cooking. This softens the fruit and makes them much juicier. Serve the lemon halves with the fish.

STUFFED PILCHARDS
Serves 4

In his student days, Zach supplemented his grant by working as a waiter, first for his godfather, Christian Gustin, at Christian's in Chiswick and later at the River Café in Hammersmith, and it stood him in very good stead. So much so that whenever a girlfriend starts moaning about how undomesticated her teenage son is, I recommend she finds him a job in a restaurant. It's great, particularly if you're a single mum, because someone else nags them into clearing up properly. They can't fail to pick up a few cooking tips too.

During his time at the River Café, Zach was their ace anchovy-filleter, faster than anyone before him, so he's a natural when it comes to filleting other small fish like sardines and pilchards. Serve the fish with brown bread and butter, or make more of meal of them with potatoes and salad.

350g spinach leaves
salt and black pepper
nutmeg
1 tbsp vegetable oil
50g pine kernels
16–24 pilchards or sardines, heads, tails, guts and bones removed
2 eggs
2 tbsp finely chopped flat-leaf parsley or coriander
4 tbsp flour
lemon wedges to serve

Bring a large pan of water to the boil. Add the spinach and 1 teaspoon of salt and boil for 1 minute until the leaves just wilt. Drain into a colander, splash with cold water and, when cool enough to handle, squash the spinach into a ball and squeeze all the water out. Roughly chop the spinach and season with salt, pepper and freshly grated nutmeg.

Heat half the vegetable oil in a frying pan and stir-fry the pine kernels for about 30 seconds until patched with gold. Tip on to a sheet of kitchen paper to drain. Stir the kernels into the spinach.

Rinse the butterflied fish (see pages 42–3), pat dry and season lightly with salt and pepper. Lay out half the fillets, skin-side down, and cover with a central mound of spinach. Press a second fish, flesh-side down, on top. Whisk the eggs thoroughly in a cereal bowl and stir in the parsley. Smear a little of the whisked egg round the inside edges of the 'sandwiches' and press the edges together.

Dust the sandwiches with flour and dip them in the egg, turning to coat all over. Heat the remaining oil and a little butter in the frying pan over a medium heat and cook the fish for 3 minutes a side until crisp and nicely browned. Serve immediately, piled up on a platter with lemon wedges.

GRILLED PILCHARDS WITH TOMATO AND ROCKET
Serves 4

I taught myself to cook in my early days as a restaurant critic for *Time Out* and this recipe is a classic example of eating something delicious in a restaurant and re-creating the dish at home. It happened in this case when Ian Bates (once Simon Hopkinson's right-hand man at *Bibendum* and now cheffing behind the scenes) was cooking at the long-gone Chiswick. It's easy enough to do at home and is an impressive as well as delicious way of serving grilled or barbecued pilchards.

> 6 ripe, fully flavoured tomatoes
> 8–12 fresh pilchards or sardines, gutted and scaled but with heads on
> 2 tbsp olive oil
>
> *for the green sauce:*
> 2 garlic cloves, peeled
> 90g rocket or watercress

a few mint leaves

scant tbsp Dijon mustard

4 anchovy fillets

1 tbsp capers, drained

7–10 tbsp olive oil

for the salad:

2 tbsp vinaigrette

1 medium shallot, finely chopped

90g rocket or watercress

Begin by making the green sauce. Put the garlic, rocket or watercress, mint leaves, mustard, anchovies and capers into the bowl of the food processor with a couple of tablespoons of olive oil. Blitz, scraping down what's thrown up against the side of the bowl and, with the machine running, add the rest of the oil in a thin stream; you're aiming for the consistency of coarse, green mayonnaise. Season with salt and pepper.

Core and thickly slice the tomatoes (peel them too if you prefer) and lay out in the middle of four dinner plates. Cover the tomatoes with a tablespoon of sauce for each serving.

Make the salad in a bowl by tossing the vinaigrette with the shallots before adding the rocket.

Rinse the fish inside and out and pat dry with absorbent kitchen paper. Smear them with olive oil and season thoroughly with salt and pepper. Pre-heat a ridged griddle (or barbecue – making sure the racks are really hot, showing white ash on the coals) and cook the fish quickly with a fierce heat. This should take a couple of minutes a side. Lay them over the sliced tomatoes and top with a mound of rocket and shallot salad. Serve with crusty bread.

OATMEAL HERRINGS WITH BACON
Serves 4

Surprising though it might seem, crisp bacon and a smear of creamy Dijon mustard go very nicely with herring. The oats give the fish a crusty coating which is a good contrast to the soft flesh and complements the other flavours. Plain boiled potatoes or a few slices of buttered brown bread with a nice cup of tea are the perfect accompaniments.

If you're not good at dealing with little bones, I'd suggest filleting the fish first.

> 100g medium or coarse oatmeal (such as porridge oats)
> salt and pepper
> 8–12 fresh herrings, heads and guts removed
> smooth Dijon mustard
> 12 rashers thin-cut smoked streaky bacon rashers
> 2–3 tbsp cooking oil

Spread the oats out on a dinner plate and season with salt and pepper. Rinse the fish under the cold tap, shake and pat dry. Season lightly with salt and pepper, then smear with a little mustard. Press the fish into the oats so that they are covered with oatmeal. Cut the bacon rashers in half. Heat the oil in a frying pan and lay out the bacon. Cook briskly until both sides are very crisp and the bacon has given up plenty of its fat. Transfer to four warmed plates. Cook the fish in the bacon fat in uncrowded batches for about 2 minutes, adjusting the heat so that the oats brown and crisp. Turn and cook the other side. Keep warm while you cook the rest. Serve the fish with the bacon, a lemon wedge and a pot of Dijon mustard.

SNOTCHED HERRING OR MACKEREL
2–3 herring or 1 mackerel per person

This is arguably the best way of cooking fresh-from-the-sea herring or mackerel. It is certainly the simplest. 'Snotch' is a Cornish term which means slashing the fish two or three times in the middle of both sides so that the plump middle of the fish cooks as quickly as the thinner ends.

The fish need to be gutted and scaled but heads and tails are left intact. If cooking under the grill, lay the fish on foil generously spread over the grill pan to avoid smelly washing-up. (The foil is also useful for wrapping up bones, etc. after you've finished.) Place the pan under a very hot grill. As the fish begin to cook, the slashes will gape open. The softer, more delicate herring take 2–3 minutes a side, mackerel probably double that, but don't overcook. Serve with lemon wedges and brown bread and butter. Gooseberry sauce is lovely with grilled mackerel. Make it by simmering topped and tailed gooseberries with a little sugar until very soft and then cooking them with a scoop of clotted cream until thick and sauce-like.

SOFT HERRING ROES ON TOAST
Serves 2

Soft herring roes are a treat we are in danger of forgetting. They come free with female herring and need nothing more than to be powdered with seasoned flour and fried in hot oil. They end up looking appetizingly like slim Chinese pot-sticker dumplings. A crusty layer is essential to their enjoyment and sets off their incredible creaminess and subtly strong flavour.

It is traditional to add cayenne pepper to the seasoning, and when you do they become devilled roes. Cayenne adds a welcome piquancy, and the roes need plenty of salt and lashings of fresh lemon juice.

The bread you choose to serve them on is important, too. Ideally, you want one with a dense crumb, but if you're an ordinary white-slice person, choose a medium or thick slice to avoid sogginess.

I've never seen soft roes in the supermarket chill counter, but they are sometimes on display with the wet fish. Most fishmongers keep them in 500g bags in their deep freeze and at home they defrost relatively quickly in a warm kitchen.

They were a favourite Saturday lunch dish, usually followed by a green salad and cheese, when Zach and Henry were growing up and they're still regarded as a treat by all of us.

    500g herring roes
    3 tbsp flour
    salt and freshly milled black pepper
    cayenne pepper (optional)
    3 tbsp cooking oil
    1 lemon
    4 thick slices of bread
    a generous knob of butter

If using frozen roes, take them out of the packet and leave in a warm place to defrost. Separate the roes and remove any dark sinews. Lay them out on a double thickness of absorbent kitchen paper and pat dry thoroughly. Sift the flour on to a large plate or suitable surface. Season generously with salt, black pepper and cayenne, if liked. Roll each roe in the flour and shake off any excess. Heat the oil in a (preferably non-stick) frying pan and when it's obviously hot, lay out the roes in a single layer without crowding the pan. They will instantly shrink and splutter, enabling a few more to fit in. Turn down the heat slightly but leave them to cook for a couple of minutes without moving. The objective of this initial, very hot cooking is to get a nice crusty outer layer with sufficient heat to almost cook the roes inside. Use two forks or tongs to turn the roes and leave to cook for a further couple of minutes, adjusting the heat so that they crisp without browning. Re-turn any roes that don't seem sufficiently done and cook for a further 60 seconds in total. If cooking the roes in batches, transfer the ones that are ready to a warmed plate and keep warm while you cook the rest. Quarter the lemon – lengthways looks nicer and is easier to 'work'. Toast the bread and butter generously while hot. To serve, load the roes on to the buttered toast and serve with lemon quarters; they need plenty of lemon juice, salt and pepper.

STARGAZY PIE
Serves 4

The story of Stargazy, or Starry Gazy, Pie is peculiar to the fishing village of Mousehole. One particularly bleak winter, many years ago, or so the story goes, the weather was so wild and the fish so scarce that no one would put to sea and the villagers faced a hungry Christmas. On 23 December only one salty sea dog risked the foul weather and Tom Bawcock become a local hero when he returned with a good catch of seven different sorts of fish, enough to feed the entire village for two weeks. Stargazy Pie celebrates this, with the seven fish baked under a pastry crust with their heads poking out.

About fifty years ago, Tom Mitchell, landlord of the Ship Inn, decided it would be nice to offer Stargazy Pie in the pub on Tom Bawcock's Eve. Peno Barnes, then living in Tregenza Studios with her little son Billy, made the first pie and set up a tradition that is still going strong. The original pie was probably made with pilchards, cod, ling, huss, haddock, coley and gurnard, but more recent pies have included salmon and Parmesan cheese in the pastry crust. What doesn't change is the singing. There used to be a procession round the village with fish-shaped lanterns, a band and everyone singing Tom Bawcock's ditty. The Mousehole male choir still pitches up each year and always sings: 'a merry place you may believe, was Mousehole hearth on Bawcock's Eve'. Butts, as everyone calls him, is the expert on Tom Bawcock. He's not Mousehole-born but has been fishing in the bay all his life, for over forty years. He told me once that all the rocks in the bay have names. Publicity has spoilt Tom Bawcock's Eve for old-timers like Butts. 'You can't get in the pub for visitors,' he says, 'and when you do, you won't know anyone, so I don't bother.' We don't either.

My version of Stargazy Pie bumps up the flavours with bacon – which goes very well with most fish, particularly strong-flavoured fish like herring, which is also less bony than pilchards – but is essentially true to the recipe given on the postcards you can buy throughout Cornwall. The result is unexpectedly delicious – particularly if your herrings have roes – and if you do the traditional thing with the heads and tails, it looks stunning in a ghoulish kind of way.

750g 'old' potatoes such as King Edward
salt and pepper
100g butter, plus extra knob
approx. 100ml milk
3 eggs
1 onion
4 rashers of smoked streaky bacon
1 tsp chopped thyme
3 plump fresh herrings, filleted, but keep heads and tails
2 tbsp chopped flat-leaf parsley
1 tbsp vegetable oil
500g firm white fish fillet such as huss, gurnard, haddock or cod
150g flour, plus extra for dusting

Pre-heat the oven to 400°F/200°C/gas mark 6. Peel and rinse the potatoes and cut them into chunks. Cook in boiling salted water until tender. Drain and mash with a knob of butter and sufficient milk to make a firm mash. Boil 2 of the eggs for 10 minutes either in with the potatoes or in a separate, small pan. Crack all over and peel. Peel, halve and finely chop the onion. Fry in 25g butter for about 8 minutes until soft and lightly browned. Chop the bacon and add to the pan, together with the thyme. Cook until the bacon fat is crisp. Scoop into a mixing bowl, leaving as much fat behind as possible. If you are lucky enough to have roes with your herrings, fry them whole for a couple of minutes a side, then mix them into the mashed potato. Tip the mash into the mixing bowl and add the parsley. Wash out the frying pan and add the vegetable oil. Chop the herring fillets into bite-size chunks (don't worry about the whiskery bones) and fry briefly in hot oil on both sides. Transfer to the mixing bowl. Now dice the white fish and fry in the same way. Chop the eggs and mix everything together. Transfer to a shallow dish. Cut the remaining butter into chunks and rub it into the flour. Add 2–3 tablespoons of water, draw together with a knife or fork and form into a ball. Dust a work surface with flour and roll the pastry to make a lid for the pie. If liked, make slits and post the herring heads and tails, using leftover pastry to make little collars. Whisk the remaining egg and use it to paint the pastry. Bake for about 25 minutes until the pastry is golden.

MARINATED MACKEREL SUSHI
Serves 6–8 as a starter or snack

I am not a big fan of raw mackerel – it is a staple of sushi menus – but love the textural and flavour changes when it is marinated in rice vinegar. I found this deliciously simple recipe in *Sushi Taste and Technique* by Kimiko Barber and Hiroki Takemur, the perfect introduction to ever-popular sushi. Although a sushi rolling mat would come in handy for a neat finish, it isn't vital. What is essential is very fresh mackerel. Serve with sake.

  4 fresh mackerel fillets, approx. 150g each, pin-boned
  8 tbsp sea salt
  500ml rice vinegar
  2 tbsp mirin or 3 tbsp caster sugar
  2 tsp salt

for the sushi rice:
300g Japanese short-grain rice
1 postcard-size piece kombu, optional
4 tbsp Japanese rice vinegar
2 tbsp sugar
½ tbsp salt

to serve:
3 tbsp rice vinegar
wasabi paste

Rub the mackerel fillets with the sea salt, arrange in a colander and leave to drain for an hour. Rinse under cold running water and pat dry with kitchen paper. Pour the rice vinegar in a bowl that can hold all the fillets flat. Stir in the mirin or sugar, immerse the fish and leave for 1–2 hours. Remove the fillets and pat dry with kitchen paper. Slowly peel away the papery skin, starting at the head end. Run over the fillets with your finger to isolate any stray bones and remove with tweezers.

Meanwhile, make the sushi rice. Tip the rice into a sieve and submerge in a bowl of water. Wash the rice, shaking the sieve and changing the water until it runs clear. Place rice, 325ml water and the kombu (if using), cut in a couple of places to release the flavour, in a pan and cover with a tight-fitting lid. Bring to the boil over a medium heat. When you hear the water boiling, turn the heat to high and cook for a further 5 minutes. Reduce the heat to low and simmer for a further 10 minutes, then remove from the heat and leave to stand for 10 minutes. Lift the lid and discard the kombu. Heat the 4 tbsp rice vinegar, sugar and salt, stirring until dissolved, without allowing it to boil. Leave to cool. Spread the hot rice out in a wide bowl and slowly, gradually mix the sugared vinegar into the rice, using a spatula and a slicing action to coat and separate the grains of rice. Continue folding and fanning the rice until glossy and cooled to room temperature.

To assemble, mix 3 tbsp rice vinegar into 250ml water. Lay out a rolling mat (if you have one) and cover with a sheet of clingfilm, or just use a sheet of clingfilm if you don't have a mat. Wet your hands with vinegared water. Place two small handfuls of rice in the centre of the clingfilm and shape into a mackerel-length log. Dab the underside of the mackerel with a little wasabi and place the fillet on top of the mound of rice, skin-side up. Lift the mat/clingfilm over the rice and mackerel to completely cover and work your hands along the length of the sushi log, squeezing firmly but gently. If the mackerel is longer than the rice, neaten by pressing the ends of the fish over so they stick to the rice. Leave to rest for 20 minutes at room temperature. Moisten a sharp knife with the vinegared water and slice the log into bite-size pieces. Neat.

DEVILLED MACKEREL WITH BEETROOT, TOMATO AND SPINACH SALAD

Serves 4

A great way of ringing the changes with grilled mackerel.

> 4 mackerel, cleaned and trimmed, but head and tail on
> 2 tbsp olive oil
> 1 tsp ground cayenne
> 1 tsp ground paprika
> 1 tsp ground coriander
> 1 tsp English mustard powder
> 1 tsp sugar
> salt and pepper
> 1 tbsp red wine vinegar
> 1 tbsp vegetable oil
> 2 lemons

> *for the salsa:*
> 3 boiled beetroot
> 250g cherry or small vine-ripened tomatoes
> 250g young spinach leaves
> handful mint leaves
> 2 tbsp best olive oil
> 1 tbsp aged balsamic vinegar

Wash the mackerel and pat dry. Cut diagonal slashes about 1cm apart on both sides of the fish, not quite cutting down to the bone. Heat the

2 tbsp oil in a small pan, remove from the heat and stir in the spices, mustard and sugar. Season with salt and pepper and add the vinegar. Stir thoroughly. Place the fish on a plate or chopping board and use a pastry brush to coat liberally with the devil sauce, painting in the slashes and the cavity. Line a grill pan with foil, smear it lightly with oil and lay out the fish. Pre-heat the grill and position the grill pan so the fish is approximately 5cm from the heat and cook for 4–8 minutes a side, depending on the size of the fish, until cooked through to the bone, with a nicely crusty skin. Meanwhile, make the salad. Peel the beetroot and cut into chunks. Halve the tomatoes. Shred the spinach and mint leaves. Season with salt and pepper and mix thoroughly on a platter. Dribble the olive oil over the top and criss-cross the salad with balsamic vinegar. Serve the mackerel with lemon wedges.

CUMIN MACKEREL WITH GOOSEBERRY COUSCOUS
Serves 4

Piling all the food on to one big platter is a very attractive way of sharing a meal with friends and standard Fish Store procedure, popular because it saves on the washing-up.

Couscous is the perfect candidate for this informal presentation and almost anything, from roasted or griddled vegetables to a whole roast chicken or a leg of lamb, looks superb served with a mound of this golden grain. Fish isn't an obvious choice to match with couscous but with a little help from complementary ground spices, it can be fantastic. Mackerel is the perfect fish for strong seasoning and works wonderfully well when grilled with a liberal scattering of cumin. The smoky flavour of this haunting spice is a good foil to the silky but oily flesh of mackerel.

Gooseberries are a time-honoured partner for mackerel and they work very well with this combination of flavours and textures. Serve the pile of gooseberry-laced couscous on a platter and arrange the grilled, whole fish around the mound, tucking lemon wedges and a few sprigs of coriander into the arrangement. A feast for all the senses.

½ chicken stock cube
generous pinch of saffron stamens

200g couscous

2 tbsp olive oil

salt and freshly milled black pepper

2 tbsp blanched almonds

4 mackerel, gutted, heads removed but tails intact

1–2 tbsp ground cumin

25g butter

200g can gooseberries

small bunch of coriander

2 lemons

Dissolve the stock cube in 350ml boiling water. Stir in the saffron, agitating the water for a few seconds until the stamens begin to soften. Place the couscous in a suitable bowl and stir in the stock together with a tablespoon of olive oil. Cover the bowl and leave to hydrate. Heat the remaining oil in a frying pan placed over a medium heat and stir-fry the almonds until golden. Tip on to a fold of kitchen paper to drain. Rinse the mackerel inside and out and pat dry with kitchen paper. Slash in two or three places in the middle of each side of the fish and then dust liberally all over the fish with cumin. Cover the grill pan with foil and smear with the butter. Lay out the fish and cook under the grill (or in a hot oven) for 4–8 minutes a side, depending on the size of the fish, until cooked through to the bone, with a nicely crusty skin. Meanwhile, fork up the couscous, stir in the almonds and loosely fold in the drained gooseberries. Pile into the middle of a warmed platter and arrange the fish around the couscous. Decorate with a few sprigs of coriander and lemon wedges and serve.

BUTTERFLIED MACKEREL WITH SMOKED PAPRIKA AND GARLIC
Serves 4

I picked up on this Spanish way of preparing mackerel from the *Moro Cookbook* by Sam and Sam Clark. I cook so much from this book that I keep a copy at the Fish Store. The Sams ate this dish in a small restaurant in a Barcelona backstreet and their description of how the raw garlic cut through the oiliness of the mackerel while the paprika gave it an unusual smoky aroma made me want to try the dish immediately. It looks and tastes stunning. Smoked Spanish paprika is a godsend and widely available in small, attractively decorated tins.

> 3 garlic cloves
> 1 medium bunch flat-leaf parsley
> 3 tbsp olive oil
> 4 portion-size mackerel, gutted and butterflied or filleted
> salt and pepper
> 2 tsp sweet smoked Spanish paprika
> 1 lemon

Pre-heat the oven to 425°F/220°C/gas mark 7. Peel and finely chop the garlic. Roughly chop the parsley. Place a large roasting tin big enough to accommodate the four butterflied mackerel or 8 fillets on the hob over a high heat. Drizzle a little oil over the dish and slide in the fish. Season with salt and pepper and place in the over for about 10 minutes until cooked through. Remove, transfer to warmed plates and sprinkle the chopped garlic, parsley and paprika liberally over the top. Serve with lemon wedges 'and something simple like braised spinach and boiled potatoes with olive oil'.

MACKEREL WITH PEAS IN WINE AND TOMATO
Serves 4

Pilchards canned in tomatoes are cheap nutritious food with an image problem. The acidity of tomato goes extremely well with the rich, meaty flesh of pilchards, herring and mackerel, and in this unusual recipe carefully boned fillets of mackerel are rolled and cooked in a highly seasoned tomato coulis with peas. The mackerel are eaten from soup bowls, with garlicky bruschetta on the side. An unexpected discovery on an old Franco Taruschio menu from his days at the land-locked Walnut Tree at Abergavenny.

> 1 onion
> 4 garlic cloves
> 2 tbsp olive oil
> 150ml white wine

2 x 400g cans chopped tomatoes
2 tbsp finely chopped flat-leaf parsley
1 sprig thyme
generous pinch of red chilli flakes or 1 red chilli (seeded but left whole)
salt and pepper
4 fresh mackerel, approx. 450g each, filleted and pin-boned
450g frozen petits pois
you will also need 8 cocktail sticks

for the bruschetta:
4 slices sourdough-type bread
1 garlic clove
olive oil

Peel and finely chop the onion and garlic. In a pan that can accommo-date all the ingredients, fry the onion and garlic in the olive oil until tender and golden. Add the wine and reduce by two-thirds. Add the tomatoes, parsley, thyme and chilli. Season with salt and pepper. Roll up the mackerel fillets and skewer with a cocktail stick. Put the mack-erel rolls in the tomato sauce, add the peas and cook gently for 10–15 minutes until the peas are tender and the mackerel cooked through. Carefully remove the cocktail sticks and serve in shallow soup bowls with bruschetta.

To make the bruschetta, toast the bread, peel the garlic and rub vigorously on one side of the toast. Splash with olive oil and season with salt. Cut in half and serve.

Flat Fish

To prepare flat fish
To fillet flat fish

Fried Plaice with Parsley
Green Fish Fingers with Cauliflower Cream
Parcels of Plaice or Lemon Sole, Courgette and Thyme
Plaice with Indian Mint Chutney
Tempura Fish with Carrot and Coriander Salad
Lemon Sole with Crushed Peas and Vine Tomatoes
Asian Fish in a Packet with Basmati Rice
Lemon Sole *à la Meunière*
Grilled Dover Sole
Turbot in Champagne and Chive Sauce

Plaice, Sole, Turbot and Brill

Turbot and Dover sole are without doubt the king and queen of flat fish, but the knights of their realm – megrim and lemon sole, witch or Torbay sole, brill and plaice – are superb fish too. They are all best cooked simply, skin and fins removed, then grilled whole with plenty of butter and lemon juice and eaten with buttered new potatoes.

Working backwards in order of perceived status, plaice is instantly recognizable by the orange–red spots on its dark brown 'back'. It is generally regarded – wrongly, I think – as dull and boring. If it isn't overcooked, fresh plaice has a lovely delicate texture and clean taste-of-the-sea flavour. I often buy a couple of fillets for quick, lone meals. I like it dusted with flour and quickly fried with a salad of young spinach leaves tossed with peas and halved cherry tomatoes and a dressing of lemon juice and olive oil. It's good, too, with a few rashers of crisp bacon or with a mound of green spring vegetables such as broad beans, green beans and courgettes. Another delicious alternative is to dust fillets with flour, dip them in egg, then into breadcrumbs and fry them quickly in hot oil. This provides a light crunch giving on to the soft, succulent fish.

I'd never heard of megrim sole until I started buying fish in this part of Cornwall. It's so abundant in these waters that fishing isn't bound by European quota restrictions. It's a small to medium flat fish and highly regarded locally, but the jury is out on whether it really measures up against lemon sole, to which it is often compared. I tend to cook it whole, either grilled or in the oven, with plenty of butter or olive oil and lemon. Unlike lemon sole, which can taste dry, dull and woolly, its loose-textured flesh is sweet and clean. Witch or Torbay sole is also prolific in south-westerly waters. It looks and tastes like a small megrim and is only worth eating if it's very fresh.

Brill is a rounder version of squat and angular turbot. Both have dark brown 'backs' and are fringed with a skirt of comparatively long fins. These two fish are highly regarded and expensive, though brill is known as poor-man's turbot. If you're pushing the boat out with turbot, be sure to chose a mature, large fish (or buy thick fillets from the middle of a large fish) rather than immature, smaller fish which are sometimes called 'turbottine', so that its flavour has had a chance to develop. Turbot is lovely steamed or poached and served with hollandaise, but the favourite way of cooking it at the Fish Store is in memory of La Croisette, a basement restaurant on the Chelsea borders opened by Pierre Martin in the eighties. We used to go regularly for Friday lunch and take Zach and Henry, who were toddlers. Often there were no other customers and Daniel, the French ex-rugby player who managed the place, really enjoyed watching the little blond English boys dealing with plateau de fruits de mer and turbot in champagne sauce.

The market fish stall where I used to shop in Hammersmith when Zach was a baby was the first place I'd ever seen tiny Dover soles, called slip soles. The lady who ran the stall once told me she fried three or four for breakfast, which I found quite impressive at the time. Grilled Dover sole – ideally fresh from the sea via Jake or Royden – is one of my favourite meals. I like it with big, chunky but golden-crisp chips on a separate plate and plenty of lemon to squeeze over the top. Unfortunately, these sleek brown slippers (with both eyes set on the right of their face) are desperately expensive, even in Cornwall where they come inshore to spawn in the spring. The only point to remember when grilling a whole Dover sole is that the flesh is incredibly dense and deep next to the bone, so it takes longer than you might expect.

To prepare flat fish

The fishmonger will gut, trim, clean and fillet any flat fish quicker than you can say 'Davy's locker' but it is as well to know how to do all these little jobs yourself. Flat fish are the easiest fish to fillet. Begin by cutting off all the fins with sharp kitchen scissors. It's rare for them to have serious scales – Dovers and brill are the exception – but if necessary, scale the fish by running a blunt knife from tail to head, vigorously, up and down in short bursts, until smooth.

Slit the soft belly and remove the intestines with your fingers. I generally leave the head on but that is a matter of preference.

Rinse thoroughly under cold running water and shake, then pat dry with absorbent kitchen paper. To skin the whole fish – fillets can be skinned later – lay the fish on a flat surface and make a small nick in the skin just above the tailbone. Prise it up slightly with knife and fingers, then grip the skin tightly, pulling towards the head, yanking it quickly as if pulling off a plaster, taking care not to tear the fish. Turn the fish and repeat on the other side. Dover sole are traditionally skinned on the dark side only; the skin is glove-tight and you may need to use a cloth to hold it. If the fish is very fresh, you might need a little salt to stop the cloth slipping.

To fillet flat fish

This can be done with the skin intact. Run a sharp knife along the middle of the fish from head to tail, following the line of the backbone on both sides of the spine. Scrape the knife over the bone, cutting from the middle to the side, starting at the head end of the fish, lifting the fillet as you cut. Run the knife round the outer edge and lift off the fillet. Turn over the fish and repeat on the other side.

To remove the skin from a fillet, place it skin-side down on a work surface, make a small slit between skin and fish at the tail end, then run the knife down the fish, pushing down towards the skin while gently but firmly lifting the fillet as you go. It should be done in a swift movement.

Often, when I'm cooking a whole flat fish per person, I don't bother to remove the skirt of fins, although it would always be done in a restaurant. This should be scraped away from the fish first, before starting to eat, otherwise all the little fin bones get caught up with the fillet.

When eating a whole flat fish, proceed exactly as if filleting it, eating one fillet at a time. When one side is eaten, lift the carcass in one piece and discard rather than attempting to turn the fish.

FRIED PLAICE WITH PARSLEY

Serves 1 or more

This is one of the simplest and quickest ways of cooking fillets of plaice or another soft flat fish such as megrim or lemon sole. Cooked this way, the fish is surprisingly satisfying, but a few sprigs of curly parsley fried at the same time are the perfect accompaniment.

Fried parsley always reminds me of Mrs (Laurina) Cornish, who lived along the road from the Fish Store. She was quite old when I first met her, before Zach and Henry were born, and she could remember the Fish Store working as a commercial operation and could recall the sound of the sails of the old luggers flapping in the wind and the wooden masts creaking as they gathered outside the harbour after a day's fishing and waited for the incoming tide. She had a quaintly poetic turn of phrase and once said that our wind-surfers looked like butterflies bobbing about on the sea. I'd pop in when we were going shopping in Penzance and she once asked me to get her some parsley with the words, 'I love a bit of fried parsley with my fish for tea.'

> 2 fresh plaice fillets, skinned
> flour for dusting
> 4 big sprigs of curly parsley
> 25g butter
> ½ tbsp vegetable oil
> Maldon sea salt and black pepper
> ½ lemon

Pat the fish dry with absorbent paper, then dust with flour, shaking away any excess. Rinse the parsley and shake dry.

Heat the butter and oil in a frying pan over a moderate heat and when the butter is bubbling lay out the fish. Cook for a minute a side, adding the parsley, which should be fried on both sides, when you turn the fish. It will crisp almost immediately and take on a glassy texture. Transfer to a warmed plate, season with salt and pepper and eat with a generous squeeze of lemon.

If making this for more than one person, cook the fish first, piling the fillets on to a platter with the lemon halves and keep warm in a low oven. Cook the parsley at the last moment.

GREEN FISH FINGERS WITH CAULIFLOWER CREAM
Serves 4

A lovely way to liven up plaice or other white fish fillets. It takes a moment or two to identify cauliflower in this fluffy, creamy and intriguingly delicious purée because it has none of the usual cabbagey flavour and it is such an unexpected way to serve this snowy-white vegetable.

    1 quantity cauliflower cream, see page 249
    100g crustless white bread
    25g flat-leaf parsley leaves
    3 tbsp freshly grated Parmesan
    4 tbsp flour
    2 eggs
    8 plaice fillets
    4 tbsp vegetable oil

Prepare the cauliflower cream before you start work on the fish.

Tear the bread into chunks and place in the food processor together with the parsley. Blitz to make green crumbs. Add the grated Parmesan and pulse briefly to mix thoroughly. Tip the crumbs into a cereal bowl. Sift the flour into a second bowl and whisk the eggs in a third bowl. Halve the plaice fillets lengthways and dip each one first in the flour, shaking off any excess, then in the egg and, finally, press into the crumbs. Lay out on a plate as you go. If necessary, the fish can be kept in this state, covered with clingfilm, in the fridge for an hour or so without harm.

Fry the fish in batches in hot oil for a couple of minutes a side until nicely crusty and cooked through. Rest on kitchen paper, then keep warm on a platter in a low oven while you finish cooking the remaining fillets.

Serve the hot cauliflower cream draped with four green fillets and accompany with buttered new potatoes.

PARCELS OF PLAICE OR LEMON SOLE, COURGETTE AND THYME
Serves 4

Never underestimate the impact of serving familiar food in unfamiliar ways. Fish, for example, cooked in a foil parcel always goes down well and people love the excitement of opening their own parcel. Plaice and lemon sole both have a delicate flavour and tender texture that contrast wonderfully well with *al dente* courgettes. Together, they achieve an interesting tension. The combined subtlety is lifted by the fresh, clean flavour of lemon and a heady, aromatic scent of thyme. Olive oil unites everything. It is a simple and very special combination. The dish doesn't really need an accompaniment but very crisp oven chips, served on a separate plate to avoid sogginess, would be great.

4 pieces of foil, each approx. 30cm square

4 tbsp olive oil

8 plaice or lemon sole fillets

4 small or 2 medium–large courgettes

1 small unwaxed lemon

1 tbsp chopped thyme

salt and freshly milled black pepper

2 tbsp extra virgin olive oil

Pre-heat the oven to 400°F/200°C/gas mark 6. Lay out the four sheets of foil and smear the middle with some of the olive oil. Arrange one fillet of fish on each square. Trim the courgettes. Slice small courgettes on the slant into three or four thick pieces approximately 1cm thick. If using larger courgettes, cut them in half lengthways first. If they contain seeds – some larger courgettes begin to look like a cucumber inside, with pronounced seeds – use a teaspoon to scrape them out. Cut them on the slant into chunky slices. Remove the zest from the lemon with a potato peeler in small wafer-thin scraps. Cover the fish with a share of the courgettes and scatter with the thyme and lemon zest. Season with salt and pepper and about half of the remaining olive oil. Make a sandwich with the other fish fillet. Smear with the last of the olive oil. Parcel up the fish and courgettes loosely but securely. Place on a baking sheet or directly on to a high shelf in the oven and cook for 20 minutes. Cut the lemon into four wedges. Serve the parcels on warmed dinner plates and let people open their own parcel. Before eating, splash with the extra virgin olive oil and squeeze over a wedge of lemon.

PLAICE WITH INDIAN MINT CHUTNEY
Serves 6

When the Bombay Brasserie opened in 1982 – Henry was a baby and I was a full-time restaurant critic – London hadn't seen anything like it. Huge and themed to convey the opulence of the British Raj, it was decorated with carved chests, lamps and other artefacts imported from the famous Chor Bazaar in Bombay. At dinner they offered valet parking and cocktails. There was a live pianist. This was an Indian restaurant to get dressed up for. The elegantly presented food was a clever mix of wholesome Punjabi fare and elaborate Moghul cuisine alongside more familiar tandoori dishes. Eighteen months later, they added a large conservatory and lined its walls with giant palms and elaborate rattan furniture. During the eighties – the real start of London's restaurant boom – fashionable places would give their regulars a customized diary enhanced with full-colour plugs for other 'in' places. It was in one such that I came across this recipe. At the Bombay Brasserie they wrap the fish in banana leaves and serve it as a starter. These days, they call it by its Parsee name of *patrani macchi*. On early menus it was made with pomfret, but any flat white fish fillets would be perfect. Two fillets per person are about right for a main course when eaten with rice, but if you're feeding bigger appetites allow three or four. Creamed coconut, incidentally, which is what I used instead of freshly grated coconut, is sold in a block that resembles frozen lard and is widely available. It crumbles easily in the hand and helps bind all the other ingredients of the spicy green paste that is smeared on the fish. Any left over will keep for a week. This treatment works with fillets of cod, haddock, huss and megrim, but leave thick fillets flat rather than folding as described for thin fillets of plaice or lemon sole.

198g block of creamed coconut

4 garlic cloves

50g fresh ginger

3 green chillies

75g bunch coriander

20g bunch mint

2 tsp ground cumin

approx. 900g plaice, whiting or cod fillets

3 limes or lemons, to serve

You will also need tinfoil

Pre-heat the oven to 400°F/200°C/gas mark 6 or half-fill a steamer pan of water and put on to boil. Grate or crumble the creamed coconut into a mixing bowl. Moisten with 100–150ml hot water, stirring to make a thick cream. Peel and coarsely chop the garlic and ginger. Trim and split the chillies, scrape away the seeds. Coarsely chop. Place coriander, mint leaves, garlic, ginger, chillies, cumin and coconut cream in the bowl of a food processor. Blitz for several minutes to make a stiff green paste. Cut twelve pieces of tinfoil approx. 24cm square. If necessary, remove the skin from the fish fillets by holding the narrowest end with one hand and quickly running a sharp knife between fish and skin. If there is a line of bones running down the fillet, cut them out in a strip.

Lightly oil the centre of six pieces of foil. Generously pile the green paste on to the fish, then fold the ends together, pressing to make a sandwich. Divide between the six oiled sheets of foil. Cover with a second sheet, folding the sides to make a secure but not overly tight parcel. Place on a baking sheet or, if steaming the fish, lay the parcels in the steamer, place over boiling water and cover with the lid. Bake or steam for 15 minutes. Serve the parcels with boiled basmati rice (see page 73) and half a lime or lemon.

TEMPURA FISH WITH CARROT AND CORIANDER SALAD
Serves 4

You can buy good fish and chips in Mousehole, but the batter is strictly traditional. This batter, from Elizabeth David's *A Book of Mediterranean Food*, first published in 1950 when eggs were still rationed, produces a crisp and light crust and is rare among batters in that the flavour doesn't intrude and it keeps its crispness perfectly. The only important point is to make sure that the oil is hot enough and you don't bring the temperature down by trying to cook too many pieces at a time. The batter will keep perfectly for 24 hours.

8 plaice, whiting or sole fillets
oil for deep frying
2 limes to serve

for the batter:
100g flour plus extra for dusting
salt and pepper
3 tbsp oil or melted butter
150ml tepid water
1 egg white

for the salad:
2 tsp sweet chilli sauce
1 tbsp Thai fish sauce
1 tbsp lime juice
4 medium carrots
4 spring onions
small bunch coriander

First make the batter. Mix the flour, a pinch of salt and oil or butter, adding the water gradually and keeping the batter smooth and liquid. Make the batter at least 30 minutes before you need it, adding the beaten egg white at the last moment. Whisk the egg white until bubbly but not firm. Fold it into the batter.

Next make the salad. Mix together the chilli sauce, fish sauce and lime juice in a bowl. Trim and scrape the carrots and slice into match-sticks. Trim the spring onions and slice the white and green parts very thinly. Stir both into the dressing. Finely chop the coriander – you want a couple of heaped tablespoons – and add that too.

Divide the fillets in half lengthways. Pat the pieces dry, dust with flour and shake away the excess. Heat sufficient oil to completely immerse the fish until very hot but not smoking. Cooking four pieces of fish at a time, dip into the batter and plunge into the hot oil – they should be crusty and golden within a couple of minutes. Drain on kitchen paper while you cook the rest. Serve the tempura with the salad and a lime wedge.

LEMON SOLE WITH CRUSHED PEAS AND VINE TOMATOES
Serves 4

This is without doubt one of my favourite fast, no-fuss fish suppers. It is as easy to make for one as it is to prepare for half a dozen people. All you need is a fillet of white fish per person, a bag of frozen petits pois, a lemon and some of your best olive oil. Presentation makes the dish, and by serving the fish over the peas with olive oil flashed over the food in a Jamie Oliver–River Café kind of a way, it looks smart, fashionable and very tempting.

When I make this for a home-alone supper, I usually fry the fish, cooking it with a dusting of flour to get a lovely crusty, golden finish. If I'm making it for more than two people, it is easier to cook the fish in the oven. An extra advantage of oven-cooking the fish means that the gorgeous cooking juices can be stirred into the peas. Another neat presentational idea, which takes the flavours in a different but very complementary direction, is to drape a vine of grilled or roasted cherry tomatoes over the top. Either way, you won't need potatoes or any other accompaniment – apart, that is, from a glass of your favourite dry white wine – because the farinaceous quality of the peas and the rich-ness of the olive oil make the dish surprisingly satisfying.

> 2 tbsp olive oil
> 4 large fillets lemon sole, cod, haddock or huss
> 2 large lemons
> salt and freshly ground black pepper
> 4 branches of cherry tomatoes on the vine (optional)
> 750g frozen petits pois
> 2 tbsp extra virgin olive oil

Pre-heat the oven to 400°F/200°C/gas mark 6 and put a large pan of water on to boil. Smear a small oven dish with half the olive oil and lay out the fish fillets. Squeeze over the juice of half one lemon and finish with the second tablespoon of olive oil. Season lightly with salt and pepper. Place the dish in the hot oven and cook, checking the thickest part of the fillets, for 8–12 minutes or until just done. If including tomatoes, put them in a separate oven dish, smear with olive oil, salt and pepper and cook at the same time on a higher shelf.

Add salt and peas to the boiling water and boil for a couple of minutes until tender. Drain the peas and return them to the pan. Carefully drain the fish cooking juices into the peas, stir well, crushing them slightly, then spoon the peas on to four warmed plates. Drape a fillet of fish over the peas, adding a spray of tomatoes if using. Finish the dish with a generous splash of extra virgin olive oil and a squeeze of lemon juice. Serve with a lemon wedge.

ASIAN FISH IN A PACKET WITH BASMATI RICE
Serves 4

I usually think of making this when there is rice left over from the day before, but it is such a lovely dish that it's worth cooking rice specially. It's another of those dishes that scales up or down as required and is great for a dinner party because all the work can be done in advance and there's very little washing-up.

300g basmati rice
450ml cold water
3 big garlic cloves
generous pinch of salt
4 tbsp vegetable oil
8 tbsp Kikkoman soy sauce
2 tbsp toasted sesame oil
10cm knob of fresh ginger
4 small pak choi, approx. 75g each, or
    300g green cabbage or spring greens
4 white fish fillets such as plaice, lemon sole, haddock or cod, approx.
    175g each, skinned
you will also need 8 sheets of tinfoil, approx. 35cm square

Pre-heat the oven to 450°F/230°C/gas mark 8.

Rinse the rice until the water runs clear. Place in a lidded pan with 450ml cold water and bring to the boil. Reduce the heat to very low. Cover the pan and cook for 10 minutes. Leave for 10 minutes without removing the lid.

Meanwhile, peel and chop the garlic. Sprinkle with salt and crush to a paste. Place in a bowl with 1 tablespoon of oil, the soy sauce and toasted sesame oil. Whisk together thoroughly.

Peel, then grate the ginger. Separate the pak choi leaves or shred the cabbage or spring greens. Rinse and shake dry.

Lay out four sheets of foil and use the remaining oil to smear the middle section. Fork up the cooked rice and spoon into the middle of the oiled foil, making piles approximately the size of the fish fillet. Top with half the ginger, then all the pak choi or cabbage, and lay the fish over the top. Sprinkle with more ginger. Give the sauce a final whisk and pour over the top. Cover with foil and fold over the edges to make a secure and snug but not overly tight package.

Place on a baking sheet in the middle of the hot oven. Cook for 15 minutes. Serve the packages on plates with chopsticks or forks.

NB If using cold, cooked rice, allow an extra 5 minutes' cooking.

LEMON SOLE *À LA MEUNIÈRE*
Serves 2

This simple and classic technique – *à la meunière* means 'miller's wife style' – can be applied to any sole.

> flour for dusting
> salt and pepper
> 4 lemon sole fillets, dark skin removed
> 75g butter
> 1 lemon
> ½ tbsp finely chopped parsley

Season the flour with a generous pinch of salt on a large plate or similar. Rest each side of the fish fillets, one at a time, in the flour and shake to remove any excess. Melt half the butter in a frying pan placed over a medium heat. As soon as it begins to bubble, arrange the fillets of fish in the pan. Cook for a couple of minutes a side until a light golden colour, then transfer the fish to two warmed plates.

Add the remaining butter to the pan. Swirl it around as it melts, continuing until it turns a light golden-brown and begins to smell nutty. Squeeze the juice from half the lemon into the butter, swirl it around again and pour it over the fish. Scatter the chopped parsley over the top and serve with a wedge of lemon.

GRILLED DOVER SOLE
Serves 2

If serving this with potatoes, have them ready and keeping warm before you start cooking the fish. Chips, cooked crisp and dry, would be my first choice, but chive game chips (see page 218) or new potatoes would be good in a different sort of way.

    75g soft or melted butter
    2 Dover sole, 350–450g each or
        1 large Dover sole, approx. 600g, cleaned and skinned, head on
    salt and black pepper
    2 lemons

Pre-heat the grill to its highest setting. Cover the grill pan with tinfoil and smear generously with butter. Lay the fish on the buttered tinfoil and smear the exposed side generously with butter. Season with salt and pepper. Grill 5cm away from the heat source until the fish is firm and cooked through. Allow 6–10 minutes a side, depending on the size and thickness of the fish. It should not be bloody next to the bone and the flesh should be firm and white, juicy and not dry. Carefully turn the fish, smear with more butter, season with salt and pepper and cook for a further 6–10 minutes until done.

Serve the fish whole or tease off the fillets on to warmed plates, lining them up to cover the plate. Cut the lemons in half lengthways and serve with the fish.

TURBOT IN CHAMPAGNE AND CHIVE SAUCE
Serves 4

Lovely. Serve with new potatoes.

4 turbot steaks, preferably middle cut, on the bone, approx. 250g each

for the court bouillon:
2 carrots
1 large onion
1 celery stick
2 cloves
2 bay leaves
a few sprigs of thyme
1 tbsp salt
2 tbsp white wine vinegar or juice ½ lemon
1.5 litres water

for the sauce:
3 shallots
300ml champagne or dry white wine
300ml fish stock
300ml thick cream
3 tbsp finely chopped chives
salt and pepper
lemon juice to taste

Trim, scrape and slice the carrots. Peel and coarsely chop the onion. Slice the celery. Place all the ingredients for the *court bouillon* in a pan with the water and bring to the boil. Reduce the heat and simmer for 20 minutes. Slip in the turbot steaks, bring back to the boil, switch off the heat, cover and leave for 10 minutes. Remove with a fish slice and drain on kitchen paper. Meanwhile, make the sauce. Peel and finely chop the shallots and place in a pan with the champagne and fish stock. Bring to the boil and reduce by half. Add the cream, return to the boil and cook until the sauce thickens to a coating consistency. Add the finely chopped chives and adjust the seasoning with salt, pepper and lemon juice. Skin the fish, place on warmed plates and pour the sauce over.

Flaky Fish

Mousehole Bouillabaisse
Cod with White Beans
Roast Cod with Watercress Crushed Potatoes
Roast Haddock with Borlotti Beans and Tomatoes
Roast Haddock with a Potato Crust
Poached Cod with Lentils and Salsa Verde
Cod and Cos Salad
Party Fish Pie
Fish Pie with Spinach and Tomatoes
Kedgeree
Smoked Haddock Risotto with Parmesan and Chives
Smoked Haddock Mornay
Smoked Haddock with Poached Egg and Mustard Sauce
Huss with Lemon and Parsley
Fillet of Hake with a Herb Crust

Cod, Coley, Pollack and Ling, Haddock, Hake and Huss

'It's only cod,' Royden used to say, when he gave me a gift of fish that was going spare after the daily auction at Newlyn Fish Market, where he works. These days, only a few years later, it's rare to see cod at all and it's usually an undersized fish with the huge price tag once reserved for wild salmon. The silky and succulent yet firm and gently flavoured flakes of cod with big, easy-to-detect bones, have made this lovely fish the national favourite. Haddock, which is generally regarded as second-best to cod, is also increasingly hard to come by. There are, though, several other members of the cod family that are pretty good alternatives.

Hake is much prized by the Spanish, who buy the majority of the hake caught in the British Isles. It's softer than cod but has similarly large bones which are easy to detect. The fishermen of Newlyn some-times land a fish they call 'plus four' or Spanish hake. No one knows why or what its real name is. It has a more speckled silver skin than regular hake, which in turn looks like a sleeker version of haddock with a thin line running down the side of its body. Coley, also known as 'pollock' – as opposed to pollack, which is also a member of the cod family – used to be known as the cat-food fish. Its grey-white flesh looks off-putting on the slab next to pearly white cod or haddock but, like once-common, brown-skinned ling and pollack, the soft, mild-flavoured flesh is perfect for a classic fish pie, the sort made with a creamy parsley sauce and whatever else – prawns, hard-boiled egg, spinach, tomatoes, mussels, leeks or onions – you might like to add under the mashed-potato topping. The odd man out is huss, which they sell down here in the chip shop as rock salmon. Most people know huss by its old name of dogfish and Marks & Spencer call it rockfish, but huss is actually a small shark. There are several varieties and it's always sold skinned to remove its sharkiness. I'm a big fan because huss is relatively inexpensive (down here, it's used as crab-pot bait) and its firm flesh makes it an acceptable alternative to cod and haddock in all recipes, not just fish pie.

All these fish are improved by sprinkling the fillets with a little salt an hour or so before cooking. This firms the flesh as well as seasoning it.

For details on filleting, boning and skinning these fish, see page 99.

MOUSEHOLE BOUILLABAISSE
Serves 4

Leon Pezzack grew up in Mousehole and his mother is one of the few surviving people who can remember the Fish Store in its original working order. In fact, her sister, Leon's aunt, Elizabeth Ann Batten, worked there: it was her first job when she left school. Leon can recall eight serious fishing boats in the Mousehole harbour when he was growing up. Two, the *Renovelle* and *Our Katie*, were owned by the Madron family and the *Mark H. Leach* was owned by Mr Downs. Others were called *Internos*, *Ocean Pride* and *Silver Dawn*. Everyone in the village was either involved with the sea, mainly, or cultivated the land, like his mother's brother, William Batten, a market gardener who employed six people to work ten acres at the top of Raginnis Hill. As a small boy, Leon remembers Mr Eddy going down to the harbour with his horse and cart to take the fish off the boats. Sometimes there would be salt, too, or coal. Mr Eddy had a son called Clayton, who was a bit simple, and a daughter called Bernice. She used to brush the gravel across the road so that the horse could go up Raginnis. Then she'd rush out and collect manure for the rhubarb. These days, Leon reckons only fifty houses here are inhabited by working-class people; the rest are second homes. Apart from singing in the Mousehole Male Voice Choir, and being heavily involved in the Rowing Club, Leon and his wife Sylvia organize a biennial Sea, Salts & Sail Festival (www.seasalts.co.uk), which takes place in the village at the beginning of summer. It's an amazing occasion, when the harbour is full of traditional sailing craft, the luggers, gaffers and crabbers which were once a common sight. These beautiful old wooden boats with their huge flapping sails have been restored to their former glory or replicated in fibreglass. A highlight of the event-filled day is Leon's photographic display, showing pictures of the village and harbour from the 1800s – not long before the Fish Store was built – to the present day. I got roped in to do a fish-cookery demonstration for the festival in 2004. Zach came along to help and we set up shop on the old quay, cooking our way through a carefully chosen menu of quick, easy dishes using fish landed that day. One lady and her husband drew up chairs and were the first to try everything and disappeared the moment they'd polished off the last of the soup invented for the occasion. No one cooks fish much these days in the village. Even 'marinaters' – the local name for herring cooked overnight in spiced vinegar and eaten cold with bread and butter (see page 44) – are a treat rather than the every-day-in-every-home standby they once were.

> 12 medium-sized new potatoes
> salt and pepper
> 1 onion
> 2 garlic cloves
> 2 tbsp olive oil
> 1 large fennel bulb
> 3 plum tomatoes
> 5cm x 1cm strip of orange zest
> ½ chicken stock cube dissolved in 350ml boiling water
> generous pinch of saffron stamens
> 400g cod, haddock, ling, huss or other thick, firm white fish fillets
> 170g raw or cooked tiger prawns
> small bunch of flat-leaf parsley

Put the potatoes on to boil in plenty of salted water. When tender to the point of a knife, drain the potatoes, then return to the pan and cover with cold water. Leave for a minute or so to cool, then drain and tear off the skin. Halve the potatoes. Meanwhile, peel and finely chop the onion. Peel the garlic, chop coarsely and sprinkle with half a teaspoon of salt. Crush in a pestle and mortar or using the flat of a knife to make a juicy paste. Heat the oil in a large frying pan or similarly wide-based pan and stir in the onions and then the garlic. Sauté gently, stirring often, for about 5 minutes without letting the onions brown. Split the fennel bulb, cut out the dense core and slice across the layers very finely, reserving the fronds. Add the fennel to the onion, increase the heat slightly and cook for a further 5 minutes. Meanwhile, pour boiling water over the tomatoes, count to 20, drain and remove the skin. Chop the tomatoes. Add tomatoes, orange zest and ½ a teaspoon of salt to the pan, together with a generous grinding of black pepper. Let the vegetables simmer gently for 6–7 minutes or until almost soft. Dissolve the stock cube in the boiling water and stir in the saffron. Pour it on to the vegetables and bring to the boil. Simmer for a couple of minutes while you slice the fish into 2.5cm wide chunks. Check the seasoning, then slip the pieces of fish under the liquid. Cook for 2–3 minutes until the fish has turned white and opaque. Add the prawns and potatoes and warm through. If using raw prawns, cook slightly longer until bright pink. Chop the fennel fronds and parsley leaves, sprinkle over the top of the soup and serve.

COD WITH WHITE BEANS
Serves 4

Neither soup nor stew, but a bit of both; a comforting dish with fresh, clean flavours. Serve with garlic bread (see page 319).

6 rashers rindless streaky bacon

1 tbsp cooking oil

1 medium onion

1 large garlic clove

1 unwaxed lemon

2 x 400g cans haricot blanc or cannellini beans

salt and pepper

1 chicken stock cube dissolved in 450ml boiling water

generous splash of Tabasco

4 ripe tomatoes, preferably plum

small bunch of flat-leaf parsley

4 x 175g fillets cod, haddock or huss

Slice across the bacon rashers to make little strips. Heat the oil in a medium-sized, heavy-bottomed pan and cook the bacon for a few minutes until the fat begins to crisp. Peel and finely chop the onion.

Add it to the bacon and cook for about 10 minutes until tender and lightly browned. Peel the garlic and chop it very finely. Remove the lemon zest in wafer-thin sheets and chop into yellow dust. Stir both into the lightly browned onion and cook for a minute or so until aromatic. Tip the beans into a sieve, rinse with cold water and shake dry. Add the beans to the pan, season generously with pepper and lightly with salt. Add the stock and Tabasco. Simmer briskly for 5 minutes.

Meanwhile, cover the tomatoes with boiling water, count to 20, drain and peel. Coarsely chop. Chop the parsley. Cut the fish into big bite-size chunks and season with salt and pepper. Stir the tomatoes and most of the parsley into the beans. Cook for a further 2 minutes, then stir in the fish, making sure it's all submerged. Cook for 5 minutes or until the fish is opaque. Check the seasoning: you may need a tad more Tabasco or a squeeze of lemon as well as extra salt and pepper. Serve in shallow soup bowls garnished with the last of the parsley and a wedge of lemon.

ROAST COD WITH WATERCRESS CRUSHED POTATOES
Serves 4

A serious contender for the most popular cod recipe. Extremely simple and very good. All credit to David Gibbs.

> 1.2kg King Edward or other 'old' potatoes
> salt and pepper
> 5 tbsp olive oil
> 4 fillets cod, haddock or hake, approx. 200g each
> 1 small lemon
> 2 garlic cloves
> 100g watercress
> splash of your best olive oil (optional)

Pre-heat the oven to 400°F/200°C/gas mark 6. Peel the potatoes, cut into even-sized chunks, rinse and put on to boil in plenty of salted water. Cook until tender and drain. While the potatoes are cooking, smear a suitable oven tray with about 1 tablespoon of the oil. Lay the fish, skin-side down, on the oil. Smear liberally with another tablespoon of oil, squeeze over the lemon juice and season with salt and pepper. Cook the fish in the oven for 10–15 minutes, depending on the thickness of the fillets, until just cooked through. Peel the garlic, chop finely, sprinkle with a little salt and work to a paste. Put the remaining oil and garlic in the potato cooking pan and heat through for a minute or so. Return the hot potatoes and watercress and use a fork to mash, mix and amalgamate; you want the potatoes crushed rather than mashed smooth. Carefully drain the juices from the cooked fish into the potatoes, season with salt and pepper and give a final mash. To serve, spoon half the potatoes on to a warmed plate and lay the fish over the top. If liked (I do), splash with some of your best olive oil.

ROAST HADDOCK WITH BORLOTTI BEANS AND TOMATOES
Serves 6

I love dishes like this which are perfect for any occasion and are easily adjusted to suit more or less people. It is mindless to prepare, looks suitably impressive, and is healthy and delicious. If you can't find cherry tomatoes on the vine, use a 500g punnet of loose tomatoes and just scatter them over and between the pieces of fish, then spoon them over the top when it comes to serving. It won't look quite as smart but is actually easier to eat and will taste just as good.

    3 x 400g cans borlotti beans
    ½ chicken stock cube
    2 tbsp coarsely chopped oregano or marjoram
    3 tbsp olive oil
    salt and pepper
    6 fillets of haddock, cod or other firm white fish, approx. 200g each
    6 sprays of cherry tomatoes on the vine
    2 tbsp balsamic vinegar
    ½ lemon

Pre-heat the oven to 425°F/220°C/gas mark 7. Tip the beans into a sieve or colander, rinse with cold water and shake dry. Place the drained beans in a medium-sized saucepan. Dissolve the stock cube in 300ml boiling water and add that too, together with half the oregano or marjoram and 1 tablespoon of olive oil. Season lightly with salt and generously with black pepper, stir well and leave to simmer gently. Smear the base of a large oven tray with olive oil and lay out the fish fillets.

Arrange the sprays of tomatoes around them and splash everything with the remaining olive oil. Sprinkle the fish with the balsamic vinegar and squeeze the lemon-half over the top. Season with salt and pepper. Place the oven tray in the hot oven and cook for 10–15 minutes, depending on the thickness of the fillets, until the fish is just cooked through and the tomatoes are beginning to split and weep. Carefully drain all the juices into the beans and stir well. To serve, divide the beans and their juices between 6 large, shallow bowls, arrange a piece of fish on top and decorate with a spray of tomatoes. Serve immediately.

ROAST HADDOCK WITH A POTATO CRUST
Serves 6

Soon after *In Praise of the Potato* was published, I was invited to lunch by Anton Edelman in his office behind a glass wall overlooking the vast Savoy kitchen. After champagne and Savoy canapés (the 'secret' of which is tomato ketchup), I was served a fillet of sea bass covered with 'scales' made from wafer-thin slices of potato. The fish and its crisp, golden scales sat on a mound of silky mashed potato made with olive oil. My simplified version of Anton's interpretation of a traditional way of cooking a whole John Dory – called *St Pierre à Parmentier* after Auguste Parmentier, who popularized potatoes in France – could be made with any firm white fish fillet. Accompany with a simply cooked green vegetable. This is also very good made with smoked haddock, in which case I would pour the fish juices into cooked petits pois and stir in a dollop of smooth Dijon mustard and another of clotted cream.

> 100g butter
> salt and pepper
> 6 haddock fillets with skin, approx. 200g each
> about 3 tbsp flour for dusting
> 3 large potatoes
> 3 lemons

Pre-heat the oven to its highest setting. Lavishly butter a heavy-duty baking sheet that can accommodate all the fillets. Season the fish on the flesh side. Sieve the flour over a plate or work surface. Wipe the fish skin through the flour, shake off excess and arrange on the buttered baking tray. Peel the potatoes and slice wafer-thin; a job simply done with a mandoline. Without being too neat about it, arrange overlapping potato slices over the fillets. Dot the 'scales' with butter and season with salt. Cook in the oven for about 20 minutes (30 for smoked haddock) or until the potato slices are crisp at the edges and the fish is just cooked. Use a fish slice to transfer the fish to warmed plates and nap with the roasting juices. Serve with a lemon wedge.

POACHED COD WITH LENTILS AND SALSA VERDE
Serves 4

Another perfect way of cooking cod, this time from *Roast Chicken and Other Stories*. This is the book I helped Simon Hopkinson write and which inspired *The Prawn Cocktail Years*, both of which get a lot of use at the Fish Store. Most of the dishes became instant family favourites – Simon is Zach's godfather and almost everything for both books was cooked in our kitchen – and this one is perfect Fish Store food because it's as easy to make for two as it is for ten. The salsa verde is made in moments, the lentils require no skill or attention and the fish is poached in salted water with the juice of a lemon. It's a dish that comes together like a dream and everyone always loves it: 'The combination of moist and succulent flakes of fish, the earthiness of the lentils and the sharp punch of the sauce gives this dish a fine balance of flavours. This is one of the most satisfying plates of food I know, both for texture and flavour.' Quite. If there is leftover salsa verde, it goes with simply cooked white fish, or all sorts of other foods, including warm new potatoes or hard-boiled eggs, or both together.

 1 small onion
 1 clove
 1 bay leaf
 225g Puy lentils
 450ml water
 ½ chicken stock cube
 salt and pepper
 2 garlic cloves
 80g bunch flat-leaf parsley, leaves only

10 basil leaves

15 mint leaves

1 tbsp Dijon mustard

6 anchovy fillets

1 tbsp capers, drained

150ml extra virgin olive oil

juice of 1 lemon

700g cod, descaled, filleted and cut into 4 pieces

lemon and parsley, to serve

Peel the onion and push the clove through the bay leaf, then into the onion. Rinse the lentils and place in a pan with 450ml water, the onion and stock cube. Bring to the boil, then reduce the heat and simmer gently for 30–40 minutes or until the liquid has been absorbed and the lentils are tender. Season with salt and pepper.

Peel and crush the garlic and place in the bowl of a food processor together with the herbs, mustard, anchovies, capers and 2 tablespoons of olive oil. Process for a couple of minutes, stopping occasionally to scrape down what is thrown up against the sides of the bowl. With the machine running, add the rest of the oil in a thin stream, as if you were making mayonnaise; in fact, the finished sauce should look like coarse, green mayonnaise. Season with pepper.

Ten minutes before you are ready to serve, bring to the boil some lightly salted water with the lemon juice added. Put in the fish, bring back to the boil and switch off. Leave for 5 minutes, then lift the fish out on to four warmed plates. Allow the excess water from the fish to drain away by tilting the plates. Add a wedge of lemon and tuck in a couple of sprigs of parsley. Pour a little olive oil over the fish, sprinkle with a little sea salt and a grinding of black pepper. Serve the lentils and salsa verde separately.

COD AND COS SALAD

Serves 2

Succulent, moist flakes of cod or haddock are lovely with crisp slices of aniseedy fennel with crunchy lettuce and a chive-flavoured mayonnaise dressing.

2 cod or haddock fillets, approx. 175g each

1 tbsp vegetable oil

flour for dusting

1 small fennel bulb

3 cos, romaine or Little Gem lettuce hearts

1 tbsp mayonnaise

salt, pepper and sugar

½ tbsp wine vinegar

1 tsp smooth Dijon mustard

1 tbsp olive oil

1 tbsp finely sniped chives

If you are counting calories, I would suggest steaming the fish. To do this, smear both fillets lightly with vegetable oil, lay them out in the steaming dish and place over a pan of vigorously boiling water. Cook, covered, checking for doneness after 5 minutes. If not, dust the fish fillets with flour, shaking away the excess. Heat a frying pan with the vegetable oil and, when hot, lay out the fillets. Cook for about 3 minutes a side, depending on the thickness of the fillets, until the fish is light golden and cooked through. Meanwhile, make the salad. Halve the fennel lengthways and use a small sharp knife to cut out the triangular core. Trim the ends and slice super-thin across the width. Trim the lettuce hearts, discarding any outer damaged leaves. Halve the hearts lengthways, halve again and cut each quarter in half. Rinse and shake dry. Spoon the mayonnaise into a mixing bowl. Season with salt, pepper and a pinch of sugar. Stir in the wine vinegar and then the mustard. Gradually beat in the olive oil to make a thick dressing. Stir the fennel into the dressing, then the salad leaves and most of the chives. Toss well. Serve the salad topped with a piece of fish and finish with a scattering of chives.

PARTY FISH PIE

Serves 10–12

Fish pie can be as simple or elaborate as you like, but is always far tastier if it includes smoked haddock. Betty made hers with ling and its firm texture is a good alternative to more familiar cod and haddock, although I've started buying huss (the little shark formerly known as dogfish) because ling often isn't available. Coley, pollack or even whiting are perfectly fine in fish pie, particularly if there is some cod and haddock. A few prawns give the pie texture and colour and add a bit of luxury, but I wouldn't normally bother. The fish is held in a parsley and hard-boiled egg sauce under a crusty mashed-potato topping and I don't know anyone who doesn't love this superior nursery food. It is the ideal party dish because it can be made up to 24 hours in advance but will have to be kept, covered, in the fridge. I have a soft spot for peas (frozen petits pois) with fish pie. Mixed with lightly cooked green beans, which I always cut in half to make serving easier, they become a bit smarter. Quantities given are generous; any leftovers will reheat perfectly. If you decide to choose coley (the cat-food fish) or hake, reduce the initial cooking time because the flesh is very soft.

1.2kg white fish fillets such as cod, haddock, coley, pollack, ling, whiting or huss, or a mixture

1.2kg undyed smoked haddock

1 litre milk

2 bay leaves

4 large eggs, preferably organic and free range

150g butter

75g flour

400g headless, raw or boiled tiger prawns

2 tbsp anchovy sauce

salt and pepper

5 tbsp chopped flat-leaf parsley

2½kg 'old' potatoes such as King Edward

50g Parmesan cheese

Pre-heat the oven to 400°F/200°C/gas mark 6. Cut the fish into big pieces and lay out in an oven dish. Pour 750ml of the milk over the fish to cover it, add the bay leaves and cook in the oven or over direct heat for about 10–15 minutes, so the fish is almost but not quite cooked. Remove the fish to a plate to cool. Strain the milk from the pan and plate into a measuring jug and top up with sufficient water or extra milk to end up with 750ml liquid. Meanwhile, boil the eggs for 10 minutes in a small pan of water. Drain, tap all over and peel. Melt 75g butter in a medium pan and stir in the flour until smooth. Gradually incorporate the 750ml milk mixture, stirring constantly as the sauce comes to the boil, giving it a good whisk if it turns lumpy. Reduce the heat immediately and simmer for 10 minutes. If using frozen prawns, slip them into a bowl of warm water and leave for 5 minutes. Drain and remove the shells. Run a sharp knife down their backs and remove the black veins. Add prawns and anchovy sauce to the hot sauce, stirring as the prawns turn pink. Taste and adjust the seasoning: you might need more pepper, but it's unlikely you'll need salt. If using cooked, peeled prawns, simply stir them through the sauce. Tip the prawn sauce into a mixing bowl. Chop the eggs and add them together with the parsley. Run your forefinger over the fish to locate then remove any bones. Flake the fish off the skin into big pieces and stir loosely into the sauce. I used two large gratin dishes with a total capacity of 6 litres, but deeper dishes would be fine. Spoon in the fish mixture and leave to get cold: this avoids the mash sinking in the middle. Meanwhile, peel, chop, rinse and cook the potatoes in boiling salted water. Drain and mash with sufficient of the remaining milk and butter to make a fluffy but dense mash. Carefully spread the mash over the fish, smooth the surface, then fluff with a fork. Grate the Parmesan over the top, and bake for 35–45 minutes until bubbling and golden.

FISH PIE WITH SPINACH AND TOMATOES
Serves 4

Another way of making fish pie, with a bottom layer of spinach and tomato hidden under the fish.

> 750g 'old' potatoes such as King Edward
> salt and freshly milled black pepper
> 100g butter, plus an extra knob
> 225g undyed smoked haddock fillet
> 500g white fish fillets such as coley, pollack or ling
> 400ml milk
> 2 eggs
> 50g flour

3 tomatoes

100g spinach

3 tbsp finely grated Parmesan

Pre-heat the oven to 400°F/200°C/gas mark 6. Peel the potatoes, cut into big, even-sized chunks, rinse and boil in plenty of salted water. Set aside 3 chunks and leave to cool, then slice them thickly. Mash the rest of the potatoes with half the butter. Meanwhile, place the fish and milk in a pan that can accommodate the fish in a single layer. Simmer gently for about 6 minutes until the fish is just cooked. Lift the fish on to a plate to cool. Boil the eggs for 9 minutes, drain, crack the shell all over, peel and chop. Melt the remaining 50g butter in a small saucepan and stir in the flour. Strain the hot fish milk into the mixture and stir briskly to make a smooth, creamy sauce. If it turns lumpy, take a globe whisk and give it a good beating. Simmer for 5 minutes to cook the flour. Taste and adjust the seasoning with salt and pepper. Pour boiling water over the tomatoes. Count to 20, drain, peel, quarter and scrape away the seeds – this is an occasion when the juicy seeds will make the mixture too wet – and dice the flesh. Shred the spinach. Smear a suitable dish – I favour a deep, 2 litre china dish – with the knob of butter. Break the fish into chunks and place in the bottom. Season with salt and pepper, then scatter tomatoes and spinach over the top. Stir the egg into the sauce and pour over the fish. Cooling the fish mixture before adding the mash avoids the possibility of the middle sinking, but if there isn't time, spoon the mash round the outside of the dish and spread it evenly towards the centre with a fork. Make a border with the discs of potato. Scatter the Parmesan over the top and bake for 20 minutes or until the top is nicely brown with crusty edges.

KEDGEREE

Serves 4

This Anglo-Indian rice and fish dish can be dry and dull. Here, it's made traditionally with smoked haddock and basmati rice but the mixture is held together in an untraditional curried cream sauce, the textures and flavours offset by hard-boiled egg and chopped parsley. Kedgeree is a favourite Saturday lunch dish at the Fish Store.

Seven-year-old Ben, oblivious to the battleships in Mousehole harbour in 1942

The view from Raginnis Hill over the Fish Store, showing the Mousehole fishing fleet and St Clement's Isle

Mousehole in 1927. The Fish Store is clearly visible *bottom right* with its distinctive inverted roof

Betty (*centre*) outside the Fish Store in 1940 with five-year-old Ben and friends

300g basmati rice
450g undyed, naturally smoked haddock (the thicker the piece
    the better)
1 bay leaf
4 black peppercorns
350ml milk
1 onion
40g butter
1 level tbsp curry powder
1 level tbsp flour
100ml single cream
black pepper
3 hard-boiled eggs
small bunch flat-leaf parsley

Wash the rice until the water runs clean and place in a saucepan with 450ml water. Bring to the boil, cover and then turn the heat as low as possible. Cook for 10 minutes, take off the heat and leave without removing the lid for 10 minutes. The rice should be light and fluffy, having absorbed all the water. Meanwhile, place the smoked haddock in a large frying pan or similar, add the bay leaf and peppercorns and pour over the milk. Simmer gently for 5 minutes or until the fish is just cooked through. Lift the fish on to a plate, peel the skin off, flake the fish into big chunks (taking care to remove all bones) and keep warm. Peel, halve and finely chop the onion. Melt the butter in a small pan and cook the onion over a gentle heat until limp and golden. Stir in the curry powder and flour and continue stirring for a minute or two to allow the curry power and flour to cook. Strain the milk into the mixture, stirring vigorously as the sauce comes to simmer. Cook, stirring every now and again, for about 5 minutes. Add the cream and bring back to simmer. Season with black pepper, remove from the heat and stir in the flaked fish. Have ready a warmed serving bowl. Tip the rice into the bowl and gently fold the sauce into the rice. Quarter the hard-boiled eggs lengthways, arrange on top of the kedgeree and sprinkle with chopped parsley.

SMOKED HADDOCK RISOTTO WITH PARMESAN AND CHIVES
Serves 4

Sublime comfort food.

750g undyed, naturally smoked haddock fillet

1 bay leaf

50g butter

1 small onion

250g arborio rice

300ml dry white wine

½ tbsp smooth Dijon mustard

2 heaped tbsp clotted cream or crème fraîche

4 tbsp finely grated Parmesan plus extra to serve

2 tbsp freshly snipped chives

Place the fish in a suitable pan that can accommodate it in a single layer. Add the bay leaf, 1 litre water and 20g of the butter. Bring the water to the boil, then turn the heat down slightly so that it simmers gently for about 10 minutes until the fish is just cooked through. Lift the fish on to a plate to cool. Discard the bay leaf, pour the liquid into a saucepan and keep just below boiling. Peel, halve and finely chop the onion. Melt the remaining butter in a wide-based pan with a capacity of at least 2 litres. Stir in the onion and cook gently for about 8 minutes until wilted. Meanwhile, flake the fish off the bones in bite-sized chunks. Stir the unwashed rice into the onion and cook for a couple of minutes until all the grains are covered with butter. Add the wine and simmer until reduced by half. Stir in the mustard and then add a ladle-ful of the hot fish water. Cook, stirring constantly, for a few minutes until absorbed into the rice. Continue thus until all the liquid is used up and the rice is creamy but still retains a bite at the centre. Stir the cream and 2 tablespoons of Parmesan into the risotto, followed by the flaked fish and any juices. Cover the pan, turn off the heat and leave for 5 minutes. Remove the lid, give a final stir, dredge with Parmesan and garnish with the chives. Serve immediately with extra Parmesan.

SMOKED HADDOCK MORNAY
Serves 2

I was writing this recipe for Jake one day when an old friend from London turned up at the Fish Store out of the blue. When I mentioned what I was doing, he asked for a copy. Everyone loves smoked haddock in a creamy, cheesy sauce, particularly when it's served with mashed potato.

2 undyed, naturally smoked haddock fillets, approx. 175g each, skinned
250ml milk
25g butter
25g flour, approx. 1 tbsp
100g mature Cheddar, grated (traditionally Gruyère is used)
black pepper
chopped parsley for garnish

Place the fish in a shallow, heavy-bottomed, heatproof dish and pour on the milk, which should more or less cover the fish. Cook over a medium-low heat for 4–5 minutes until just cooked through. Cover with foil to keep warm.

Melt the butter in a small pan and stir in the flour until smooth. Remove from the heat and carefully strain the fish-cooking milk into the pan. Return to the heat and use a globe whisk to thoroughly beat the sauce as it warms through, whisking continually as it comes to the boil. Reduce the heat to quite low and keep whisking until smooth and thick. (You can do this with a wooden spoon, but using a whisk guarantees no lumps.) Leave to cook for 3–4 minutes. Stir in the grated cheese with a wooden spoon and heat through. Season with black pepper. If you want to pep the sauce up a bit, add a pinch of cayenne pepper and/or a pinch of grated nutmeg. To make the sauce richer, beat a couple of egg yolks with a couple of tablespoons of single cream and stir into the sauce. Do not let it boil once the eggs are added.

Lift the fish on to two warmed plates and pour over the sauce. Garnish with the chopped parsley and serve with mashed or boiled potatoes and green veg, if liked.

Another idea is to spoon mashed potato around the fish in the cooking dish, smooth/fluff it with a fork and pour the sauce over the top. Cover with more grated Cheddar and pop into a hot oven – 400°F/200°C/gas mark 6 – for about 15 minutes until the top is crusty and golden.

This method means the dish can be made up to 24 hours in advance and popped into the oven when you're ready.

You could vary this recipe by using fresh haddock or cod, and substitute a tablespoon of Dijon mustard or a couple of tablespoons of finely chopped parsley for the cheese.

SMOKED HADDOCK WITH POACHED EGG AND MUSTARD SAUCE
Serves 2

If you are lucky to come across a fine piece of undyed, naturally smoked haddock, then this way of cooking it, with a soft-poached egg, a creamy mustard sauce and a few potatoes, is hard to beat.

8 medium-sized new potatoes
salt and pepper
2 fillets undyed, naturally smoked haddock, approx. 175g each
250ml milk
salt and pepper
1 large shallot
25g butter
1 small glass of white wine
1 tbsp thick cream
1 tbsp vinegar
2 large eggs
½ tbsp Dijon mustard
1 tbsp chives or chopped flat-leaf parsley

Scrub or scrape the potatoes and cook in plenty of boiling, salted water. Leave, covered in the cooking water, until ready to serve. Place the fish in a frying pan or similarly wide-based pan that can hold the fillets in a single layer. Pour over the milk and season with pepper. Now begin the sauce. Peel and finely chop the shallot. Melt the butter in a small pan and stir in the shallot. Cook over a low heat for about 10 minutes until the shallot is golden and tender. Add the wine, which will bubble and seethe, and cook until reduced and syrupy. Stir in the cream and remove from the heat. Cook the fish over a medium heat for 5–6 minutes until cooked through. Meanwhile, boil a small pan of water. Add the vinegar. Crack an egg into a cup and slip it into the boiling water. Repeat with the second egg and cook for 1–2 minutes until the egg white is set and the yolk still runny. Turn off the heat. Strain 150ml of the cooking milk into the sauce, add the mustard and cook briskly, stirring constantly to finish the sauce. To serve, drain the potatoes, cut them into thick slices and arrange in the middle of two warmed dinner plates. Place a fillet of fish over the potatoes, season with black pepper and place an egg (lifted from the water with a perforated spoon) on top. Pour the sauce over the egg and around the fish and potatoes. Garnish with chives or parsley and serve.

HUSS WITH LEMON AND PARSLEY
Serves 2

When the Cornish Range reopened as Mousehole's answer to Rick Stein's Seafood Restaurant, they put a version of this dish on their early menus, made with John Dory. I had a go with inexpensive huss and its firm but tender, sweet meat is perfect for this delicious, simple dish. Good with very creamy mashed potato.

    2 huss fillets, approx. 175g each
    juice of ½ a large lemon
    handful of flat-leaf parsley
    50g unsalted butter
    salt and pepper

Slice each fillet on the slant to make three or four thin, long pieces. Pat the slices dry and place in a bowl. Squeeze the lemon juice over the top and toss around so that all the pieces come into contact with the juice. Finely chop the parsley. Add 30g of butter to a frying pan placed over a medium heat. As soon as the butter bubbles but before it gets a chance to brown, lay out the fish. Cook for a couple of minutes a side until the fish cooks through whilst adjusting the heat so neither butter nor fish browns. Now add the parsley, any lemon juice left in the dish and the last of the butter. Turn the pieces around a couple of times, so the parsley wilts, season with salt and pepper and serve on warmed plates.

FILLET OF HAKE WITH A HERB CRUST
Serves 6

Another lovely recipe from *Roast Chicken and Other Stories*.

When I haven't had all the herbs required for the crust mixture, I've resorted to just using parsley and it works deliciously well on its own with the zip of garlic and lemon zest. Firm white fish such as haddock, huss or cod would work similarly well in this recipe.

1 garlic clove
4 heaped tbsp fresh breadcrumbs
2 tbsp chopped parsley
½ tbsp chopped tarragon
½ tbsp chopped dill
1 tbsp chopped chives
grated rind of 1 lemon
6 x 175g skinned hake fillets
salt and pepper
flour for coating
1 egg
olive oil
1 quantity *beurre blanc* (see page 104)

Pre-heat the oven to 425°F/220°C/gas mark 7. Peel and finely chop the garlic. Mix together with the breadcrumbs, herbs and lemon rind. Season the fish fillets with salt and pepper and dip one side of them only first into the flour, then into the beaten egg and finally into the herb-and-breadcrumb mixture. Lay on a buttered baking sheet and, if there are any bald spots, fill in with more of the breadcrumb mixture. Drizzle with a teaspoon or so of olive oil.

Bake in the top of the oven for 10–15 minutes or until golden and crusty. Serve on warmed plates with *beurre blanc*.

Inshore Fish

To prepare sea bass
To fillet sea bass

Chinese Sea Bass with Ginger and Spring Onions
Sea Bass with *Sauce Vierge* or *Beurre Blanc*
Roast Sea Bass with Balsamic Vinegar
Sea Bass Carpaccio with Fennel Salad
Grilled Sea Bass with Cucumber Noodles and Sushi Ginger
Gurnard with Minted Pea Purée and Bacon
Fish Stock
Snotched Red Mullet with Garlic Butter
Red Mullet with Saffron Tomatoes and Green Beans
Red Mullet Wrapped in Parma Ham with Garlic and Rosemary
Provençal Fish Soup with Rouille and Croûtes
Braised John Dory with Sorrel

Sea Bass, Red Mullet, Gurnard and John Dory

In France they call sea bass *bar* or *loup de mer* and regard it as one of the finest fish in the sea. We called it plain bass until recently, adding 'sea' to differentiate between the increasingly ubiquitous farmed bass and the real thing. Bass is a sleek and elegant silvery fish and when you see lots of them swimming together, as they do, like the mackerel, pilchards and herring they chase for food, they look too beautiful to catch. There are millions out there in the sea – so no quota controls – but they have a reputation for being difficult to catch and are expensive in the shops. In the summer they're caught by hand – little boats can catch seventy or eighty a day – but leading up to Christmas they become worthless down here because there are so many. The flesh of sea bass is, to my mind, perfect. It has a silky texture and clean, fresh flavour that is complemented by its particularly rich skin, which bubbles and crisps spectacularly when grilled. I love to cook it whole, either steamed or wrapped in foil and baked in the oven. A grilled whole fish looks stupendous and the burnished skin is delicious to eat. Grilled fillets are good with rich buttery sauces like hollandaise and *beurre blanc*. It is also a lovely fish to eat raw.

The average weight of a mature sea bass is 1kg, which feeds four perfectly, but they are often landed much smaller than this. Perhaps it is the increased availability of small farmed bass – as popularized by Chinese restaurants – that has led to inshore fishermen landing immature bass which average 600g. These smaller fish feed two comfortably, three at a push, probably with leftovers.

Sea bass isn't an obvious fish to eat cold, but one of the River Café signature dishes is roast sea bass with lentils and salsa verde and on more than one occasion mine has been served cold. It was so good, I didn't demur.

To prepare sea bass

Watch out for vicious spiky fins, particularly on the 'backs' of sea bass, which should be snipped off with kitchen scissors before scaling. Sea bass are thickly covered with a layer of big scales. It's sensible to line the sink with newspaper before you start scaling because the thin little plastic discs go everywhere and stick to everything. Work up the body from the tail end, scraping a blunt knife vigorously backwards and forwards, until they're all gone. Having removed the scales, slit the belly from the anal fin to the head and pull out the guts with your fingers. Gutting a sea bass can be an alarming process because you often find undigested whole pilchards, baby squid or young, soft-shell crabs in their big bellies. Give the cavity a good wash under cold running water. To remove the head, cut in a V-shape rather than straight across so that none of the precious fillet is wasted.

To fillet sea bass

It takes practice and confidence to fillet a large, so-called round fish like bass and it's an expensive fish to spoil. Practise first on smaller and cheaper similar fish such as gurnard, herring or mackerel.

Use a very sharp thin-bladed knife, preferably a filleting knife.

Lay the fish on its side with its tail towards you and its backbone to your right (unless you are left-handed). Cut across the top of the fish below the head in a V-shape to release the top of the fillet. Turn the knife and slice close to the backbone, cutting all the way down to the tail in one swoop, but gently stroking the flat of the knife across the rib cage towards the belly as you slice. It helps to lift the fillet with your left hand as you move down the fish, so that you can see what you're doing. Turn the fish over and repeat on the other side. I find it easier to run the knife from tail to head on this side.

Keep the debris for the stockpot.

Bass is usually cooked with its skin on because it eats so well, but if you want to remove it, follow the instructions for skinning flat fish fillets (see page 65).

I've come late in life to appreciate red mullet. I had always found it bony, dry and rather too strongly flavoured, but recently I've discovered what a special little fish it is. It looks like a giant goldfish and is covered with a thick layer of scales and viscous dorsal fins which should be snipped off before scaling. Most red mullet landed weigh about 200g, which is exactly the right size for one person. It's often cooked with its liver in place, flavouring the fish in a rich, gamy way that suits the firm flesh. Most of the time it's cooked simply at the Fish Store – whole, either grilled or quickly roasted with butter or olive oil – and eaten with plenty of lemon juice, black pepper and Maldon sea salt. It's good like this with a smear of pesto or black olive paste and roasted red peppers and aubergine too, if you're in a Mediterranean mood. Another good idea is to tuck a sprig of rosemary in the cavity to encourage the gamy flavours. Whatever you do, take care not to overcook red mullet because it can be dry. Slashing the fish on the diagonal in a couple places, cutting down to the bone, helps it cook evenly. The local term for this is 'snotching'. For more preparation and filleting advice, see Oily Fish, pages 42–3. Red mullet skin is considered a delicacy.

Gurnard is not related to red mullet, but the pink/red colour of its skin is very similar. It's a prehistoric-looking fish with a big, beaky, hard face and surprisingly intricate snowflake etching on its huge, duck-like head. Although most fish are quite small, they can grow as large as 2kg, and whatever the size of the fish, a gurnard's head seems curiously at odds with its slim tapering body and long, beard-like side jaw fins. It's used for crab bait in this part of Cornwall and is essentially a stock and soup fish, but deserves greater acknowledgement (not least because it's very cheap). I'm a recent convert and buy it whole, using the head and carcass for the stockpot – they add an essential taste to Mediterranean fish soup – and I cook the fillets simply, either grilling or frying, using them as a cheap alternative to red mullet. It's quite a bony fish, similar to red mullet, mackerel, herring and pilchards, and needs to be pin-boned by running a finger over the flesh to locate bones and using tweezers to whip them out. If I'm filleting any of these fish, I take an old tip from Rick Stein and cut lines of bones out in a strip.

John Dory is a bit of a weirdo to look at. It's immediately recognizable by the black 'thumb prints' on either side of its stumpy but thin, flat body, which give it its other name – St Peter's fish or St Pierre.

The faded spot is said to denote the place where St Peter put his thumb when picking it up. It has a viscous Mohican-fin 'hairdo' which fringes to a tail that resembles a spiky Afro comb, but it is the pouting Mick Jagger lips which make St Pierre so distinctive. It has a smooth skin with no scales and firm, delicate tasting snowy-white meat. Big heavy bones make it easy to fillet but leave little room for flesh, so expect to get around 300g fillet from a 1kg fish. The two fillets divide naturally into three thin strips rather than the usual two and are small compared with the size of the fish. When buying from a fishmonger, always ask for the carcass to make stock, but if you want to have a go at filleting John Dory, follow the instructions for flat fish. It is less hassle to cook John Dory whole – either grilled or in a hot oven – but because the delicate, firm flesh suits creamy sauces, it means last-minute filleting and a quickly made cream and butter sauce. Summer and autumn are the best times for local John Dory.

CHINESE SEA BASS WITH GINGER AND SPRING ONIONS
Serves 4

There are so many lovely ways to cook a whole sea bass, but this one wins hands down most of the time at the Fish Store because it is so easy to make and so good to eat. The fish are cooked in the oven in foil and the foil can then be used to collect bones and other detritus destined for the bin.

Apart from being a lovely, simple dish to share with friends, this is perfect diet food. It tastes delicious, requires minimal preparation and cooking, and is healthy and satisfying, leaving you feeling light and elegantly fed.

The ideal accompaniment is boiled basmati rice and this way of cooking it gives perfect results every time. I specify toasted sesame oil in the list of ingredients. Any oil would do, but this one, sold as a condiment in Chinese and oriental ranges of food, gives the dish a rich, nutty flavour. Confusingly, it is often labelled as sesame oil. A small bottle with an oriental logo is usually the clue. If it's more appropriate, this recipe can be made in a steamer.

2 sea bass, 450–600g, head on, scaled and gutted

2 tbsp vegetable oil, preferably toasted sesame oil

2 bunches of spring onions

2 garlic cloves

50g piece fresh ginger

soy sauce

250g basmati rice

8 sheets of foil approx. 30 x 20cm

Pre-heat the oven to 400°F/200°C/gas mark 6. Cut two short diagonal slashes across the middle of both sides of the fish, cutting almost to the bone. Wash out the fish cavity and pat dry. Lay out four sheets of foil and use your hands to oil the fish all over. Lay the fish on a sheet of foil. Trim and cut the spring onions in long, thin diagonal slices. Peel the garlic and slice in wafer-thin rounds. Peel the ginger and slice into thin pieces and then into batons or small scraps. Mix spring onions, garlic and ginger together. Divide between the body cavity and the slashes on both sides of the fish. Working on one fish at a time, splash with soy sauce, adding any leftover oil. Place a second sheet of foil over the fish and loosely fold and crimp the edges to make a secure but not overly tight parcel. Place the fish on a baking tray and cook in the hot oven for 15 minutes. The parcels can be kept waiting for 5–10 minutes without harm. Meanwhile, rinse the rice until the water runs clean and place in a pan with 375ml cold water. Bring to the boil, reduce the heat immediately to very low, cover the pan and cook for 10 minutes. Turn off the heat but leave the lid for a further 10 minutes for the rice to finish cooking in the steam. Fork up the rice and serve. Remove the skin and fillet the fish at the table, serving one fillet per person with a share of the spring onions, ginger, garlic and juices. Serve with soy sauce.

POACHED SEA BASS WITH *SAUCE VIERGE* OR *BEURRE BLANC*
Serves 6

Many summers ago, I was served this at a dinner party in St Tropez and was so captivated by the combination of flavours, textures and colours on the plate that I've been making it ever since. In the summer it is even more popular at the Fish Store than the previous recipe. *Sauce vierge* –

vierge means virgin and is a term for olive oil made from first-pressed olives – originates, I think, from Michel Guérard's seminal *Cuisine Gourmande*, and is really a tomato vinaigrette. When I make this for a family supper, I usually cook a whole bass in foil in the oven and serve the fillets from the fish at the table, but for a dinner party it's less hassle to poach individual fillets.

6 fillets sea bass, approx. 175g each

for the sauce vierge:
6 ripe but firm tomatoes
2 plump new-season garlic cloves
1 tbsp red wine vinegar
200ml best possible olive oil
handful of basil leaves

for the court bouillon*:*
1 onion
1 stick celery
1 carrot
1 bay leaf
1 tsp salt
1 litre cold water
1 tbsp white wine vinegar

Place the tomatoes in a bowl, cover with boiling water and count to 20. Drain, peel, halve, scrape out the seeds and slice the flesh into dice. Peel the garlic and slice in wafer-thin rounds. Mix together the vinegar and garlic in a large bowl. Stir the chopped tomatoes into the bowl and leave to macerate for 30 minutes. Stir the olive oil into the salad and tear or snip the basil over the top. Stir and serve.

Meanwhile, peel and chop the onion, thinly slice the celery, scrape and chop the carrot and place in a pan with the bay leaf, salt, water and white wine vinegar. Bring to the boil and simmer for 20 minutes.

Cook the fish by slipping the fillets into the boiling *court bouillon*. Bring back to the boil and switch off the heat. Leave, covered, for 5 minutes. Carefully lift the fillets of fish out of the pan. Drain on absorbent kitchen paper and remove the skin.

To serve, place a fillet of fish on a warm dinner plate, spoon over the sauce and serve with mashed or new potatoes and perhaps green beans. Alternatively, serve with *beurre blanc*.

BEURRE BLANC
Serves 4–6

4 shallots
225g cold, unsalted butter
75ml white wine vinegar
salt and pepper
a squeeze of lemon juice

Peel, halve and finely chop the shallots. Cut the butter into cubes. Place shallots, vinegar and 50ml cold water in a small non-reactive pan. Season with salt and pepper and place over a high heat. Cook until all the liquid has evaporated. Turn the heat to very low and whisk in the butter, piece by piece, until it is incorporated and the sauce has the consistency of thin cream. Taste for seasoning and add lemon juice to taste.

ROAST SEA BASS WITH BALSAMIC VINEGAR
Serves 4

It's probably my background as a restaurant critic that accounts for it, but I've definitely got a 'nose' for sniffing out worthwhile restaurants. Take the short stay my sister and I had in Verona. I purposely didn't arrive armed with guidebooks and, although I had a few dining recommendations from friends up my sleeve, I wanted to do my own restaurant sleuthing. Bottega del Vino is tucked away down a side street off one of the main shopping drags and it drew me like a magnet. From the outside it doesn't look much, but once inside the place is a hive of activity. The tightly packed tables edge up to the busy bar and a proliferation of preoccupied but attentive waiters work the deep, L-shaped room. Wine, as you can tell from the name of the place, is serious business here and the bar is lined with bottles of various vintages from local names like Masi, noted for its Valpolicella. The wine list is a thick book, but the menu is far more manageable. It was my sister who chose sea bass with balsamico but I was the one who wanted the recipe. Our waiter tossed his blond locks as he sniffed the cork from our Soave Classico, poured a mouthful into a glass, deftly decanted it into another, sniffed and passed it on for confirmation of acceptability. Minutes later, he was back telling me in his perfect English that the sea bass is splashed with balsamico, roasted, filleted and then the juices poured over the top. So, you can either do it like that or use fillets as I have done in this recipe; mine is quick and stunningly good. Aged balsamic vinegar is thick and syrupy and clings to the fish, giving it a sweet, rich and beguiling succulence. Serve with chive game chips (see page 218), made with 2 tablespoons of finely chopped flat-leaf parsley instead of chives, and a green vegetable. Peas with young leaf spinach added for the last 30 seconds of cooking and served with a splash of olive oil go particularly well with this.

> 4 sea bass fillets, approx. 200g each
> 2 tbsp olive oil
> 4 tbsp aged balsamic vinegar
> salt and pepper

Pre-heat the oven to 400°F/200°C/gas mark 6. Place a sheet of foil in a small, shallow metal oven pan. Smear the skin side of the fish with olive oil and lay the fillets skin-side down in the pan. Dribble the flesh with the balsamico and a splash of olive oil. Season with salt and pepper. Cook in the hot oven for 10 minutes. Transfer to warmed plates and dribble any juices left in the foil over the top. Serve immediately.

SEA BASS CARPACCIO WITH FENNEL SALAD
Serves 8–10

The *Spectator* is a not a magazine I usually see, but when I do I always check out the Dear Mary 'Your Problems Solved' column. 'During May,' a letter in a copy discarded in the Fish Store log basket began, 'I attended an exceptionally good party given in Venice.' The letter requested enlightenment on 'the unusual and gratifyingly texture' of one of the dishes served. The recipe, described by MW of Wiltshire as 'a kind of sea bass carpaccio', was prepared by Renato Piccolotto, the chef of the Hotel Cipriani, and is a masterpiece of simplicity. Carpaccio

in this context means thin slices and in this instance the fish is marinated in lemon juice for a couple of hours. This has the effect of 'cooking' the fish and thus changing its colour and texture. It is quite safe to
eat and surprisingly delicious. Here, it is served with a crunchy salad
garnish which has been doused in extra virgin olive oil with a few
shredded basil leaves. The dish is a perfect dinner-party starter in that
it can be prepared in advance, assembled quickly and easily at the last
minute and has enormous appeal even to those who've never fancied
the idea of raw fish. The first time I made it, I followed the recipe slav-
ishly (500g sea bass, 60g each diced tomato, cucumber and fennel, 3
basil leaves plus a few more when it's served) but everyone agreed that
the salad garnish was so agreeable that next time I upped the quantities considerably.

When sea bass is available, especially during its summer season,
this is a favourite Fish Store dinner-party starter. Particularly if someone can persuade Jake to fillet it. This recipe is also good with salmon.

> 500g sea bass fillet
> 2 lemons
> 200g ripe plum or vine tomatoes
> 200g cucumber
> 200g fennel
> about 12 flourishing basil leaves
> Maldon sea salt flakes and black pepper
> 6 tbsp extra virgin olive oil

Check over the fish with your index finger to locate stray bones and
remove them with tweezers. Using a sharp, thin-bladed knife, cut across
the fillets, at an angle, to make very thin slices. Lay the slices out in a
single layer on a large plate and squeeze over the lemon juice. Cover
with clingfilm and leave in the fridge for 30 minutes to 'cook'.
Meanwhile, place the tomatoes in a bowl, cover with boiling water and
count to 20. Drain, splash with cold water to stop the flesh softening,
then remove skins and core. Quarter the tomatoes, scrape out the
seeds and dice the flesh. Use a potato peeler to skin the cucumber, split
lengthways and scrape out the seeds and their watery surrounds with a
teaspoon. Dice into similar-sized pieces. Trim the fennel, cut out the

dense core and finely dice the layers of flesh. Shred 3 of the basil leaves. Place tomatoes, cucumber, fennel and shredded basil in a bowl, season with salt and pepper and add 4 tablespoons of olive oil. Toss and leave to marinate until ready to serve. Drain the lemon juice from the fish, season lightly with salt and pepper and add the remaining olive oil. Place the salad over the top, garnish with the remaining basil and serve.

GRILLED SEA BASS WITH CUCUMBER NOODLES AND SUSHI GINGER
Serves 2

Cucumber is terrific in slurping noodle dishes, adding a clean, crisp taste and texture which goes well with the slippery noodles. Ready-to-go rice noodles sold in sealed plastic packs are a useful standby, but any of the round (as opposed to flat) rice noodles would be good for this dish. Sushi ginger has become an essential relish and is used in all sorts of fish dishes. It's sold by health food shops, some supermarkets and many fishmongers. To make this for more people, just multiply the ingredients in proportion.

½ cucumber
2 spring onions
½ chicken stock cube
3 tbsp soy sauce
6 slices sushi ginger
150g soaked Udon or other round rice noodles
2 sea bass fillets, approx. 175g each
1 tbsp olive oil
salt and pepper

Use a potato peeler to peel the cucumber. Cut it in half lengthways and use a teaspoon to scrape away the seeds and their watery surround. Slice into chunky half-moons. Trim the spring onions and then finely slice them. Dissolve the stock cube in 300ml boiling water. Add the soy sauce, cucumber and spring onions to the stock. Cover and leave for 5 minutes. Add the ginger to the broth.

At the same time, place the noodles in a separate bowl and cover with boiling water. Leave for 5 minutes. Drain the noodles and divide between two deep bowls. Strain the stock over the top, then stir the cucumber and onions into the noodles.

Pre-heat the grill. Brush the bass with olive oil and season with salt and pepper. Grill on both sides, finishing with the skinned side, allowing the skin to blister and crisp but taking care not to overcook the fish. Allow a couple of minutes each side and up to 5 minutes, depending on thickness. Lay the fish skin-side up over the noodles and serve.

GURNARD WITH MINTED PEA PURÉE AND BACON
Serves 4

A lovely combination of textures and flavours. There is sufficient minted pea purée for 6–8 servings but it keeps well and reheats perfectly.

    1 recipe minted pea purée (see page 284)
    8 gurnard fillets without skin
    salt and pepper
    flour for dusting
    8 rindless, thin rashers smoked streaky bacon
    groundnut oil for frying
    1 lemon

First make the pea purée.

Run your finger over the gurnard fillets to check for stray bones, pulling them out with tweezers or pliers, or divide them in two lengthways, cutting out the bony strip. Season both sides of the fish with salt and pepper, then dust with flour, shaking away the excess. Grill the bacon on both sides until very crisp. Rest on absorbent kitchen paper to drain and keep warm. Heat a couple of tablespoons of oil in a frying pan and cook four fillets at a time so the fish isn't crowded and can cook quickly and evenly. Allow a couple of minutes a side, until golden and just cooked through. Serve the fish fillets over the hot pea purée, with the bacon on top of the fish and a lemon wedge on the side.

FISH STOCK
Makes approx. 2 litres

Fish stock is quick and cheap to make. Most of the goodness and flavour comes from the bones and trimmings of fish, but the heads and skin are good too. All white fish and most crustaceans make satisfactory fish stocks, but oily fish such as mackerel, herring, pilchards and sardine aren't suitable, except in special circumstances, and give an oily, bitter flavour. Different combinations of fish and shellfish can give marked differences in flavour. The *crème de la crème* combination is sole (particularly Dover), turbot or halibut carcass, head and tail, with cod trimmings. Sole, whiting, turbot and monkfish, which are among the few fish that yield substantial amounts of gelatine, provide stocks with the most body. Red mullet and gurnard give it a noticeable Mediterranean flavour, and crab and lobster debris give it a depth of flavour and richer colour. It's easy to scrounge carcasses, heads and tails and small damaged fish from fishmongers, particularly those in Newlyn who are wholesalers too. In fact, some of them close to the fish market maintain a help-yourself box next to the wet fish display and will help you pick out the best of the bunch if they're not busy.

Traditionally, fish stocks are seasoned with finely diced onion, carrot and leek, with a bouquet garni of parsley, thyme and a bay leaf. Because fish stocks cook quickly, the vegetables should be finely sliced or diced to release the flavour in the shortest possible time.

Fish stock is never as clear as meat and vegetable stocks, but the clearest stocks are made with very fresh bones and trimmings. They should be used immediately and washed thoroughly under running water. The carcass should be chopped across the backbone into 5cm pieces.

Fish stock is not improved by increasing the length of cooking. To intensify the flavour of fish stock, reduce it by gentle simmering (without the bones, etc.) and by adding new bones and trimmings for old.

Fish stock should be stored covered and will keep for a few days in the fridge but the flavours begin to fade after 12 hours. It can be kept successfully for up to 1 month in the freezer.

900g carcasses, heads, tails and trimmings of non-oily fish
1 onion
1 carrot
1 stick celery
1 leek

knob of butter
salt and pepper
glass of white wine
sprig of thyme
small bunch of parsley stalks
½ bay leaf

Leave the fish debris to soak in cold water for an hour. Drain and chop the carcasses across the backbone in 5cm widths. Meanwhile, peel and chop the onion, scrape and chop the carrot, trim and finely slice the celery and leek. Melt the butter in a spacious pan and stir in the chopped vegetables, season with salt and pepper, cover and cook gently for 10 minutes. Stir the fish trimmings into the vegetables, then add the wine. Cook on a fierce heat for a few minutes until reduced, then add 2.3 litres of cold water. Bring to the boil, skim well, add the thyme, parsley and bay leaf, reduce the heat and simmer for 25 minutes. Strain. To concentrate the flavour, simmer gently until reduced by a third.

SNOTCHED RED MULLET WITH GARLIC BUTTER
Serves 4

Smearing the slashes or 'snotches' cut in the mullet with garlic butter is an idea borrowed from Jake Freethy, skipper of *Go For It*. The sweet, garlicky flesh is delicious with some very crisply fried or roasted potatoes tossed with masses of chopped flat-leaf parsley.

4 red mullet, scaled, trimmed, gutted with heads on
4 big garlic cloves
salt
100g soft butter
squeeze of lemon
1 lemon, to serve

Pre-heat the oven to 400°F/200°C/gas mark 6. Cut two or three diagonal slashes on either side of the fish, cutting down to the bone. Rinse the fish and pat dry with absorbent kitchen paper. Peel and finely chop the garlic. Sprinkle with a little salt and use the flat of a knife to work to a juicy paste. Place the butter in a bowl. Add the garlic paste and a squeeze of lemon. Beat the garlic into the butter. Spread the garlic butter in the cavity and slashes on both sides of the fish. Line a baking tray with tinfoil and lay out the fish. Cook in the oven for 15–20 minutes until just cooked. Serve the fish whole with a lemon wedge.

RED MULLET WITH SAFFRON TOMATOES AND GREEN BEANS
Serves 4

A rather smart-looking, restaurant-style high-rise layered dish which is also good without the beans, served over rice. Adding saffron to the tomatoes gives the sauce a Moorish flavour. I like it with a few buttery new potatoes tossed with mint.

750g ripe tomatoes
4 garlic cloves
4 tbsp olive oil
salt and pepper
generous pinch of saffron softened in 1 tbsp hot water
400g fine green beans
8 red mullet fillets, approx. 75g each
extra virgin olive oil
2 tbsp chopped flat-leaf parsley

Place the tomatoes in a bowl. Cover with boiling water, count to 20, drain and peel. Cut out the cores, discard the seeds and chop. Peel and finely chop the garlic. In a large frying pan, fry the garlic in 3 tablespoons of olive oil until aromatic and lightly coloured. Add the tomatoes, salt, pepper and saffron, and simmer for 10 minutes. Top and tail the beans and cook in a big pan of salted water for 2 minutes. Drain and keep warm. Meanwhile, brush the red mullet fillets with olive oil and season with salt and pepper. Grill for 2 minutes a side until just cooked through. Make a nest of beans in the middle of four serving plates, top with tomato sauce and arrange the fish, skin-side up, over the sauce. Swirl over and round the fish with olive oil, garnish with parsley and serve.

RED MULLET WRAPPED IN PARMA HAM WITH GARLIC AND ROSEMARY

Serves 2

Here's an Italian way of preparing red mullet which suits the robust flavour of this lovely fish. It smells wonderful as it cooks and is good with buttered new potatoes tossed with mint or very crisp roast potatoes, started before the fish goes into the oven.

> 2 red mullet, scaled, trimmed, gutted, with heads on
> 2 garlic cloves
> 1 tbsp fresh rosemary leaves
> 4 tbsp olive oil
> salt and pepper
> 1 lemon
> 4 slices Parma ham
> extra virgin olive oil

Pre-heat the oven to 400°F/200°C/gas mark 6. Wash the fish inside and out and pat dry. Have ready a small roasting tin. Peel and finely chop the garlic. Chop the rosemary leaves until they resemble green dust. Mix the two together with the juice from half the lemon, 2 tablespoons of olive oil and some salt and pepper. Spoon some of the mixture into the cavity of each mullet and smear the rest all over them. Wrap two slices of ham around each fish and arrange in the roasting tin. Dribble the remaining oil over the fish. Cook in the oven for 15–20 minutes until the fish is just cooked through and the ham is crisp. Serve with a lemon wedge and a bottle of your best olive oil to splash over the fish.

PROVENÇAL FISH SOUP WITH *ROUILLE* AND *CROÛTES*

Serves 6

A good fish stock, nurtured over several days from the debris of many crab and fish meals, tends to lead me to make this rich and luscious soup at the Fish Store. Unlike bouillabaisse, the other famous French fisherman's soup, which is made with pieces of fish, this one is a thick, smooth(ish) purée. It was originally made with the fish left behind in the nets, either damaged or too small for sale, all boiled up with garlic, tomatoes and other soup vegetables. It ends up a deep brick colour and has a back flavour of anise, saffron and orange zest, and the merest hint of chilli from the cayenne pepper. It's extremely rich and filling, particularly as it is always served with a spankingly fiery *rouille* or mayonnaise, grated Gruyère cheese and slices of oven-toasted bread. It's fun to load the toasts with *rouille* and cheese and float them in the soup, where they melt and merge with the gorgeous fish nectar. A feast. Follow with cheese and salad. And something indulgent from the pudding section.

1 onion

1 carrot

6 garlic cloves

1 leek, white part only

1 large fennel bulb

olive oil for frying, approx. 100ml

salt and pepper

approx. 1.3kg mixed fish, which must include:

    gurnard, red or grey mullet, huss, monkfish, rascasse if you can get them, but also conger eel, sea bream, hake or any non-oily fish and small, soft-shell crabs

6 very ripe tomatoes or 400g can peeled whole tomatoes

½ tsp cayenne pepper

bouquet garni made with:

    1 bay leaf, 1 sprig thyme, 1 sprig rosemary, small bunch parsley, particularly the stalks, and leek greens

5cm strip dried orange zest

1 tbsp tomato purée

½ glass Pernod, Ricard or similar if possible

2.5 litres fish stock (see page 108)

very generous pinch of saffron stamens softened in 1 tbsp boiling water

for the croûtes:

1 day-old baguette or similar

olive oil

for the rouille:

2 red peppers

1 thick slice white bread

2 large garlic cloves

1 small red chilli

salt and pepper

pinch saffron stamens softened in 1 tbsp boiling water

100ml olive oil

freshly grated Gruyère, approx. 200g

Peel and chop the onion, carrot and garlic. Trim and slice the leek and fennel. Heat the oil in a heavy casserole that can hold the finished soup and stir in the prepared vegetables and garlic. Season with salt and pepper, cover and cook, stirring a couple of times, over a low heat for 15–20 minutes until soft but not brown. Meanwhile, wash all the seafood and chop – heads, bones and all – into pieces about 6cm long. Coarsely chop the tomatoes (it's easiest to chop canned tomatoes in the can). Sprinkle the cayenne over the vegetables, then pile the fish over the top, adding the tomatoes, bouquet garni (tied up with string), orange zest, tomato purée and Pernod, if using. Increase the heat and cook, stirring a couple of times to avoid sticking, for a further 5 minutes. Add the stock and saffron and bring up to the boil – this will take quite a while – as quickly as possible. Reduce the heat and simmer for 30–45 minutes until everything is thoroughly cooked and falling to bits. Liquidize the soup in batches, then return through a sieve or Mouli-legumes, pressing and scraping under the sieve so nothing is wasted, into another pan or bowl. Stir well, then return to the original (clean) pan and discard the debris. You want the soup to be smooth and without lumps or bone. Reheat, taste and adjust the seasoning.

To make the croûtes: pre-heat the oven to 400°F/200°C/gas mark 6. Slice the loaf, brush both sides generously with olive oil, lay out the slices on a baking sheet and bake, turning once, for about 6 minutes until crisp and golden.

To make the rouille: core, deseed and quarter the peppers lengthways. Grill, skin-side up, until the skin chars and blisters. Peel off the skin. Soak the bread in water, leave for a few minutes, then squeeze out the excess. Peel and chop the garlic. Trim and split the chilli. Scrape away the seeds and finely chop. Pound or process the bread with the peppers, garlic, chilli, salt, pepper and saffron to make a paste, and gradually incorporate the oil to make a smooth, thick, shiny sauce. Transfer to a bowl. Cover with clingfilm, to stop a crust forming, if not using immediately.

BRAISED JOHN DORY WITH SORREL
Serves 2

If preferred, this lovely dish could be made with turbot or brill (see Flat Fish, page 63) and mushrooms could be used in place of sorrel.

    900g–1kg John Dory, gutted, gills and fins removed
    100g young sorrel
    2 shallots
    salt and pepper
    25g butter cut into small pieces, plus an extra knob
    75ml dry white wine
    75ml thick cream

Pre-heat the oven to 400°F/200°C/gas mark 6. Wash the fish thoroughly and pat dry. Check over the sorrel, discarding discoloured leaves and any tough central stems. Wash and shake dry. Make piles of leaves, roll up like a cigar and cut into very fine ribbons to make a chiffonade. Peel and finely chop the shallots. Season the fish on both sides. Smear a baking dish that can hold the fish snugly with the knob of butter and sprinkle with the shallots. Place the fish on top and pour in the wine. Cook in the oven for 20 minutes. When the fish is cooked, transfer to a platter and keep hot. Pour the cooking liquid and shallots into a saucepan over a high heat. Boil until the liquid is syrupy and reduced to 2–3 tablespoons. Add the cream and bring briefly to the boil, then stir in the sorrel (or cooked, sliced mushrooms). Bring back to the boil and season to taste. Remove from the heat and beat in the butter, little by little.

Peel the skin from the fish and remove the fringe of bones by running a sharp knife around the edge of the fish and pushing the bones outwards. Lift the fish on to a warmed serving plate, spoon the sauce over the top and serve. Alternatively, remove the fillets before saucing.

Fish without Bones

Roast Monkfish Tail with Garlic and Onion
Monkfish in the Style of *Coq au Vin*
Monkfish Chowder with Green Beans and Thyme
Monkfish and Chorizo Paella with Prawns
Monkfish Thai Green Curry
Saffron Monkfish and Leek Puff Pastry Pie
Monkfish Mollee
Picasso's *Matelote* of Monkfish
Roast Monkfish Satay with Cucumber Relish
Skate with Black Butter

Monkfish and Skate

Monkfish is a vicious-looking creature – it has a huge head, vast jaw and rapier teeth – which is why it is rare to see anything more than the tail on the fishmonger's slab. In the supermarket it is sold in fillets, cut from either side of its cartilaginous spine. Its dense, meaty, no-bones flesh is excellent for kebabs and can stand up to any marinade or flavouring you might use for chicken. It can be grilled, barbecued, fried, stewed or cooked in the oven.

There are two things to watch out for when it comes to monkfish. One is to be sure to remove (or ask the fishmonger to remove) the slimy membrane that covers the surface of its skinned tail. It's not hard to do but it can be tricky and entails running a knife under the surface and cutting it away in sheets. If this isn't done, the membrane shrinks as it cooks and ruptures the fish, leaving an unattractive rubbery pucker. The other point to watch is that monkfish tail is very dense and meaty and doesn't suit being undercooked. Nor does it suit overcooking. So, when it comes to monkfish, keep a weather eye.

Occasionally it is possible to buy monkfish cheeks. My fishing deep-throat tells me that it's quite common for fishermen to cut out the cheeks from those horrible faces. These steaks are sweeter than the tail and are very good dipped in egg and breadcrumbs and then fried.

Skate or ray (or *raie*, as its spelled in France) looks like a spaceship and moves through the water waving its wings up and down. It's rare to see the big ones: they can be 100 or 110kg a piece. Mostly they average the size of the Fish Store windows – about 1.5m square. Sometimes they get caught in a tangle net (which has a 76mm-odd centimetre mesh), along with monkfish, turbot and brill and, occasionally, spider crabs, crayfish and lobsters. Only the wings ever appear on the wet slab and they're normally skinned for sale. The mild-flavoured, meaty flesh is supported by cartilaginous long, knobbly finger 'bones' and it looks like snowy-white jumbo cord when the wing is cooked. It is pleasingly satisfying to 'stroke' the fish off the cartilage and not have to worry about bones. Skate wings are an occasional treat at the Fish Store and they are always served with black butter – *raie au beurre noir* – although I am occasionally tempted to batter and deep-fry them (to eat with minted pea purée and chips). Avoid buying skate with a strong smell of ammonia and, given the choice, choose wings which weigh approximately 450g and divide them in half down the cartilage to feed two.

ROAST MONKFISH TAIL WITH GARLIC AND ONION
Serves 4

This is without doubt my favourite way of cooking monkfish tail because it is so easy and so delicious. The fillet is spiked with garlic in the same way as you might prepare a joint of lamb. Don't be shy about this. Monkfish can soak up quite a lot of garlic before you will notice any effect. If you wish, you could also add a bay leaf and a small bunch of thyme, but neither is necessary. The fish is laid over very finely sliced onions and both are liberally doused with olive oil. The fish ends up tender and succulent and the onions soft, juicy and sweet. All you need with this is a lemon wedge to squeeze over the top and chive game chives (see page 218), which can be cooked in the oven at the same time.

> 4 monkfish tail fillets, approx. 250g each
> 2 garlic cloves
> 4 tbsp olive oil
> 4 medium onions, approx 250g
> salt and pepper
> best olive oil for serving
> lemon wedges to serve

Pre-heat the oven to 400°F/200°C/gas mark 6. Remove any trace of the slimy membrane covering the monkfish. Peel the garlic and slice very thinly in rounds. Using a small sharp knife, make several slashes in the monkfish, as if you were preparing to garlic a lamb joint. Post the garlic in the slashes. Use one tablespoon of the oil and smear it all over the fish. Set aside. Generously smear a baking tin with some of the oil. Peel and halve the onions. Slice them very thinly. Spread them out in the baking tin to make a bed for the monkfish and lay the fillets on top, lining them up side by side. Season the fish with salt and pepper and splash with the remaining olive oil. Roast in the oven for 25 minutes until the fish is cooked through and the onions tender and browned slightly at the edges. Give the monkfish tails and their juicy onion goo a generous seasoning of sea salt and black pepper and a lavish swirl of your best olive oil before serving with lemon wedges.

MONKFISH IN THE STYLE OF *COQ AU VIN*
Serves 6

When I turned up at the Fish Store on Easter Monday one year, I overlapped with my eldest son Zach and his girlfriend. 'Don't bother to bring anything for supper,' he said. 'Royden's given us some monkfish.' The lovely thing about a gift of fish from Royden is that we're likely to be favoured when there is a serious seasonal glut, so it gives me the opportunity to experiment *ad infinitum*. There aren't many fish that can tolerate being cooked in a stew like chicken or beef, but monkfish is one of them. Its mild flavour and dense, meaty texture make it perfect for this relatively quick yet comforting dish cooked in the style of *coq au vin* or *boeuf bourguignonne* with masses of garlic and strong-flavoured smoked bacon. It is very good with frozen peas and boiled new potatoes. Boiled basmati rice is another option.

8 rashers rindless smoked streaky bacon or 150g diced pancetta

4 large shallots

4 garlic cloves

1kg monkfish tail fillet

4 tbsp flour

150g small mushrooms

4 medium carrots, approx. 350g in total

4 tbsp olive oil

1 bay leaf

500ml red wine

1 chicken stock cube

salt and pepper
2 tbsp chopped flat-leaf parsley

Chop the bacon into small pieces. Peel, halve and finely slice the shallots. Peel the garlic and slice in thin rounds. Remove any trace of the slimy membrane covering the monkfish and cut into kebab-size chunks. Toss the fish in the flour. Wipe away any dirt from the mushrooms and slice thinly. Trim and scrape the carrots, then cut in thick slices. Heat half the oil in a medium-sized, heavy-bottomed pan over a medium heat and stir in the bacon. Cook, stirring after a couple of minutes, for about 5 minutes, until the bacon is nicely crisp. Add the shallots, garlic and bay leaf and adjust the heat so that the shallots cook gently for a further 5 minutes until limp. Move the contents of the pan to the sides and add the remaining oil. Add the fish and brown briefly, piling the bacon and shallots over the top when you turn the pieces. Pile the sliced mushrooms on top and add the wine. Let it bubble up over the food, then stir to loosen the flour from the fish and thicken the sauce. Dissolve the stock cube in 600ml boiling water and add to the pan. Bring to the boil, stirring constantly, then add the carrots. Season with salt and pepper, partially cover the pan and cook for about 15 minutes until the carrots are tender, the fish is cooked through and the sauce is reduced and thickened. Adjust the seasoning with salt and pepper, discard the bay leaf, garnish with the parsley and serve immediately or reheat later.

MONKFISH CHOWDER WITH GREEN BEANS AND THYME
Serves 2–4

There couldn't be a much simpler and quicker way of making a comforting and satisfying yet chic and healthy fish supper than this soup-cum-stew. It's roughly based on a New England chowder. These chunky soups usually contain seafood and potatoes and are always made with milk. There is plenty for two as a main dish and sufficient for four if following with something else. Serve with crusty bread and butter for dunking.

600g new potatoes
salt and freshly milled black pepper

500g monkfish fillet

1 trimmed leek, approx. 125g

1 shallot

25g butter

sprig of thyme

1 bay leaf

100g extra fine green beans

400ml milk

1 tbsp finely chopped flat-leaf parsley

Boil the potatoes in plenty of salted water until tender. Drain, return to the pan, cover with cold water and leave for a couple of minutes. Drain again, remove the skins and cut into chunks. Remove any trace of the slimy membrane covering the monkfish and cut into small kebab-size chunks. Trim the leek, split lengthways and then slice across to make chunky half-moons. Tip into a colander, rinse under cold water and shake dry. Trim and finely chop the shallot. Melt the butter in a heavy-bottomed, lidded pan placed over a medium-low heat. Stir in the leek and shallot. Add a generous seasoning of salt and pepper, the thyme and bay leaf. Adjust the heat so that the vegetables soften gently, cover the pan and cook for 10 minutes. Top and tail the beans, then cut them in half. Stir the beans into the leek and shallot mixture, cover the pan and cook, stirring a couple of times, for a further 5 minutes. Now add the fish. Stir as it firms and turns snowy white. Add the potatoes and the milk. Simmer for about 10 minutes to finish cooking the fish. Taste and adjust the seasoning. Remove the thyme and bay leaf, sprinkle with the chopped parsley and serve.

MONKFISH AND CHORIZO PAELLA WITH PRAWNS
Serves 6

I finally gave in to Jake's pleas for me to make a paella. The deal was that he would provide the seafood and I would do the rest. On the appointed day, he dropped off a huge monkfish tail and a bag of frozen shell-on prawns. Thanks to Tessa, the friend who persuaded me that I should write this book, we have a big paella dish at the Fish Store. It's about 40cm wide and feeds six greedy appetites. If you are not so fortunate, use two large frying pans and divide the ingredients between them. Paella is a dish that is good whatever the weather. If it's hot and balmy and you don't fancy cooking indoors, it could be cooked outside on the barbecue. If it's fine but there's a chill in the air, it is the perfect al fresco meal because it doesn't matter if the last few mouthfuls are lukewarm. When it's rainy and cold, it's a dish that conjures up thoughts of hot, sunny days. This version matches bland but meaty monkfish with spicy chorizo, the whole enriched in the traditional paella way with onion, garlic, peppers and a hint of saffron. It looks stunning garnished with prawns, lemon wedges and chopped flat-leaf parsley. A lovely treat for all the senses. If traditional calasparra or arborio risotto rice isn't available, you will get very good results with basmati.

1 large onion
4 large garlic cloves
salt and pepper
4 tbsp olive oil
100g sliced chorizo
2 red peppers, preferably the pointy, sweet Italian type
1 large beef tomato
2 very generous pinches of saffron stamens, softened in 1 tbsp
    hot water
1kg monkfish tail fillet or 500g monkfish tail and 500g prepared squid
350g calasparra, arborio or basmati rice
1 litre fish stock or 2 chicken stock cubes
8 large shell-on cooked prawns or 12 medium-sized ones
1 large lemon
1 tbsp chopped flat-leaf parsley

Keeping separate piles, peel, halve and finely chop the onion and garlic. Sprinkle the garlic with ½ tsp salt and use the flat of a small knife to crush it to a paste. Heat the oil in a 35cm diameter paella pan or in two large frying pans placed over a medium heat. Stir in the onion and garlic and cook for 3–4 minutes before adding the chorizo. Cook for a further couple of minutes to release some of the fat and flavour from the chorizo. Meanwhile, dice the peppers, discarding core, seeds and white filament. Pour boiling water over the tomato. Count to 20, drain and remove the skin. Chop the tomato. Add peppers to the onion. Stir well and cook for 5 minutes before adding the tomato and saffron. Leave to cook while you remove any trace of the slimy membrane covering the monkfish and chop it into kebab-size pieces. Stir the fish into the onion mixture. Increase the heat slightly and cook for 5 minutes to seal the fish. Season with salt and pepper. Stir in the unwashed rice and cook for a couple of minutes while you heat up the fish stock or dissolve the stock cubes in 1 litre of boiling water. Stir the stock into the pan, return to the boil, then reduce the heat to a steady simmer. Cook for 20 minutes or until all the liquid has been absorbed into the rice and the grains are swollen and tender. Fold the food together rather than stir it, encouraging the paella to cook evenly. Garnish with the prawns and lemon wedges and leave to sit, covered, for 5 minutes before scattering over the parsley and serving the paella from the pan. Another good last-minute addition to this paella is a handful of green beans which have been cut in half and boiled for 2 minutes.

MONKFISH THAI GREEN CURRY
Serves 4

Everyone loves Thai green curry and monkfish is perfect for the dish. The vital ingredient, apart from a decent curry paste, is *nam pla* or *nuoc nam*, as they call this pungent, salty liquor in Vietnam. It gives the spicy coconut broth that haunting sour back flavour which singles out the good green Thai curry from the mediocre. Serve with basmati rice.

800g monkfish tail fillet
3 shallots or 1 onion
1 garlic clove
2 green chillies
2 lemon grass stalks
200g fine French beans
2 tbsp vegetable oil
2 heaped tbsp Thai green curry paste
2 x 200ml carton coconut milk or
    400g can coconut milk
2–3 tbsp Thai fish sauce (*nam pla*)

1–2 limes
2 kaffir lime leaves
½ chicken stock cube
300ml boiling water
big bunch of coriander
handful of Thai basil, if possible

Get everything ready and assembled before you start cooking. Remove any trace of the slimy membrane covering the monkfish and cut into kebab-size pieces. Peel and chop the shallots and garlic. Trim the chillies, split lengthways, scrape away the seeds and slice into long, thin strips. Chop into tiny dice. Smack the lemon grass stalks with something heavy to crack their woody exterior. Trim the French beans and halve. Heat a wok, large frying pan or 2 litre capacity pan and add the oil, garlic, shallots and chillies and cook for a couple of minutes. Stir in the curry paste and 3 tablespoons of coconut milk. Add 2 tbsp fish sauce, a couple of strips of lime zest if you haven't been able to find kaffir lime leaves (available freeze-dried from Bart Spices) and the remaining coconut milk. Dissolve the stock cube in the boiling water and add that too. Adjust the heat and leave to simmer, stirring occasionally for about 10 minutes. Taste and adjust the seasoning with lime juice and fish sauce, salt shouldn't be necessary. Stir in half the chopped coriander (stalks are fine) and the beans. Cook for a couple of minutes and add the fish. Cook steadily for about 10 minutes or until the fish is just cooked through. Stir in the rest of the coriander and Thai basil, if you have some, and serve. The curry reheats perfectly, but add the beans at the last moment. Serve with basmati rice.

SAFFRON MONKFISH AND LEEK PUFF PASTRY PIE
Serves 6

It's hard to believe, when you look at the hefty price tag of a neatly trimmed fillet of monkfish tail, that only a few years ago this giant of the ocean was cheap and unfashionable. It is the perfect fish for people who think they don't like fish because it has no bones to get anxious about. It makes a terrific hash and is delicious in this double-crust fish pie. Apart from the visual treat of the wonderfully puffed pastry – I always go a bit over the top, using the trimmings for decoration – the flavours and textures are superb. The monkfish remains firm, the leeks silkily soft and, together with chunks of hard-boiled egg, chopped parsley and a hint of sage, it is all held in a thick, luscious cream. I got the idea for cooking fish with sage from Michel Roux at a private lunch he gave a few years ago at three-Michelin-starred Waterside Inn at Bray. I'd been looking for an opportunity to copy this clever, unexpected idea and now I have. Serve the pie hot, warm or cold, with hot new potatoes and peas or beans. It would make a lovely al fresco supper dish and is robust enough to transport for a picnic.

500g monkfish tail fillet
salt and pepper
300g trimmed leeks
250ml clotted cream or crème fraîche or half milk
1 bay leaf
25g butter
25g flour
100ml milk
4 large sage leaves
handful of flat-leaf parsley leaves
2 eggs
500g ready-made puff pastry
1 egg whisked with a splash of milk

Remove any trace of the slimy membrane covering the monkfish and cut the fish into small kebab-size pieces. Season with salt. Trim the leeks and slice into 2.5cm thick rounds. Wash and shake dry. Heat the crème fraîche with the bay leaf and a generous seasoning of salt and pepper in a medium-sized pan. Once it boils, reduce the heat immediately and simmer for a couple of minutes. Increase the heat again and add the fish, stirring it round to keep immersed. Simmer for 5 minutes, then remove the fish with a slotted spoon to a plate. Add the leeks and simmer for 10 minutes until just tender. Melt the butter in a second pan and stir in the flour. Strain the cream (or cream and milk) into the mixture, adding the extra milk too. Stir or whisk thoroughly to avoid lumps as it comes to the boil. Reduce the heat. Chop the herbs and add to the sauce. Simmer for 5 minutes. Pour the sauce over the fish and leeks and stir gently but thoroughly. Meanwhile boil the eggs for 9 minutes. Shell and chop the eggs and stir into the mixture. Pre-heat the oven to 425°F/220°C/gas mark 7. Flour a surface and roll slightly more than half the pastry to fit a non-stick or greased 23cm loose-bottomed, high-sided flan tin, leaving a 2.5cm overhang. Spoon in the cooled filling. Roll the remaining pastry into a 25cm circle. Paint the overhang with egg wash, position the lid and pinch the two edges together, rolling it inwards to make a secure seal. Paint the surface with egg wash. Make a central hole and, if liked, etch the surface decoratively. Use trimmings for decoration and glaze with egg wash. Transfer to a baking sheet and bake for 15 minutes before reducing the heat to 375°F/190°C/gas mark 5. Cook for a further 20 minutes until puffed and golden. Rest for 5 minutes before removing the collar.

MONKFISH MOLLEE
Serves 4

This South Indian sauce reminds me of Thai curries. The same principles apply in that you make a highly seasoned base to which you add coconut milk. The spices – cinnamon, turmeric, cloves and cardamom – are common enough and onion and garlic are probably in the house already. I love the fact that all the preparation can be done in advance and the dish finished and ready to serve within 15 minutes from when the fish is added to the sauce. Serve it with boiled basmati rice and sit back to receive the compliments.

800g monkfish tail fillet
1 tbsp turmeric
salt
1 onion or 2 shallots
1 garlic clove
2 small green chillies or 2 dried red chillies
3cm piece fresh ginger
12 cardamom pods or 1 flat tsp seeds
6 cloves
50g butter

5cm cinnamon stick
400g can coconut milk
squeeze lemon juice
torn coriander leaves to serve

Remove any trace of the slimy membrane covering the monkfish and slice the fish into 3cm wide strips. Mix the turmeric and 1 teaspoon of salt on a plate and roll the fish in the mixture. Leave while you prepare the sauce. Peel, halve and finely chop the onion or shallots. Peel the garlic and crush to a paste. Trim fresh chillies and finely chop. If using dried chillies, crush them into small pieces. Peel and grate the ginger. Crush the cardamom and cloves to dust. Melt the butter in a 2 litre capacity pan and stir in the onion, garlic, chillies, ginger, cardamom, cloves and cinnamon stick. Cook gently for about 15 minutes until the onion is soft but hardly coloured. Add the coconut milk 15 minutes before you're ready to serve, then add the fish to the hot sauce, gently stirring it to loosen the turmeric so that it colours the sauce, and immerse all the pieces of fish. Cook for 10 minutes until the monkfish is just cooked through. Stir in the lemon juice and serve with coriander leaves.

PICASSO'S *MATELOTE* OF MONKFISH
Serves 4

Dining with Picasso by Ermine Herscher with Agnes Carbonell gives an intriguing glimpse into the great man's domestic life. There's a terrific photo of Picasso having a meal with Jacqueline at La Californie, in the Midi, in 1955. I like to think they'd been eating Jacqueline's *matelote*, made with eels. It's the subject of a stunning oil on canvas painted five years later, showing several black eels wriggling about on a white plate flanked by a well-worn knife and huge red onion. I used firm, meaty monkfish for my adaptation of this interesting soup-cum-stew. Picasso ate it with garlic *croûtons*, but you get the same effect with far less effort by toasting French bread in the oven and rubbing it with garlic.

12 shallots or small onions
50g butter
1 tbsp sugar
salt and pepper

150g rindless, streaky bacon or 100g pancetta

2 onions

2 carrots

1 celery heart

2 leek whites

3 garlic cloves

2 tbsp olive oil

3 monkfish tails, approx. 800g in total

1 glass dry white wine

350ml fish or chicken stock (a decent cube is fine)

1 small bay leaf

sprig of fresh thyme or 2 pinches dried thyme

1 tbsp finely chopped flat-leaf parsley

for the croûtes:

1 day-old baguette or similar

olive oil

2 garlic cloves

Peel the shallots, melt the butter with the sugar and a seasoning of salt and pepper and cook the shallots, covered, over a low heat for about 25 minutes until tender. Meanwhile, chop the bacon. Peel the onions and finely chop. Scrape the carrots and slice into thin strips. Slice finely across the celery and rinse thoroughly. Slice the leeks into thin strips. Crush the garlic to break the skin. Heat the oil in a heavy-bottomed pot and cook the bacon until very crisp. Scoop the bacon out of the pan and add all the vegetables, cooking for about 10 minutes until tender but not browned. Remove any slimy membrane from the fish and slice it off the cartilaginous 'backbone' into large kebab-size chunks. Stir the fish into the vegetables, cooking for a couple of minutes until noticeably firm. Add the wine, stock, bay leaf, thyme and bacon. Season with salt and pepper and cook over a low heat, stirring gently, for 10 minutes or until the fish is cooked through. Add the shallot mixture. Stir in the parsley and serve in bowls with the *croûtes* on the side.

To make the *croûtes*: pre-heat the oven to 400°F/200°C/gas mark 6. Slice the loaf, brush both sides generously with olive oil, lay out the slices on a baking sheet and bake, turning once, for about 6 minutes until crisp and golden. Rub one side with peeled garlic.

ROAST MONKFISH SATAY WITH CUCUMBER RELISH
Serves 4

Although monkfish is perfect for kebabs, there is always the risk that it will end up dry. Coconut cream solves the problem, giving these Thai-style kebabs an unexpected succulence. Served with a spicy peanut satay sauce and a crunchy relish-cum-salad, this is yet another example of the versatility of monkfish. Serve it with basmati rice or tagliatelle-style rice noodles tossed with chopped coriander, butter and toasted sesame oil.

> 800g monkfish tail fillet
> 1 small lime
> 200ml carton coconut cream
> 1 tsp ground cumin
> 1 tsp ground coriander
> 16 wooden kebab sticks soaked in cold water for 1 hour

> *for the peanut sauce:*
> 1 tbsp Thai green curry mix
> 150g chunky peanut butter
> 1 tbsp tamarind pulp
> 1 tsp cane sugar paste or 1 tbsp runny honey
> 1 tbsp lime juice
> 2 tbsp sesame oil

> *for the cucumber relish:*
> 1 small cucumber
> 1 tbsp pickled sushi ginger
> 1 shallot
> 2 small red chillies
> 2 tbsp Thai fish sauce (*nam pla*)
> 2 tbsp lime juice
> ½ tsp sugar
> 1 tbsp chopped coriander

Remove any trace of the slimy membrane covering the monkfish and cut the meat into kebab-size chunks. Remove the zest from half the lime in paper-thin strips. Stir the zest into the coconut cream with the cumin and coriander in a bowl that can hold the fish. Mix thoroughly and leave for at least 1 hour, preferably 2.

Pre-heat the oven to 400°F/200°C/gas mark 6. Thread the monkfish on to the sodden skewers (regular skewers are fine but wooden ones are more *simpatico*, although they must be soaked in water to avoid burning in the oven). Line a baking sheet with foil, lay out the kebabs and cook for 15 minutes until they are cooked through. Arrange on a platter, spoon the peanut sauce over the kebabs and serve with lime wedges, and the relish and rice or noodles in separate bowls.

To make the peanut sauce, warm all the ingredients together, adding just sufficient water to make a thick, creamy mixture with pouring consistency.

To make the relish, halve the cucumber lengthways, scrape away the seeds and watery pulp and slice thinly. Chop the slices into small scraps. Chop the sushi ginger into similar-sized scraps. Peel and finely chop the shallot. Trim and split the chillies, scrape away the seeds, slice into skinny strips and then into tiny dice. Pour the fish sauce and 2 tbsp lime juice into a bowl, stir in the sugar to dissolve, then add all the other ingredients. Stir well.

SKATE WITH BLACK BUTTER
Serves 4

The combination of bland and slightly chewy skate with the sharp but nutty, buttery sauce and its bursts of sour capers is one of those marriages made in heaven. I would suggest boiled potatoes with this.

    1 quantity *court bouillon* (see page 103)
    2 x 450g skate wings, skinned
    175g butter
    50ml red wine vinegar
    1 tbsp finely chopped flat-leaf parsley
    2 tbsp capers in vinegar

Follow the recipe for *court bouillon*, cooking it for 20 minutes.

Meanwhile, divide the two wings in half lengthways – or ask the fishmonger to do it for you – and slip them into the simmering *court bouillon*. Return to the boil and simmer for 15 minutes or until cooked through at the thickest part of the wing. Drain the fish on absorbent kitchen paper, place on four warmed plates and keep warm. Melt the butter in a frying pan, swirling the pan as the butter foams and turns a deep brown with a nutty smell. Add the vinegar, swirling the pan again, and let the mixture boil for a few seconds, then add the parsley and capers. Cook for a few more seconds, then pour and spoon the sauce over the fish.

Crab, Lobster and Crayfish

Buying crab
Dealing with a live crab (crayfish and lobster)
Dressing and picking cooked crab

Fish Store Dressed Crab
Brown Crab Mayonnaise
Crab Claws with Aioli
Crab Bruschetta
Crab Bisque
Crab and Cucumber Linguine
Betty's Crab Jambalaya
Crab Tart with Leeks and Saffron
Cantonese Crab with Ginger and Spring Onions
Thai-style Crab Cakes with Cucumber Relish
Lobster (or Crayfish) with Mayonnaise

Fresh crab is everyone's favourite food at the Fish Store. We eat so much of it that the preparation sometimes seems like a conveyor belt of boiling, cooling, cracking, picking and eating. It's not uncommon for the big double butler's sink to be full of crabs either awaiting their fate or draining afterwards. Most of the time, crab gets eaten cold with no embellishment, the creamy brown meat seasoned with a little vinegar and the silky white meat providing a blissful contrast of taste and texture. It might be made into sandwiches, but usually it's eaten with brown bread and butter and some salad or other. There are only a handful of deviations from this joyous combination, but they are all Fish Store diehards. For a special occasion, there might be an attempt at a *plateau de fruits de mer*, with winkles, oysters, mussels, shrimps and sea urchins, piled over seaweed and crowned by a crab or two. The only rule then is to work from the smallest winkles up to the crab, which is the *pièce de résistance*. With this there would be French bread and butter and a shallot vinegar made by mixing together a finely chopped shallot with about three tablespoons each of red wine and red wine vinegar.

Crayfish – or 'cray' as it's called at the Fish Store – and lobster are reserved for high days and holidays, not just because they are so expensive but because everyone prefers crab. When we do have one or the other, they are always bought raw, boiled and served lukewarm or cold. They are rarely turned into a thermidor or another fancy restaurant dish. Hot new potatoes or potato salad with home-made mayonnaise and a crisp green salad are the usual accompaniments. The shells, however, will be saved – sometimes frozen – to add to a fish stock or to be boiled up for bisque.

Buying crab

Crab is available in Newlyn at any time of the year, but the best time to buy it is in the autumn, from September to Christmas. Crabs come inshore to breed in spring and become scarce during July, when they burrow under the rocks and get busy. Although everyone wants to eat crab at the height of the summer, this isn't a great time to buy hen crabs because they will be full of eggs or roe, commonly called coral, which looks like dark red wax. It is stunning the first time you see it, but, although edible, I find it boringly waxy to eat. It can be turned into coral butter, but I don't like it enough to bother. In August and September the crabs 'march', so that's the best time to catch them. Knobbly, long-legged spider crabs have a slightly later season, between January and May.

No one knows how long crabs live – probably twenty to thirty years – and they're very slow-growing. They cast their shell every year, to be replaced by a bigger one, giving themselves a sort of annual facelift. Spider crabs do it twice. Never buy a brown crab with a pale, soft shell. This means it has just cast its shell and it will be sloshing around with water instead of meat.

The best advice when buying live or boiled whole crab is to choose one that feels proportionately heavy for its size, with a dark, hard shell. This shows the crab hasn't moulted recently, as do signs of wear and tear on the shell, a missing leg and the odd barnacle. Chose a feisty, lively crab which is waving its antennae and looking for a fight rather than a sleepy, docile one which seems resigned to its fate.

On average, the yield of meat from a crab will be one-third of its whole weight and about two-thirds of that will be brown meat. Male crabs – cocks – have larger claws than the female – hen – and as it's the claws and legs that contain most of the white meat, males are generally thought to be the best buy. The sex of a crab is determined by its tail, which is curled up under the body. The female is broad and round, while the male is narrow and pointed.

Spider crabs have a relatively small, knobbly body and long, long legs. Weight for weight, they're never as good value as the common edible brown crab because there's not much meat in the body and most of it is brown. They are prized for their legs and claws – known as quiddle claws locally – with their silky, sweet meat.

Although crabs are traditionally caught in pots, they often get tangled up in fishing nets. Frequently when the nets are hauled in, brown crabs and spider crabs will have gripped their claws into the monofilament nets and the only solution for the fisherman is to snap them off and throw the body back into the sea. This results in buckets full of raw claws, which, inevitably, many people prefer to the whole crab. They only need about 10 minutes in boiling salted water.

Dealing with a live crab (crayfish and lobster)

It is always best to buy crabs live. They should be cooked as soon as possible, but if necessary live crabs can be kept, covered with a damp tea towel, in the bottom of the fridge for a couple of days, provided they were lively when you bought them. Keep an eye on them, though, and if they die, cook them immediately because crabmeat deteriorates extremely fast once the crustacean is dead. There is much debate about the most humane way of killing a crab. The Fish Store way is to drop them into a very big pan of vigorously boiling, generously salted water. We keep one saucepan with big lugs and a close-fitting lid specially for the job. It's one of Betty's original Fish Store pans and must have been responsible for cooking thousands of crabs over the years since 1939. It's important to cook crab in plenty of water so that the time taken to come back to the boil once the crab has gone in is minimized. The cooking time starts from the moment the water returns to the boil.

A good-sized crab weighs an average 1–1.5kg and we boil them for 20 minutes in approximately 5 litres of water with 5 tablespoons of salt. For smaller crabs, up to 900g, allow 15 minutes.

Live crayfish and lobsters are always sold with wide rubber bands round their claws, otherwise they attack each other. We cook them in exactly the same way as crab, plunging them into a big pan of heavily salted boiling water, allowing 20 minutes unless they are very small or very big. A 750g lobster is a good, generous size for two people. Crayfish are generally landed slightly larger.

Dressing and picking cooked crab

When you buy dressed crab, the white and brown meat is usually neatly laid out, often divided by a sprig of parsley or slice of lemon, in the crab shell. Occasionally the white meat might be laid out in a wide strip between the brown meat on either side. Shops and restaurants often tidy the shell first, washing it out and then cracking along an obvious line that runs round the edge, to make a neat, open finish. It will seem very expensive for what you get, even at the height of the season, and that's because picking crab is a tedious and laborious job. These days, the work is done by an imported Polish work-force, often students, happy to earn the minimum wage for work that no one local wants to do. The white meat will have been carefully picked from the body cavities and the spindly legs, ensuring that none of the thin bony cavity shell gets in among the silky strands of white meat. The silkiest white meat is in the legs and the joints of the claws closest to the body.

It is good fun, though, if you are going to eat the crab yourself, to do the initial preparations and then pick as you eat at the table. This is how we usually eat freshly boiled crab laying the cracked legs and claws out on a platter along with the halved or quartered body. The brown meat is mixed with the picked white meat from the body cavities, then seasoned and served separately in a bowl. Everyone digs in, theoretically starting with the legs, slathering the brown meat on to buttered brown bread, graduating to the work-intensive body, with the occasional reward of a claw. Some people add freshly made brown breadcrumbs to the brown meat to make it go further, and finely chopped hard-boiled egg white to the white meat. Cooked and picked crab will keep, covered, for a couple of days in the fridge but soon starts to dry out and lose its fresh flavour. You will know if it is off by the smell.

FISH STORE DRESSED CRAB

> 2 decent-sized crabs, approximately 1.5kg each, is about right for
> 4 people

Boil the crab as described above. Leave to drain and cool in the sink and then transfer to several sheets of newspaper. Place the crab on its back and, using your fingers, twist the claws from the body. Twist off the bony, tail flap and discard. Prise the body from the main shell by pressing hard with the full weight of your thumb opposite the eyes where the carcass obviously dovetails into the shell. Remove the stomach bag and the grey, crêpey 'dead man's fingers'. Remove the legs and cut the body in two. Cut each half in two again, cutting across to expose the meat in the leg chambers. Scrape the firm creamy meat round the edge of the shell and then the brown meat and slush in the middle into a small bowl. This is extremely rich and tasty and might be a bit watery. If so, drain off or into the stockpot. Season with a little salt and pepper and a splash of wine vinegar or lemon juice – not too much, just enough to season the meat – and stir thoroughly. Pick the white meat from the body cavities and stir it into the seasoned brown meat. Crack the claws and legs slightly – we use a small wooden mallet, but special claw-crackers are available from any cookshop – taking care not to crush the meat inside. Arrange on a platter and serve the brown meat separately. If special crab picks aren't available, the white meat can then be picked with the pointed end of a teaspoon. All you need with this is brown bread and butter, salt and pepper, and a cucumber and lettuce salad.

To make a crab sandwich, butter brown bread generously, spread thickly with brown crabmeat and pile the white on top. Season with salt, pepper and a squeeze of lemon juice. If liked, add very thin slices of cucumber and lettuce or cress.

BROWN CRAB MAYONNAISE
Serves 4

This is a delicious way of making brown crabmeat less rich and more palatable to more people. Serve it on or with toast, perhaps with pickled cucumber (see page 323), or in curls of lettuce with a chopped parsley garnish. This is great with drinks.

> 6 tbsp brown crabmeat (approx.)
> salt and pepper
> 1 tbsp fresh lemon juice
> 1 tsp tomato ketchup
> 2 tsp English mustard
> 2 tbsp mayonnaise

Place the crabmeat in a bowl. Season with salt and pepper and mix in the lemon juice, ketchup and mustard, breaking up any lumps of creamy white meat or roe with a wooden spoon. Use a fork to whisk in the mayonnaise. Taste and adjust the seasoning if necessary. Chill before serving.

CRAB CLAWS WITH AIOLI
Serves 4

Serve the claws on a platter with the bowl of aïoli in the middle, a pile of crusty toast and a few lemon wedges to squeeze over the claws. If the claws are raw, drop them into a big pan of generously salted boiling water. Boil for 10 minutes. Drain and cool before cracking.

> *For the aioli:*
> 6 garlic cloves
> salt and pepper
> 2 large egg yolks
> 1 tsp smooth Dijon mustard
> 300ml olive oil plus a little extra
> lemon juice
> 12 crab claws
> 3 lemons

First make the aioli. Ensure all ingredients are at room temperature. Peel and finely chop the garlic. Sprinkle with a little salt and use the flat of a knife to work the garlic to a smooth, juicy paste. Place the egg yolks, mustard and a generous seasoning of salt and pepper in a mixing bowl. Beat with a whisk until thick. Stir in the garlic paste and add the oil in a thin stream, beating continuously, adding a little lemon juice and then more oil until all is used up and the mayonnaise is thick and glossy.

Crack the crab claws lightly without crushing the meat, so that the meat is easy to extract. Pile the claws on to a platter. Plant the aioli in the middle. Decorate with lemon wedges.

CRAB BRUSCHETTA
Serves 4

So moreish and great with chilled white wine on a hot summer evening.

1 red chilli

approx. 200g dressed crab, preferably with some chunky white meat

1 tbsp lemon juice

6 tbsp olive oil

2 tbsp finely chopped coriander

Maldon salt and black pepper

4 slices sourdough bread

1 big garlic clove

Trim and split the chilli. Scrape away the seeds, slice into skinny strips and then into tiny pieces. Stir the chilli into the crab. Add half the lemon juice and stir in 4 tablespoons of olive oil in a steady trickle. Stir in the coriander, season lavishly with black pepper and lightly with salt. Taste and adjust the seasoning with more lemon juice. Toast the bread, rub one side vigorously with peeled garlic and dribble with the remaining olive oil. Spread the bruschetta with crab. Cut the slices into quarters and serve.

CRAB BISQUE

Serves 4–6

The thing about crab bisque is that in order to be authentic it must be flavoured by the shell as well as the meat from the crab. It's an incredibly rich soup made with brandy, white wine and cream, and a little goes a long way. It can be made with live or boiled crab and it can be a thick, smooth soup or a thinner soup with chunks of white crabmeat floating around in it. At the Fish Store a crab bisque is usually created after several crabs have been boiled in the same water and the picked carcasses, legs and shells go back in the pot. This stock is then built up with other fish carcasses, so that the soup is virtually made before the real cooking begins. The danger with this continual stockpot, particularly in hot weather, is that if the pan isn't constantly monitored – i.e. sieved, boiled, cooled and refrigerated – the stock goes off. *Ben, please note.*

This recipe starts from scratch with live crabs but can be modified with boiled crab.

2 live crabs, approx. 900g each

1 small onion

1 carrot

1 stick celery

1 trimmed leek

50g butter

1 bay leaf

salt and pepper

2 tbsp cognac, brandy or whisky

4 ripe tomatoes

1 tbsp tomato purée

50g white rice

1 glass dry white wine

1.75 litres fresh fish stock

2 tbsp thick cream

cayenne pepper

squeeze of lemon juice

Drop the crabs into a large pan of generously salted boiling water. Boil for 15 minutes. Lift the crabs out of the water, set aside to drain and cool slightly. Twist the legs and claws from the crab, joint and crack them. Discard the tail and remove the body from the shell of the crab. Cut the body into four pieces. Meanwhile, peel and finely chop the onion. Trim, scrape and finely chop the carrot. Finely chop the celery and slice the leek. Melt the butter in a spacious, heavy-bottomed pan and stir in the prepared vegetables and bay leaf. Season with salt and pepper, cover the pan and leave to soften, stirring occasionally, without browning for about 10 minutes. Scrape the brown meat out of the shell and into the vegetable mixture, and stir the body pieces, legs and claws into the pan. Put the shell between several layers of newspaper and smash with a wooden rolling pin. Stir the shell into the vegetables. Add the brandy. Allow to boil away. Chop the tomatoes coarsely and add to the pan with the tomato purée, rice, white wine and stock. Bring to the boil, turn down the heat, partially cover the pan and simmer for 45 minutes. Remove the tough claws and large pieces of shell from the pan and pulse the rest in 3–4 batches in a food processor or pass through a mouli. The idea is to loosen any crabmeat clinging to the shell, particularly in the body section, rather than pulverize the shell itself. Strain the soup through a fine sieve, pressing down to extract as much juice and crabmeat as possible and scraping under the sieve so that nothing is wasted. Discard the debris. Pass the soup through the sieve a second time into a clean pan. Bring to the boil, add the cream, then adjust the seasoning with cayenne pepper, lemon juice, salt and black pepper.

CRAB AND CUCUMBER LINGUINE
Serves 4–6

The firm texture and thin, flat strands of linguine give exactly the right level of resistance to the bite against silky and creamy crabmeat and thin slices of peeled cucumber which wilt against its heat. Serve this lovely summer pasta supper with a glass of chilled white wine. It is rich and luscious; do not be tempted to serve it with Parmesan or any other grated cheese.

> 2 live male crabs, approx. 1.5kg each, or
>   250g white and 200g brown crabmeat plus 6 large claws
> 1 tsp dried red chilli flakes or 2 fresh red chillies
> 1 small or ½ large cucumber
> juice of 2 large lemons
> 2 tbsp coarsely chopped flat-leaf parsley
> Maldon salt and freshly ground black pepper
> 6–8 tbsp extra virgin olive oil
> 400g linguine

Cook the crabs in a big pan of generously salted boiling water for 20 minutes. Drain in the sink and allow to cool. Remove the brown meat from the shell into a large bowl. Crack the legs and pick the meat directly into the bowl. Scrape the meat off the flat central 'bone' of the claws, leaving it in big chunks, adding it to the brown. Cut the body into four pieces and pick out the white meat. Add that to the bowl. Meanwhile, place the chilli flakes in an eggcup, just cover with boiling water and leave for a few minutes until soft. If using fresh chillies, trim and split them, scraping away the seeds. Slice into skinny strips and then into tiny dice. Use a potato peeler to remove the skin from the cucumber. Split it in half lengthways and use a teaspoon to scrape out the seeds and their watery pulp. Thinly slice the cucumber into half-moons. Mix together the drained chilli, dressed crab, juice from 1½ lemons and chopped parsley. Season lightly with salt and generously with pepper. Slowly stir in 4 tablespoons of olive oil to make a thick but slack mixture.

Put a large pan of water on to boil. Cook the pasta until *al dente*, then drain and return to the saucepan. Stir the cucumber and 2 table-spoons of olive oil into the drained pasta, stirring to mix thoroughly and encouraging the cucumber to wilt slightly. Now add the crab mix-ture, adding more lemon juice or oil to taste. Stir thoroughly before serving.

BETTY'S CRAB JAMBALAYA
Serves 6–8

Jambalaya is a spicy rice dish from Louisiana and this crab version won my mother-in-law a fiver in the fifties in a *Daily Telegraph* cookery com-petition. Betty would almost certainly have used the crab cooking water as the basis for a stock in which to cook the rice, but if you are making this with shop-bought dressed crab, a decent chicken stock works out all right. Serve the jambalaya risotto-style; I quite like green beans on the side.

> 2 live male crabs, approx. 1.5kg each, plus a few extra claws, or
>   250g white and 200g brown crabmeat plus 6 large claws
> salt and black pepper
> 2 red onions, approx. 250g
> 2 garlic cloves
> 2 tbsp vegetable cooking oil
> 2 red peppers
> 1 bay leaf
> 3 dried chillies
> 250g basmati rice
> 400g fresh tomatoes or 400g can tomatoes
> 600ml chicken or fish stock (cubes are fine) or jar of Mediterranean
>   fish soup
> 1 small lemon
> Tabasco and parsley to serve

Boil the crabs in plenty of generously salted and vigorously boiling water for 20 minutes. If the claws are raw, add them to the pan for 10 minutes. Drain, cool and pick the meat as described above, leaving the claw meat in big chunks. Keep the brown meat separate from the white.

Meanwhile, peel and dice the onions and garlic. Heat the oil in large frying pan or similarly wide-based pan and stir in the onions and garlic. Cook gently for 5 minutes or so while you dice the peppers, discarding seeds, white filaments and stalk. Stir the pepper into the onions, together with the bay leaf and chillies, cooking for about 15 minutes until the onion is soft and slippery, the pepper partially softened and the chillies crumbled.

Meanwhile, rinse the rice in several changes of water. If using fresh tomatoes, place them in a bowl and cover with boiling water. Count to 20, drain, remove the skins, cut out the core and coarsely chop them. Stir the rice into the vegetables, then add the brown crabmeat. Cook for a couple of minutes, then add the tomatoes and their juices, ½ teaspoon of salt and plenty of pepper. Add the stock, bring the liquid to the boil, stir, reduce the heat, cover the pan and cook for 15 minutes. Turn off the heat and leave the pan without removing the lid – the rice will finish cooking in the steam – for 10 minutes. Stir in the white crabmeat and the extra claw meat. Taste the juices, adjust the seasoning with salt, pepper and lemon juice, adding a shake or two of Tabasco if it isn't hot enough. Stir in the parsley and serve.

CRAB TART WITH LEEKS AND SAFFRON
Serves 6–8

A slice of this creamy crab tart with its saffron back flavour and muddle of soft slippery leeks is perfect for any occasion. I have served it hot as a main course with new potatoes and peas, and cold as a starter with a cucumber salad. Using yoghurt rather than water in the pastry gives it a springy texture which works wonderfully well with the soft voluptuousness of the crab filling in this rich and interesting tart. It will keep, covered in the fridge, for a couple of days but bring it back to room temperature before eating.

200g flour plus a little extra

125g butter plus a little extra

2–3 tbsp natural yoghurt or water

2 trimmed leeks, 350g in total

pinch of saffron stamens

salt and pepper

3 large eggs

200g thick cream or crème fraîche

2 tsp smooth Dijon mustard

350g brown and white crabmeat

100g Gruyère cheese

Pre-heat the oven to 400°F/200°C/gas mark 6. Sift the flour into a mixing bowl. Add 100g of the butter in chunks and rub into the flour until it resembles breadcrumbs. Add 2 tablespoons, possibly 3, of yoghurt or water, quickly work into the flour mixture and form it into a soft ball. Rest for 30 minutes. Rub butter round the inside of a 23cm flan tin with a removable base and dust with flour, rolling the tin round in your hands to completely cover. Tip out any excess flour. This, incidentally, makes it non-stick. Roll out the pastry to fit, pressing down gently into the base edges and trimming with a bit of an overhang to allow for shrinkage. Cover loosely with foil, fill with baking beans or rice and bake in the oven for 10 minutes. Remove the foil and cook for a further 5 minutes to firm and lightly brown the pastry. Meanwhile, prepare the leeks. Trim and split them lengthways and slice across to make half-moons. Rinse thoroughly and shake dry. Melt the remaining 25g butter in a spacious frying pan or similarly wide-based pan. Stir in the leeks, cover and cook, stirring occasionally, for about 10 minutes until juicy and wilted. Stir in the saffron, season with salt and pepper and cook uncovered for a few minutes to drive off the liquid. Set aside to cool. Whisk the eggs in a mixing bowl, stir in the cream and mustard and then the crab, breaking up any big pieces. Season with salt and pepper. Stir the cooled leeks into the egg mixture. Using the small hole of the cheese grater (this is an ideal occasion for a Microplane grater), grate two-thirds of the cheese across the base of the pastry case. Place the case on a baking sheet. Spoon the crab mixture into the pastry case; it should fit exactly, going right up to the top but without danger of spillage. Grate the remaining cheese over the top. Cook in the oven for 35 minutes or until the top is golden and billowing and feels firm but springy. Cool for 10 minutes before removing the collar. Serve hot, warm or cold.

CANTONESE CRAB WITH GINGER AND SPRING ONIONS
Serves 4

This is a hands-on greed-fest. Yum.

>   4 garlic cloves
>   50g fresh ginger
>   6 spring onions
>   2 cooked crabs, approx. 1.5kg each
>   2 tbsp groundnut oil
>   3 tbsp Kikkoman soy sauce
>   2 tbsp Shaoxing rice wine or dry sherry
>   250ml chicken stock (cube is fine)
>   2 tsp toasted sesame oil

Peel and finely slice the garlic in rounds. Peel the ginger and slice into thin matchsticks. Trim the spring onions and slice in long chunks, on the slant, including all the green unless obviously tough. Twist the claws and legs off the main body of the crabs. Crack the shell lightly without crushing the crabmeat. Remove the body from the shell (see above, pages 138–9, for more details). Use a cleaver or heavy chef's knife to cut the body into four pieces. Heat a wok over a high heat. Add the groundnut oil, swirl it round the wok and when it is very hot and slightly smoking, toss in the garlic, ginger and spring onions and stir-fry for 20 seconds. Add the brown crabmeat, soy sauce, rice wine or sherry and chicken stock. Stir thoroughly, letting everything bubble up together and then add the crab pieces. Stir-fry over a high heat for about 5 minutes, letting all the pieces get coated in garlic, ginger, spring onion and the soy/brown meat/stock sauce. Turn on to a large, warmed platter, dribble with the sesame oil and serve with finger bowls and paper napkins.

THAI-STYLE CRAB CAKES WITH CUCUMBER RELISH

Serves 4

Despite its delicate flavour, crab goes extremely well with chilli and coriander and other South-east Asian flavourings. This mixture of flavours makes delicious little crab fishcakes to eat with thin slices of cucumber seasoned with salty, sour Thai fish sauce and a green salad made with rocket, avocado, spring onions and coriander.

1 large or 3 small red chillies
4 spring onions
4 kaffir lime leaves
1 large bunch of coriander
2 heaped tbsp mayonnaise (bought is fine)
450g crabmeat, brown and white mixed
4 tsp Thai fish sauce (*nam pla*)
100g breadcrumbs made from stale bread
flour for dusting
1 small cucumber
1 tbsp fresh lime juice
½ tsp sugar
sweet chilli dipping sauce and lemon or lime wedges to serve
oil for frying

Trim the chillies, split, scrape away the seeds, slice into skinny batons and then into tiny dice. Trim and finely slice the spring onions. Cut the central vein from the lime leaves, roll together and slice very finely and then into tiny scraps. Finely chop the coriander, discarding any roots and stalk ends, and reserve some to use as a garnish. Transfer chilli, spring onions, lime leaves and coriander to a mixing bowl. Add the mayonnaise, crabmeat and 1 teaspoon of fish sauce and stir together. Add the breadcrumbs and stir again thoroughly. Cover the bowl with clingfilm and chill for at least an hour to encourage the mixture to firm up. Dust a work surface with flour and, working quickly, take tablespoons of the mixture and form into cakes-cum-patties, patting the tops and sides to flatten, transferring to a plate as you go. You will end up with 12–15 pieces. Cover with clingfilm and chill the crab cakes until required.

Meanwhile, make the cucumber relish. Peel the cucumber, split lengthways and use a teaspoon to scrape out the seeds and their pulp. Thinly slice in half-moons. Pour the remaining fish sauce and lime juice into a bowl, stir in the sugar to dissolve and then stir in the cucumber. Chill until ready to serve. When you are ready to serve, stir the reserved coriander into the cucumber relish.

Fry the crab cakes briefly in batches in shallow hot oil, just long enough to make a thin, golden crust. Lift carefully from the pan and serve with a lime or lemon wedge.

LOBSTER (OR CRAYFISH) WITH MAYONNAISE
Serves 2

Although there are plenty of lobster pots in the sea around the rocks in Mousehole and Lamorna, most of what is caught goes to restaurants or is sent abroad, live, in special water-tank lorries, where it fetches such a high price that no one can afford to eat lobsters or crayfish down here. Lots of people bait a pot or two during the season, usually for crab, but daily disappointment is usual when the bait is changed. In any case, unless the boat is licensed and the owner has a permit, fishing laws prevent the sale of these valuable crustaceans; the catch is for private consumption only.

Lobster and crayfish always remind me of a giant prawn with a hard carapace and big pincer claws. They are far easier to eat than crab because most of the dense, rich meat is in the tail, although the body section and where the legs join the body hold a surprisingly large amount. We don't eat lobster or crayfish that often at the Fish Store and it's rare these days (unlike when Ben was a boy) for a gift of one to turn up on the doorstep.

For a special treat, it's hard to beat this simple way of eating lobster with freshly made mayonnaise, a few hot new potatoes tossed in butter and a salad of mixed leaves or thinly sliced cucumber seasoned with vinegar. I would always try to coordinate things so that the lobster is at room temperature rather than chilled. To make a lobster supper for four people, you will need two lobsters. Either cook the lobsters one after the other or use a larger pan, more water and more salt and bring the water back to the boil after the first lobster has been immersed before plunging the second one into the pan.

4 litres water

4 tbsp salt

1 live lobster or crayfish, weighing approx. 750g

1 quantity mayonnaise (see page 170)

Bring the water to the boil in a large pan and add the salt. When the water is boiling vigorously, plunge the lobster into the water, tail first. Boil for 20 minutes, timed from when the water returns to the boil. Drain and leave to cool.

To cut the lobster in half, drive a large, heavy knife through the head and in between the eyes down the main body section, lengthways. Lever the knife in your hand, moving the blade down the body towards the tail, cutting down the tail to split it in half. Discard the black intestinal tract which runs along the back and remove the stomach sac behind the mouth. Cut the rubber band binding the claws. Crack each section of the claws with a short, sharp tap and do the rest of the cracking and picking at the table with the help of lobster crackers and a lobster pick, or improvise with a mallet or rolling pin and fork or teaspoon.

Limpets, Winkles and Mussels, Scallops and Squid

Winkles with Shallot Vinegar
Mussels with Garlic Butter
Dijon Moules Marinière with Clotted Cream
Thai Mussels
Marazion Mussels with Fettuccine
Griddled Scallops with Pea Purée and Mint Vinaigrette
Chinese Scallops on the Half-Shell
Coquille St Jacques with Bacon
Scallop or Squid Provencal with Basmati Rice
Squid with Tomatoes and Peas

All the boys growing up in Mousehole in the war years had nick-names: 'Big Boo', 'Shonolly', 'Strom', 'Jinx', the two 'Nabos', 'Wackers' and 'Ben banger'. They would play cricket and rounders in the harbour at low tide, collecting the balls from under the hulls of the fishing boats. Another favourite pastime was collecting limpets and cooking them on a metal sheet over a fire on the rocks, when they weren't fishing for whistlers and bull cats in the rock pools. The limpets didn't taste particularly good – rubbery and salty – but they were edible and the thrill of knocking these clinging, conical molluscs off the rocks and cooking them over a fire by the sea more than compensated. I have a special relationship with one row of limpets, glued to the base of my favourite sunbathing rock. Where the 'wall' rock naps the flat rock, a row of limpets has been lined up like pointed, ridged pyramids for years. They don't move much, but they are quite vocal. Every now and again they make a squelching noise, a sort of grinding which sounds a bit like little bubbles bursting. I imagine the limpets are stamping their tiny feet in unison, but as the sun beats down and the water laps against the rocks my mind begins to wander. There's a particular bit of cliff nearby which is the courting ground for gulls and other birds. I watch the lovebirds smooching and pecking and finally nesting, as they always do, on the earthy crevices of the cliff. Once I woke from a little sunbathing snooze to see the beady, bright yellow eyes of a gull blinking perilously close to my face. I couldn't get rid of him. When the tide goes out from my flat rock haven, the sea uncovers a mass of seaweed called sea-thong or thong-weed, which looks exactly like green spaghetti. Sometimes the gentle put-put of an outboard motor or the regular swish of an oar brings someone up close to check a lobster pot or shoot a line for mackerel. Occasionally the chalky backbone of a cuttlefish gets washed up on the rocks, or tiny soft-shell crabs, but the only reliably acceptable free seafood for landlubbers is winkles. They used to grow abundantly on the steps in the harbour below the village clock (the old sewage outlet) and less conveniently in the cracks of the rocks by Dicky Daniel's Cove, out towards Lamorna.

People used to collect them for sale and there was one particular man who worked the shore between the old Penryn quarry and the lighthouse quay at Newlyn.

The tiny grey-black winkles need to be carefully washed – agitated in several changes of cold water – to remove sand and mud before boiling briefly in salted water. Their little flat, shiny trapdoor is removed before they are 'winkled' out with a pin. Some people dip them in vinegar. Betty preferred shallot vinegar, the sort that goes with oysters, and served them for tea with bread and butter. Winkles are the starting-point for a *plateau de fruits de mer* and are usually served with a cork stuck with pins for winkling.

Tiny little mussels grow on the big rocks by the sea at Mousehole and, like winkles, must only be picked and eaten from clear, clean water. The mussels inside are so tiny they aren't worth collecting, but it's possible to find farmed mussels from nearby Falmouth. The beautiful black-blue shells come relatively clean but it's wise to hack off any barnacles with a blunt, old knife. To clean the mussels, tip them into a sink of cold water and agitate thoroughly, repeating a couple of times until the water runs clean. Discard any mussels that are cracked or open. Their little whiskery 'beards' can be removed with a sharp tug.

There are vast quantities of scallops moving about on the sea-bed in local waters during the summer and fishermen come from all over the country for scallop fishing. The best are diver-caught, hand-sorted and graded. If they aren't on sale graded as diver-caught, the scallops have probably been scooped up by a beamer which trawls the sea-bed with a chain mat attached to two big steel shoes. Many fishermen think beamers should be banned because they are systematically ripping up the sea-bed. The scallops they catch are likely to be full of sand.

There are two types: king scallops are large with one flat shell and one curved one; 'queenies', which are smaller and rated for their exceptionally sweet flavour, have two curved shells. The best way to buy them is live on the shell. Avoid frozen scallops, which are often soaked in water before freezing to pump up the size and make them seem better value for money.

To prepare fresh scallops, hold the curved shell in your cupped hand

and slide a sharp, thin-bladed flexible knife between the two shells, keeping the blade pressed against the top shell. Feel for the muscle which joins the meat to the shell, slicing through it and thus releasing the shell. Pull away the frilly 'skirt' that surrounds the white scallop and orange coral. Rinse away any sand. To remove the scallop from the shell, slide the knife under the scallop. Cut off the thin white ligament at the side of the white meat, which is hard and tough.

Squid is quite common down here but still underrated and therefore extremely good value. The snowy-white, tube-like body or sac of this mollusc is tender and sweet and comes without a shell. It belongs to a group which also includes cuttlefish and octopus, called cephalopods or 'head-footed', referring to the way their tentacles come out of their head. If you are squeamish, most fishmongers will clean squid for you; but it's a painless and simple enough job – just a bit slimy and messy. I like the bald description in *The River Café Cook Book*: 'clean the squid by cutting the body open to make a flat piece. Scrape out the guts, keeping the tentacles in their bunches, but remove the eyes and mouth.' If you want to keep the squid in its tube shape, begin this (slightly more detailed) cleaning process by holding the body with one hand and gently pull the head away from the body, taking the slippery, creamy intestines with it. If you want to retain the ink sac, look among the intestines for a silvery-white slim sac and carefully cut it away. Squid ink, incidentally, is sold in plastic pouches by most fishmongers. Cut the tentacles off just in front of the eyes and discard the head. Squeeze out the hard mouth from the centre of the tentacles and discard. Cut the tentacles in half if they are very big. Pull out the transparent plastic 'quill' inside the body and wash out the sac, removing any soft white goo. Pull off the two fins on the side of the body and remove the skin in sheets.

To cook flat sheets of squid, score it with a close cross-hatch on the inner side, taking care not to cut all the way through. Oil it lightly and griddle or fry. Slice into 5cm strips for stir-frying or deep-frying.

NEWLYN

TIMES OF
HIGH WATER

13 FT 4 INS

Barbecuing just-caught mackerel
on the Fish Store steps

WINKLES WITH SHALLOT VINEGAR

Carefully wash freshly picked winkles in cold water as described above. Put a pan of well-salted water on to boil, just sufficient to cover the winkles, and when boiling throw in the winkles. Return to the boil and boil for a couple of minutes, then drain and cool under the cold tap. Serve with the vinegar (see page 135 for dipping and slices of buttered brown bread. To eat, use a pin to remove the 'lid' and deftly hook them out.

MUSSELS WITH GARLIC BUTTER
Serves 4

A bit of a palaver to make – although virtually everything can be done in advance – but well worth the effort. Serve as a snack or first course with crusty bread.

   1kg cleaned mussels
   3 garlic cloves
   handful parsley
   75g butter

Cook the mussels, covered, with half a cup of water over a high heat, shaking the pan a couple of times, until they are all opened. Drain in a colander and leave to cool. Meanwhile, peel and finely chop the garlic. Finely chop the parsley leaves. Chop the two together and then mash them into the butter with a fork. Remove the empty shell from each mussel and put a teaspoon of garlic butter on each mussel. Arrange in a grill pan and flash under a pre-heated grill for a few seconds until the butter is bubbling hot. Serve immediately.

DIJON MOULES MARINIÈRE WITH CLOTTED CREAM
Serves 4

There are many ways of ringing the changes with moules marinière and this is one of them. Serve with crusty bread and butter or garlic bread (see page 319).

2kg cleaned, closed, uncracked mussels
1 large onion
3 garlic cloves
50g butter
1 flat tbsp flour
1 tbsp smooth Dijon mustard
300ml dry white wine or cider
4 tbsp chopped flat-leaf parsley
pepper
150g clotted cream

Leave the mussels to drain in a colander. Peel and finely chop the onion and garlic. Heat the butter in large, lidded saucepan that can accommodate all the mussels. Stir in the onion and garlic and cook gently until soft and transparent. Sift the flour over the top and stir with a wooden spoon until it disappears into the buttery onions. Stir in the mustard, then add the wine in a steady stream, stirring to make a smooth sauce. Simmer gently, stirring occasionally, for 3–4 minutes. Tip in the mussels, put on the lid and, holding the handle and the lid in both hands, shake the pan around a bit. Turn the heat very high and cook for 3 minutes. Lift the lid to check that all the mussels are open; if not, put the lid back on, shake again and continue for a few more minutes. Repeat again if necessary, continuing until most of the mussels are open. Add the parsley, several grinds of pepper and stir everything around for the last time. Tip into a large bowl or eat from the pan. Serve the clotted cream separately for people to stir into their soup.

THAI MUSSELS
Serves 4

The broth of this spicy version of moules marinière has all the hall-marks of a coconut-milk Thai soup, being all at once creamy, sour, chilli-hot and citrus-scented. This basic recipe can be changed with other seasonings – leeks, for example, instead of onion, with curry spices or saffron and cream – but Thai seasonings are the current favourite.

 2kg mussels, cleaned, broken and unopened shells discarded
 1 red onion
 3 garlic cloves
 1 small unwaxed lemon
 2 red bird's eye chillies
 2 tbsp vegetable oil
 2 tbsp Thai fish sauce (*nam pla*)
 200ml coconut cream
 freshly milled black pepper
 50g bunch of coriander

Leave the mussels in a colander to finish draining while you prepare the broth. Peel, halve and finely chop the onion and garlic. Using a zester or potato peeler, remove the zest from the lemon in wafer-thin strips. Chop quite small. Trim and split the chillies, scrape away the seeds, slice into thin strips and then across into tiny scraps – don't forget to wash your hands to remove the chilli juices that will burn eyes and other sensitive parts. Heat the oil in a large pan with a good-fitting lid. Stir in the onion, lemon zest, garlic and chilli and cook, adjusting the heat so nothing burns, for 6–7 minutes until the onion is soft. Add the *nam pla*, coconut cream and juice from half the lemon. Season generously with black pepper. Chop the coriander, including the stalks, which should be sliced very finely. Add the stalk half of the coriander to the pan. Simmer for a couple of minutes, taste and adjust the seasoning with lemon juice. Tip the drained mussels into the pan, stir a couple of times with a wooden spoon, clamp on the lid and cook at a high heat for 5 minutes. Lift off the lid, have a look to see if the mussels are opening – it doesn't take long – and give the pan a good shake or another stir, trying to bring the already opened mussels on the bottom to the top. Replace the lid and cook for a few more minutes. Check again that all the mussels are open, returning the lid for a couple more minutes if necessary, add the rest of the coriander, give a final stir and then tip the contents of the pan into a warmed bowl. Do not eat any mussels which haven't opened.

MARAZION MUSSELS WITH FETTUCINE
Serves 4–6

Marazion is a long, sandy beach opposite St Michael's Mount beyond Penzance. It was there, one freezing, windy, rainy Sunday in October, that friends and I took shelter at an imposing pub overlooking the sea. As the rain lashed down outside and the sky blackened over the Mount, we chose our food from one of those impossibly ambitious pub menus. We were mindful to chose local produce and the grilled sardines (actually pilchards) were very good, but the Newlyn crab salad was spoilt for me by an overdose of fancy lollo rosso and chunks of raw green and red pepper. The best choice by far was pasta with mussels in a creamy sauce flecked with tomatoes. This is my interpretation of the dish, which owes a lot to a recipe in Rowley Leigh's book *No Place Like Home*.

> 2kg mussels, cleaned, broken and unopened shells discarded
> 1 glass white wine or cider
> 1 medium onion
> 3 garlic cloves
> 2 tbsp olive oil
> ½ tsp fresh thyme leaves
> 6 ripe plum tomatoes
> 200ml thick cream
> 500g fettuccine or tagliatelle
> salt and pepper

Cook the mussels in the wine in a large lidded pan over a very high heat for 3–4 minutes. Lift the lid to check that all the mussels are open; if not, return the lid, give the pan a good shake and continue for a few more minutes until the mussels are open. Tip into a colander but retain the juices. Leave to cool and then shell the mussels. Meanwhile, peel and finely chop the onion and garlic. Soften gently in the olive oil. At the end of cooking, stir in the thyme. Cover the tomatoes with boiling water, count to 20, drain, core and peel. Scrape the seeds into a sieve placed over a bowl and chop the flesh into small, neat dice. Add the strained mussel liquor (taking care to hold back any shell, etc. towards the end) and tomato juices into the onion. Boil until the liquid is reduced to less than a cupful, then beat in the cream. Reduce the heat and simmer until thick and unctuous. Cook the pasta in plenty of boiling salted water until just *al dente*. Drain and return to the pan. Stir in the mussels and tomato. Season with black pepper, stir again and serve.

GRIDDLED SCALLOPS WITH PEA PURÉE AND MINT VINAIGRETTE

Serves 4–6

Clever Rowley Leigh, chef of Kensington Place, who invented this fantastic combination of crusty, sweet scallops with a creamy pea purée, the whole dribbled with a mint vinaigrette. It is inspired. Serve with crusty bread as a starter. Leftover mint vinaigrette keeps well in the fridge and is excellent with lamb chops on another occasion.

3–5 scallops per person, cleaned, corals intact
a little vegetable oil

for the pea purée:
4 spring onions
50g butter
1 small lettuce
250g peas, fresh or frozen
a few mint leaves
salt and pepper
½ tsp sugar
150 ml dry white wine
150ml thick cream
squeeze lemon juice

for the mint vinaigrette:
small bunch of mint
1 tsp sugar
salt and pepper
50ml cider vinegar or white wine vinegar
125ml sunflower or groundnut oil

Begin by making the pea purée. Trim and slice the spring onions and stew them in 50g butter. Shred the lettuce leaves and add to the pan, then stir in the peas. Add a few mint leaves and season with salt and pepper and a little sugar. Add the white wine and stew, covered, on a low heat for 30 minutes. Add the cream and simmer briskly to reduce until it is in danger of catching on the sides of the pan. Remove from the heat and purée in a blender until very smooth. Sharpen the seasoning with lemon juice and salt and pepper. Transfer to a small pan and keep warm.

To make the vinaigrette, chop 6 or 7 sprigs of mint roughly and put in the blender. Add a teaspoon of sugar and a big pinch of salt. Bring the vinegar up to the boil and pour over the mint. Switch on the blender and add the oil in a steady trickle. Check the seasoning and adjust with lemon, salt and pepper if necessary.

To cook the scallops, salt them lightly, leave for 10 minutes and then pat dry with kitchen paper. Lightly brush them with a little oil. Heat a heavy, dry frying pan or griddle until it is very hot and put the scallops in one by one. Do not move them for a couple of minutes, but let them brown well. Turn and cook for another 2 minutes, then remove. They should be just hot in the middle, but very moist. To serve, arrange the scallops around a mound of pea purée on each plate and drizzle the vinaigrette between them, taking care not to drown the scallops.

CHINESE SCALLOPS ON THE HALF-SHELL
Serves 4

In my early days a restaurant critic I was taken to Chinatown by a Singaporean friend and introduced to this stunningly simple, utterly fabulous way of cooking scallops. The scallops are cooked in the shell and served with an exquisite 'gravy' made from the shellfish juices mingled with soy, toasted sesame oil and ginger, with a garnish of spring onions and coriander.

> 50g fresh ginger
> 16 scallops, cleaned but on the shell
> 3 spring onions
> 4 or 5 sprigs coriander
> 4 tbsp toasted sesame oil
> 2 tbsp Kikkoman soy sauce

Leave the scallops attached to the shell. Peel and finely slice the ginger and then cut into skinny matchsticks. Half-fill a steamer pan with water and bring to the boil with the lid on. Sprinkle the scallops with ginger and place in the steamer. Cover and cook for about 4 minutes until just set. Trim and finely slice the spring onions and coarsely chop the coriander leaves. Quickly heat together the sesame oil and soy sauce. Serve four shells per person. Sprinkle with spring onions and coriander and pour over the hot sauce.

COQUILLE ST JACQUES WITH BACON
Serves 2–4

This variation on Coquille St Jacques, the classic French way of cooking and serving scallops in their shell, makes a few scallops go a long way. The creamy mash acts as a wall to contain the smooth, silky scallops in their white wine sauce, a sublime combination. And when there are a few scraps of crisp, salty bacon with each mouthful and a crunchy, cheesy topping, it is hard to resist. Quantities given are for four starter portions or two main dishes.

500g maincrop potatoes

salt and black pepper

50g butter

100ml milk plus 3 tablespoons

8 scallops, cleaned, round shells retained

1 bay leaf

150ml dry white wine

4 rashers rindless smoked streaky bacon

1 tbsp vegetable oil

bunch of spring onions or 1 leek

25g flour

4 tbsp freshly grated Parmesan

Pre-heat the oven to 400°F/200°C/gas mark 6. Peel the potatoes, cut into even-sized chunks and cook in plenty of salted water. Drain and mash with half the butter and 3 tablespoons of milk. Meanwhile, cut the orange corals off the scallops and slice each scallop into three thick pennies. Place the bay leaf and wine in a small pan and bring to the boil. Reduce the heat immediately and add the scallops and their corals. Cook gently for a couple of minutes, then scoop the scallops out of the pan and drain the wine into a cup. Discard the bay leaf. Slice across the bacon rashers to make skinny strips. Fry the bacon in the vegetable oil until nicely crisp. Scoop the bacon out of the pan and drain on kitchen paper. Trim and finely slice the spring onions or, if using a leek, trim, then quarter it lengthways and slice into small scraps. Cook the onion or leek in the bacon oil for about 5 minutes until soft. Add the remaining butter and, when melted, stir in the flour until smooth. Then gradually incorporate the wine, followed by 100ml milk, stirring constantly to make a smooth sauce. Season with salt and pepper and cook for 5 minutes before returning the scallops and bacon. Edge four scallop shells – the mixture may require more, depending on the size of the shells – with a wall of potato. Spoon the sauce in the middle and use leftover mash to fork a thin lid. Dredge lavishly with Parmesan. Cook in the oven for 15–20 minutes until the top is crisp and gorgeous.

SCALLOP OR SQUID PROVENÇAL WITH BASMATI RICE
Serves 2–4

The combination of smooth, sweet scallops and fresh, vibrant cherry tomatoes with a quickly made garlicky, lemon–wine sauce flecked with flat-leaf parsley is as easy on the tongue as it is on the eye. There is a huge amount here for two, but it is so light and delicious that everyone always seems to eat more than expected. Serve it with bread and butter as a starter or with rice for a main course. Another simpler version is to slice the cleaned squid into rings or strips and fry it briefly in olive oil flavoured with garlic crushed to a paste with a little salt. Serve with a squeeze of lemon and a shower of freshly chopped flat-leaf parsley.

 300g basmati rice
 12 plump, fresh, cleaned scallops or 400g cleaned squid
 salt and pepper
 2 garlic cloves
 250g cherry tomatoes
 50g butter
 1 tbsp olive oil
 juice of ½ lemon
 ½ glass dry white wine
 flourishing bunch of flat-leaf parsley
 1 lemon

Rinse the rice until the water runs clean and place in a pan with a tight-fitting lid with 450ml cold water. Bring to the boil, then reduce the heat to very low, cover the pan and cook for 10 minutes. Remove from the heat but leave the lid in place for a further 10 minutes so that the rice finishes cooking in the steam. Meanwhile, cut the white part of each scallop into two rounds, or three if they are very big. Put the corals in a separate pile. Season both with salt and pepper. If using squid, slice the sacs in chunky rings, approximately 1cm wide. Divide the tentacles into two or three pieces, depending on their size. Peel and chop the garlic, sprinkle with a generous pinch of salt and use the flat of a knife to crush to a juicy paste. Quarter the cherry tomatoes, then slice across the quarters. Heat butter and oil in a spacious frying pan, stir in the garlic and almost immediately the scallop pennies or squid, moderating the heat so that it cooks gently, turning the scallops to cook evenly. After a couple of minutes, add the scallop corals, cook for a few more seconds, turning to cook both sides, then squeeze in the lemon juice and add the white wine. Let everything bubble up, then add the tomatoes. Cook for 2–3 minutes for everything to mix and merge. Pick the leaves off the parsley stalks and coarsely chop; you need at least 4 heaped tablespoons. Stir the parsley into the dish before the tomatoes have had a chance to collapse. Season generously with black pepper and lightly with salt. Serve over rice with lemon wedges.

SQUID WITH TOMATOES AND PEAS

Serves 4

Apart from a few bungled attempts at re-creating the deep-fried squid rings I'd eaten in Spain, this was the first squid recipe I ever cooked and it's slightly adapted from Marcella Hazan's *Classic Italian Cookbook*. It tastes fresh and luscious and converts would-be squid haters. Serve it with plenty of crusty bread to scoop up the wonderful juices.

> 1 medium onion
> 2 garlic cloves
> 8 ripe, firm tomatoes
> 2 tbsp olive oil
> 800g small squid, cleaned
> salt and black pepper
> 350g frozen petits pois
> lemon wedges and parsley to serve

Peel, halve and finely chop the onion and garlic. Pour boiling water over the tomatoes. Count to 20, drain, peel, cut out the core and halve the tomatoes. Scrape out the seeds and chop the flesh. Heat the oil in a heavy-bottomed, medium-sized pan that can hold all the ingredients. Sauté the onion over a medium heat, stirring occasionally, for about 10 minutes until it begins to soften and turn golden. Add the garlic and cook for a couple of minutes before adding the tomatoes. Cook at a gentle simmer for about 15 minutes until the tomatoes begin to thicken and the onions melt into them to make a cohesive sauce. Meanwhile, slice the squid sacs (its body) into 1cm-wide rings. Cut off the tentacles. Squeeze out the hard mouth from the centre of the tentacles – it will pop out easily – and discard everything else. Divide the tentacle clusters in half. Add the rings and tentacles to the casserole. Season with salt and pepper, stir well, cover and cook at a gently simmer for about 20 minutes or until the squid is tender. Taste and adjust the seasoning. Stir in the peas and cook for a few more minutes until tender. Taste and adjust the seasoning, stir in the parsley and serve with lemon wedges.

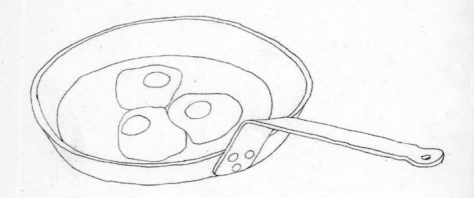

Eggs

James Bond's Scrambled Eggs
Oeufs en Cocotte à la Crème
Fromage des Oeufs
Mayonnaise
Hollandaise Sauce
Quiche Lorraine
Penne alla Carbonara

During the war, one of the luxuries of living in a small fishing village with inland farms and meadows was the inevitable trade in black-market food. In Mousehole it was possible, amongst other things, to get a supply of fresh, black-market eggs. Ben remembers visiting Will Harvey at Raginnis Farm. They might come back with a chicken wrapped up in old newspapers, but eggs, lovely big brown speckled eggs, are what he particularly remembers. Betty would make eggs Florentine or, best of all, bake the eggs with cream in buttered ramekins for supper.

Several nearby farms sell fresh eggs from the farm door but good local free-range, organic eggs are sold by the village shop. The yolks are creamy and dark yellow and the eggs taste, well, eggy. Proper job, as Lionel might say. So much tastier than the eggs from the various supermarkets.

JAMES BOND'S SCRAMBLED EGGS
Serves 4

Ian Fleming wrote the Bond books in food-rationed, post-war Britain and it occurred to me, after trawling several books for food references, that James was an egg man, so much so that he specified the type of egg – speckled brown – and the sort of hen – French Maran – for his boiled egg when breakfasting in London. The eggs had to be boiled for precisely 3 minutes. Bond – or was it Fleming? – liked his scrambled egg made with plenty of butter, and his secret was to add extra butter just before the eggs were finished. A few finely snipped chives or *fines herbes* – parsley, tarragon, chervil and chives – is another preference, and they make a terrific difference. Perfect with smoked salmon.

    12 fresh eggs
    salt and pepper
    75g butter
    ½ tbsp finely snipped chives or parsley
    hot buttered toast for serving

Break the eggs into a bowl. Beat thoroughly with a fork and season well with salt and pepper. In a heavy-bottomed saucepan, melt 50g of the butter. When melted, pour in the eggs and cook over a very low heat, whisking continuously with a small whisk or beating with a wooden spoon. When the eggs are slightly more moist than you would wish for eating, remove the pan from the heat and add 25g butter. Continue whisking or beating for about 30 seconds, adding the chopped chives.

OEUFS EN COCOTTE À LA CRÈME
Serves 6

A lovely way to enjoy a new-laid egg. Betty would serve these for supper with bread and butter, but they are a treat for breakfast or high tea.

> 150ml thick cream
> 6 fresh eggs
> salt and pepper
> 25g butter

Pre-heat the oven to 375°F/190°C/gas mark 5. Bring a kettle full of water to the boil. Place six cocotte dishes, ramekins or tea cups in a roasting tin and pour in sufficient boiling water to come halfway up the sides of the dishes. Put a spoonful of cream in each dish and break in an egg. Season with salt and pepper and divide the butter in small pieces over the top. Position a baking sheet (or tinfoil) to cover and 'poach' in the oven for 6–8 minutes until the white is set and the yolk creamy. Lift the dishes on to plates and serve with a spoon.

FROMAGE DES OEUFS
Serves 6–8

I discovered this alternative way of making eggs mayonnaise in *Poor Cook* by Caroline Conran. The eggs set like a round of Brie and can be cut like one. The top is covered with a lattice of anchovies and the mayonnaise is served separately. Perfect for a party.

50g butter

12 fresh eggs

salt

2 x 50g cans anchovies in olive oil

cayenne pepper

mayonnaise (see recipe, below)

Pre-heat the oven to 350°F/180°C/gas mark 4. Bring a kettle full of water to the boil. Butter a round, flat dish lavishly so the eggs won't stick and carefully break the eggs into the dish. Sprinkle a little salt over the eggs, place the dish in a small oven dish and pour on sufficient boiling water to reach halfway up the side of the dish. Cover the dish with foil and bake for about 20 minutes or until the eggs are just set. Allow to cool in the dish, then turn out on to a plate and decorate the top with a criss-cross of split anchovy fillets. Sprinkle with cayenne pepper. Serve the 'Brie' with the mayonnaise separately. Eat with thinly sliced brown bread and butter.

MAYONNAISE

Ensure all ingredients are at room temperature.

2 egg yolks

1 tbsp smooth Dijon mustard

salt and pepper

300ml light olive oil, or half olive oil and half groundnut oil

juice of ½ lemon

Place the egg yolks, mustard and a generous seasoning of salt and pepper in a mixing bowl. Beat with a whisk or wooden spoon until thick. Add the oil in a thin stream, beating continuously, adding a little lemon juice and then more oil until all is used up and the mayonnaise is thick and glossy.

HOLLANDAISE SAUCE

Serves 4

A creamy, buttery, slightly tart sauce to serve with poached turbot, halibut or sea bass.

225g butter
3 egg yolks
juice of 1 lemon
salt and white pepper

First clarify the butter. Melt the butter in a small pan and leave to settle. Remove the frothy scum with a spoon, then pour the clear butter in a bowl, leaving behind the milky residue. Choose a small stainless-steel pan and place it over the lowest possible heat. Add the egg yolks and a splash of water and whisk until the eggs are thick and creamy – you do *not* want them to scramble. Add the clarified butter in a thin stream, whisking all the time until the sauce has the consistency of mayonnaise. Season with the lemon juice, salt and pepper. Serve warm.

QUICHE LORRAINE
Serves 4–6

A lot of rude things have been said about quiche, but when you eat a good one, made properly with rich cream, fresh eggs, smoky bacon or ham and a thin, crisp pastry base, it is a slice of heaven.

150g plain flour plus a little extra
90g butter
salt
100g rindless, smoked, streaky bacon or 3 thick slices decent ham
½ tbsp vegetable oil
8 fresh, large eggs
400ml thick cream
3 tbsp finely snipped chives
salt and pepper
freshly grated nutmeg

Sift the flour into a mixing bowl or food processor. Cut 80g of the butter into chunks directly into the flour. Blend together the flour, chunks of butter and a pinch of salt in the processor or by hand until it resembles damp breadcrumbs. Tip into a mixing bowl and add 2–3 tablespoons of cold water, just sufficient to make a cohesive, pliable dough. Chill for 30 minutes before rolling thinly to fit a non-stick or greased and floured 20cm x 4cm deep flan tin (preferably one with a removable base). Cover loosely with tinfoil or greaseproof paper, fill with pie weights or rice and bake for 10 minutes. Remove the foil and cook for a further 10 minutes. Meanwhile, slice the bacon across the rashers into strips and fry in vegetable oil until very crisp. Scoop on to kitchen paper to drain. Alternatively, tear the ham into small pieces. Whisk together 4 egg yolks and 3 whole eggs, stir in the cream, add the chives, and season with salt, pepper and nutmeg. Plug any cracks in the pastry case with spare pastry and paint with spare egg white to seal. Strew the bacon over the base of the pastry case, pour on the custard and cook for 30–40 minutes until the custard has just set. Serve hot, warm or cold.

PENNE ALLA CARBONARA
Serves 4

This is the favourite store-cupboard supper at the Fish Store, probably because it tastes so good when made with fresh eggs and rich clotted cream. The idea is to cook the pasta *al dente* and then, at the last minute, to toss it with beaten raw egg mixed with cream, tiny specks of garlic and very crisp scraps of bacon. The egg is warmed rather than cooked and holds the garlic and bacon in a delicious cream which clings to the pasta. If the eggs end up solid like scrambled eggs, the whole point of the dish is lost. This is good with quick garlic bread (see page 319).

400g dried penne
4 eggs
4 tbsp thick cream
salt and pepper
6 rashers smoked streaky bacon
1 tbsp olive oil
4 garlic cloves
4 tbsp freshly grated Parmesan
2 tbsp chopped flat-leaf parsley

Cook the pasta according to packet instructions in plenty of salted boiling water. Meanwhile, using a wooden spoon, beat the eggs with the cream and season with a pinch of salt and several grinds of pepper. Discard the rind and chop the bacon into thick matchsticks. Ten minutes before the pasta is ready, heat the olive oil in a frying pan and cook the bacon gently so that it releases most of its fat, then turn up the heat until both bacon and fat are very crisp. Peel the garlic and chop very finely. Add the garlic to the bacon right at the end of cooking, stirring quickly for a few seconds until aromatic. Don't let the garlic brown. When the pasta is ready, drain it thoroughly and tip it back into the saucepan. Combine immediately with the hot bacon, its oil and the garlic, then pour in the egg mixture. Stir to coat the pasta evenly so that the heat of the pasta cooks the egg slightly. Finally, add the Parmesan and parsley.

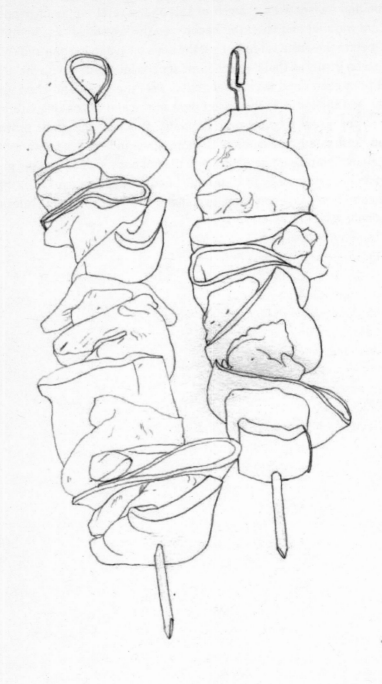

Chicken

Thai-style Chicken Meatloaf
Lemon and Garlic Chicken Kebabs
Pot-roasted Chicken with Onions
Leek, Chicken and Parsley Pie
A Simple Chicken Curry
Chicken Kdra with Almonds and Chickpeas
Coronation Chicken
Vietnamese Chicken Salad
Malaysian Chicken Rendang
Picasso's Valencienne Rice
Chicken Liver Pâté
Devilled Chicken Livers on Toast with Onion Marmalade

When I was little and my family came to Cornwall for our summer holidays, I used to look forward to visiting my aunt Rene. She was tall, with a distracted little smile playing on her lips. She looked like a female version of my dad, her brother. She always wore khaki-coloured, well-worn cotton dungarees tucked into wellington boots, a man's navy cardigan with leather elbow patches and a moth-eaten navy-blue French beret. My dad called her 'Tom' and she and her husband, Harold, owned lots of fields, some close by, others having to be visited in a jeep. They grew blackcurrants, raspberries and gooseberries, but their main thing was rearing rare-breed chickens and beautiful, creamy-pink pigs. Sometimes the pigs grew so big we could sit on them like a pony, but I preferred hanging around the pig pens watching the wiggly little piglets. Most of the chickens were secured in giant wire playpens, but her particular favourites, including a handsome cockerel with petrol-green feathers, wandered and pecked wherever they wanted. In those days it was a special treat to eat chicken but I don't recall ever associating my aunt's chickens with our Sunday roast.

In those post-post-war days, when rationing was over but no scrap of food was wasted, we might have had chicken once a month, maybe less. My father carved it wafer-thin – even the legs and thighs were carved to make it go further. The remains would be turned into curry or a gratin or made into a pie and the bones cooked up with carrots and onions for soup. This was in the days before battery-reared broilers and chicken portions; it was only possible to buy a whole chicken, complete with giblets. These days, we are used to cooking up a tray of supermarket chicken legs or thighs without even thinking about what happened to the rest of the bird. I'm gradually going backwards towards that old attitude to chicken; I'd rather eat it less often and pay more for one that has been properly reared. I don't want to eat chicken stuffed with hormones, pesticides and anitibiotics. The difference in taste, texture and size of joints between organically reared chickens and an ordinary broiler with no particular pedigree is immediately obvious. The fact that organically reared birds take nearly twice as long to mature –

12–14 weeks as opposed to 6–8 weeks – and are fed a natural diet is obviously reflected in the price. I prefer the stronger flavour and the dense, almost chewy texture of these birds. Our propensity for chicken portions and whole chickens without giblets means that local butchers, as well as supermarkets, have an abundance of wings and livers in their fridges and freezers and sell them remarkably cheaply. The wings are great for making stock but are also a lip-smacking treat cooked fast and furiously over the barbecue. Livers make creamy smooth pâtés and are delicious fried for pasta sauce or piled on to toast.

One of the great by-products of a chicken dinner is the bones. I make stock every time I roast or cut up a whole chicken, or bone several legs or thighs (bones, chopped onion, carrot, bay leaf and any other useful vegetables or herbs are covered with water and left to simmer for a couple of hours, strained, chilled and de-fatted before use), but most of the time I use stock cubes or granules. Stock granules, sold in a tub, are brilliant. It's laziness really; you stir a scoop into hot water or directly into whatever you are making and it dissolves like instant coffee. It also avoids all those half-finished cubes that everyone has mouldering at the back of the shelf, slowly oozing out of their foil. Best brands are Knorr, Just Bouillon, Marigold and Telma (Kosher soup cubes). A can of consommé, which is really superior stock, is another useful standby.

THAI-STYLE CHICKEN MEATLOAF
Serves 8

Meatloaf isn't a name that does a dish many favours. This reworking of that much-maligned feed-the-five-thousand dish works on all sorts of levels. It's more of a terrine, really, and eaten cold. It's great for a help-yourself meal, bundling up slices in soft and floppy rice-flour pancakes with lettuce, cucumber, coriander and wafer-thin red onion, the whole dribbled with sweet chilli sauce. It's also excellent in wraps, on toast, with rice noodles tossed with butter and chopped coriander, or in Thai and other salads.

Rice pancakes, incidentally, also known as crystal pancakes in Thai restaurants, are brittle in their cellophane pack but once dipped into warm water they soften and become malleable. If using fresh onions instead of super-convenient canned, fried onions, allow an extra 15 minutes for the preparation time and add an extra tablespoon of oil.

Eazy fried onions are a *must* for the store-cupboard, giving you instant meltingly soft onions fried in olive oil.

2 garlic cloves
salt and black pepper
2 small red chillies
25g fresh ginger
1 small unwaxed lemon
3 tbsp vegetable oil
200g canned Eazy fried onions
90g bunch of coriander
50g couscous or fresh breadcrumbs
2 eggs
1 tbsp Thai fish sauce
500g minced pork
500g minced chicken

Pre-heat the oven to 350°F/180°C/gas mark 4. Peel and finely chop the garlic. Sprinkle with ½ a teaspoon of salt and use the flat of a knife to work to a juicy paste. Trim and split the chillies. Scrape away the seeds, slice into skinny strips and then into tiny scraps. Peel the ginger, slice thinly and then chop into small scraps. Use a potato peeler to remove the zest from half the lemon in small, paper-thin pieces. Heat two tablespoons of oil in a frying pan and stir in the onions, garlic, chillies, ginger and lemon zest. Cook, stirring often, for 5 minutes or so, until the garlic is aromatic and the chillies, ginger and lemon zest wilted. Meanwhile, chop the coriander. Start at the stalk end and chop very finely to begin with, slackening as you get to the leafy part. Add the chopped stalks to the pan, stir and allow to wilt before turning off the heat. Pour 125g boiling water over the couscous, leave for 5 minutes to hydrate, then fork up to separate the grains. Whisk the eggs in a mixing bowl with the fish sauce. Mix in the chicken and pork, the onion mixture, the hydrated couscous or breadcrumbs and the rest of the coriander, dispersing everything thoroughly. Oil a 1 litre capacity gratin dish with half the remaining oil. Pat the mixture into the dish, making a slight mould, then smear with the remaining oil. Cook in the oven for 60 minutes. Leave to cool in the dish, then chill, covered, in the fridge. Serve sliced from the dish.

LEMON AND GARLIC CHICKEN KEBABS
Serves 4–6

The standard marinade for chicken or lamb kebabs. Good with just about everything. For a change, add a fold of sliced chorizo and squares of red pepper between some of the pieces of chicken.

> 800g boned chicken
> 2 large garlic cloves
> salt
> 2 sprigs of thyme
> 1 tbsp lemon juice
> 3 tbsp olive oil

Slice the chicken into kebab-sized pieces. Peel the garlic and chop. Sprinkle with salt and use the flat of a knife to work to a juicy paste. Transfer to a suitable container that can hold the chicken. Add the thyme, stir in the lemon juice and then the olive oil. Mix the chicken into the marinade, stirring to coat all the pieces thoroughly. Cover and chill for at least 1 hour and up to 24 hours. If cooking the kebabs over barbecue coals, ensure the coals are covered with white dust and thus ready for the cooking to begin. If using a griddle, place it over a high heat and leave for several minutes to get very hot. Meanwhile, thread the chicken on to skewers, shaking off excess marinade. When coals or griddle are ready, lay out the skewers and cook for about 3 minutes a side, turning as the chicken forms a thick golden crust. Continue to cook all the surfaces. Take care not to overcook.

POT-ROASTED CHICKEN WITH ONIONS
Serves 4–6

This is a completely brilliant way of cooking a chicken in the oven. It is even simpler than roasting the bird and actually smells more delicious. The result is moist juicy chicken with floppy, sweet onion 'gravy'. Serve with mashed potato.

> 4–5 large onions
> salt and pepper
> 1 medium–large chicken
> sprig of thyme (optional)
> 6 tbsp olive oil

Pre-heat the oven to 350°F/180°C/gas mark 4. Peel and halve the onions and slice very thinly. Season generously inside the chicken cavity. Add the thyme, if using. Pour 2 tablespoons of olive oil into a deep casserole – a big Le Creuset is ideal – and add all the onions. Add 2 more tablespoons of oil and season with 1 teaspoon of salt and plenty of pepper. Place the chicken, breast-side down, on top of the onions, pressing it down firmly. Pour the final 2 tablespoons of oil over the top. Position the lid or use foil to make an efficient leak-free lid. Cook in the middle of the oven for 60–90 minutes depending on the size of the chicken. Remove from the oven. Leave covered for 15 minutes before lifting the chicken on to a plate for carving in thick slices. I usually discard the skin (which will be flobby and unappetizing). Serve the chicken topped with some of the onions and their juices.

LEEK, CHICKEN AND PARSLEY PIE
Serves 4–6

One of the best pie combinations: buttery pastry giving on to chicken and leek held in a creamy parsley sauce. This pie is good with roast potatoes – which can cook at the same time as the pie – and peas or buttered cabbage. Or boiled new potatoes and carrots. It is excellent, too, eaten cold with salad.

225g flour plus 2 tbsp extra

125g butter

3–4 tbsp cold water

2 leeks

1 shallot, or 1 small onion and 1 garlic clove

salt and pepper

800g boned chicken

150ml milk

150ml thick cream

4 tbsp coarsely chopped flat-leaf parsley

1 egg whisked with 1 tbsp milk

Pre-heat the oven to 400°F/200°C/gas mark 6. Sift 225g flour into a mixing bowl. Cut 100g butter into pieces and use your fingertips to work it quickly into the flour until it resembles heavy breadcrumbs. Stir in sufficient cold water to enable the dough to cling together. Knead lightly to form a ball. Cover and chill. Trim and slice the leeks in 1cm rounds. Rinse and shake dry. Peel, halve and finely chop the shallot or onion and garlic. Melt 25g butter in a spacious frying pan or similarly wide-based pan and stir in leeks and shallot or onion and garlic. Season with salt and pepper and cook, stirring often, for 5 minutes, then lower the heat, cover the pan and cook for 10 minutes until the leeks are soft. Meanwhile, cut the chicken into chunks. Increase the heat and stir the chicken into the pan, stirring for a few minutes until all the pieces are white. Sift 1 tablespoon of flour over the top, stir vigorously until it disappears, then stir in the milk and cream to make a thick, smooth sauce. Reduce the heat and cook gently for a few min-utes to cook the flour. Stir the parsley into the pan, check the season-ing and cool – 10 minutes in the freezer is a quick solution. Dust a work surface with flour and roll two-thirds of the pastry to fit a non-stick or oiled 20cm flan tin. Spoon in the filling. Roll the remaining pastry and fit the lid, crimping the edges to seal. Paint with the egg wash, prod with a fork to make steam holes and bake for 30–40 minutes until the pastry is golden and cooked through. If the pie seems to be browning too quickly, reduce the heat slightly and cover with a sheet of foil.

A SIMPLE CHICKEN CURRY

Serves 4

There is no grinding of spices or careful measuring of ingredients in this curry recipe. Flavour and heat come from two little jars that most kitchens seem to collect along the way: curry powder and chilli powder. The curry is finished with spinach and Greek yoghurt, which give it a freshness and richness that belie the simplicity of the recipe. Make a treat of this surprisingly subtle cheat's curry by serving it with boiled rice, mango chutney, poppadoms and home-made cucumber raita.

    2 medium onions
    2 large garlic cloves
    salt and pepper
    2 tbsp cooking oil
    ½ tsp chilli powder
    3 heaped tsp curry powder
    800g boned chicken
    200ml carton coconut cream
    ½ chicken stock cube dissolved in 250ml boiling water
    1 tbsp lemon juice
    200g young spinach leaves
    4 tbsp thick Greek yoghurt
    1 tbsp toasted flaked almonds

Peel, halve and thinly slice the onions. Peel and chop the garlic. Sprinkle the garlic with ½ a teaspoon of salt and work to a juicy paste. Heat the oil in a spacious pan and stir in the onions and garlic. Cook briskly, stirring frequently, for about 10 minutes until the onion is wilted and browned in places. Add the chilli and curry powders and cook, stirring constantly, for about a minute. Meanwhile, cut the chicken into large, bite-size pieces. Stir the chicken into the onion, turning it around until all the pieces have changed from pink to white. Increase the heat slightly and let the chicken brown a little. Add the coconut cream and stock. Bring to the boil and simmer for about 20 minutes until the chicken is cooked through. Increase the heat, stir the lemon juice into the sauce, taste and adjust the seasoning if necessary before pushing the spinach between the chicken pieces. When wilted – a matter of seconds – loosely stir the yoghurt into the curry. Scatter with the toasted almond flakes and serve.

CHICKEN KDRA WITH ALMONDS AND CHICKPEAS
Serves 6

Moroccan kdra is a type of tagine, or stew, flavoured and thickened with onions. The chicken should end up so tender it almost falls off the bone into the herb-flecked, saffron-scented gravy. Whole almonds, boiled to get rid of bitterness, and chickpeas make it very satisfying. Serve with couscous (300g hydrated in 700ml boiling chicken stock, stirred with 1 tablespoon lemon juice and 2 tablespoons olive oil) or boiled (peeled) new potatoes finished in butter, saffron and chopped flat-leaf parsley.

> 150g whole blanched almonds
> 3 garlic cloves
> 1 tsp salt
> juice of 2 large lemons
> 1 tbsp olive oil
> 6 organic chicken legs, jointed
> 5 large onions
> 2 x 400g cans chickpeas
> 75g flat-leaf parsley
> 40g butter
> 750ml chicken stock
> 1 large cinnamon stick
> large pinch saffron stamens softened in a little boiling water
> ground black pepper

Place the almonds in a small saucepan, cover with water and leave to simmer, topping up the water as necessary, while you prepare the dish.

Peel and crush the chopped garlic with 1 teaspoon salt to make a juicy paste. Stir in 1 teaspoon lemon juice and 1 tablespoon olive oil. Smear this over the chicken pieces and set aside. Peel, halve and finely slice four of the onions. Finely chop the fifth. Tip the chickpeas into a colander, rinse with cold water and rub between your hands to remove the skins. Discard the skins. Coarsely chop the flat-leaf parsley. Melt the butter in a large casserole over a medium heat. Fry the pieces of chicken on both sides without browning. Stir in the chopped onion and cook for a few minutes. Add the stock, cinnamon, half the saffron and a generous seasoning of black pepper. Bring to the boil, turn down to simmer, cover the pan and cook for 30 minutes. Add 50g chopped parsley and the sliced onions, poking them down between the chicken pieces and leaving some on top. Cover again and cook for a further 30 minutes.

Remove the chicken pieces to a plate, scraping the onion back into the pan. Add the chickpeas, drained almonds, remaining saffron and juice of 1 lemon. Boil rapidly for 10 minutes to reduce and thicken the sauce. Taste and adjust the seasoning with salt, pepper and lemon juice. Return the chicken pieces and cook for a few minutes until heated through. Five minutes before serving, stir in the remaining parsley.

CORONATION CHICKEN
Serves 6

To describe coronation chicken as cold chicken in a creamy, lightly curried yet curiously nutty sauce doesn't do it justice. It is the addition of a little mango chutney and slices of juicy, crisp cucumber which transform this pale but interesting combination beyond belief.

I like to decorate this darling of the buffet table with toasted almonds and white grapes, but that's strictly untraditional. It is a good dish to serve with rice and a crisp green salad.

> 1 small cucumber
> salt, pepper and 4 black peppercorns
> 1 carrot
> 1 medium onion
> small bunch thyme
> 1 garlic clove
> 1 medium chicken or 6 large chicken thighs
> 1 glass of white wine (optional)

1 tbsp vegetable cooking oil or 20g butter

1 heaped tbsp curry powder or paste

1 heaped tbsp tomato purée

1 large lemon

1 bay leaf

4 tbsp mango chutney or chunky apricot jam

100ml mayonnaise

100ml thick cream

150g seedless white grapes

50g toasted almonds flakes

lemon wedges to serve

Peel the cucumber, split it lengthways and use a teaspoon to gouge out the seeds and their watery pulp. Cut the cucumber in ½cm-thick slices, sprinkle with 1 teaspoon salt and leave to drain in a sieve or colander. Peel and chop the carrot. Peel and halve the onion and coarsely chop half of it. Place carrot, chopped onion, thyme, bruised garlic, 4 peppercorns and ½ teaspoon salt in a 2 litre saucepan. Arrange the chicken, breast-side down if using a whole chicken, on top, pour over the wine if using and top up with water until the chicken is just submerged. Bring to the boil, reduce the heat so that the liquid simmers gently and cook, semi-covered, for 20 minutes. Turn off the heat and leave for 20 minutes. Meanwhile, finely chop the remaining onion and soften in the oil or butter in a small saucepan without letting it brown. Stir in the curry powder or paste and cook for a minute or two, before stirring in the tomato purée, juice from the lemon, 100ml water and the bay leaf. Season with salt and pepper and simmer until reduced by half. Remove from the heat. Chop the lumps in the chutney or jam and stir into the sauce. Allow to cool. Stir in the mayonnaise. Whip the cream softly in a mixing bowl. Fold into the sauce. Taste and adjust the seasoning. Discard the bay leaf. Squeeze the cucumber dry. Remove the chicken from the stock, discard the skin and tear the meat into bite-size chunks. Toss cucumber and chicken in the sauce, then transfer to a serving dish and decorate with halved grapes and almonds. Serve with lemon wedges.

VIETNAMESE CHICKEN SALAD

Serves 6

An excellent way of using up leftover roast chicken, but interesting enough to make from scratch.

    3 tbsp oriental fish sauce
    3 tbsp fresh lime juice
    1 heaped tsp sugar
    2 small red chillies
    4 spring onions
    1 small white cabbage or iceberg lettuce
    4 medium carrots
    1 cucumber
    1 poached chicken (see recipe above, pages 184–5) or 3 portions roast
       chicken
    small bunch coriander
    small bunch mint

Mix together the fish sauce and lime juice in a large salad bowl. Dissolve the sugar in the mixture. Trim and split the chillies lengthways, slice into skinny batons and then into tiny scraps. Trim and finely slice the spring onions. Stir the chilli and onions into the salad dressing.

Core then finely shred the cabbage or lettuce. If using white cabbage, mix it into the dressing immediately; softer lettuce goes in later. Trim and scrape the carrots, trim and peel the cucumber. Slice both very thinly on the slant to make ribbons rather than slices. Stir carrot and cucumber into the salad. Remove the skin from the chicken and tear it into bite-size pieces. Coarsely chop the coriander and mint to make approximately 2 tablespoons of each. Add chicken, lettuce (if using), mint and coriander to the salad, toss thoroughly and serve.

MALAYSIAN CHICKEN RENDANG
Serves 4

Rendang is a very hot, medium-dry curry which is so famous in Malaysia that it's eaten for breakfast and proudly regarded as the national dish. It originates in nearby Indonesia and Western Sumatra, where they make it even spicier and hotter, so much so that it keeps at room temperature for a week. Despite the vast quantities of chillies in this somewhat tame version, the heat is softened by coconut milk, resulting in a curry that won't blow your head off. Serve with basmati rice, cucumber raita and Indian bread.

    2 onions
    20g fresh ginger
    2 lemon grass
    8 small or 2 long red chillies
    1 tsp ground turmeric
    1 tsp ground coriander
    salt
    2 tbsp vegetable oil
    1kg chicken thigh fillet
    400ml can coconut milk
    2 limes or small lemons
    4 tbsp desiccated coconut

Peel and quarter the onions. Peel the ginger and coarsely chop. Trim the lemon grass and peel away the tough outer layers. Coarsely chop the tender inner stem. Trim and split the chillies. Scrape away the seeds and coarsely chop. Place all these ingredients in the bowl of a food processor and add 150ml cold water. Blitz to make a smooth paste flecked with red chilli. Add the turmeric, coriander and 1 teaspoon salt to make a carrot-coloured purée. Pulse briefly to mix thoroughly. Heat the oil in a *karahi* (Indian wok), wok or other spacious, wide-based pan over a medium heat and stir in the purée. Cook briskly, adjusting the heat so it doesn't splutter, whilst stirring every so often for 10–15 minutes until the water evaporates, the purée darkens and becomes more paste-like and all the ingredients cook thoroughly. Meanwhile, cut the chicken into bite-size pieces. Stir the chicken into the paste and stir-fry for about 5 minutes until the pieces are all sealed. Stir in the coconut milk and bring the sauce to the boil. Adjust the heat so that the curry simmers steadily and cook, stirring often, for about 20 minutes until the chicken is cooked through and the sauce has thickened considerably and darkened in colour. Taste and adjust the seasoning with salt and lime juice. While the curry cooks, dry-roast the desiccated coconut in a frying pan, stirring constantly for a couple of minutes until evenly golden brown. Tip on to a plate to cool and arrest cooking. Just before serving, stir the juice of 1 lime into the curry, followed by the desiccated coconut. Serve with a lime wedge.

PICASSO'S VALENCIENNE RICE

Serves 4–6

Valencienne rice is really paella and the recipe is adapted from *Dining with Picasso* by Ermine Herscher. The book divides Picasso's life between his youth in Spain, early days as an artist in Paris and his years living in the Midi. It is large-format and lavishly illustrated, with a predominance of his food-related work, but also includes a terrific collection of photographs of Picasso meal times.

    2 onions
    3 garlic cloves
    3 large ripe tomatoes or 200g canned chopped tomatoes
    6 tbsp olive oil
    1 small chicken cut into 8 pieces, or 8 thighs or 8 legs
    4 Toulouse or other densely packed spicy sausages
    4 pieces rabbit back
    2 tsp soft/sweet paprika
    250g arborio or other short-grain risotto rice
    generous pinch saffron softened in 1 tbsp boiling water
    salt and pepper
    1 chicken stock cube dissolved in 750ml boiling water
    125g fresh or frozen peas
    1 lemon

Peel and slice the onions and garlic. Peel, seed and coarsely chop the tomatoes. Heat the oil in a paella pan or large frying pan and sauté the chicken, sausages and rabbit on a low heat, turning them to brown on all sides. You may need to do this in batches and transfer to a plate.

Drain away some of the oil and stir in the onions and garlic, cooking gently until soft but uncoloured. Add the tomatoes and paprika and cook for approximately 10 minutes. Return the meat to the pan. Add the rice, saffron, salt and pepper and the chicken stock. Stir once and raise the heat. As soon as the stock comes to a boil, lower the flame so that the stock is at a simmer. Cover and cook over a low heat for 15–20 minutes or until the rice has absorbed most of the stock. Stir in the peas, cover and cook for about 5 more minutes until the peas are tender. Adjust the seasoning, cover and leave for 5 minutes before serving with lemon wedges.

CHICKEN LIVER PÂTÉ
Serves 4–6

A simple and rather delicious pâté which is a useful thing to have in the fridge. If you're feeling posh, serve it with Melba toast made by lightly toasting sliced bread, removing the crusts and splitting the slices in half through the slice and then briefly grilling one side until it curls.

    1 shallot
    1 garlic clove
    salt and pepper
    50g butter
    250g chicken livers
    ½ tsp finely chopped fresh thyme leaves
    dash of brandy, whisky, sherry, port or white wine
    1 bay leaf or couple sprigs thyme

Peel and chop the shallot very, very finely. Peel the garlic, chop then sprinkle with a little salt and use the flat of a knife to work to a paste. Melt 25g butter in a frying pan and gently soften the shallot, cooking for a few minutes until soft but not coloured. Meanwhile, sort through the livers, discarding sinew and any green, blemished or fatty bits.

Spread them out on a chopping board and chop thoroughly whilst trying to stop them leaving the area. Season the livers with salt and pepper and tip them, the garlic and thyme into the pan. Increase the heat a little and stir/mash constantly with a wooden fork or spoon as the livers begin to crumble. Add the alcohol and keep stirring/mashing for about 5 minutes until the livers are pinkish-brown. Remove from the heat and stir/mash until smooth. Pour into a dish or little dishes. Melt the remaining butter in a small pan. Place the bay leaf or thyme sprigs over the pâté and pour the melted butter over the top. Chill to set the butter. It will keep, thus, for about a week.

DEVILLED CHICKEN LIVERS ON TOAST WITH ONION MARMALADE

Serves 4

It's easy to take food for granted and assume that what you like will go down well with your friends. When I dished this up as a starter to 'the Badcock girls', aka Fiona Gray and Mimi Connell, who run Badcocks Gallery in Newlyn, it turned out that chicken livers were a first for Fiona and probably Mimi too. Once they'd got over what they were eating, they didn't look back (perhaps the wine helped), but it wasn't until we'd polished off Mimi's gift of three fat monkfish tails (which I studded with garlic and roasted over sliced onions, see page 118) and cooked up some game chips with chives (page 218) followed by balsamic strawberries (page 365) that they told me.

> 250g chicken livers
> flour for dusting
> cayenne pepper
> salt
> 25g butter
> 2 tbsp vegetable oil
> 4 thick slices sourdough/country-style bread
> approx. 4 tbsp onion marmalade, see page 305

Pick over the livers, discarding sinew and any green, blemished or fatty bits. Pat the livers dry with absorbent kitchen paper and then dust with flour seasoned with cayenne pepper and salt, shaking away any excess. Heat the butter and oil and fry the livers in batches, encouraging them to brown quickly yet remain pink and tender inside. Toast the bread, pile with onion marmalade and top with the chicken livers. Dust with extra cayenne.

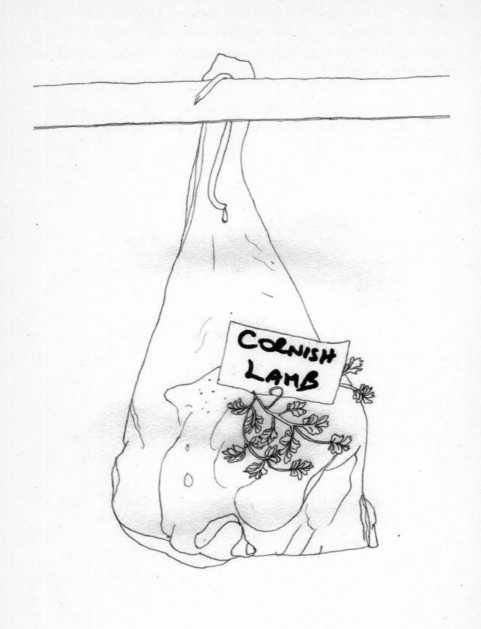

Lamb

Mediterranean Meatballs with Basil Tomato Sauce
Middle-Eastern Lamb Burgers with Lime Couscous and
   Courgettes
Arabian Shepherd's Pie
Shepherd's Pie
Robert's Gypsy Stew
Chilean Lamb Stew with Pumpkin and Sweetcorn
Slow-braised Lamb with Flageolets
Lamb Khoresh with Rhubarb
Anchovy and Rosemary Roast Lamb
Lamb *Boulangère*
Desert Lamb with Brown Rice Pilaff

Some people in Mousehole can remember when Dylan Thomas and his young wife Caitlin lived in the village. It's possible, it is often said, that he was inspired by the backstreets of Mousehole for the tittle-tattle 'voices' in the mythical village *Under Milk Wood*. One of the main gossiping spots in Mousehole used to be outside the butcher's when it was at the top of Brook Street. These days, the corner shop is called Cornish Rock and sells gemstones. You can't buy fresh meat in Mousehole except on Thursdays, when Vivian Olds, a butcher from neighbouring St Just, drives round the village in his special refrigerated van. You see him parked up at different spots, or striding around in his white pork-pie hat and cotton coat delivering orders. If you buy from the back of the van, which I often do, the order is dealt with on a minia-ture butcher's block. The chill cabinet is surprisingly well stocked and it is generally possible to buy eggs, home-cured bacon and collar joints, organic chickens, steak for pasties and minced meats, but lamb is the local speciality. Cornish lamb, particularly if has been reared in fields close to the sea, is exceptionally fine.

MEDITERRANEAN MEATBALLS WITH BASIL TOMATO SAUCE
Serves 4

There is something gently therapeutic about making meatballs. It is so satisfying to roll them between your hands, turning a mound of minced meat into neat little balls. These are cooked in a tomato sauce and served, Italian-style, over pasta. The mixture can be doubled or trebled to feed more: just scale everything up in proportion.

  1 large onion
  50g butter
  ½ tsp fresh thyme leaves
  400g can chopped tomatoes
  sugar
  salt and pepper
  20 basil leaves

15 pitted black olives

1 thick crustless slice of bread

2 milk or thin cream

1 egg yolk

500g minced lamb

400g linguine

chunk of Parmesan to serve

Peel, halve and finely chop the onion. Melt half the butter in a large frying pan or similarly wide-based pan and gently soften the onion, stirring frequently and adding the thyme after 5 minutes. Cook for about 15 minutes in total until the onions are limp and soft but hardly coloured. Tip half of the onions into a mixing bowl and add the tomatoes to the onions left in the pan. Season with ½ a teaspoon of sugar, a generous seasoning of salt and pepper and about 150ml of water. Simmer the sauce for 10 minutes. Shred half the basil leaves and stir them into the sauce.

Chop the olives quite finely. Shred the remaining basil. Tear the bread into pieces and soak in the milk or cream until soggy. Give the soggy bread a squeeze to get rid of excess liquid and add it, remaining basil, olives, egg yolk, meat and a generous seasoning of salt and pepper to the onion in the mixing bowl. Mix and mulch everything together with your hands, pressing the mixture into a ball. Rinse your hands, leave them wet – this helps prevent the meat from sticking to your hands – and pinch off small lumps of mixture, rolling between your palms into cherry-tomato-size balls. Lay the balls out on a plate as you go. The dish can be kept waiting at this point; simply cover the plate with clingfilm and chill in the fridge. It's quite a good idea to chill the balls for about 20 minutes anyway, to encourage them to firm up.

Coordinate the pasta cooking time with the final stage of cooking the meatballs. Reheat the tomato sauce and when bubbling away nicely, drop in all the balls, shaking the pan so that they are all immersed in tomato sauce. When the sauce has returned to boiling, reduce the heat and cover the pan. Cook for 6–8 minutes or until the balls are firm and cooked through. Pile the meatballs and sauce over the drained pasta. Serve immediately, with Parmesan to grate over the top.

MIDDLE-EASTERN LAMB BURGERS WITH LIME COUSCOUS AND COURGETTES

Serves 4

It's lovely, sometimes, to serve a meal on one big platter, letting everyone tuck in without fuss and formality. Meals like this one, which are quick and easy to prepare but look stunning and appear complicated, are perfect for such treatment. The lamb burgers are loaded with interest and their small size makes them extra appealing. It's important, incidentally, in order to achieve the intended textures and flavours, for the courgettes to be *al dente* and the burgers pink in the middle.

> 3 tbsp olive oil
> 50g pine kernels
> 1 red onion
> 50g bunch of coriander
> 500g minced lamb
> salt and freshly milled black pepper
> 750g courgettes
> ½ chicken stock cube
> generous pinch of saffron stamens
> 200g couscous
> 2 limes or small lemons
> 100g feta or soft goat's cheese

Heat ½ a tablespoon of the olive oil in a frying pan over a medium heat and, when hot, stir-fry the pine kernels for a couple of minutes until pale golden. Tip on to a double fold of kitchen paper to drain. Peel, halve and finely chop the red onion. Wash the bunch of coriander and shake dry. Set aside a few sprigs and chop the bunch, stalks and all, very finely. Place meat, onion, pine kernels and coriander in a mixing bowl. Add 1 tablespoon of the olive oil. Season generously with salt and pepper, then use your hands to mix and mulch the ingredients, forming them into a ball. Rinse your hands and, with wet fingers, divide the ball into four equal pieces. Divide each quarter into four pieces again and use your hands to roll and pat into small patties-cum-burgers. Set aside on a plate as you go. Cover the patties with clingfilm and store in the fridge for at least 10 minutes to chill and firm up while you prepare the couscous and courgettes. The patties can be kept safely for up to 24 hours and will freeze perfectly.

Trim the courgettes and cut lengthways into 3 or 4 thick slices. Dissolve the chicken stock cube in 400ml boiling water. Stir in the saffron. Place the couscous in a bowl, stir in the stock, juice of ½ a lime and 1 tablespoon of olive oil. Cover and leave for about 10 minutes to hydrate. Heat a griddle pan for several minutes until very hot. Smear the courgette slices with the remaining oil and cook briefly on both sides on the griddle. Arrange on a large platter and season with salt, pepper and the remaining lime half. Cook the burgers without moving for 3–4 minutes a side. Arrange the burgers next to the courgettes. Fork up the couscous and pile it next to the burgers and courgettes. Crumble the goat's cheese over the courgettes and strew over the reserved coriander sprigs. Serve with lime wedges to squeeze over the top.

ARABIAN SHEPHERD'S PIE
Serves 6

Reinventing favourite dishes like shepherd's pie is a dodgy business. The whole point about them is that they are reassuringly familiar. This pie, made with leftover roast lamb or chicken, provides the all-important comfort-food factor, with just enough spin to excite the jaded palate. Adding saffron-soaked sultanas and couscous instead of flour to thicken the pie, with chickpeas and ground coriander and cumin, transforms the mood of what used to be a way of finishing up the remains of the roast. Topping the pie with crushed rather than smooth mashed potato and seasoning it with more hauntingly flavoured cumin completes the makeover.

1kg similar-sized potatoes

salt and pepper

3 tbsp sultanas

pinch of saffron stamens

4 carrots

1 chicken stock cube

400g can chickpeas

400g can Eazy fried onions or 2 medium onions and 2 tbsp olive oil

2 tsp ground coriander

3 tsp ground cumin

600g roast lamb or chicken

2 tbsp couscous

1 lemon

50g bunch coriander

2 tbsp olive oil

Pre-heat the oven to 400°F/200°C/gas mark 6. Boil the unpeeled potatoes in plenty of salted water until tender. Drain, return to the pan and cover with cold water. Leave for a minute or so, drain and remove the skins. Crush the potatoes into chunky pieces. Meanwhile, place the sultanas in a cup, add the saffron and just cover with boiling water. Leave for a few minutes to soften. Trim and scrape the carrots, then grate on the large holes of a cheese grater. Dissolve the stock cube in 500ml boiling water. Drain the chickpeas, rinse with cold water and shake dry. If using Eazy fried onions, tip them into a spacious, heavy-bottomed pan placed over a medium heat and stir in the ground coriander and 2 teaspoons of cumin. Cook, stirring to distribute the spices, for a couple of minutes before adding the carrots. Stir thoroughly, season with salt and pepper, cover the pan and cook for 5 minutes. If using fresh onions, peel, halve and finely chop them and cook for about 15 minutes in 2 tablespoons of olive oil to soften before proceeding with the recipe. Tear the lamb or chicken into bite-size chunks and stir into the pan. Add the sultanas and their saffron soaking water. Stir in the couscous and then the stock. Simmer, uncovered, for about 10 minutes until the couscous has hydrated and thickened the mixture. Taste the gravy and adjust the seasoning with salt, pepper and lemon juice.

Coarsely chop the coriander and stir into the mixture. Tip into a suitable gratin-style, ovenproof dish. Spoon the crushed potato over the top. Season with the remaining cumin and dribble with 2 tablespoons of olive oil. Cook in the oven for 15 minutes until the potatoes are crusty and the filling is piping hot and bubbling up round the edge.

SHEPHERD'S PIE
Serves 4–6

Serve with Chang's cabbage (page 260) or frozen peas.

    1 large onion
    3 medium carrots
    1 celery heart
    2 tbsp dripping or lard
    leaves from 4 sprigs of thyme
    1 bay leaf
    salt and pepper
    750g good-quality minced lamb
    1 tbsp flour
    2 tsp tomato ketchup
    1 dsp anchovy essence
    150ml water

    for the mash:
    1.5kg floury potatoes
    100ml milk
    50g butter
    freshly grated nutmeg
    extra butter

Pre-heat the oven to 360°F/180°C/gas mark 4. Peel, halve and finely chop the onion. Scrape, trim and grate the carrots on the largest holes of a cheese grater. Finely chop the celery. Heat most of the dripping in a heavy casserole and fry the onion over a medium heat for a few minutes. Add the celery, carrot, thyme and bay leaf, season with a little salt and pepper and cook until the vegetables are tender. Transfer to a plate. Add the remaining lard to the pan and briskly fry the meat, stirring until it changes colour. Sprinkle over the flour, stirring it in thoroughly, add the ketchup, anchovy essence and then the water. Cook for a few minutes and then return the vegetables to the pan. Leave to simmer for 30–45 minutes until thick and nicely amalgamated. Adjust the seasoning. Remove the pan from the heat, tip the contents into a suitable shallow earthenware dish and leave to cool and firm.

Peel the potatoes, cut into even-sized pieces, rinse and boil in salted water until tender. Drain into a colander. Heat the milk and butter in the potato pan until the butter melts, then return the potatoes (putting them through a Mouli-legumes gives perfect mash) and crush to make a fluffy but firm mash. Season with black pepper and nutmeg. Spoon the mashed potatoes over the cooled minced meat, fork the potato up and dot with butter.

Bake the pie for 30 minutes until the top is golden and crusted and the meat is beginning to bubble up around the edge.

ROBERT'S GYPSY STEW
Serves 6

Artist Bob Osborne's long relationship with St Ives inspires his work in many different ways. After a particularly heavy sea storm in Mousehole, when lots of boats were smashed to pieces in the harbour, he collected a huge pile of wood from the wreckage and stored it in the garage below the Fish Store. Almost a year later, he ended up with a series of works which he exhibited in a mixed show at the Royal West of England Academy in Bristol. Bob cooks in much the same way as he makes his art, flinging things together in an inspired way. He introduced this robustly flavoured lamb stew to the Fish Store. It cooks slowly in the oven while you do something else and is a lovely dish to come back to after a coast walk on a cold, wintry day. It's one of those dishes where exact quantities and timings are irrelevant. Serve with jacket potatoes cooked at the same time. Like all stews, it is even better the next day.

10 garlic cloves

6 neck or shoulder chops

flour for dusting

2 tbsp olive oil

salt and freshly milled black pepper

10 carrots

2 x 400g can of chopped tomatoes or bottled passata

½ bottle red wine

3 medium onions

200g fine green beans

2 tbsp chopped flat-leaf parsley

Pre-heat the oven to 325°F/170°C/gas mark 3. Peel the garlic, leave them whole and place in a spacious, heavy-bottomed pan with a tight-fitting lid that can accommodate all the ingredients. Trim the chops of excessive fat. Dust with flour, shaking away the excess. Brown the chops in batches in hot oil in a frying pan. Place the chops over the garlic cloves and season with salt and pepper. Scrape and trim the carrots and then cut into big, chunky pieces. Add to the pan and pour over the chopped tomatoes or passata. Season again with salt and pepper and then add the red wine. Peel, halve and thinly slice the onions and add them to the pan, pushing them down under the liquid. Season for a final time. Cover and put the pan in the oven. Cook for at least 2 hours. Remove the lid and check that the onions have wilted into a soft slop and that the carrots are tender. If not, return to the oven for a further 30 minutes. When you are satisfied that the stew is done, remove it from the oven; it can sit happily, covered, for up to 30 minutes. Top and tail the beans and cook in plenty of boiling, salted water for 2 minutes. Drain and loosely stir into the stew with a garnish of parsley.

CHILEAN LAMB STEW WITH PUMPKIN AND SWEETCORN
Serves 4

A colourful autumn stew with a high proportion of vegetables to meat. Oregano gives the gravy a haunting flavour. Serve with garlic bread (see page 319).

1 large onion

1 bay leaf

4 tbsp vegetable oil

400g pumpkin

salt and pepper

1 leek

3 large carrots

2 corn on the cob or 340g can sweetcorn

1 tbsp dried oregano

500g diced lamb fillet

½ tbsp ground cumin

500g small new potatoes

1 chicken stock cube dissolved in 600ml boiling water

2 tbsp finely chopped flat-leaf parsley

Peel and dice the onion. Place onion and bay leaf in a spacious heavy-bottomed pan with 2 tablespoons of vegetable oil and stir. Cook over a medium heat for 5 minutes while you peel, seed and cut the pumpkin into kebab-size chunks. Stir the pumpkin into the onion, season with salt and pepper, cover the pan and cook for a further 5 minutes. Trim and slice the leek. Rinse under cold running water, shake dry. Scrape the carrots and cut into chunky rounds. Hold the sweetcorn upright on a work surface and slice the corn off the cobs with a sharp knife. Stir leek and carrot into the onion together with the oregano, cover and cook for a further 5 minutes. Dust the meat with cumin. Heat the remaining 2 tablespoons of vegetable oil in a frying pan and quickly brown the meat in batches. When all the meat is browned, add it to the pan with the sweetcorn, potatoes and chicken stock. Bring to the boil, reduce the heat so the stew simmers steadily, cover the pot and cook for 30 minutes or until the meat is tender. Adjust the seasoning with salt and pepper, stir in the parsley and serve. Reheats perfectly.

SLOW-BRAISED LAMB WITH FLAGEOLETS
Serves 6

A rather wonderful chemical reaction seems to take place when lamb shoulder is stewed with tomatoes. The acidity in the tomatoes liberates and mingles with the fat in the meat and results in a particularly luscious gravy. When the succulent sweetness of slowly cooked onions and buttery, mellow flavour of garlic are added to the equation, the result is rich and subtle. These gorgeous juices are absorbed by the pretty green flageolet beans.

2 large onions

12 shallots

12 garlic cloves

350g dried flageolet beans, soaked overnight in plenty of water or
    2 x 400g cans flageolet beans

2 bay leaves

4 branches of rosemary or a small bunch of thyme

2 branches of sage

salt and pepper

300ml red wine or half-wine, half-water

2 x 400g cans Italian tomatoes

1 lemon

1 shoulder of lamb or 2 half-shoulders

2 tbsp anchovy essence

Peel, halve and thinly slice the onions. Trim the root end of the shallots, peel and separate the sections, leaving the shoot-end intact. Smack the garlic cloves with your fist to loosen the skin, then peel it away. Tip the canned flageolet beans into a colander or sieve, rinse under running water and drain. If using dried flageolets, boil them in plenty of unsalted water for 15 minutes and drain. Tip the beans into a large casserole or ovenproof earthenware dish. Push the sliced onions amongst the beans with the shallots and herbs and all but two of the peeled garlic cloves. Season very generously with pepper but lightly with salt. Pour over the wine, tomatoes and their juice, breaking up the tomatoes a bit, and squeeze over the lemon juice. Trim away any flaps of fat from the lamb and make several incisions in the fleshy parts with a small sharp knife. Peel and slice the two remaining garlic cloves and post the slivers in the gashes. Smear the anchovy essence over the lamb (this adds a subtle, salty pungency) and push the joint into the beans. Cover the casserole or use foil to make a lid and cook for 4 hours in the lower part of the oven at 275°F/140°C/gas mark1. Remove the lid, increase the oven temperature to 425°F/220°C/gas mark 7 and cook for another hour. Serve directly from the dish, carving the meat in chunky pieces. Serve with green beans.

LAMB KHORESH WITH RHUBARB
Serves 6

Rhubarb gives this herby, saffron-scented Persian lamb stew a haunting sharp, fresh, clean flavour. The meat cooks until it is meltingly soft but ends up curiously pink. The dish reheats perfectly and suits being served with rice, which in Persia is cooked, burnt-style, to make a golden crust on the bottom. A scoop of creamy yoghurt works well with this.

  2 large onions
  75g butter
  salt and pepper
  1.3kg boned lamb shoulder, scrag end of neck or chump chop
  2 tbsp olive oil
  2 generous pinches of saffron stamens
  juice of 1 lemon
  600ml chicken stock
  80g bunch flat-leaf parsley
  handful mint leaves
  500g rhubarb
  400g basmati rice
  600ml cold water
  Greek yoghurt to serve

Peel, halve and finely slice the onions. Melt just under half of the butter in a spacious, lidded casserole dish and stir in the onions. Season with ½ a teaspoon of salt, cover the pan and cook gently, stirring once or twice, for 15–20 minutes until soft, sloppy and hardly coloured. While the onions are cooking, cut the meat into big cubes, trimming away excess fat and gristle. Using half the remaining butter and the olive oil, brown the meat in batches in a frying pan – this ensures the meat browns rather than sweats – transferring to a plate as you go. Soften the saffron in a little boiling water. Add meat and saffron to the sloppy onions, season generously with pepper, and add half the lemon juice and the stock. Bring the liquid to the boil, immediately turn down the heat to very low and simmer gently for an hour. Finely chop the parsley and mint leaves, setting aside about 1 tablespoon of parsley. Melt the last of the butter in the frying pan and gently stir-fry the chopped herbs for a couple of minutes. Trim the rhubarb and cut into 5cm lengths, discarding any silky skin that presents itself. Stir the rhubarb and herbs into the pot and cook, uncovered, for a further 20–30 minutes until the sauce has reduced slightly and thickened, and the rhubarb disintegrated. Taste and adjust the seasoning with salt, pepper and the rest of the lemon juice. Just before serving, stir in the remaining parsley. Twenty minutes before you are ready to serve, wash the rice in several changes of cold water. Place in a lidded pan with the water, bring to the boil, immediately turn the heat to its lowest level, clamp on the lid and cook for 10 minutes. Turn off the heat, do not remove the lid, and leave the rice for 10 minutes to finish cooking in the steam.

Serve the khoresh with rice and a scoop of yoghurt to stir into the juices and mix with the rice.

ANCHOVY AND ROSEMARY ROAST LAMB
Serves 6

This is a deeply savoury, particularly special way of roasting lamb. Anchovy, garlic and rosemary are all posted, together, in little slits over the joint and it's cooked in the Italian wet-roast style, with lemon juice and white wine. The idea is that the meat roasts and steams all at once and you end up with ready-made gravy and noticeably moist, tender meat. We cook this over and over again. Mashed potato is good with it. Mint sauce isn't. The recipe comes from *Roast Chicken and Other Stories*.

4 garlic cloves

small bunch of rosemary

1.8kg leg of lamb

2 x 50g can anchovies

75g soft butter

½ bottle white wine

juice of 1 lemon

black pepper

Pre-heat the oven to 425°F/220°C/gas mark 7. Peel the garlic and slice lengthways into 3 pieces. Divide the rosemary into 12 little sprigs. Make twelve 5cm-deep cuts over the lamb and stuff half an anchovy, a piece of garlic and a sprig of rosemary into each cut. Cream the butter with the remaining anchovies to make a soft, smooth paste and smear this all over the joint. Make a bed for the lamb in a roasting tin with any remaining rosemary. Pour over the wine, squeeze the lemon juice over the top and season generously with black pepper. Roast in the hot oven for 15 minutes, then reduce the temperature to 350°F/180°C/ gas mark 4 and roast the lamb for a further hour or slightly more, depending how well done you like your meat. Baste with the winy juices from time to time during cooking. Remove from the oven and rest for 15 minutes before carving. Drain the meat juices into a jug to serve as gravy; if it seems too thin, a quick bubble on the hob first will do the job.

LAMB *BOULANGÈRE*
Serves 6–8

This is a useful roast to know because it can be adapted to suit any number of people. I have made it for two, using a small half-shoulder, and as many as twelve, when two legs of lamb were perched over the finely sliced potatoes. All you need to remember is to prepare approximately the same weight of potatoes as the weight of the lamb. The secret of its success is making sure that the potatoes and their aromatic seasoning are completely cooked and all the water absorbed before the lamb goes into the oven. The potatoes under the lamb end up soft and imbued with juices from the meat, while the uncovered potatoes will be gorgeously crusty. I usually serve it with a big bowl of green beans and redcurrant jelly rather than mint sauce.

approx. 2kg large potatoes
1 large onion
3 large sprigs thyme
2 bay leaves
6 garlic cloves
100g butter
salt and pepper
approx. 2kg leg or shoulder of lamb

Pre-heat the oven to 450°F/230°C/gas mark 8. Peel the potatoes and slice them no thicker than a 50p coin. Some food processors have an attachment that will do this in a trice; I use a mandoline, which takes slightly longer but is far quicker than a knife. Rinse the potatoes and leave to soak in cold water. Peel, halve and finely chop the onion. Strip the leaves off the thyme stalks and finely chop. Finely chop the bay leaves, discarding the stalk. Peel the garlic and finely chop 3 cloves. Mix all the chopped ingredients together. Use 25g of the butter to grease a large earthenware gratin-type dish or roasting pan. Cover the bottom of the dish with one-third of the drained potatoes. Season with salt and pepper and scatter half the onion mixture over the top. Make another layer of potatoes and onion and finish with a layer of potatoes. Smooth the top and press down evenly with the flat of your hand. Dot with butter and season with salt. Add sufficient hot water to almost cover the potatoes and cook for about 90 minutes until all the liquid has been absorbed and the top layer of potatoes is nicely browned.

Meanwhile, prepare the lamb. Peel and thinly slice the remaining garlic and post it in slits cut in the flesh. Use the rest of the butter to smear over the lamb. Season with salt and pepper. Calculate the cooking time, allowing between 15 and 25 minutes per pound (450g), depending how pink you like your lamb. Place the joint on top of the potatoes and turn halfway through cooking. Remove the joint to a warmed serving platter and rest for 15 minutes, leaving the potatoes in the oven.

Carve at the table, giving everyone some of the meat juices and letting people help themselves to potatoes – there are never enough!

DESERT LAMB WITH BROWN RICE PILAFF
Serves 6

The combination of garlicky roast lamb with a garlic and cumin crust and nutty brown rice pilaff eaten with a dollop of creamy Greek yoghurt seems particularly Arabian as the seagulls squawk and swoop around the Fish Store.

    8 garlic cloves
    salt
    2 tbsp olive oil
    1.8kg shoulder or leg of lamb
    3–4 tbsp ground cumin

    for the pilaff:
    50g flaked almonds
    50g butter
    handful of broken vermicelli or fine thread egg noodles
    300g brown rice
    50g raisins
    1 chicken stock cube, dissolved in 750ml boiling water
    2 decent-sized onions
    2 garlic cloves
    2 tbsp olive oil
    ½ tsp ground cinnamon
    salt and pepper
    Greek yoghurt to serve

Pre-heat the oven to 350°F/180°C/gas mark 4. Peel all the garlic and slice three cloves lengthways into 3 pieces. Chop the remaining garlic, sprinkle it with a little salt and use the flat of a knife to crush it to a paste. Stir the paste into the olive oil and smear this all over the joint. Dust the joint liberally with ground cumin. Place in a roasting tin and roast, turning once during cooking, for about an hour and a half or slightly more, depending how well done you like your meat, until crusty and brown on the outside. Rest for 15 minutes before carving.

While the lamb is cooking, make the pilaff. Sauté the almonds in a little butter in a medium-sized, lidded pan until browned. Set aside. Sauté the vermicelli until golden and set aside. Add the last of the butter and stir in the rice, tossing until glossy and golden. Return the nuts, raisins, vermicelli and stock to the pan and bring to the boil. Reduce the heat immediately, cover the pan and simmer gently for about 45 minutes until the rice is tender.

Meanwhile, peel, halve and finely slice the onions and garlic cloves. Cook gently, stirring often, in the olive oil, adding the cinnamon and a generous seasoning of salt and pepper. Cook until very limp. Fork the onions into the cooked rice and tip on to a platter to serve.

Vegetables

Barry Cornish was born, bred and is still living in Mousehole. He was the village postman from the mid-1960s until he retired thirty-odd years later. Every morning he walked eight miles, or four furlongs, and developed legs like a footballer. He lives in a little cottage built in 1835, around the same time as the Fish Store, by master mariner Harry Wright, in a terrace in the middle of the village named after a two-masted schooner which used to trade between Penzance and Jamaica. Barry's cottage still has its original floor and once, when he had the floor up, he found part of a fossilized lid of one of the barrels used for keeping the oil from pilchards. Apart from big fish stores like ours, there were lots of small cellars for curing and storing fish. The oil produced was used for lighting lamps. During the war, it was sent up to London. Most of the fish went to Italy.

Shopping, particularly food shopping, has changed dramatically during Barry's lifetime. In his youth there were two post offices. One had a grocery store attached (now Mousehole's *second* estate agent). There was a chemist (now an ice-cream shop), a butcher (now a rock and gemstone shop), two fruit and vegetable shops (both now gift shops), a baker (now a restaurant), two general stores (one now a gift shop, the other a gallery), and Nigel Brockman's grandfather used to go round the village with a horse-drawn cart, delivering fish. Rationing imposed limitations but fish was always available and the rocks beneath the Old Quay were pink with crab shells. These days, there is only one shop selling food.

The Mousehole News and Stores overlooks the harbour and has replaced the pub as the nerve centre of the village. Everyone goes there at least once a day, even if it's only for a paper or tobacco or a fizzy drink. It caters valiantly to the villagers in a corner-shop kind of way, offering the basics, including canned and frozen groceries, daily fresh bread and pasties from a local baker and a limited range of fresh fruit and vegetables. There is always a big sack of locally grown, earthy potatoes. In the spring and summer these will be delicious little new potatoes and in the winter months they will be big, mealy so-called old potatoes. There are always a few onions and swedes (essential for home-made pasties) and a small selection of seasonal local speciali-ties. Parsnips, leeks, cauliflower and broccoli might come from local allotments or market gardeners. Runner beans, tomatoes, ridge cucumbers and occasionally spinach almost certainly do. It's much the same at the nearby shop-cum-post office in Paul, which, usefully, does local deliveries.

Occasionally, people sell their excess fruit and vegetables outside their house. I've bought runner beans and tomatoes this way, but a more reliable source is from the market gardeners who have fields and meadows on the roads leading out of the village towards Lamorna, Porthcurno, Sennen and Land's End. There is a particularly good one at the junction of the B3315 and B3283 at the turn to Treen. The best shop in the area for fruit and vegetables is Tregenza's in the Green Market part of Penzance, at the top of Market Jew Street and very bottom of Causeway Head.

Potatoes

Champ with Caramelized Onions
Baked Potatoes with Maldon Sea Salt
Furrowed Field Roast Potatoes
Sydney Opera House Roast Potatoes
Chive Game Chips
Cracked Potatoes with Guacamole
Gratin Dauphinoise
Potato *Pithiviers*
Buttery Potato Pie with Thyme
Potato Rösti with Field Mushrooms and Bacon
The Favourite Potato Salad
Greek Potato Salad with Coriander
Curried Potatoes
Thai-style Potato and Spinach Soup
Anchovy and Potato *Gratin*
Spanish Omelette with Chorizo

Lots of people grow a few new potatoes in Mousehole. Some are lucky enough to have an allotment or vegetable garden or use a corner of the flower garden. But I've seen potatoes growing in (highly desirable) discarded butler's sinks and in old dustbins. I've even seen them growing in one of the dark back alleys in a specially designed stout green bin made in the style of a parsley crock, with slits at intervals out of which the sturdy leaves seek the light of day.

Cornish new potatoes, particularly those grown close to the sea, with a southerly aspect to the land and light soils which warm up early, can be planted in December and are ready for harvesting in early April, sometimes even earlier. You see neatly tucked furrows of polythene-covered potatoes in fields around the village and you can hear the bedding crackling in the wind. The first time I was struck by their delicious flavour was at a special awards lunch given by Rick Stein soon after the Seafood Restaurant won its first accolade in the seventies. The potatoes had that special just-dug, intense potato flavour, rather like the best Jersey Royals. Royden keeps me supplied with new potatoes from his perfectly located allotment overlooking the sea. Otherwise I buy from the Mousehole shop, which has a fast turnover of local new potatoes still earthy from the ground.

Cornish maincrop potatoes taste good too, and when the Fish Store is in full-on entertaining mode it is worth buying a big sack direct from the farm or from a roadside sale.

Potatoes, incidentally, are 81 per cent water, fat-free (that's why they need butter and cheese), high in vitamin C and have low levels of vitamins B1 and B6. They contain trace elements including folic acid, potassium and, of course, fibre. An average serving without add-ons averages 150 calories.

CHAMP WITH CARAMELIZED ONIONS
Serves 4

Champ is extra-luscious mashed potato made with spring onions cooked in the mashing milk. Many vegetables and other flavourings go well with mashed potato. Apple gives it a lightness, parsnip makes it sweeter and spinach, nettles and parsley, sweated first in butter, turn it green. Saffron turns it pale yellow and so does Dijon mustard, but the flavours are quite different. Mash is also delicious with a topping of slowly cooked caramelized onion. Try it with roast cod or a similar white fish, or with sausages, chops or roast chicken.

2 large onions
100g butter
1 tbsp vegetable oil
8 decent-sized mealy potatoes, preferably Irish or King Edward
100g bunch spring onions
225ml milk
salt and pepper

Peel, halve and finely slice the onions. Heat 50g butter and 1 table-spoon of cooking oil in a frying pan over a high heat and, when the butter is bubbling, stir in the onions. Cook, tossing constantly, for about 5 minutes until the onions are starting to wilt and brown. Turn the heat down low and leave to cook very gently while you attend to the potatoes.

In Ireland, potatoes are always cooked in their skins, drained and then left in the hot pan for the skins to dry and crack before they are peeled away and the potatoes mashed. As most of the goodness in potatoes lies just beneath the skin, this makes sense. Either do it the Irish way or peel, chunk and rinse the potatoes and boil in salted water until tender. Drain and mash the potatoes, preferably passing them through a vegetable press (Mouli-legumes).

While the potatoes cook, trim and slice the spring onions, including all the dark green. Place in a pan with the milk and simmer until tender. Tip the milk, onion and 25g of the butter into the mash and beat with a wooden spoon until light and fluffy. Season to taste with salt and pepper. Serve the mash in a mound, top with the remaining butter and cover with the onions. Serve immediately.

BAKED POTATOES WITH MALDON SEA SALT
Serves 6

I am a baked potato addict. I'm always trying out slightly different ways of cooking them and this one, when the potatoes are cut in half and dipped in Maldon sea salt, is an all-time favourite. I put them in a cold oven turned to its highest setting and speed up the cooking by rubbing the potatoes with olive oil and laying them on a foil-lined oven tray. Cutting tramlines or a criss-cross pattern gives them an even better crusty finish and looks very pretty.

Never throw away leftover baked potatoes. Pop them back in the oven for 10 minutes or so when you need them and they will be perfect. This is worth remembering if you are cooking jacket potatoes for a party: cook them in advance and reheat as and when required.

> 12 medium-sized potatoes
> approx. 50ml olive oil
> Maldon sea salt flakes
> you will also need tinfoil

Turn the oven to its highest setting and line a roasting tin with tinfoil. Tip some of the Maldon salt flakes on to a plate. Cut the potatoes in half lengthways. If liked, cut a shallow criss-cross without cutting the skin. Pour some of the oil into the palm of one hand and roll the potatoes through the oil, then dip the cut edge in salt and lay it cut-side uppermost on the foil-lined tin.

Don't wait for the oven to come up to temperature before cooking. Check for doneness after 30 minutes.

FURROWED FIELD ROAST POTATOES
Serves 6

The best roast potatoes have shaggy, crusty outsides and fluffy insides. Most recipes suggest parboiling them, but I like the results when the potatoes are completely cooked and a bit waterlogged and beginning to break down. Roughing them up a bit in a colander is another good way of encouraging rough surfaces that will crisp up in the oven. Running a fork over boiled potatoes makes lovely fluffy edges. It's unfashionable to collect dripping these days, but beef or pork dripping was once used for roasting potatoes. Goose fat gives the finest results and you can buy that in cans.

I often add scraps of bacon for the last 10 minutes of roasting if the potatoes are going with chicken, along with blanched, peeled garlic cloves. Peeled pickling onions, unpeeled garlic cloves and aromatic herbs such as rosemary and thyme are other good additions. The smaller you cut the potatoes, the faster they cook; this is another way of ringing the changes with roast potatoes. One favourite way is to cut the potatoes small, roast them until golden and then strew with finely chopped garlic mixed with flat-leaf parsley or rosemary, sometimes adding lemon zest too.

> 9 (or more) large potatoes
> salt and pepper
> dripping, lard or olive oil

Scrub the potatoes but don't bother to peel them. Cook in salted boiling water until tender and their skins are beginning to burst. Drain and leave to cool slightly before peeling. Pre-heat the oven to 400°F/200°C/gas mark 6.

Heat a decent amount of dripping, lard or oil in a roasting tin in the oven. Cut the potatoes in half, arrange in the hot oil and roll through it until covered. Run a fork down the length of each potato a couple of times to make furrows. Return the tin to the oven and cook, turning once during cooking, for 45–60 minutes, depending on size and what else is in the oven, until crusty and golden. Season with salt and pepper before serving.

SYDNEY OPERA HOUSE ROAST POTATOES
Serves 6

These are my 'posh' roast potatoes and this is the only time I don't boil potatoes for roasting. Slicing down the golden-brown crusty layers of the 'opera house' is particularly pleasing.

> 9 (or more) medium-sized potatoes
> olive oil

Peel the potatoes and cut in half through their middles. Use a small sharp knife. Stand the potato on its flat surface and make diagonal slashes approximately 1cm apart, cutting halfway through the potato. Leave to soak in cold water for at least 15 minutes.

Pre-heat the oven to 400°F/200°C/gas mark 6. Oil a roasting tin and stand the potatoes in the tin. Paint the 'opera house' lavishly with olive oil. Cook in the oven without moving for 1 hour, checking after 40 minutes, until the potatoes are golden and the slices fanning slightly.

CHIVE GAME CHIPS
Serves 4

No one can get enough of these potatoes. They are quick to prepare and cook and they go with everything. The flavour can be fine-tuned with other assertively flavoured soft herbs such as rosemary (which should be chopped to dust, otherwise it gets caught in the teeth), thyme and flat-leaf parsley. Garlic and lemon zest (also chopped to dust) are good, too. What you use depends on what you intend to eat them with. Because the potatoes are cooked at such a high temperature, it's essential to cook them in a heavyweight roasting tin to avoid buckling.

> 4 potatoes, approx. 200g each
> olive oil
> salt and pepper
> 4 tbsp chopped chives

Finely slice the washed but unpeeled potatoes as if making crisps. If you don't have a suitable attachment on a food processor, the next best thing to use is a mandoline (a blade set in a metal or wood frame), or, failing that, it can be done (very frustratingly) on the cucumber slicer at the side of a box cheese grater. It's hard to get the slices thin enough with a knife and they need to be fairly uniform. Rinse and pat dry.

Smear one or more 5cm deep heavyweight roasting pans approx. 37 x 27cm with a little of the oil. Add the potatoes and the rest of the oil. Toss thoroughly to coat with oil, then spread out evenly. Roast for 15 minutes until crisp and golden. You might need to turn the pan round or turn some potatoes during the cooking. Don't worry about them cooking unevenly: you just want to end up with plenty of crusty edges but a bit of soft middle.

Remove from the oven, rest for a couple of minutes (this helps loosen stuck potato) and use a fish slice to chase them off the pan. Sprinkle with chives, season with salt and pepper and toss before serving.

CRACKED POTATOES WITH GUACAMOLE
Serves 4

I came across this way of cooking small, new potatoes years ago in a small and modest café-restaurant near Balmoral beach on the outskirts of Sydney. They called them New York fries and served them with a big scoop of crème fraîche. The combination of tongue-scorchingly hot crusty potatoes and cold slippery cream was utterly compulsive. Back home, I matched them with guacamole and have been making the combo regularly ever since. They are great alone but go well with simply cooked salmon or white fish and are an excellent accompaniment to whole poached chicken.

> 1kg ready-washed baby new potatoes
> Maldon sea salt flakes and black pepper
> 2 large or 4 small ripe avocados
> 2 limes
> 3 medium tomatoes
> 1 small red onion
> 1 or 2 red bird's eye chillies
> 1 large garlic clove
> handful of coriander leaves
> oil for deep frying

Boil the potatoes in plenty of salted water for about 10 minutes until tender. Drain and leave to cool while you make the guacamole. Run a sharp knife round the length of the avocados. Twist apart and remove the stone. Dice the avocados in their shells, then use a spoon to scoop all the flesh into a bowl. Squeeze over the juice of one lime. Season with salt and pepper. Use a small sharp knife to remove the core from the tomatoes in a small, pointed plug shape. Halve the tomatoes, slice in strips and then into small dice. Peel, halve and finely chop the onion. Add tomatoes, their juices and the onion to the avocado. Trim and split the chillies. Scrape away the seeds. Slice into skinny strips and then into tiny dice. Peel and chop the garlic. Sprinkle with a little salt and use the flat of a knife to work to a paste. Stir the garlic into the avocado, coarsely mashing the fruit as you do so; you want it lumpy rather than smooth. Add the tomatoes, onion and chilli to the avocado and mix thoroughly. Taste and adjust the seasoning with salt, pepper and more lime. Stir in the coriander. Cover with cling-film, allowing it to sag against the guacamole, if you need to keep it waiting for more than 30 minutes. This stops the avocado turning black.

Use your thumbnails to split the potatoes in half. It's important not to use a knife for this because you want to achieve an uneven, slightly shaggy edge to the potato halves. Get the oil really hot, deep-fry the potatoes in batches – overcrowding will stop them browning evenly – and cook until really crusty. Drain on kitchen paper, tip into a serving bowl, sprinkle with salt and keep warm in the oven. Serve crusty hot potatoes and cold, chilli-hot guacamole together.

GRATIN DAUPHINOISE
Serves 4–6

The ultimate potato *gratin*, originally from the Alps and adopted throughout France. The business. It is hard to believe that potatoes and cream could taste so good.

> 750g potatoes
> 1 garlic clove
> 50g butter
> salt and pepper
> 400ml thick cream or crème fraîche
> freshly grated nutmeg

Pre-heat the oven to 325°F/175°C/gas mark 3.

Thinly slice the potatoes (I use a mandoline rather than a knife), soak in cold water and drain. Crush the garlic with your fist and rub it all over the inside of a suitable gratin dish, then smear it with about half the butter. Make layers with the potatoes, seasoning each layer with salt and pepper and the final layer with nutmeg and adding a few scraps of butter, filling the dish to approximately 1.5cm from the top. The gratin should be about 5cm deep. Heat up the cream and pour it over the top. Cook for approximately 1½ hours. During the last 10 minutes of cooking, turn the oven up fairly high to get a fine golden crust on the potatoes.

POTATO *PITHIVIERS*
Serves 6–8

Pithiviers is the name of a distinctively etched puff-pastry pie filled with almond cream. This one is made with sliced potato cooked in cream seasoned with garlic, bay and nutmeg. It's a fabulous dish to make for a party, picnic or barbecue and is good hot, warm or cold.

    2 garlic cloves
    600ml thick cream or half-cream, half-milk
    1 bay leaf
    salt and pepper
    nutmeg
    900g potatoes
    25g butter
    flour for dusting
    500g puff pastry
    1 egg beaten with 2 tbsp milk

Peel and finely chop the garlic. Place the cream in a large saucepan – later it will also hold the potatoes – with the bay leaf and garlic. Season generously with salt and pepper and add nutmeg. Bring to the boil gently (to avoid scorching the bottom), then turn down the heat and simmer for 10 minutes to thicken slightly. Turn off the heat and cover the pan for the flavours to infuse.

Meanwhile, peel and slice the potatoes very thinly, about the thickness of a £1 coin, then rinse and drain. Stir the potatoes into the cream and simmer for 15–20 minutes until the potatoes are tender to the point of a knife. Cool slightly.

Lavishly butter a 25.5cm x 5cm deep flan tin/pie dish with a removable base, dust with flour and shake away the excess to make it non-stick. Set aside one-third of the pastry. Dust a work surface with flour and roll out the larger piece to fit the pie tin with a generous overhang.

Roll out the reserved pastry and cut it to make a generous-sized lid. Pour the cooled potato and cream mixture into the pastry case and fold the edges over, nipping and tucking to prevent leakages – this is very important. Use a pastry brush to paint the dough flaps with egg wash, then cut and fit the lid. Paint the lid with the rest of the egg wash. Use a small sharp knife to etch a pattern into the pastry.

Pre-heat the oven to 475°F/240°C/gas mark 8 and place a pastry sheet in the middle. Put the pie on the hot pastry sheet – this ensures the pastry base cooks thoroughly – and cook for 10 minutes. Lower the temperature to 325°F/160°C/gas mark 3 and bake for a further 45 minutes. Remove the pie from the oven, discard the collar and slip the pie on to a plate.

BUTTERY POTATO PIE WITH THYME
Serves 4

It is incredible that slices of potato layered up with onion, butter and thyme taste so delicious. Lovely with lamb.

> 800g medium large potatoes
> 2 large onions, approx. 400g in total
> salt and pepper
> 1 tsp fresh thyme leaves
> 100g butter

Pre-heat the oven to 400°F/200°C/gas mark 6. Peel or scrape the potatoes, then slice wafer-thin as if you were making crisps. Use a mandoline or the appropriate slicer attachment of your food processor rather than a knife. Rinse the potatoes and shake dry in a colander. Peel and halve the onions, then slice as thinly as you can manage. Don't separate out the layers. In a suitable *gratin* or pie dish, make layers of potato, a generous seasoning of salt, pepper and a sprinkling of thyme, followed by onion and finishing with potato. As you make the layers, cut pieces of butter and scatter them over the top, making sure there is a decent amount for the final layer. Cover the top of the dish with foil, pierce a few times so that steam can escape, and cook in the oven for

45 minutes. Remove the foil and cook for a further 30 minutes or until the top is golden and the potatoes are tender all the way through when pierced with a knife or skewer.

POTATO RÖSTI WITH FIELD MUSHROOMS AND BACON
Serves 4

There used to be a café in nearby 'miles of golden sand' Hayle with an all-day breakfast menu which revolved around rösti. The pancakes were made to order by the Swiss wife of the couple who ran the Harbour Café and she cooked them to perfection: both light and elegant yet big and substantial.

Rösti is great for breakfast and was one of the first things I ever cooked – invented, I thought, by me, out of necessity when the cupboard was bare. We used to eat indecent quantities of them with nothing more than salt and tomato ketchup, but rösti go with everything from fried eggs to lambs' kidneys in red wine. They're good, too, with apple purée and bacon instead of mushrooms.

You can make rösti as thick or thin and as large or small as you like.

    4 large potatoes, approx. 700g
    vegetable oil
    50g butter
    salt and pepper
    4 large field mushrooms
    2 tbsp olive oil
    12 rashers smoked streaky bacon

Parboil the potatoes for 10 minutes and allow to cool in their skins. Peel, then grate the potatoes with a coarse grater. Divide the mixture into four heaps.

For perfect rösti results, use a heavy, non-stick frying pan and heat up half a tablespoon of vegetable oil and a knob of butter. When the oil is very hot, spread one heap of potato evenly into the pan. Turn down the heat and cook for between 2 and 10 minutes depending on the thickness of the rösti. To turn the pancake over, put a plate that fits snugly inside the pan, flip it over and slip the pancake back into the pan with a bit more oil and a little more butter. It might not sound like it, but it makes the turning operation easier when a bread board is placed on top of the plate. Cook on this side as before. Slip on to a plate and keep warm while you cook the other rösti.

Wipe, then halve the mushrooms. Melt 25g butter and a little oil in a frying pan and stand the mushrooms on their cut sides. Cook for a few minutes until nicely browned, turn so the gills are uppermost, and cook the base for a few more minutes. Drape the bacon over the mushrooms and cook under a hot grill, turning the bacon to cook the other side.

Serve the rösti with the mushrooms and bacon alongside. A fried egg would be good with this.

THE FAVOURITE POTATO SALAD
Serves 6

Simple and superb.

> 750g small new potatoes
> salt and black pepper
> 2 tbsp Hellmann's mayonnaise
> ½ tbsp smooth Dijon mustard
> 3 tbsp vinaigrette (see page 280)
> small bunch of chives

Scrub the potatoes and boil in salted water until tender. Meanwhile, spoon the mayonnaise into a bowl, stir in the mustard and gradually beat in the vinaigrette to make a smooth, thick dressing.

Leave very small potatoes whole, halve or thickly slice medium ones and add to the bowl. Season with black pepper. Toss the hot potatoes thoroughly in the dressing and leave until ready to serve. Snip most of the chives over the top, stir again and serve with a final flourish of chives.

GREEK POTATO SALAD WITH CORIANDER
Serves 4–6

I love potatoes so much that I wrote a book about them and I'd happily do it again. There is a whole chapter on potato salads and I know that it only scratched the surface. This one, called *patata salata* in the book, is a particular favourite that goes with everything from a slab of feta and a hard-boiled egg to fish, chicken or lamb. This latest version ups the quantity of coriander and specifies red rather than any other onion. The result is a very pretty salad, streaked with red and thick with green leaves. It is the perfect thing to knock up for a barbecue, when you might echo the Greek theme with hummus, a Greek salad and lamb kebabs or grilled red mullet.

    750g similar-sized new potatoes
    salt and black pepper
    1 red onion
    2 garlic cloves
    60g bunch of coriander
    2 tbsp wine vinegar
    4 tbsp Greek or other fruity olive oil

Scrub the potatoes, rinse and cook in salted boiling water until tender. Drain. Leave small potatoes whole, halve medium potatoes and chunk large ones. Meanwhile, peel, halve and finely slice the onion. Peel and chop the garlic. Trim the coarse stalk ends of the bunch of coriander. Keeping the bunch shape, finely chop the stalks and let the chopping get progressively coarser as you work up the bunch into the leaves. Pour the vinegar into a salad bowl, add a generous pinch of salt and several grinds of pepper. Swirl the vinegar around the bowl until the salt dissolves. Whisk in the olive oil to make a thick and luscious dressing. Stir in the garlic and onion and then add the hot potatoes. Stir thoroughly and then add the chopped coriander. Stir again and serve hot, warm or cold, giving a final stir just before serving.

CURRIED POTATOES
Serves 6

This take on Bombay aloo is adapted from a much less healthy version from *In Praise of the Potato*. Like all curries, it is possibly even better eaten cold the next day. The potatoes end up bathed in a pale yellow aromatic cream laced with silky strands of onion, scraps of green chilli and fresh coriander. It is interesting enough to serve on its own, or with rice, pickles and poppadums, but works well as part of a curry blow-out. I often serve it with dal and discovered by accident that if you cook the seasonings – chillies, garlic, turmeric and cumin seeds – first and stir them into the lentils with the oil they are cooked in, at the beginning of cooking, rather than adding them at the end, you end up with the best ever dal.

1.4kg small salad potatoes
salt and black pepper
1 large onion
40g butter
2 green chillies
5cm fresh ginger
3 large garlic cloves
200ml Greek yoghurt
1 tsp each ground cloves, cumin and coriander
½ tsp turmeric
50ml water
2 tbsp chopped coriander

Boil the unpeeled potatoes in salted water until tender. Drain, return to the pan and cover with cold water. Leave for a couple of minutes for the potatoes to cool, then drain and skin them. While the potatoes are cooking, peel, halve and finely slice the onion. Melt the butter in a frying pan over a medium-low heat and add the onion. Stir until thoroughly coated with butter. Season with salt, cover the pan, reduce the heat and cook, stirring every so often, until wilted, juicy and lightly coloured. Allow at least 15 minutes for this. Meanwhile, split the chillies, scrape away the seeds, slice into skinny batons and then into tiny dice. Peel the ginger and grate or chop. Peel the garlic and chop. Pulverize these ingredients into a smooth paste – easily done with a pestle and mortar or by improvising with something heavy and a chopping board. Stir the paste into the yoghurt, along with the ground cloves, cumin, coriander and turmeric. Pour the yoghurt into the softened onions, add the water and the potatoes. Stir well and simmer for at least 10 minutes. Adjust the seasoning with salt and pepper, stir in the fresh coriander and serve.

THAI-STYLE POTATO AND SPINACH SOUP
Serves 4

An almost store-cupboard soup which delivers all the whizz-bang flavours of an authentic Thai soup without any special ingredients.

    1 large red onion
    1 garlic clove
    2 tbsp vegetable oil
    2 small red chillies
    1 unwaxed lemon
    750g potatoes
    2 chicken stock cubes dissolved in 1 litre boiling water
    salt and pepper
    100g young spinach leaves
    generous handful of coriander leaves

Peel, halve and finely chop the onion. Peel the garlic and slice in wafer-thin rounds. Heat the oil in a 2 litre capacity pan and gently fry the onion and garlic for 5 minutes, giving them a good stir halfway through. Meanwhile, trim and split the chillies and scrape away the seeds. Slice into skinny batons and across into tiny scraps. Remove two strips of wafer-thin zest from the lemon. Stir the chilli and lemon zest into the onion and cook for a further 5 minutes. Peel the potatoes and cut into even-sized chunks or thick slices. Rinse and shake dry. Stir the potatoes into the onions and cook for a couple of minutes before adding the hot water in which you've dissolved the stock cubes. Bring the soup to the boil and turn the heat down immediately. Add 1 tablespoon of lemon juice, ½ teaspoon of salt and a generous grinding of pepper. Partially cover the pan and leave to simmer for about 15 minutes until the potatoes are done. Taste and adjust the seasoning with salt and lemon juice. Squash the spinach under the liquid, coarsely chop the coriander and add that too. The soup is ready when the spinach has wilted.

ANCHOVY AND POTATO *GRATIN*

Serves 4–6

This comforting gratin is perfect rainy-day food. Grated potatoes are layered up with super-thin slices of onion and anchovies preserved in olive oil. The mixture is moistened with a little cream or milk and topped with breadcrumbs. The potatoes melt against the slippery onions and their gentle flavours are given a briny savour with soft anchovy, so soft, in fact, that the little fish disintegrate into a brown blur. A crunchy breadcrumb topping, enriched with the olive oil from the can, offsets this surprisingly delicious dish. It is good on its own but the perfect accompaniment to grilled herring or mackerel.

   50g butter
   2 medium onions
   100ml thick cream or crème fraîche and
      100ml warm water or 200ml milk
   1 thick slice bread
   750g potatoes
   salt and black pepper
   60g canned anchovy fillets in olive oil

Pre-heat the oven to 450°F/230°C/gas mark 8. Use half the butter to generously smear a 2 litre capacity gratin dish. Peel, halve and slice the onions very, very finely. Mix together the cream and water. Cut the crust off the bread, tear into pieces and blitz in the food processor to make a handful of breadcrumbs. Peel, then grate the potatoes on the large holes of a cheese grater. Strew a third of the unrinsed potatoes in the buttered dish. Season lightly with salt and generously with pepper. Arrange half the anchovies over the top, tearing them in half for uniform distribution, then cover with half the onions and then with a second third of potatoes. Season with salt and pepper and then place the rest of the anchovies over the potatoes. Cover with the remaining onions and finish with the rest of the potatoes. Press the mixture down with the flat of your hand and pour the cream and water or milk mixture over the top; it will moisten rather than cover the potatoes. Season again with salt and pepper, then strew the breadcrumbs over the top. Dribble the anchovy oil from the tin over the breadcrumbs and dot with the remaining butter. Place the dish in the oven and cook for 10 minutes. Reduce the heat to 425°F/220°C/gas mark 7 and cook for 35 minutes until the top is crusty and golden and the onions and potatoes are very soft. If the top seems to be browning too much and too quickly, cover the dish loosely with a sheet of tinfoil. Serve hot from the oven or allow to cool slightly to avoid burning your mouth.

SPANISH OMELETTE WITH CHORIZO
Serves 4–6

They sell decent-sliced chorizo at the delicatessen counter of the 24-hour Safeway at Penzance. It's particularly meaty and its orange colour delivers a spicy punch. I love it with the delicious new potatoes they grow down here and hit on the idea of combining the two in a Spanish omelette. My way of making this thick omelette has always been to boil the potatoes before they are sliced, but Maria-Jose Sevilla, the expert on Spanish cooking, tells me that they should be gently fried in lots of olive oil. I followed her advice but cooked the chorizo first with the onions and their flavour permeated through the potatoes, making the omelette unbelievably good. Spanish omelette is great picnic food.

    1kg potatoes, preferably large new ones
    5–6 tbsp olive oil
    400g can of Eazy fried onions or 2 Spanish onions
    150g sliced chorizo
    salt and pepper
    6 large, fresh eggs

Pre-heat the oven to 400°F/200°C/gas mark 6. Scrape or peel the potatoes and slice as thick as a 50p coin. Leave the potatoes in a bowl of cold water. Heat 4 tablespoons of the oil in a large frying pan or similar-shaped ovenproof pan placed over a medium heat. Add the onions and cook for a couple of minutes. If using fresh onions rather than canned fried onions, chop them finely and fry until soft with the extra tablespoon of olive oil. Meanwhile, make a pile of the chorizo and cut the slices in quarters. Separate the pieces and add them to the pan. Cook, stirring as the slices melt into the onions, for a further couple of minutes. Drain the potatoes, shake dry and stir them into the onions and chorizo. Season with ½ a teaspoon of salt. Stir again, reduce the heat, cover the pan and cook for 10 minutes. Give the potatoes another stir, return the lid and cook for a further 10 minutes or until the potatoes are tender. Crack the eggs into a mixing bowl. Season lightly with salt and generously with pepper. Whisk until smooth, then tip the contents of the frying pan into the eggs and stir thoroughly. Quickly wipe out the pan – you don't want any food stuck to the bottom – and smear all over the inside of the pan with the remaining oil. Tip the mixture into the pan and smooth the top so the surface is level and the potatoes are just covered by the egg. Place the omelette pan in the oven and reduce the temperature immediately to 350°F/180°C/gas mark 4. Cook for 10–15 minutes until the omelette is just set. Allow to cool in the pan and then run a spatula round and under the sides to loosen. Place a large plate over the pan and quickly invert to remove the omelette. Serve in wedges. Excellent warm or cold.

Spinach, Sorrel, Watercress and Nettles

Spinach Soup
Spinach *Gratin*
Eggs Florentine
Spinach with Chickpeas
Spinach and Caramelized Onion Tart
Cream of Sorrel Soup
Sorrel Sauce
Watercress Soup
Pear and Watercress Soup
Watercress Pesto
Watercress Sauce
Stinging Nettle Soup with Bacon *Croûtons*

'Mr MacClary worked for Mr Giles, the market gardener who lived in Asphodel (which means daffodil) at the top of Raginnis Hill. Mr MacClary lived in Gurnick Street but had meadows 'up the Crackers' and we got lots of vegetables from him, but I just remember the spinach. His wife was ill and prescribed lots of spinach to make her better, so he grew plenty and used to bring it down specially for Betty. So we had this huge bunch of freshly picked spinach. She would probably make eggs Florentine with it, using some of the black-market eggs from Raginnis Farm. And cream of spinach soup.

During the war the fields up there would be covered with strips of silver paper, called mirror, which was dropped from airplanes to simulate aircraft. Nowadays, you hear a crackling sound up Raginnis but it's because the fields are covered with polythene. The Germans were looking for Porthcurno radio station. Our troops used blow-up lorries in rows to simulate troop activity in order to take them off the scent away from Porthcurno. Places like Paul and Newlyn were badly hit by bombs because the Germans on their return journey didn't want to take their bombs back to Germany, so they dropped them anywhere.'

Ben John

Wild sorrel seems to flourish in temperate Cornwall, particularly in the sheltered hedgerows on the roads 'up and over' between Mousehole and Paul. This is one of my favourite walks, which I often do at the end of the day when the light is beginning to fade. It's a typical Cornish country road walk, with fields on either side of thick, overgrown hedgerows. Each stretch of hedge is different, but all are fringed with wide grasses that sweep the road and clumps of pale green wild sorrel. The sorrel season begins in spring and seems to go on indefinitely, constantly renewing itself through summer and late into the year.

You have to be careful when picking sorrel because it looks rather like a clump of young dock leaves. Sorrel leaves are often compared with spinach, but they are a far lighter green and their texture is flimsy, like basil. Another distinctive quality is the scabbard shape of the sorrel leaf and its spindly stalk. The leaves, particular young ones, melt down to nothing once heated and, like basil, don't take well to being cut. Sadly their vibrant apple-green colour is lost to heat, but cooking accentuates sorrel's lemony flavour.

Behind the hedgerows on Raginnis Hill are large sloping fields planted with all manner of vegetables. I've seen potatoes, cabbages, corn on the cob and cauliflower. Sometimes there are black and white cows grazing in one particular field. They stop chewing the cud or flicking flies with their long pointy tongues (which fit neatly up their wide nostrils) and stare as you walk past. I like it when a tractor is working the fields, leaving behind a field full of black crows eager to poke their sharp beaks into the newly ploughed earth in search of worms. They crowd the sky at the sound of footsteps, gathering in small armies to swoop and weave, making graceful patterns in the sky before settling on the sagging telegraph wires and stretching them taut with their weight. The occasional tree grows out of the hedgerow, but its spiky branches have been shaped to a gradual slant by years of hard, blustery winds. In the distance the distinctive turreted L-shaped spire of Paul church beckons me onwards, and way beyond I can just make out the sea. It takes about forty-five minutes to walk this walk and if there's sorrel to be had, I pick some to make sorrel soup or Betty's creamy sauce to serve with sea bass. The distinctive citrus spinach flavour is particularly good with cream and eggs. The (French) chef at the Cornish Range, Mousehole's only 'posh' restaurant, recommends using the young leaves in salads.

At the top of Raginnis Hill, when the road turns sharply to the right, a stream runs down both sides of the road in the grassy verge which edges a short stretch of hedgerow. This is where wild watercress grows. The leaves are smaller than usual and the flavour noticeably fresh and peppery. This is true of other wild watercress I've eaten.

Watercress is one of the world's most ancient and vital foods and is thought to have originated in Greece. One of the top three most healthy vegetables – along with dandelions and nettles – it is high in vitamins C and the B group, and contains sulphur, potassium, phosphorus, iodine, calcium, beta-carotene and folic acid. It has a positive anti-cancer link and aids digestion. Watercress gets its pungency from the mustard oil present in all members of the nasturtium family. The bigger the leaf and darker the green, the stronger the flavour. Delicious in salads, or chopped and treated like a herb, it is interchangeable in any recipe that calls for rocket.

Irrepressible nettles flourish from March onwards in the hedgerows and edges of fields, along the coast path, everywhere, in fact, where they can get a foothold. Young nettles are delicious food for free and make excellent green soups. They taste a bit like spinach and are rich in iron, formic and silicic acid and natural histamines. Young nettle shoots are tender enough to cook whole, but as the plants become more forceful, just the crown of leaves at the top should be harvested. As spring turns to summer and the plants get coarser and develop seed heads and flowers, they are no good for the pot. But when established plants have been strimmed or mown, they quickly renew themselves and new growth is ready for picking within a few days.

Pack your Marigolds or a stout pair of gloves and a plastic carrier bag when you go nettle-picking. If you do get stung by their soft, furry serrated leaves, rub the sting vigorously with a dock leaf. A clump of these stout wide green leaves always grows conveniently nearby wherever 'stingers' grow.

SPINACH SOUP
Serves 6

Spinach makes a velvety, dark green soup, but unless it is very young and soft, it needs lengthy liquidizing to get rid of its fibrous nature. This spinach soup has a luscious texture and citrus creaminess because it's finished in the Greek *avgolemono* style with egg yolks and lemon juice.

750g spinach leaves
1 medium onion
1 lemon
50g butter
salt and black pepper

1.5 litre boiling chicken stock or 2½ chicken stock cubes dissolved in
   1.5 litre boiling water
3 egg yolks
cream and nutmeg to serve

If necessary, cut out thick central stems from the spinach, wash the leaves, shake dry and coarsely chop. Peel and finely chop the onions. Remove 6 strips of wafer-thin lemon zest from the lemon and squeeze 2 tablespoons of lemon juice.

Melt the butter in a suitable pan and stir in the onion. Season with salt and pepper and sweat very gently until soft and slippery. Add the spinach and let it sweat until it has wilted. Add the boiling chicken stock and simmer for about 10 minutes until the spinach is completely tender but still bright green. Liquidize the soup in batches for several minutes until very smooth. Pass through a sieve or the finest disc of a Mouli-legumes food mill directly into a clean pan. Taste and adjust the seasoning with salt and pepper

Beat the egg yolks in a bowl with the lemon juice, then gradually beat in a cupful of hot soup, beating all the time. Return this mixture to the soup and heat very gently, stirring all the time until thickened. Do not let the soup boil once the egg mixture has been added.

Place a strip of lemon zest in each serving bowl and serve the soup with a swirl of cream and a little freshly grated nutmeg.

SPINACH *GRATIN*
Serves 2–4

This is a lovely solution to an excess of spinach. Usefully, it can be made ahead and cooked as required. We like it on its own with roasted tomatoes – which can be cooked at the same time – but it goes further with lamb chops, sausages or chicken and is perfect to serve with simply cooked fish.

big bunch spinach, 600–750g
salt and pepper
50g butter
25g flour
300ml milk

nutmeg

1 heaped tbsp thick cream

2 eggs

40g fresh breadcrumbs

Pre-heat the oven to 350°F/180°C/gas mark 4. Squash the spinach into a large pan of boiling salted water and boil for a couple of minutes until wilted. Drain, splash with cold water and spread out in a colander to drain thoroughly and cool.

Meanwhile, make a thick white sauce by melting 25g of the butter in a medium-sized pan. Stir in the flour until it is amalgamated with the butter, then add the milk, stirring constantly to avoid lumps as it comes up to the boil. If it does turn lumpy, beat vigorously with a wire whisk. Reduce the heat, season generously with salt, pepper and nutmeg and leave to simmer gently for 5 minutes. Remove the pan from the heat and stir in the cream. Add the eggs, beating one at a time.

Squeeze the spinach against the sides of the colander or between your hands to remove as much liquid as possible. Chop the ball of spinach a few times and stir it into the sauce until evenly distributed. Tip the mixture into a 750ml capacity gratin dish. Smooth the surface and sprinkle with the breadcrumbs. Dot with the remaining butter.

Cook in the oven for 30 minutes until puffed and risen, with the top evenly crusted. Serve immediately.

EGGS FLORENTINE

Serves 2–4

Eggs Florentine is a comforting but rather elegant little baked egg and spinach dish. People used to make it for dinner parties and serve it in white ramekins, but it's one of those simple dishes that can go disastrously wrong. What you're after is soft, slippery spinach held in a well-seasoned, creamy white sauce. Just below the surface, hidden from view, is an egg, and the skill of the dish is serving it when the egg white has set but before the yolk has hardened.

One of my little innovations is to gratinée the top with a thin, crisp layer of grated Parmesan and breadcrumbs. I love the contrast of all that silky, smooth food with the crisp, thin crust on top, but I'm equally keen on the original. This version makes a great snack lunch or supper for two but quantities are also perfect for four starters.

    1 small onion
    300ml milk
    2 cloves
    1 bay leaf
    salt and pepper
    500g spinach
    50g butter
    freshly grated nutmeg
    25g plain flour
    2 tbsp thick cream
    vinegar
    4 eggs
    3 tbsp fresh breadcrumbs
    3 tbsp freshly grated Parmesan

Peel, halve and finely chop the onion. Place in a pan with the milk, cloves and bay leaf and a decent seasoning of salt and pepper. Bring to the boil, reduce the heat immediately and simmer for 5 minutes. Remove from the heat, cover the pan and leave to infuse for 15 minutes or longer.

Meanwhile, pick over the spinach, discarding any yellowing leaves and thick stalks. Shred mature spinach, but leave young spinach intact without bothering to discard stalks. If necessary, wash and shake dry.

Melt 25g butter in a large, shallow pan until it is just turning nut-brown. Put in the spinach, turning it through the butter. Season generously with salt, pepper and nutmeg and cook until the spinach is limp and just-cooked. Drain in a colander, pressing gently to extract excess moisture.

Melt 25g butter in a medium-sized pan and stir in the flour to make a smooth roux. Strain the seasoned milk into the roux, stirring constantly as the milk comes up to the boil. Whisk thoroughly to disperse any lumps and leave to simmer gently for 5 minutes until the flour is cooked and the sauce thick. Stir in the cream, taste and adjust the seasoning. Stir the spinach into the sauce. Keep warm. Half-fill a medium-sized pan with water and bring to the boil. Add the vinegar. Crack one egg after another into a cup and slip them, one by one, into the simmering water. After about 1 minute, when the egg white has set but before the eggs are completely cooked, lift them out of the water and rest on kitchen paper to drain. Tip just over half of the sauced spinach into one or two shallow ovenproof dishes, or four ramekins, making indentations for them. Slip the eggs into the hollows, and spoon the reserved sauce over the top to cover them. Mix the breadcrumbs with the Parmesan and scatter over the surface.

Flash under a hot grill or pop into a very hot oven (425°F/220°C/gas mark 7) for 4 minutes to crisp the surface.

SPINACH WITH CHICKPEAS

Serves 4

In Spain they serve this warm or cold as tapas. It's a great thing to have in the fridge as standby food – it will keep covered for a few days – for emergency meals. It's good piled on to toast rubbed with garlic and dribbled with olive oil. Add a fried or poached egg and it's even better. Or serve with grilled white fish or chicken kebabs.

500g spinach
1 small onion
2 garlic cloves
1 small red chilli
3 tbsp olive oil
400g can chickpeas
1 tsp ground cumin
juice of ½ lemon
salt and pepper
juice of ½ lemon

Three-quarters fill a large pan of water and put it on to boil. If necessary, pick over the spinach, removing any thick stalks and yellowing leaves. Wash thoroughly and shake dry. As soon as the water boils, stuff the spinach into the pan and let it boil for a couple of minutes. Drain and splash with cold water so that it is cool enough to handle. Leave in a colander to drain.

Meanwhile, peel and finely chop the onion and garlic. Split the chilli in half, discard stalk and white seeds and chop very finely. (Remember to wash your hands.) Heat the oil in a frying pan over a moderate heat. Stir in the onion, garlic and chilli, and cook, stirring every so often, until the onion is tender and beginning to brown in places. While the onion is cooking, tip the chickpeas into a sieve and rinse thoroughly under cold running water.

By now the spinach will be cool enough to squeeze between your hands to get rid of the remaining water. Shred it with a knife.

Stir the cumin into the onion, let it cook for about 30 seconds, then add the spinach and chickpeas. Stir everything together, season with salt, pepper and lemon juice. Serve hot, cold or tepid.

SPINACH AND CARAMELIZED ONION TART
Serves 6–8

This rich tart makes a terrific dinner-party starter which can be made in advance and is perfect served before fish. As a supper dish, serve it with baked potatoes and stewed leeks which you've stirred with ribbons of Parma ham.

150g flour plus a little extra
salt and pepper
100g butter plus an extra knob
2–4 tbsp cold water
1 large onion
1 tbsp cooking oil
350g young spinach
2 eggs
300g Cornish clotted or other thick cream
50g grated Parmesan plus a little extra
nutmeg

To make the pastry, sift the flour into the bowl of a food processor. Add a pinch of salt and process briefly to mix. Cut the butter into small pieces directly into the bowl. Using the pulse button, blitz until the mixture resembles coarse breadcrumbs. With the food processor running, slowly add the water and process just until combined and crumbly. You may prefer to do this by hand (I do), rubbing the cold butter into the flour and salt and then stirring in sufficient water to make a cohesive dough.

Turn the dough on to a lightly floured surface and press into a ball. Leave to sit, covered, for at least 30 minutes, to allow the gluten to stretch and thus avoid the pastry shrinking when it cooks.

Pre-heat the oven to 425°F/220°C/gas mark 7. Smear the inside of a 24cm tart tin (preferably one with a removable base) with butter and dust with flour, shaking out any excess. This makes it non-stick. Roll out the pastry on the floured surface to fit and gently press in place, trimming the rim. Cover the pastry case loosely with foil and fill with pastry weights or rice and cook for 10 minutes. Remove the foil and cook for a further 10 minutes and leave to cool. Reduce the oven to 350°F/180°C/gas mark 4.

Meanwhile, peel, halve and finely chop the onion. Heat the oil in a frying pan and cook the onion for about 12 minutes until soft and golden brown. Bring a large pan of water to the boil. Add 1 teaspoon of salt and the spinach, pushing it under the water. Boil for 2 minutes until wilted. Drain, splash with cold water and squeeze dry with your hands. Chop roughly.

Break the eggs into a mixing bowl and beat with the cream until smooth. Add the Parmesan and season generously with nutmeg and lightly with salt and pepper. Add the spinach and onion and mix thoroughly. Smooth the mixture into the cooled tart case and bake in the oven for about 30 minutes until risen and browned but slightly wobbly in the centre of the tart. Rest for 5 minutes before removing the collar. Serve this hot, warm or cold. It looks attractive dusted with grated Parmesan.

CREAM OF SORREL SOUP
Serves 4

Creamy and lemony.

>	1 onion
>	25g butter
>	salt

4 or 5 new potatoes, approx. 350g

500ml chicken stock (cube is fine)

3 large handfuls of young sorrel

2 egg yolks

150ml thick cream

Peel and finely chop the onion. Melt the butter in a medium saucepan placed over a moderate heat and stir in the onion. Season with salt, give the onion a good stir, then reduce the heat, cover the pan and leave to soften gently, stirring occasionally, for several minutes. Scrape the potatoes, cut into small cubes and rinse with cold water. When the onion is soft and slippery, add the potato and stock. Bring to the boil, partially cover the pan and cook for about 10 minutes until the potato is tender. Meanwhile, pick over the sorrel, discarding stalks and discoloured leaves. Wash thoroughly and shake dry. Add to the pot. It will wilt and turn dark green as it hits the hot liquid. Pass the soup through a Mouli-legumes or blitz to liquidize. Return to the pan. Scoop a little soup into a bowl. Add the eggs and cream and whisk thoroughly. Stir back into the soup, stirring constantly without letting the soup boil for a minute or so. Taste and adjust the seasoning with salt.

SORREL SAUCE
Serves 4

A lovely food-for-free sauce to serve with sea bass.

2 very large handfuls of sorrel

salt and pepper

75g cold, diced butter or thick cream

Pick over the sorrel, discarding stalks and discoloured leaves. Wash thoroughly and shake dry. Place in a medium-sized pan over a moderate heat. Turn with a wooden spoon as it melts down into a dark green purée. Once the wateriness has evaporated, season with salt and pepper and stir in the butter or cream. Serve immediately.

WATERCRESS SOUP

Serves 6

Essence of watercress with potatoes and cream.

> 3 small onions
> 100g unsalted butter
> 400g floury potatoes
> salt and pepper
> 1.2 litre water or light chicken stock
> 6 bunches watercress, approx. 500g
> 250ml whipping cream

Peel and chop the onions. Melt the butter in a suitable heavy-bottomed pan, stir in the onions and cook gently until soft and slippery. Meanwhile, peel the potatoes, chop them into large chunks, rinse and add to the soft onions. Season with salt and pepper and cook for 3 or 4 minutes. Now add the water or stock and simmer briskly for about 15 minutes until tender.

Pick over the watercress, discarding any woody stems, rinse thoroughly and shake dry. Add the cream to the pot, return to simmer and then add the watercress. Liquidize immediately. Pass through a fine sieve, adjust the seasoning and serve.

PEAR AND WATERCRESS SOUP

Serves 6

The combination of succulent sweet pears and peppery watercress is a triumph. Serve hot or cold.

> 2 flourishing bunches of watercress, approx. 200g
> 3 large, ripe pears
> 900ml light chicken stock
> salt and pepper
> juice of ½ lemon
> 175ml thick cream

Pick over the watercress and set aside the leaves. Peel, quarter and core the pears and cut into chunks. Bring watercress stalks, pears and stock quickly to the boil in a pan with a generous pinch of salt and a few grinds of black pepper. Turn down the heat, cover and simmer gently for 15 minutes. Process in batches with the watercress leaves, then pass through a sieve or Mouli-legumes to catch the fibrous debris. Stir in the lemon juice and cream, taste and adjust the seasoning. Serve hot or cold.

WATERCRESS PESTO
Makes approx. 10 tbsp

Pesto is really prepared with basil, but a delicious peppery version can be made with watercress or rocket. It has all sorts of uses and is a great thing to have in the fridge on standby. Stir it into pasta with a few grilled cherry tomatoes or spread it thickly on garlic-rubbed, olive-oil-dribbled bread and top with tomatoes and roasted red peppers. Try it slackened with extra olive oil to make dressings for boiled potatoes, streamed fish and poached chicken. It keeps, covered, in the fridge for days.

  3 tbsp pine kernels
  2 plump garlic cloves
  decent bunch of watercress, approx. 90g without big stalks
  7 tbsp virgin olive oil
  3 tbsp freshly grated Parmesan

Heat a small, heavy frying pan and briefly stir-fry the pine kernels until lightly golden. Peel the garlic. Place the pine kernels, garlic and watercress in a food processor and blitz. When evenly chopped, with the motor still running, gradually add the olive oil and continue until nicely amalgamated. Transfer to a bowl and stir in the grated Parmesan.

WATERCRESS SAUCE
Serves 4–6

This is a good alternative to parsley sauce and goes with simply cooked white fish such as cod, haddock, huss, ling or gurnard. It's good, too, with boiled gammon or over cauliflower.

2 small onions
a few cloves
1 bay leaf
salt
500ml milk
2 flourishing bunches of watercress, approx. 200g
25g butter
25g flour
3 tbsp thick cream

Peel the onions and cut in half. Use a couple of the cloves to spear the bay leaf on to one of the onion halves. Place in a milk pan with a generous pinch of salt and the milk. Bring to the boil, simmer for 5 minutes, remove from the heat, cover and leave for at least 20 minutes.

Meanwhile, pick over the watercress, discarding yellowing leaves and woody stalks. Plunge into boiling water for 1 minute. Drain and refresh under cold water, then drain again before chopping finely.

Melt the butter in a second pan, stir in the flour until it disappears and then, away from the heat, strain the milk into the pan. Return to the heat and whisk until it thickens. Stir in the cream and simmer for a few minutes before you taste and adjust the seasoning. Stir in the blanched watercress, gently reheat and serve.

STINGING NETTLE SOUP WITH BACON *CROÛTONS*
Serves 4–6

You'll need to wear washing-up gloves to prepare this soup. The 'sting' disappears once the nettles begin to cook. Leeks, incidentally, give a silky and creamy texture to puréed soups like this one.

500g young nettles
1 trimmed leek or 4 plump spring onions
25g butter
salt and pepper
1 scant tbsp flour
1 litre light chicken stock or 1 chicken stock cube dissolved in
    1 litre boiling water

2 egg yolks

2 tbsp cream or creamy milk

for the croûtons:

6 rashers rindless smoked streaky bacon

3 tbsp vegetable oil

2 slices bread

to serve:

thick cream and freshly snipped chives

Wearing washing-up gloves, pick over the nettles, discarding damaged leaves, then rinse thoroughly in a colander and shake dry. Discard gloves, trim and finely slice the leeks or spring onions and sweat in the butter in a suitable pan until limp. Stir in the nettles, season with ½ teaspoon of salt, cover and cook for 5 minutes. Remove the lid and boil hard for 30 seconds to evaporate excess liquid before sifting in the flour. Stir thoroughly as you pour in the hot stock. Simmer for 5 minutes and liquidize in batches. Return to a clean pan, scoop out a little of the broth and mix it with the egg and cream or milk. Stir the mixture back into the soup. Simmer gently for 30 seconds without letting the soup boil. Taste for seasoning.

To make the *croûtons*, slice the bacon across the pile of rashers into little strips. Heat the oil in a frying pan and stir in the bacon, adjusting the heat so that the fat melts as the bacon crisps. Scoop the bacon on to a plate, leaving all the fatty oil behind. Cut the bread into chunky squares and quickly fry in the bacon fat, tossing until crisp and golden. Return the bacon and toss again

Serve the soup with a dollop of cream, some of the *croûtons* and a shower of chives.

Cauliflower, Broccoli and Cabbage

Cauliflower Soup with Lemon and Thyme
Cauliflower Cream
Superior Cauliflower Cheese with Baby Jacket Potatoes
Green Cauliflower Cheese with Grilled Vine Tomatoes
Orechiette with Cauliflower
Breadcrumbed Cauliflower with Mustard Mayo
Sprouting Broccoli with Prosciutto
Broccoli with Chilli and Anchovy Dressing
Thai Broccoli
Portuguese Cabbage Soup with Rosemary Bruschetta
Cabbage with Chickpeas
Chang's Cabbage
Red Cabbage with Tomatoes and Caraway

Late one afternoon in early December, Henry and I decided to explore the coast path leading out of Marazion towards the Lizard. As the light faded – you get an extra hour of light this far south-west – there was the most amazing sunset which brought the rocky beach and imposing image of St Michael's Mount rising out of the sea into sharp relief. Shafts of bright sunlight shone through a painted sky of greys and purple-pink, flecking the sea with golden effervescence and making a dramatic backdrop for distant Newlyn and the promontory which hides Mousehole from view. On the way back, we edged round a field of rejected cauliflowers in various stages of decay and Henry couldn't resist stuffing a few of the better ones up his jumper. I've done it many times myself because it seems criminal to waste perfectly good cauliflower presumably not quite perfect enough for the marketplace.

Cauliflower and broccoli are part of the brassica family and both are richer in vitamins and minerals than cabbage, sprouts or kale and that's saying something. The distinctive 'head' of both vegetables is actually made of flowers that have begun to form but stopped growing at the bud stage. The stems leading up to the florets act as storage organs for nutrients intended for the flowers and eventual fruit. In cauliflowers, the buds grow tightly from short, stumpy stems into the distinctive white head which nestles inside vigorous cabbagey green leaves. Broccoli 'branches' and buds look more like a bushy tree, and in so-called sprouting broccoli, or 'tenderstem', as supermarkets would have us call it, each group of buds has its own stem and can be eaten like asparagus.

It's unclear which was developed first, cauliflower or broccoli, but these curious cabbages are thought to have originated in the Near East and been introduced into Britain via Arabs who took it to Europe after the fall of the Roman Empire. There are various types of broccoli. The most common is known in Mousehole by its correct name of calabrese and it flourishes locally, ready for harvesting in early summer. Sprouting broccoli arrives slightly earlier. Cauliflower is even more common in these parts and by late November or early December the main crop has been harvested and the imperfect cauli left to rot in the fields. I'm sure I'm not the only one to have helped myself. Cauliflower has a less assertive flavour than broccoli but can still taste quite cabbagey. Some people like the florets raw as crudités with a creamy dip or in salads, but most of all we love it in a cheese sauce. Cauliflower is unexpectedly good in soup, particularly puréed cream soups which end up with a lovely fluffy texture and delicious, subtle flavour.

Broccoli is big in Italy and has always had a posher image than cauliflower in the UK. Lately it's been hailed as a health food because it is one of the most nutritious green vegetables around. It's high in vitamin C and E, and rich in antioxidants, which can help prevent heart disease and cancer. Broccoli first arrived in the UK in 1720 but wasn't grown here on any scale until the 1970s. It was originally marketed as calabrese, which refers to Calabria, but the name didn't catch on and was changed to broccoli, referring to '*braccia*', which suggests 'little arms' or 'little shoots' in Italian.

Two to three portions of any brassica per week reduces cancer risk by 30 per cent, and to gain the maximum nutritional benefit it must be cooked briefly. Broccoli is tricky to cook well because the buds are soft and cook faster than the 'little arms' and the stalk. One chef I know cooks each part – the florets, the 'little arms', the turned stalk and the leaves – separately. You can be bold with broccoli, pairing it with strong flavours like anchovy, chilli and garlic. Thais stir-fry it with carrot, sweet chilli sauce and soy. It makes a lovely green soup with fish or cheese.

CAULIFLOWER SOUP WITH LEMON AND THYME

Serves 4

There is an Italian tradition of combining thyme with garlic and lemon zest and that must have been at the back of my mind when I came up with this utterly beguiling soup. It ends up fluffy and creamy with a haunting back taste of thyme that is lifted by occasional little bursts of citrus. The frugal housewife came into force when I found myself boiling up the cauliflower stalks to make a quick stock. If you can't be bothered with this way of strengthening the cauliflower flavour, I wouldn't blame you. The soup will be quite delicious without this burst of domestic goddessticity.

1 large cauliflower

salt and pepper

1 onion or 150g bunch of spring onions

1 plump garlic clove

1 small unwaxed lemon

25g butter

1 tsp chopped fresh thyme

1 or 2 tsp Marigold Swiss vegetable bouillon

2 tbsp chopped flat-leaf parsley

100g thick cream or crème fraîche

Cut the stalks off the cauliflower and cut out the dense core in a cone shape. Chop the stalks into short lengths and place in a large pot with the core, 1 teaspoon of salt and any discarded thyme and parsley stalks. Cover with just over a litre of water and boil, uncovered, for 10 minutes.

Meanwhile, peel and finely chop the onion or trim the spring onions and finely chop, including all the tender green. Peel the garlic and coarsely chop. Remove the zest from the lemon in wafer-thin scraps. Melt the butter in a 2-litre-capacity pan and stir in the onion, garlic, lemon zest and thyme. Season with salt and pepper, toss thoroughly, cover the pan and sweat, stirring occasionally and checking that nothing burns, for 6 or 7 minutes until the onion has begun to soften.

While that is happening, cut the cauliflower into small florets, each with a bit of stalk. Stir the cauliflower into the onion mixture. Drain the stock (or 1 litre of hot water) into the soup, add 1 teaspoon of stock granules (2 teaspoons if you're using water), bring to the boil, then turn down the heat slightly, partially cover the pan and cook for 10–15 minutes until the cauliflower is tender. Add the parsley. Blitz in batches, return to the pan, stir in the crème fraîche, reheat, taste and adjust the seasoning with salt, pepper and lemon juice.

CAULIFLOWER CREAM
Serves 6

A cauliflower just past its prime – you find lots of these abandoned in the ground they were grown in during late November in these parts –

inspired this superb dish. It's best described as puréed cauliflower cheese, but that undersells a fluffy, creamy and intriguingly delicious purée. It takes a moment or two to identify cauliflower because it has none of the usual cabbagey flavour and it is such an unexpected way to serve this snowy-white vegetable. The purée is perfectly matched with anything salty – believe it or not, it is wonderful cold on toast with caviar – and particularly good with fillets of white fish dipped in green breadcrumbs (see page 67).

> 1 cauliflower
> salt
> 150ml thick cream or crème fraîche
> 75g mature Cheddar
> squeeze of lemon

Remove and discard the stalks and leaves from the cauliflower. Cut into quarters and then into florets. Bring about 10cm of water to the boil in a medium-sized saucepan, add 1 teaspoon of salt and the cauliflower. Return to the boil, cover the pan and cook for about 5 minutes until completely tender. Drain but reserve 2 tablespoons of cooking water. Place cauliflower, reserved water, cream and grated Cheddar in the bowl of a food processor and blitz to make a smooth, thick, creamy white sauce. Taste and adjust the seasoning with salt and a squeeze of lemon. Reheats perfectly, but stir well before serving.

SUPERIOR CAULIFLOWER CHEESE WITH BABY JACKET POTATOES
Serves 4

Who can resist cauliflower cheese? And who can resist jacket potatoes? Both these favourite dishes go down well however they are cooked – and goodness knows, they can both vary greatly. It's good, though, isn't it, to come across an unexpected way of preparing a familiar dish that turns it into something special? Little potatoes, for example, aren't usually baked in their jackets. And cauliflower cheese is usually an ordinary sort of dish made simply with cauliflower and a cheese sauce. There is an obvious advantage to baking small potatoes and it's because they cook very quickly. Rubbing the potatoes with oil and

Mediterranean Meatballs with Basil Tomato Sauce

crab sandwich

Crab Bruschetta

Left: Roast Monkfish Tail with Onion and Chive Game Chips
This page: Royden Paynter

placing them on reflective tinfoil speeds up the cooking even more and so does threading them on kebab sticks. It is extraordinary the difference it makes to the flavour of cauliflower cheese if the sauce is made with cauliflower cooking water and a small amount of milk instead of the more usual milk on its own. When you also add white wine and Dijon mustard, you end up with a really tasty sauce. Masses of chopped flat-leaf parsley make another good addition and look very attractive too. This, then, is deluxe comfort stodge: two of our favourite foods given a great makeover. Enjoy alone or with lamb, chicken, sausages or simply cooked fish.

32 new potatoes

2 tbsp olive oil

Maldon sea salt and freshly milled black pepper

2 large cauliflower

50g butter

50g flour

1 tbsp smooth Dijon mustard

150ml white wine

150ml milk

200g grated Cheddar

2 tbsp flat-leaf parsley

3 tbsp finely grated Parmesan

Pre-heat the oven to 425°F/220°C/gas mark 7. Pour half the olive oil into your cupped palm and roll half the potatoes through the oil. Repeat with the rest of the oil and potatoes. Thread the potatoes on to 4 kebab sticks. Season lavishly with Maldon sea salt. Line a baking sheet with foil and lay out the kebab sticks. Place in the oven, not worrying if it hasn't come up to temperature. Cook, testing after 30 minutes, until tender with a crusty skin.

Divide the cauliflower into large, bite-size florets, discarding stalk and core. Cook in boiling, salted water for 3–4 minutes until just tender. Drain, reserving 150ml cooking water. Tip the cauliflower into a suitable ovenproof dish. Melt the butter in a medium-sized pan and add the flour, stirring until smooth. Stir in the mustard. Add the reserved cooking water, wine and milk. Stir constantly whilst bringing the sauce to the boil. Reduce the heat, season with salt and pepper and simmer for a few minutes to cook the flour. Stir in the grated Cheddar and then the parsley. Pour the sauce over the cauliflower. Scatter the Parmesan over the top and cook in the oven for about 15 minutes until the cheese is crusty. Serve potatoes and cauliflower together with extra butter and grated Cheddar.

GREEN CAULIFLOWER CHEESE WITH GRILLED VINE TOMATOES
Serves 4

Cauliflower cheese is an endlessly versatile dish that can be presented in so many different ways. The cheese you use – everything from Cheddar to Roquefort, even feta, halloumi or mozzarella – changes the dish completely. I love adding extras such as onions, peas, tomatoes, olives or a garnish of very crisp streaky bacon or Parma ham. A handful of fresh herbs added to the sauce – and almost any soft green herb from basil to savory would do – changes its mood completely. This sort of cauliflower cheese doesn't go back in the oven or under the grill for a crusty topping; it's a more gentle dish in risotto style. In this take on a favourite dish I've left the cauliflower whole. It looks very attractive with grilled vine tomatoes draped over the cauliflower.

> 1 large cauliflower or 4 Romanesco cauliflower
> salt and pepper
> 50g butter
> 50g flour
> 600ml milk
> 100g Gruyère cheese
> 50g freshly grated Parmesan
> 10g chives
> handful of basil leaves
> 200g cherry tomatoes, preferably on the vine
> 1 tbsp olive oil

Half-fill a lidded pan that can hold the cauliflower snugly and put it on to boil. Trim the leaves of the cauliflower and use a small sharp knife to cut out the core in a cone shape. Add 1 teaspoon of salt to the boiling water and lower the trimmed cauliflower into the water. Cover and boil hard – the stalks and leaves will be in the water and the florets will steam – for about 15 minutes, checking after 10, until the cauliflower is tender. Drain, saving about 100ml of the cooking water, and transfer to a warmed serving dish.

Meanwhile, make the sauce. Melt the butter in a small saucepan and stir in the flour. Add the milk gradually and stir constantly to avoid lumps as it comes to the boil. Add the reserved cooking water and season generously with salt and pepper. Simmer gently, stirring occasionally for 5 minutes, then stir in the cheese. Snip the chives and basil directly into the sauce and pour it over the cauliflower.

To cook the tomatoes, smear them with olive oil, season with salt and pepper and grill for a few minutes until the flesh softens and the skins begin to pop. Tumble or drape the tomatoes over the cauliflower and serve.

ORECHIETTE WITH CAULIFLOWER
Serves 4

Proof that cauliflower works with pasta!

> 1 cauliflower or 450g cauliflower florets
> salt and black pepper
> 350g dried orechiette or caserecce pasta
> 1 large onion
> 3 tbsp olive oil
> 1 red chilli
> 4 anchovy fillets
> 400g can chopped tomatoes
> about 15 pitted black olives
> 2 tbsp chopped flat-leaf parsley
> lump of Pecorino or Parmesan cheese

Half-fill two large pans with water and put on to boil.

If using a whole cauliflower, remove the outer leaves, cut in half and divide into bite-size florets. Add 1 teaspoon of salt and the cauliflower florets to the boiling water in one pan and 1 teaspoon of salt and the pasta to the other. When the water returns to the boil, adjust the heat so it simmers. Cook the cauliflower for 3 minutes, drain and keep warm. Cook the pasta until *al dente*, drain, covered, and keep warm.

Meanwhile, peel, halve and thinly slice the onion. Heat the olive oil in a large, heavy-bottomed frying pan or similarly wide-based pan and cook the onion for about 8 minutes until tender and beginning to colour.

Split the chilli, scrape out the seeds and chop finely. Chop the anchovies. Add both to the pan and stir-fry for a minute or two until the anchovy melts into the onions. Add the tomatoes. Simmer, uncovered, for about 6 minutes, until thick and sauce-like. Stir in the cauliflower. Cover the pan and cook for 5 minutes.

Tear the olives in half. Add olives and chopped parsley to the sauce. Taste and adjust the seasoning with salt and pepper. Stir the sauce into the drained pasta and serve the Pecorino or Parmesan for people to grate over the top.

BREADCRUMBED CAULIFLOWER WITH MUSTARD MAYO
Serves 4

A good snack or something different to serve with drinks, either on their own with a squeeze of lemon or like this with mayonnaise or a chunky tomato sauce.

    1 cauliflower
    1 tsp salt
    flour
    2 large eggs
    200g breadcrumbs made from stale bread
    oil for deep frying
    1 tbsp smooth Dijon mustard
    4 tbsp Hellmann's mayonnaise
    squeeze of lemon juice

Divide the cauliflower into florets. Rinse in a basin of cold water, drain and shake dry. Bring a large pan of water to the boil, add the salt and cauliflower and boil for 2 minutes. Drain thoroughly and pat dry. Dust the florets with flour, shaking away the excess. Beat the eggs in a bowl and place the breadcrumbs in a second bowl. Dip the floured florets first in egg and then press into the breadcrumbs to entirely cover. Transfer to a plate as you go. Cook a few florets at a time in hot oil, turning so that they end up a light golden brown all over. Rest on kitchen paper before serving. Stir the mustard into the mayonnaise, pointing up the flavours with a squeeze of lemon.

SPROUTING BROCCOLI WITH PROSCIUTTO
Serves 4

A lovely starter adapted from a recipe in *Chez Panisse Cooking* by Paul Bertolli with Alice Walters. The original is made with a mixture of greens such as spinach, rocket, frisée and bok choi, but it works wonderfully well with sprouting broccoli or asparagus. In fact, I often make a cheat's version by wrapping the lightly boiled veg in Parma ham with a dressing of balsamic vinegar and olive oil splashed over the top.

> 1¼ tsp salt
> approx. 450g sprouting broccoli/tenderstem
> 1 large shallot
> 1 garlic clove
> 2 tbsp red wine vinegar
> pepper
> 4 tbsp olive oil

Bring a large pan of water to the boil. Add 1 teaspoon of salt and the broccoli. Boil for 1 minute, then drain. Peel and finely chop the shallot and garlic. Dissolve the remaining salt in the vinegar, stir in the shallot and garlic, add pepper and stir in the olive oil. Put the vinaigrette in a wok or pan large enough to hold the broccoli comfortably. Place over a medium-high heat. Add the drained broccoli and toss continually with a pair of tongs or two forks for a couple of minutes to just finish cooking. Remove from the heat and, working directly from the bowl, place some of the broccoli on a slice of prosciutto. Roll up and serve while still warm.

BROCCOLI WITH CHILLI AND ANCHOVY DRESSING
Serves 4

It is difficult to convey just how wonderful this dish tastes. It looks marvellous, the tiny scraps of red chilli caught up in the 'hair' of broccoli florets, and the smells as the sauce is prepared are guaranteed to kick-start even the most jaded of palates. Quite why anchovy goes so well with broccoli is mysterious, but the salty intensity of the fish brings out the best in this cabbagey vegetable. To expand this dish, tip the whole lot into 200g of cooked pasta tossed with a little olive oil. Either way, it goes very well with fillets of simply cooked white fish.

    salt
    2 flourishing heads of broccoli, approx. 450g each
    2 big garlic cloves
    8 anchovy fillets
    2 small red chillies
    2 tbsp lemon juice
    4 tbsp olive oil
    black pepper

Bring a large pan of water to the boil. Add 1 teaspoon of salt.

Meanwhile, use a small sharp knife to cut all the broccoli florets off the main stalk. Divide the stalk into sections – depending on its thickness, it may need splitting – that will cook at the same rate as the florets. Drop the broccoli into the boiling water and cook until just tender, allowing about 3 minutes for this. Drain and reserve 1 tablespoon of the cooking water. Peel the garlic and roughly chop. Chop the anchovy fillets. Trim and split the chillies. Discard the seeds. Slice the chilli in thin batons, then chop into tiny dice. Make the dressing by pounding the garlic with a little salt to make a juicy paste. Incorporate the anchovy, pounding with the lemon juice and hot broccoli cooking water. Whisk in the olive oil to end up with a thick vinaigrette. Stir in the chilli and season with black pepper. Tip the broccoli into a warm bowl and pour over the dressing. Toss thoroughly and eat immediately.

THAI BROCCOLI
Serves 4

I don't know if broccoli is big in Thailand, but this curious member of the cabbage family takes to Thai seasonings very well. What you're aiming for with this dish is to cook the broccoli until just tender but still with a bite, yet before the delicate florets dull in colour. The role of the carrot is really to act as a contrast to the vibrant green of the broccoli, but it too should remain *al dente*. As with all stir-fries, once all the preparations are done, the actual cooking is fast and furious. Most of the liquid evaporates or is soaked into the vegetables and what remains is the point of the dish. Don't be tempted, as I was the first time I made this, to cover the pan to speed up the cooking. It's not necessary and trapping the steam quickly robs the broccoli of its colour. I like this on its own with boiled basmati rice, but it is good with poached or griddled chicken or steamed fish. If not, remember it as a side dish for a full-on Thai feast.

    2 heads of broccoli, approx. 450g each
    1 large carrot
    2 garlic cloves
    3 tbsp sesame oil
    250ml chicken or vegetable stock (a decent cube is fine)
    2 tbsp oyster sauce
    1 tbsp soy sauce
    black pepper
    pinch of sugar

Cut the florets off the main broccoli stalks, dividing them into bite-size pieces to resemble little trees. Place in a colander, rinse with cold water and shake dry. Peel or scrape the carrot, quarter lengthways and slice across to make little chunks. Peel and finely chop the garlic. Have all the other ingredients to hand. Heat the wok over a high flame. Add the oil, swirling it round the pan, and then add the garlic. Stir briefly with a spatula until aromatic but before it starts to brown, then add the broccoli and carrot. Toss everything around a few times, then add the stock. Keep tossing and turning the vegetables through the hot liquid for about 30 seconds, then add the oyster sauce. Toss constantly for a couple of minutes, then add the soy sauce and season generously with black pepper and a generous pinch of sugar. Cook for another minute or until the vegetables are almost *al dente*. Tip into a warmed serving dish and eat immediately.

PORTUGUESE CABBAGE SOUP WITH ROSEMARY BRUSCHETTA

Serves 4

Caldo verde is Portugal's national soup and the combination of potato, cabbage and water with a little spicy sausage such as chorizo is addictive. All the supermarkets down here – Co-op, Tesco and Safeway – sell sliced chorizo. If it's not available, the soup is still good without the peppery sausage but I would add a dash of Tabasco to liven up the flavours.

    1 onion, approx. 125g
    2 large garlic cloves
    3 tbsp olive oil
    3 large potatoes, approx. 600g in total
    1½ tsp salt
    1½ litres cold water
    1 Savoy or other green cabbage, approx. 700g
    80g sliced chorizo
    ¼ tsp black pepper
    approx. 3 tbsp extra virgin olive oil
    4 thick slices sourdough
    1 branch fresh rosemary

Peel and finely chop the onion and 1 garlic clove. Heat the olive oil in a large, heavy-bottomed, lidded pan and stir in the onion and garlic. Cook, stirring occasionally, for a couple of minutes until the onion is glassy and beginning to colour.

Meanwhile, peel, slice and rinse the potatoes. Stir them into the glassy onions, season with 1 teaspoon of salt, cover and cook for a couple of minutes before adding 1½ litres cold water. Bring to the boil, partially cover the pan and boil for 15 minutes until the potatoes are soft and beginning to disintegrate. While the potatoes cook, quarter the cabbage, cut out the dense core and thick stems from the centre of the leaves. Make a pile of about 6 leaves, fold over and slice filament-thin. Rinse with cold water and shake dry. Briefly fry the chorizo, tossing it around in a frying pan until crusty.

When the potatoes are soft, remove the pan from the heat and mash a few times to break down any big pieces. Add the chorizo, remaining salt and the black pepper. Cover and cook for 5 minutes. Add the shredded cabbage and boil uncovered for a further 5 minutes until the cabbage is tender. Add a tablespoon of extra virgin olive oil and taste the soup for salt and pepper.

To make the bruschetta, toast the bread and rub one side with rosemary and then with peeled garlic. Douse with the remaining extra virgin olive oil.

Serve the soup with spoon and fork.

CABBAGE WITH CHICKPEAS
Serves 4

The trick with this dish is to cook the cabbage lightly so that its texture is still apparent but let the onions virtually melt until slippery and caramelized. Garlic – and you need quite a lot of it – lemon juice and fresh mint, added towards the end of cooking, lift the flavours in a surprisingly subtle way. Excellent with sausages or chicken kebabs.

3 onions, approx. 300g in total
1 unwaxed lemon
3 tbsp olive oil
400g can chickpeas
300g cabbage
4 large garlic cloves
salt and pepper
handful of fresh mint leaves (about 30)
Greek yoghurt to serve

Peel, halve and finely slice the onions. Remove the wafer-thin zest from the lemon in little scraps. Heat the oil and, when very hot, stir in the onions, continuing to stir for 4 or 5 minutes until they begin to flop and show patches of light brown. Reduce the heat, add the lemon zest and cook, stirring occasionally, for at least 15 minutes until the onions have melted into a slippery, reduced, lightly coloured slop.

Meanwhile, tip the chickpeas into a sieve or colander and rinse thoroughly with cold water. Shake dry. Remove the core from the cabbage and shred into strips approximately 7cm long. Wash and shake dry. Crush the garlic cloves and flake away the skin. Chop, then sprinkle them with ½ a teaspoon of salt and crush to a juicy paste with the flat of a small knife. Gather up the mint leaves and shred finely.

When the onions are ready, stir in the chickpeas together with ½ a teaspoon of salt and a generous amount of pepper. Cook for a few minutes, then add the cabbage. Increase the heat and stir for 2–3 minutes as the cabbage wilts and merges into the other ingredients. Add 3 tablespoons of lemon juice, 100ml water, the garlic paste and shredded mint. Stir well and cook for 3 or 4 minutes before turning off the heat. Taste and adjust the seasoning with salt and pepper. Leave to rest and cool slightly before serving with a dollop of yoghurt.

CHANG'S CABBAGE
Serves 6

I have been cooking this for years from Caroline Conran's recipe in *Poor Cook* and it makes a change from boiled cabbage. 'This is a lovely sweet-sour cabbage, very Chinese but rather good with Shepherd's Pie or chops. It is also very quick – cooked in seconds.'

    1 tsp salt
    3 tsp sugar
    2 tbsp vinegar
    750g cabbage, green or white
    2 tbsp oil
    few drops soy sauce

Mix the salt, sugar and vinegar together. Slice the cabbage as finely as you can, discarding the tough stalks and outer leaves. Wash well and then shake as dry as possible in a cloth, as you would salad. Heat the oil in a large frying pan over a fairly high heat and when it is really hot (but not burning) fling in the cabbage. Keep it moving about with a wooden fork, if you have one, or a spoon. As soon as it is all covered with oil, shake a few drops of soy sauce over it, then pour on the vinegar mixture. Let it cook for a minute or two and serve at once, hot, crisp and juicy.

RED CABBAGE WITH TOMATOES AND CARAWAY
Serves 4–6

Red cabbage is obviously easy to grow in Cornwall because Royden is always giving it to me. I came up with this recipe after a gift of three (!) cabbages from his allotment and it's so good, I immediately made it again and a few days later I made it again. It's got quite a kick and is surprisingly interesting with pasta. It would be good with sausages or rabbit casserole but is possibly best of all eaten cold as a relish with cheese. Remember it, too, for sandwiches and under cheese on toast for a new savoury called Mousehole rarebit.

> 500g red cabbage
> 2 large red onions
> 2 garlic cloves
> 1 lemon
> 2 tbsp olive oil
> ½ tsp caraway seeds
> salt
> 1 tsp dried chilli flakes
> 400g can chopped tomatoes

Halve, core and shred the cabbage. Soak in cold water while you prepare everything else, then drain thoroughly. Peel, halve and finely slice the onion. Peel the garlic and cut into thin rounds. Use a potato peeler to remove the zest from the lemon in small scraps. Heat the oil in a heavy-bottomed pan over a moderate heat and stir in the onions and caraway seeds. Season with 1 teaspoon of salt, reduce the heat slightly, cover and cook, stirring a couple of times, for 10 minutes. Stir in the cabbage, add another teaspoon of salt, stir again, cover and cook for a further 10 minutes. Add the lemon zest and chilli flakes. Return the lid and cook over a very low heat for 30 minutes. Add the tomatoes and cook, covered, for 20 minutes. Add the juice from the lemon, then taste and adjust the seasoning with salt.

Serve hot, warm or cold.

Beetroot, Swede, Carrots and Parsnips

Borscht with Soured Cream and Chives
Beetroot and Sweetcorn Soup with Oregano and Chilli
Stewed Beetroot with Lemon Tomatoes
Hot Grated Beetroot
Bruno Loubet's *Betteraves Aigres*
Turkish Beetroot and Yoghurt Salad with Coriander
Russian Salad with Chicken
Roast Beetroot Risotto with Beetroot Crisps
Cornish Pasty
Carrot and Cumin Soup with Coconut Milk
Curried Parsnip Soup with Bacon *Croûtons*

The gift of six large beetroot, just dug from Royden's allotment, and then three more a couple of days later taxed my love of beetroot to the max. Fortunately beetroot keeps well and wrinkled specimens can be firmed up by soaking in cold water. Beetroot is fabulous in soups – borscht, obviously, but other chunky vegetable soups too – and can be used to colour food because its distinctive purple colour leaches out when it's boiled. If cooking a whole beetroot, don't cut or scrub with a stiff brush because the colour will flood out if the skin is damaged. Just twist off the leaves and leave about 5cm of stem and any root intact. Baked beetroot has a deeper, earthier flavour than boiled beetroot. Try it with roast chicken, or rub away the soft skin, then purée it with lemon juice or balsamic vinegar. Beetroot greens can be cooked and eaten like spinach and are delicious dressed with olive oil and a squeeze of lemon. Beetroot and its greens are much revered in Greece.

There have been many attempts by chefs and food writers to raise the profile of beetroot, but it remains misunderstood and underused by home cooks. We think of it as a salad ingredient, usually bought boiled and eaten sliced with vinegar. It's a sweet root vegetable, like carrot, and needs to be balanced with acidic ingredients such as lemon, vinegar or tomatoes to make it interesting. It also loves spices, particularly cumin and chillies, and is spectacularly offset by soured cream. Lately beetroot has been hailed as the 'new' broccoli – a 'good' vegetable and a health food which stimulates the immune system. It's thought to be particularly good at enhancing the body's resistance to chronic infectious diseases and possibly cancer.

You can always pick up root vegetables in the most unpromising Cornish food shop because they are essential for home-made pasties and stews. I've singled out onions and potatoes for their own chapters but meanly limited myself to one favourite recipe each for swedes, carrots and parsnips.

BORSCHT WITH SOURED CREAM AND CHIVES
Serves 6–8

The first time I met Karl Weschke was when I was out walking on Clodgy Moor. I was Ben's new young wife and as he approached Ben told me he was an artist. While they caught up on gossip, I stood silent, not knowing anyone they were talking about. Jeremy LeGrice, another artist, was the main topic of conversation. I remember that quite clearly because it is such an unusual name. I thought Karl looked a lot like Picasso but his eyes were steely, bright blue, unlike Picasso's, which were limpid black. He wore nice clothes, I remember, beautiful cotton corduroy trousers and a French peasant jacket. The next time I met Karl was one bright summer day many years later. I was with Henry in the inevitable queue at Tregenza's, the 'posh' greengrocer in Penzance. This time Henry introduced me and I was a lot more sociable. Again I thought how like Picasso he looked and noticed his old-fashioned shopping basket, a proper wicker basket, worn and gnarled, the sort of basket that someone had once woven, probably from the local willow used to make lobster pots years ago. I think it was on the strength of that meeting that we decided to invite him to supper. Ben, Henry and I were all at the Fish Store together and we thought it would be good fun to round up a few other people too. Rose and Bo Hilton came and I think that was a weekend when my friend Tessa blew down from London for a short weekend, arriving one day and leaving the next.

The evening kicked off with crab bruschetta and some delicious dry white wine brought by Karl and his 'consort' Petronilla. The meal started with chilled, clear borscht, which I followed with sea bass and *sauce vierge* (see page 102), new potatoes and green beans. We had cheese and then gooseberry frangipane tart (page 370) with Jelbert's ice cream. That was the evening when it slipped out that Karl and Petronilla were about to get married. Everyone got very drunk and I missed my footing on the steep Fish Store steps, saying goodbye as the intendeds bickered, as they always did in a very affectionate way, about who would drive home. It was a spectacular backward fall which I miraculously corrected, landing on my feet without pain or injury. Several months later, we were invited back for supper in Karl's studio at their stupendously positioned house overlooking the sea at Cape Cornwall. Karl cooked his special stuffed potato dumplings, which we ate surrounded by huge canvases of disturbing paintings of figures and animals in claustrophobic landscapes awaiting his impending retrospective at Tate St Ives. The private view for his show was the last time Henry and I saw Karl. He died in February 2005.

This version of magenta-coloured borscht is served hot with the vegetables. For a clear, cold broth, sieve the soup, then refresh the colour with freshly grated raw beetroot. Sieve again and serve very cold with a glass of chilled vodka and black rye bread and butter.

1 large onion

2 large garlic cloves

2 tbsp olive oil

salt and pepper

2 large raw beetroot, approx. 350g each and
   2 small raw beetroot, approx. 150g each

350g new potatoes

3 medium carrots

2 free-range chicken legs or 4 large thighs or drumsticks

½ chicken stock cube

300ml beer

250g red cabbage

400g chopped canned tomatoes

2 tbsp balsamic or other good red wine vinegar

1–2 tsp sugar

soured cream and dill or chives to serve

Peel, halve and finely slice the onion. Peel the garlic and slice very thinly. Heat the oil in a large pan and stir in the onion and garlic. Add ½ a teaspoon of salt and cook for about 10 minutes until floppy and golden. Meanwhile, peel the large beetroot and chop into small dice. Do the same with the potatoes and carrots. Stir the diced beetroot and potato into the onion, cook for a couple of minutes, then add the carrot and chicken. Pour on the beer and 1 litre of cold water. Crumble the stock cube into the liquid. Bring the soup to the boil – this takes several minutes – and adjust the heat so that it simmers steadily when three-quarters covered with a lid. Cook for 15 minutes. Meanwhile, quarter and core the cabbage and slice as thinly as possible. Add cabbage, tomatoes, vinegar and 1 teaspoon of salt to the soup. Stir well, increase the heat and return to the boil. Adjust the heat and cover as before, and simmer for a further 15 minutes or until all the vegetables are tender. Taste the broth and adjust and balance the seasoning with salt, pepper, sugar and possibly a dash more vinegar. Grate the peeled beetroot directly into the soup to inject deep colour and fresh flavour. Cook for a further 5–10 minutes. Remove the chicken and (to make more of a meal of the soup) flake the meat off the bones into the soup (or garnish individual servings). Alternatively, chop the chicken, stir it with chopped dill and soured cream, make tiny pasties with thinly rolled puff pastry and serve these *piroshki* with the soup.

Serve the soup immediately or, better still, allow to sit, covered, for up to 30 minutes before serving with a blob of soured cream and a final garnish of snipped herbs.

BEETROOT AND SWEETCORN SOUP WITH OREGANO AND CHILLI
Serves 4–6

This soup looks like coloured jewels bobbing around in a magenta broth; a lovely autumn treat which is easy to make and hard to resist. The broth has a background snap of chilli and an enticingly aromatic aroma from oregano. Look out for Cretan oregano which has been dried on the stalk, imported by specialists Gaea. It has such an intense smell that it will waft you back to your last Greek holiday.

    3 corn on the cob
    1 onion
    2 large garlic cloves
    2 red bird's eye chillies
    1 tbsp olive oil
    salt and pepper
    1 yellow, orange or red pepper
    3 medium-sized raw beetroot
    2 tsp dried oregano

2 chicken or vegetable stock cubes

2 large plum tomatoes

1 small lemon or 2–3 tbsp wine vinegar

2 tbsp chopped flat-leaf parsley or coriander leaves

Rub away any silky strands clinging to the corn cobs, then stand one after the other on a work surface and run a sharp, heavy cook's knife down the cob, slicing off the kernels. Peel, halve and finely chop the onion. Crack the garlic with your fist, flake away the papery skin and finely chop. Trim and split the chillies, scrape away the seeds, slice into skinny strips and then into tiny dice. Heat the oil in a spacious, heavy-bottomed pan over a medium heat and stir in the onion, garlic and chilli. Season with salt and pepper, cover the pan and cook for 5 minutes. Meanwhile, quarter the pepper, discard stalk, white seeds and filament and chop into dice. Stir the pepper into the onion mixture, return the lid and cook for a further 5 minutes. Peel the beetroot with a potato peeler and cut into sugar-lump-size dice. Stir the beetroot and then the corn kernels into the onions together with the oregano. Dissolve the stock cubes in 1 litre of boiling water and pour into the vegetables. Bring the soup to the boil, reduce the heat slightly, partially cover the pan and simmer for 15 minutes or until the vegetables are tender. Pour boiling water over the tomatoes, count to 20, drain, remove the skin and dice the tomatoes. Add to the pan, taste and adjust the seasoning with salt, pepper and lemon juice or vinegar. Simmer for a couple of minutes, stir in the flat-leaf parsley or coriander and serve.

STEWED BEETROOT WITH LEMON TOMATOES

Serves 6

If you are stuck in a beetroot rut, this is *the* dish to try. The tomatoes end up a background slush, but together with lemon juice and zest they provide just the right acidity to counterbalance the sweetness of the beetroot. A background hint of chilli and cumin give the dish a subtle but interesting flavour. Serve it hot, warm or cold. It goes with everything from fish to chicken or pork, hard-boiled eggs and cheese. I also like it – cold – piled into curls of crisp lettuce with a dollop of minted yoghurt.

3 medium beetroot, approx. 700g in total

salt and pepper

1 small lemon

1 red onion

750g ripe tomatoes

2 tbsp vegetable oil

½ tsp cumin seeds

½ tsp dried red chilli flakes

Rinse the beetroot to remove any mud without scratching the skin. Place in a suitable saucepan, add 1 teaspoon of salt and cover generously with water. Bring to the boil, partially cover the pan and cook at a brisk simmer for 30 minutes. Drain and, when cool enough to handle, trim the beetroot and rub off the skin. Cut into dice the size of a sugar lump. Meanwhile, remove the wafer-thin zest from the lemon and shred finely. Peel, halve and finely slice the onion. Pour boiling water over the tomatoes, count to 20, drain, remove skin and core. Chop. Heat the oil in a medium-sized saucepan over a medium flame. Stir the cumin seeds and chilli flakes into the hot oil and then add the onion. Cook, stirring frequently, until the onion is tender but hardly coloured. Add the lemon zest, tomatoes and juice from the lemon to the pan. Season with salt and pepper and cook, uncovered, for 15 minutes or until the tomatoes are sloppy and the lemon zest soft.

Add the diced beetroot to the pan and cook, partially covered, for about 15 minutes until the beetroot is completely tender. Taste and adjust the seasoning.

HOT GRATED BEETROOT
Serves 4

Years ago, in my restaurant-reviewing days, I ate this simple but stunning way of preparing beetroot at the legendary Carved Angel (now a quite different place, owned by John Burton Race) on the waterfront at Dartmouth in Devon. If you ever see a copy of *The Carved Angel Cookery Book* by Joyce Molyneux with Sophie Grigson (published in 1990 and long out of print), snap it up. Joyce cooks like angel.

2 medium-sized raw beetroot
40g butter
red wine vinegar
salt and black pepper

Wash the beetroot and wrap in foil. Bake in a pre-heated oven, 400°F/200°C/gas mark 6, for about 45 minutes until tender to the point of a knife. Alternatively, boil in salted water for up to 1 hour until tender. Rub the skin from the root and grate into a saucepan with the butter and 2 teaspoons of vinegar. Season generously and reheat, adding extra vinegar if you think it necessary.

BRUNO LOUBET'S *BETTERAVES AIGRES*
Serves 4

In the early eighties a young Bordelais called Bruno Loubet was the chef at a modest restaurant in Parsons Green called Gastronome One. His menu, three different *prix-fixe* meals, was a novelty in itself. Even more unusual, for those times, was a French restaurant specializing in fish. Bruno used a lot of underrated seafood and is almost single-handedly responsible for making monkfish fashionable. He went on to work with Raymond Blanc at the same time as Marco Pierre White and earned a Michelin star for the Inn on the Park as head chef of its flag-ship restaurant, Four Seasons. It was there that he served jellied eels with a cauliflower mousse and caviar (this was the dish that impressed me so much that I took Elizabeth David to try it). This is Bruno's way with beetroot. It is very good with grilled mackerel.

600g raw medium-sized beetroot
3½ tbsp red wine vinegar
2 tsp roughly chopped fresh sage
5 tbsp water
2 garlic cloves
2 tbsp soured cream
½ tbsp chopped dill
salt and pepper

Pre-heat the oven to 400°F/200°C/gas mark 6.

Wash the beetroot and wrap tightly in a large, doubled sheet of foil with the vinegar, sage and water. Bake for about 45 minutes or until the beetroot are tender to the point of a sharp knife. Peel and finely chop the garlic. Unwrap the tender beets and rub away the skin. Cut into quarters. Toss with soured cream, garlic, dill and some salt and pepper. Serve immediately.

TURKISH BEETROOT AND YOGHURT SALAD WITH CORIANDER
Serves 6

Possibly my favourite way of cooking beetroot. It's great with barbecues and other salads and goes exceptionally well with tomatoes in any form and roasted red peppers. Good, too, with hummus.

   750g even-sized raw beetroot
   salt and pepper
   1 small lemon
   50g bunch coriander or flat-leaf parsley
   1 garlic clove
   300g Greek yoghurt
   1 tbsp olive oil

Wash the beetroot and cook in salted boiling water for between 30 and 60 minutes depending on their size. Drain when tender to the point of a knife and rub away the skin, trimming root and shoots.

Cut in chunky pieces directly into a serving bowl. Squeeze lemon juice over the beetroot and season with salt and pepper. Chop the coriander or parsley leaves and scatter over the seasoned beetroot. Crack the garlic with your fist, flake away the skin, chop finely and then sprinkle with a little salt. Use the flat of a knife to crush the garlic to a juicy paste. Stir the paste into the yoghurt. Spoon the yoghurt over the beetroot and garnish with a swirl of olive oil.

RUSSIAN SALAD WITH CHICKEN
Serves 2–4

Russian salad is one of the dishes that beetroot always brings to mind. Escoffier's original included lobster, lean ham, truffles and mushrooms along with the vegetables and mayonnaise dressing; beetroot *and caviar* was the garnish. This version uses chicken (a great sequel to the remains of a roast chicken) instead of lobster and the garnish is finely grated hard-boiled egg and freshly snipped chives. It looks marvellous with the skinny batons of beetroot arranged around the salad and tastes fresh and interesting enough to warrant a revival. Quantities given are sufficient for a starter for four healthy appetites – six if you're small eaters – and two main meal portions.

salt and pepper

50g fine green beans

50g frozen petits pois

1 carrot, approx. 100g

2 tbsp Hellmann's mayonnaise

1 tsp smooth Dijon mustard

1 tbsp lemon juice

3 medium-sized boiled new potatoes

1 large portion of roast chicken

1 tbsp capers

4 gherkins

1 large egg

1 medium-sized beetroot, freshly boiled

1 level tbsp freshly snipped chives

Put a large pan of salted water on to boil. Cut the beans in half and drop into the water. Boil for 1 minute and scoop out of the water. Add the peas and boil for 2 minutes. Add them to the beans. Scrape the carrots and cut into matchstick strips. Drop the carrots into the boiling water and boil for 2 minutes. Drain and reserve 1 tablespoon of the cooking water. Put the mayonnaise in a mixing bowl. Add the mustard, 1 teaspoon of lemon juice and the cooking water. Stir to mix, then add the beans, peas and carrots. Cut the potatoes into dice and the chicken into bite-size chunks and add them too, together with the lightly squeezed capers and sliced gherkins. Mix thoroughly. Boil the egg in a small pan of water for 9 minutes. Drain, crack all over and peel under cold running water. Pile the salad in a low mound on a platter. Cut the beetroot into strips, season with salt and pepper and toss with the remaining lemon juice. Arrange the beetroot around the salad. Use the second-smallest hole on the cheese grater to grate the egg over the top. Scatter with chives and serve.

ROAST BEETROOT RISOTTO WITH BEETROOT CRISPS
Serves 4–6

Dramatic and deliciously different; serve alone, either as an appetizer or main dish, or as an accompaniment to simply cooked fish. Beetroot crisps are an optional extra. They look very pretty and, like parsnip crisps – which, incidentally, are brilliant with roast grouse – the flavour and sweetness of the vegetable are intensified by the cooking process.

> 750g even-sized raw beetroot
> 4 tomatoes
> 1½ tbsp olive oil
> salt and pepper
> oil for deep frying
> 1 medium red onion
> 1 garlic clove
> 75g butter
> 400g arborio or carnaroli risotto rice
> large glass red wine
> 1 tbsp balsamic vinegar
> 1½ litres hot chicken stock or
>   2 chicken stock cubes dissolved in 1½ litres boiling water
> 150g clotted cream
> 2 lemons
> 1 tbsp snipped chives or chopped flat-leaf parsley

Pre-heat the oven to 400°F/200°C/gas mark 6.

If making beetroot crisps, set aside 2 medium or 1 large beetroot and wrap the others in a sheet of foil. Halve the tomatoes, poke out their seeds with your finger and lay out on the foil, cut side up. Season the cut surfaces with a little olive oil, salt and pepper. Put the beetroot on the top shelf, the tomatoes on the bottom. Remove the tomatoes after 30 minutes and cook the beetroot until tender to the point of a knife.

Trim the beetroot, rub off the skin and coarsely chop. Scrape the tomatoes off their skins.

Meanwhile, peel the reserved beetroot, slice wafer-thin, as if making crisps (you are!) and deep-fry in hot oil for about 30 seconds until crisp. Drain the beetroot crisps on kitchen towels and season lightly with salt.

Peel and finely chop the onion and garlic. Heat 50g of the butter and 1 tablespoon of olive oil in a spacious wide-based pan over a medium heat. Stir in the onion and garlic and cook until tender without letting it colour. Stir in the unwashed rice, cook for about 30 seconds and then add the wine and balsamic vinegar. Let it bubble up into the rice until absorbed. Stir in the tomato and beetroot, season with salt and pepper, then add a ladleful of hot stock, stirring constantly, cooking until absorbed into the rice before adding another ladleful. Continue thus: the risotto is done when the rice grains are tender and creamy on the outside yet still have a bite in the middle. Stir in the remaining butter and half the cream, cover and leave for 5 minutes. Adjust the seasoning with salt and lemon juice, stir in the remaining cream and serve with a garnish of chives or parsley and a lemon wedge.

CORNISH PASTY
Serves 4

There are two places to buy pasties in Mousehole, Pam's Pantry and the general store opposite the harbour, but plenty of people make their own. For something that involves so few ingredients, it is amazing how many 'correct' recipes there are. Pasties were invented as a way for miners to take their lunch to work. The thick seam that runs over the top of their midday meal was originally the handle – and as such, chucked away – and each man had his initials written with scraps of pastry in the corner of the pasty. Half was filled with beef and vegetables, the other half, for pudding, with fruit.

Aficionados reckon it is made with skirt or chuck beef, potatoes, swede and onion, and that's it. Whether the ingredients are diced or sliced is also debatable but everyone agrees that they must go in raw and that seasoning is restricted to salt and pepper; preferably a mixture of black (for flavour) and white (for pungency). The pastry is traditionally shortcrust and made with lard. I often cheat and use ready-rolled puff pastry, which makes light and flaky pasties.

for the pastry:
350g block lard
450g strong plain flour
pinch of salt
ice cold water to mix

for the filling:
400g flank, skirt or chuck beef, trimmed and diced
200g onion
200g swede
600g floury potatoes
salt and black and white pepper
a little water
butter
egg wash
salt and black and white pepper

Place the piece of lard in its wrapper in the freezer and leave for about an hour until hard.

Sift the flour and salt into a mixing bowl. Remove the lard from the freezer, peel back the paper, dip into the flour and grate it into the bowl, dipping back into the flour every now and again to make the grating easier. Mix the grated lard evenly into the flour by making sweeping scoops with a palette knife until it resembles heavy breadcrumbs. Stir in 1 tablespoon of water at a time until the dough clings together, then form it into a ball. Place the dough in a polythene bag and chill in the fridge for 30 minutes.

Pre-heat the oven to 400°F/200°C/gas mark 6. Trim the beef and cut into small dice. Keeping separate piles, peel and coarsely chop the onion and peel and dice the swede and potatoes. Roll out the pastry and cut out four circles about the size of a small dinner plate. Sprinkle onion and swede across the centre of the pasty in an oval shape, leaving a 2cm border at each end. Season with salt and pepper. Cover with the meat and then with half the potato. Season again and then add the remainder of the potato.

Moisten half the pastry border with a little water, bring up each side of the circle of pastry to enclose the filling, and press together to form a ridge. Crimp with your fingers to form what looks like the backbone of a stegosaurus.

Butter a flat baking sheet and sprinkle with water. Transfer the pasties to the baking sheet, prick them in a few places on either side of the seam with a fork and paint all over with egg wash. Use pastry trimmings to cut out initials and press on the pasties, covering with egg wash. Bake for 15 minutes, then lower the temperature to 300°F/150°C/gas mark 2 and cook for a further 30–40 minutes.

Serve wrapped in a paper napkin: a *paasty* is *never* eaten with a knife and fork.

CARROT AND CUMIN SOUP WITH COCONUT MILK
Serves 4–6

A surprisingly good soup with complex, intriguing flavours which are all at once creamy, spicy and citrus fresh.

> 1 medium onion
> 2 garlic cloves
> 1 small red chilli
> 1 unwaxed lemon
> 8 medium carrots
> 2 medium tomatoes
> 1 tbsp vegetable oil
> ½ tsp cumin seeds
> salt and black pepper
> 200ml coconut cream or milk
> 2 chicken stock cubes dissolved in 1 ½ litres boiling water
> 1 tbsp finely chopped coriander

Peel and finely chop the onion and garlic. Trim and split the chilli, scrape away the seeds and finely chop. Remove the zest from half the lemon. Peel, trim and chop the carrots. Pour boiling water over the tomatoes, count to 20, drain, remove the skin and chop.

Heat the oil in a spacious, heavy-bottomed pan and stir in the onion, garlic and chilli. Cook, stirring a few times, for about 5 minutes, then add the cumin. Stir-fry for 30 seconds and add the carrot and lemon zest. Season with ½ a teaspoon of salt and several grinds of pepper, cover the pan and cook for 5 minutes. Stir in the tomato and then add the stock. Bring to the boil, stir thoroughly, reduce the heat, partially cover the pan and cook for 15–20 minutes until the carrots are tender. Liquidize in batches and pour through a sieve into a clean pan, scraping under the sieve so nothing is wasted. Add the coconut cream or milk, reheat and adjust the seasoning with salt and pepper.

Serve with a generous squeeze of lemon and a coriander garnish.

CURRIED PARSNIP SOUP WITH BACON *CROÛTONS*
Serves 6

I once served this soup to a sophisticated Parisian and asked him what he thought it was made of. Artichoke, he wondered, or potato and carrot? The guessing game went on until he'd run out of vegetables. My triumphant revelation of parsnip left my friend dumbfounded. In France, he explained, parsnips are cattle feed and rarely turn up on the dinner table. Apart from this sublime soup, what a lot of treats the French are missing. I'd hate to forgo crusty roast parsnips (peel and parboil, quarter, then roast in olive oil, turning once during cooking), parsnip mash (superb with rabbit) and parsnip game chips ('sliced' with a potato peeler and deep-fried).

It turns out that as well as tasting good, parsnips have some interesting properties. A high glycaemic index, higher than chocolate and almost as high as glucose, means that they boost energy faster than a quick sugar fix. Like potatoes, which they resemble, parsnips are virtually fat-free and very low in calories.

The soup is thick and creamy with a background hint of curry that is perceptibly lifted by lemon zest and juice. The fresh citric zing is reinforced with a garnish of crème fraîche and complemented by scraps of crisp smoked bacon and chives. Serve with crusty bread and butter for a really satisfying soup supper.

1 tbsp vegetable oil

150g smoked bacon lardons or chopped rashers streaky bacon

2 medium onions

2 big garlic cloves

750g parsnips

1 small unwaxed lemon

25g butter

1 tbsp curry powder

2 chicken stock cubes dissolved in 1 ½ litres water

salt and pepper

150ml crème fraîche

small bunch chives

Heat the oil in a spacious, heavy-bottomed pan and add the bacon. Cook, stirring a couple of times, for about 5 minutes until the fat is very crisp. Scoop out of the pan on to absorbent kitchen paper to drain.

Meanwhile, peel, halve and chop the onions. Peel and chop the garlic. Peel the parsnips, quarter lengthways and chop. Remove the zest in wafer-thin pieces from the lemon. Add the butter to the pan and, when melted, stir in the onion, garlic and lemon. Cook gently, stirring a couple of times, for a few minutes and then stir in the parsnips. Cover the pan and cook for 5 minutes, stir again and cook for a further 5 minutes. Add the curry powder to the vegetables, stirring until it has disappeared into the juices, and cook for a couple of minutes. Add the stock, bring to the boil, partially cover the pan and cook at a steady simmer for 15–20 minutes until the parsnips are tender. Liquidize in batches, return to the pan and adjust the seasoning with salt, pepper and lemon juice. If the soup seems too thick, add a little water. Serve with a swirl of cream or crème fraîche, the bacon croutons and a sprinkling of freshly snipped chives.

Beans, Peas and Sweetcorn

Runner beans grow like wildfire in the gardens and vegetable patches of Mousehole. There's one particular allotment on the sea-facing slope just before you come into the village which always has an especially fine show. The vines look so pretty climbing up their wigwam of supports with their bright red flowers standing out against the fresh, green leaves. Runners are so popular that it's often possible to buy them in the village shop. We can't get enough runner beans. I slice them in the old-fashioned way, thinly and on the slant. I often use them in salads and ring the changes by slicing them down the length of the bean so they look like green spaghetti. After cooking, they can be pushed into pretty mounds or into a nest for crab in a herbed mayonnaise or poached monkfish in mayonnaise which has been coloured pink with tomato ketchup and Tabasco.

Broad beans grow from pretty white flowers but are notoriously difficult to cultivate because blackfly love them so much. Fortunately, Royden is very successful with them and has passed on his excesses on many occasions. Not everyone likes the mealy texture and strong flavour of broad beans and they aren't a commercially successful crop because their furry-lined pods are heavy and often don't hold many beans. Consequently they seem expensive for what you get. Young, tender bean pods can be eaten whole, but if they are old and tough, it is wise to remove the crescent attached to the bean and even their outer skin. This skin cooks up like a rubbery sheath and peels away easily. Inside, the beans are a vivid bright green.

Fresh garden peas are increasingly a luxury. Fewer people grow peas these days, although Mousehole gardens are full of scented sweet peas and their pretty pastel-coloured flowers. The reality is that frozen petits pois have spoilt us for the real thing.

Corn on the cob or sweetcorn is a common crop around these parts of the south-west peninsula and gluts, happily, are inevitable. We never tire of boiling them for about 10 minutes and biting the corn off the cobs with a slathering of butter and plenty of freshly ground black pepper. They are possibly even better cooked in their husks on the barbecue.

BEAN AND SHALLOT SALAD WITH LYONNAISE VINAIGRETTE
Serves 6–8

Unlike most salads, this one actually improves if left to sit for an hour or so. It is particularly good with terrine, either as a relish or served more generously for a main course with baked potatoes. I love the simplicity of this salad but it is also very good with diced (peeled and seeded) tomatoes stirred in just before serving.

There will be more vinaigrette than required for the recipe but as it's a useful all-rounder it will soon be used up. Store in a screw-top jar in the fridge.

4 shallots
2 tbsp Hellmann's mayonnaise
1kg green beans
salt and pepper

for the Lyonnaise vinaigrette:
pinch of caster sugar
generous pinch of salt
2 tbsp red wine vinegar
1 generous tbsp smooth Dijon mustard
black pepper
approx. 250ml vegetable oil
1 tbsp cold water

First make the vinaigrette. Stir the sugar and salt into the vinegar until dissolved and then pour into the bowl of a food processor with the mustard, garlic, if using, and several grinds of black pepper. Blitz at high speed and add the oil in a gradual stream, followed by the water, to give the vinaigrette a pale, glossy emulsion and a creamy texture.

Peel, halve and finely chop the shallots. Place the mayonnaise in a salad bowl, gradually beat in about a cupful of vinaigrette into the mayo with a wooden spoon to make a thick, creamy dressing. Stir in the shallots and leave to sit for at least 15 minutes

Top and tail the beans. I usually cut them in half because it seems to make them go further and they are easier to eat. Cook the beans in 3 or 4 batches in plenty of boiling salted water for a couple of minutes (from boiling) until slightly undercooked. Scoop the beans out of the pan and into a sink of cold water to arrest cooking. Drain and pat dry.

Add the beans to the salad bowl, stir thoroughly and stir again just before serving.

BROAD BEANS IN THEIR OWN SAUCE
Serves 4

Broad beans and gooseberries have a lot in common. Both enjoy an old-fashioned charm and a short season and both have always been popular with people who grow their own food but not with market gardeners. It would be a pity to miss out on this delicious way of cooking broad beans in a creamy sauce with a little ham. Lovely with fish and chicken.

> 400g shelled broad beans or young beans in their pods
> salt and pepper
> 25g butter
> ½ tbsp flour
> 100ml cooking water
> 200ml milk
> squeeze of lemon juice
> 2 tbsp chopped flat-leaf parsley
> 2 slices good ham (optional)
> nutmeg, optional

If the beans are young and tender, include a section of the pod around some of them. Drop the beans into boiling salted water. Return to boil and cook for 1 minute. Drain, reserving 100ml water. Melt the butter in a medium–small saucepan and stir in the flour until smooth. Add the reserved cooking water and the milk. Bring the sauce to the boil whilst constantly stirring to make a smooth sauce. If it turns lumpy, give the sauce a good beating with a whisk. Reduce the heat immediately. Season with salt and pepper and cook at a gentle simmer for 6 or 7 minutes to make a thick and smooth sauce.

If the beans are big and old, remove the now wrinkly, rubbery covers to reveal bright green beans. Stir the beans into the sauce. Add a squeeze of lemon juice and the parsley. Use scissors to chop the ham directly into the pan. Stir well to separate the pieces of ham and warm through the beans. Taste the sauce and adjust the seasoning, adding a little nutmeg if liked.

BROAD BEAN RISOTTO
Serves 4–6

This way of making risotto takes all the stress and labouring over a hot stove out of the dish. It is a strictly unethical recipe but ends up as good, if not better, than many restaurant risottos I've been served. The rice should be soft and creamy on the outside with a slight bite on the inside. If it isn't, just add a little more hot water and continue simmering for a few more minutes before you add the cream. This recipe, incidentally, works brilliantly with fresh or frozen peas. If you do use peas, pre-cook them but don't add them until the risotto is cooked, otherwise they will dull in colour and turn very sweet.

> 1 litre hot chicken stock or 2 chicken stock cubes
> 400g shelled broad beans
> 125g bunch of spring onions
> 50g butter
> 300g arborio risotto rice
> glass of white wine
> salt and pepper
> 150g thick cream
> handful of mint leaves
> freshly grated Parmesan to serve

Put the kettle on to boil, measure off 1 litre of boiling water into a saucepan and dissolve the stock cubes into it, if using. Bring the liquid back to the boil and add the broad beans. Boil for 2 minutes, then scoop the beans into a colander to drain without wasting any stock. Leave the beans to cool slightly, remove the stock from the heat and cover the pan. Trim and finely slice the spring onions, including as much green as possible. Melt the butter in a medium-sized, heavy-bottomed pan with a tight-fitting lid and cook the onions gently for 2–3 minutes until wilted and tender. Stir the rice into the buttery onions and cook, stirring constantly, for a further 2 minutes until the rice is glistening. Add the wine and cook, stirring frequently, until absorbed by the rice. Season with salt and pepper. Remove from the heat. Remove the rubbery and wrinkled skins from the cooled beans. Set aside about one-third of the beans and stir the rest into the rice. Now pour all the stock into the rice. Bring the rice liquid to the boil, stir and, when there are bubbles all over the surface, turn off the heat and clamp on the lid. Leave untouched for 30 minutes. Cook for a further 10 minutes if the rice is still chalky. Remove the lid, add the cream and reserved beans. Stir whilst gently reheating. Shred the mint, stir it into the risotto and serve with grated Parmesan.

PEA SOUP WITH BACON
Serves 6

This is one of the most useful recipes ever. It is such a simple soup and one that you can vary and jazz up with minimal trouble. And so quick. I often add a little mint sauce or a handful of fresh mint, but it's not really necessary. Other soft herbs like basil, chervil and chives make it quite different and it's very good with the South-east Asian combination of garlic, chilli and coriander.

    4 slices rindless streaky bacon
    1 leek or 2 bunches of spring onions
    1 small lemon
    50g butter
    salt and pepper
    750g frozen peas
    1 chicken stock cube

Slice across the rashers of bacon to make chunky, short ribbons. Place in a medium-sized heavy-bottomed pan and cook, gently at first, increasing the heat as the fat runs, until very crisp. Scoop from the pan and set aside. Meanwhile, trim the dark-green end of the leek and quarter it lengthways, stopping just short of the root. Wash under cold water, hold the leek together and slice across to make tiny scraps. If using spring onions, trim and finely slice. Grate the zest from the lemon or remove in small scraps with a potato peeler. Add the butter to the pan and stir in the leeks or spring onions and lemon zest. Season with salt and pepper, cover the pan and cook over a medium-low heat for 5 or 6 minutes until soft. Fill the kettle and boil. Measure off 1½ litres water. Add the stock granules or cube and stir to dissolve. Add the stock to the onions, return to the boil and add the peas. Boil for 2 minutes. Liquidize in batches and pour into a clean pan. Reheat and adjust the seasoning with salt and lemon juice. Serve with a garnish of bacon.

MINTED PEA PURÉE
Serves 6–8

A deliciously useful complement to simply cooked fish. Tweak the flavours with other herbs and try adding bacon or ham with the onion. It looks very pretty with white fish and turns peas into a quick, posh sauce. Excellent with fish fingers made by dipping pieces of fish fillet first in flour, then in beaten egg and then in breadcrumbs.

> 1 large shallot or medium onion
> 25g butter
> 400g frozen peas
> about 20 mint leaves
> salt and pepper
> 2 tbsp clotted or thick cream

Trim, peel and finely chop the shallot. Soften gently in the butter. Add the peas, 150ml water and the mint. Season and cook for about 10 minutes until the peas are tender. Add the cream and blitz to make a smooth purée, adding a little extra water or cream if it seems too stiff.

PEA GUACAMOLE WITH PARMESAN BRUSCHETTA
For 20 snack servings

Pea guacamole is a great party snack. It's quick to make and good at any time of the year. Apart from being delicious on toast (bruschetta), it makes a terrific dip with tortilla chips or strips of toasted pitta bread.

> 2 bunches of spring onions
> 2 tbsp olive oil
> 7-slice pack of Speck, Parma or Serrano ham
>   or 5 tomatoes

big handful of fresh mint leaves (about 75g)

750g frozen petits pois

salt and black pepper

1 lemon

200g feta cheese (optional)

for the bruschetta:

30 slices country-style bread

2 large garlic cloves

approx. 100ml olive oil

approx. 30g freshly grated Parmesan

Trim the spring onions and finely slice. Heat the olive oil in a large saucepan over a medium heat and add the spring onions. Using scissors, snip two slices of ham into shreds directly into the onions, together with 2 tablespoons of chopped mint leaves. Cook for about 3 minutes, stirring often, until the onion is tender. Add the peas, 350ml cold water and 1 heaped teaspoon of salt. Bring to the boil, then reduce the heat so the peas simmer gently for about 5 minutes until just tender. Tip the peas into a colander placed over a bowl to catch the liquid.

Place two-thirds of the peas in the bowl of a food processor/blender and pour in the liquid. Add the remaining mint leaves, the lemon juice and several grinds of black pepper. Blitz briefly to make a chunky cohesive mixture. Use a potato masher to crush the reserved peas. Tip both sets of peas into a bowl. Stir well, taste and adjust the seasoning with salt and pepper. Snip the remaining ham into little pieces over the peas and stir. If including feta, crumble it over the top and stir that in too. If using tomatoes, cover them with boiling water, count to 20, drain and remove the skin. Cut them in half, scrape away the seeds, chop them quite finely and stir into the peas. Leave to cool.

To make the bruschetta, toast the bread then rub one side with garlic and dribble a little olive oil over the top. Dust each bruschetta with Parmesan. Cut into 2 or 3 pieces and pile with a generous scoop of guacamole.

PETITS POIS À LA FRANÇAISE

Serves 6

The French way of eating peas, traditionally served with a spoon and eaten as a course on its own. Both peas and lettuce dull in colour and the flavour is purposely sweet. Lovely with fish.

> 16 silverskin or other small onions
> 100g butter
> 750g frozen petits pois
> 1 tsp salt and ½ tsp black pepper
> 1 tsp white sugar
> 3 Little Gem lettuce hearts
> small bunch flat-leaf parsley

Place the onions in a bowl and cover with boiling water. Leave for a couple of minutes, drain, trim and peel. Cut a shallow cross in both ends of the onions to stop them collapsing. Bring 100ml salted water to the boil, drop in the onions, cover and boil for 5 minutes. Drain. Meanwhile, melt 75g butter with 150ml water in a wide-bottomed pan, then stir in the frozen petits pois. Cook, tossing the peas constantly for a couple of minutes until they have defrosted and the butter that has solidified around them has melted. Add the salt, black pepper and sugar. Quarter the lettuce hearts lengthways, rinse under cold running water, shake dry, then shred finely across the quarters. Stir the lettuce and onions into the peas. Set aside a couple of sprigs of parsley and bundle up the rest with cotton or string and bury in the peas. Simmer uncovered for about 10 minutes until peas, onion and lettuce are thoroughly cooked. Discard the parsley bundle, stir in the remaining butter and, when melted, adjust the seasoning with salt and pepper. Chop the remaining parsley, stir into the peas and serve immediately.

SWEETCORN CHOWDER

Serves 4

Sweetcorn comes to life with a burst of chilli, garlic, lemon zest and fresh coriander leaves. A favourite quick soup.

1 onion, approx. 200g

2 tbsp olive oil

2 garlic cloves

1 small unwaxed lemon

2 small red chillies

1 red pepper

4 corn on the cob

salt and pepper

2 chicken stock cubes

handful of coriander leaves

Peel, halve and finely chop the onion. Heat the oil in a 2 litre capacity heavy-bottomed pan and stir in the onion. Cook, stirring occasionally, over a medium heat for 5 minutes while you prepare the seasoning. Trim and peel the garlic and slice into super-thin rounds. Using a pota- to peeler, remove the zest from half the lemon in paper-thin scraps. Trim and split the chillies. Scrape away the seeds, slice into skinny strips and then into tiny scraps. Wash your hands immediately before you forget and rub your eye or another sensitive part of your body with lethal chilli juices. Stir garlic, lemon zest and chilli into the onions. Quarter the pepper, discard the stalk, seeds and white filament, then cut into small chunks. Stir the pepper into the onions. Adjust the heat so that everything cooks without burning. Trim the corn on the cob and stand on the flat end. Using a sharp knife, slice down the cobs to remove the kernels. Stir the corn into the onion mixture. Season gener- ously with salt and pepper. Dissolve the stock cubes in 1 litre of boiling water and add to the pan. Bring the liquid to the boil, reduce the heat immediately, partially cover the pan and cook for about 15 minutes until everything is tender. Coarsely chop the coriander leaves and stir into the soup. Taste and adjust the seasoning with salt, pepper and lemon juice.

SWEETCORN FRITTERS
Serves 4

Sweetcorn fritters are so good, it's difficult to stop people eating them straight from the pan. They go with everything from sausages and simply cooked chicken or fish to roast tomatoes and cauliflower cheese. I've even eaten them with *foie gras* (at Kensington Place).

> 3 corn on the cob
> 50g flour
> 2 eggs
> 150ml milk
> handful of coriander leaves and 1 small red chilli,
>   or 2 slices of good ham and 25g watercress leaves
> salt and black pepper
> vegetable oil for frying

Trim the corn on the cob and stand on the flat end. Using a sharp knife, slice down the cobs to remove the kernels. Drop the kernels into boiling water, boil for 10 minutes and drain.

Sift the flour into a mixing bowl. Add the egg yolks, breaking the whites into a separate mixing bowl or the bowl of a blender with a whisk attachment. Use a wooden spoon to stir the egg yolks into the flour, gradually adding the milk. Replace the spoon with a whisk and whisk vigorously until the batter is smooth and has the consistency of pouring cream. If including coriander and chilli, coarsely chop the coriander leaves. Split the chilli, scrape away the seeds and remove the stalk. Slice into skinny strips, then cut across the strips to make tiny dice. If using ham and watercress, dice the ham quite small and finely chop the watercress. Stir sweetcorn, coriander and chilli or ham and watercress into the batter. Add ½ a teaspoon of salt and a generous seasoning of pepper. Whisk the egg whites until they hold firm but not stiff peaks. Fold into the batter until amalgamated. Heat a frying pan over a medium heat, swirl a little oil round the pan and drop spoonfuls of batter into the pan. Don't crowd the pan; you should be able to fit about 3 big fritters and 5 or 6 small ones. Cook for 2–3 minutes until you see little bubbles appearing in the fritters and when you lift an edge you can see that the bottom is brown and the fritter is beginning to set. Using a fish slice or blunt knife, quickly flip the fritter over and cook for a further 1–2 minutes. Eat immediately or keep warm in a single layer in a very low oven.

Tomatoes

Some of the tastiest tomatoes I've eaten were grown in Cornwall. The mild climate and prematurely hot, sunny weather – Easter is often more like summer than August – bring the tomatoes on early. Few houses have much of a garden in Mousehole but it's common to see potted tomato plants struggling for life in the most unpromising positions. The yield, when it comes, is always amazingly good, producing deep, dark red tomatoes with an intense sweet flavour. It's thought that the combination of sun and sea spray has something to do with it.

Sometimes people sell their excess tomatoes bagged up on the doorstep with an honesty box and others supply the general store, along with home-grown runner beans and watery marrows that nobody wants. On the roads out of the village, particularly up Raginnis Hill and towards Land's End, you'll see signs for just-picked tomatoes, lettuces and cucumbers. They are always worth buying.

SLOW-ROAST TOMATOES

I tend to make a tray or two of these at a time because they are so delicious and so useful. The intense tomato flavour is wonderful with soft-boiled or poached eggs, but they are also the perfect standby for things on toast. They particularly suit bruschetta-style compilations with tapenade or pesto, Parma ham and mozzarella or goat's cheese, which are just the ticket for serving with early evening drinks.

I make them into a roast tomato salad with an olive oil and balsamic vinegar dressing. I add them to mixed salads and layer them up with other grilled Mediterranean vegetables such as red peppers, aubergines and courgettes. They go extremely well with cauliflower cheese and leek or spinach gratin. They're great, too, with fish pie. Best of all, perhaps, is when they're folded into hot pasta. In fact, if you have some of these in the fridge you are never far from a delicious meal. They can be puréed, skin and all, to make instant sauces which will liven up a potentially dull supper of poached chicken or boiled cauliflower. They are excellent in sandwiches but come into their own with puff pastry. Try making a roast-tomato pizza tart, for example, by baking a thin circle of puff pastry, then spreading it with pesto and topping it with roast tomatoes.

I ring the changes whenever I make these slow-roast tomatoes. Sometimes I season the unpeeled tomato halves with salt, pepper and a little sugar, then add a dribble of olive oil. Other times, I add a few drops of balsamic vinegar too. I quite often lay branches of thyme or rosemary over the tomatoes. This has a surprisingly powerful effect on the final result. Any medium-sized tomato can be prepared like this but the most successful are plum (Roma) tomatoes or another dense-fleshed variety. It is a good way of adding interest to and intensifying the flavour of dull supermarket tomatoes. The juices should not be wasted.

10 medium tomatoes
3 tbsp olive oil
salt and pepper
1 tsp caster sugar
small bunch thyme or rosemary, optional

Pre-heat the oven to 300°F/150°C/gas mark 2. Halve the tomatoes, cutting through the core if using plum tomatoes and through the circumference if using round tomatoes. Spread a baking sheet with foil and smear it lightly with oil. Lay the tomato halves out, cut-side up, on the foil. Sprinkle the tomatoes with salt, pepper and caster sugar, then dribble with a little olive oil; just a few drops for each tomato.

If you wish to flavour the tomatoes with thyme (or another herb), either sprinkle the herbs over the top or – and this way avoids the possibility of burnt and thus bitter herbs – lay the thyme twigs across the tomatoes. Cook in the oven for at least an hour, probably two, until the tomatoes have softened and collapsed, and the surfaces are lightly caramelized. You want them completely soft but moist and juicy and not the least bit dry. Remove from the oven and leave to cool before trying to lift them.

The tomatoes will keep for a couple of days if they are covered with clingfilm and kept in the fridge. Alternatively, pile them into a glass jar and cover completely with olive oil. They will keep longer, in the fridge, but I find that they disappear into sandwiches, salads, etc., before they have a chance to go off. The oil will taste terrific.

ROAST TOMATO SOUP WITH SAFFRON AND HONEY
Serves 6

This is such an easy soup to make and tastes slightly different each time, depending on the quality and ripeness of the tomatoes. The slower the tomatoes are cooked, the more intense the flavour. Seasoning tomatoes with saffron and honey is a Moroccan idea and gives this soup a subtly exotic flavour which is balanced with creamy roast garlic and caramelized roast onions, the whole underpinned with a smidgen of Tabasco.

It's the perfect soup to make with a glut of overripe tomatoes. Crusty bread is good with this, but garlic bread or a big pile of bruschetta is even better.

    2kg medium-sized tomatoes
    olive oil
    salt and black pepper
    3 medium onions
    3 big garlic cloves
    2 heaped tsp honey
    6 drips Tabasco
    1 Knorr or Just Bouillon chicken stock cube
    800ml boiling water
    generous pinch saffron stamens

Pre-heat the oven to 300°F/150°C/gas mark 2. Halve the tomatoes round their middles and lay out, cut-side uppermost, on a large baking sheet covered with tinfoil smeared with olive oil. Sprinkle the tomatoes with salt and pepper, then dribble with a little olive oil; just a few drops for each tomato. Halve the onions and arrange them, cut-side down, on a second, smaller baking sheet also lined with tinfoil smeared with olive oil. Smack the garlic cloves with your fist and place them in the middle of the tray of onions. Dribble everything with a little olive oil.

Place both trays in the oven and check after an hour to see if the onions and garlic are tender. Continue cooking the tomatoes until they are meltingly soft. Leave to cool.

Discard the onion skin and place the flesh in the bowl of a food processor. Squeeze the garlic out of its skin directly into the bowl. Slip the tomatoes out of their skins and tip tomatoes and juices into the food processor bowl. Blitz to make a thick, smooth purée. Pass through a sieve into a heavy-bottomed saucepan, scraping under the sieve so nothing is wasted. Add the honey and Tabasco. Dissolve the stock cube in the boiling water and add the saffron stamens. Leave for a minute or two for the saffron to soften and leach its colour before adding to the soup.

Bring the soup gently to the boil whilst stirring to dissolve the honey and disperse the saffron. Simmer gently for several minutes before tasting. Adjust the seasoning with salt, pepper and a little more honey if you think it needs it. Serve immediately or reheat later.

GAZPACHO WITH ALL THE TRIMMINGS
Serves 6–8

Gazpacho, my Cypriot greengrocer in London once told me, means left-overs. Mr Adamou is probably right because this group of chilled, bread-based, olive oil-enriched, usually cold, Spanish soups is made with stale bread. *Gazpacho Andaluz* is the most famous and is often called the salad soup because that's exactly what it is, even down to the vinaigrette and the bread.

Gazpacho is a rough-and-ready peasant soup and the super-smooth, no pips, silky version we've become used to owes much to the food processor. We love it with a full complement of diced ingredients to add when it's served. What you choose is up to you. Either echo the soup, as I've done here, with more cucumber, tomato, onion, etc., or inject protein with white crab meat or a few quickly fried scallops. Diced avocado seasoned with lemon or lime juice is also delicious. Gazpacho is surprisingly satisfying – ideal, in fact, before grilled fish and fresh fruit – but if you want to go native, try serving it with Catalan tomato bread. This is a bit like bruschetta, but instead of rubbing the toast with garlic a ripe tomato is squashed against the toast and rubbed until all that's left is the tomato skin. Splash with olive oil, season with salt and pepper and enjoy.

When really ripe tomatoes aren't available, a very good but sweeter and less complex gazpacho can be made with cherry tomatoes.

4 thick slices white bread without crusts, approx. 150g

3 big garlic cloves

1 cucumber

1 red chilli

2 red peppers, preferably the pointed 'extra-sweet' type

1 red onion

1kg very ripe tomatoes or cherry tomatoes, or half and half

2 tbsp sherry or wine vinegar

300ml iced water

about 20 mint leaves

100ml best olive oil plus 2 tbsp extra

salt and pepper

3 plum or vine tomatoes

squeeze of lemon juice

Tabasco

Tear the bread into pieces. Place it and the peeled garlic in the bowl of a food processor and blitz to make fine breadcrumbs. Meanwhile, peel the cucumber. Halve it horizontally and use a teaspoon to scrape out the seeds and their watery pulp. Roughly chop one half. Trim and split the chilli. Scrape out the seeds. Set aside half of one red pepper and chop the rest, discarding the seeds and white filament. Peel and halve the onion. Coarsely chop one half and add to the breadcrumbs together with the chopped cucumber, chilli and chopped red pepper. Remove the stalks from the tomatoes. Roughly chop regular tomatoes, leave cherry tomatoes whole.

Add the ripe tomatoes to the food processor bowl together with the vinegar, water, most of the mint, 100ml olive oil, $1/2$ a teaspoon of salt and a generous seasoning of black pepper. Blitz for several minutes until liquidized.

Meanwhile prepare the garnishes. Keeping separate piles, finely dice the remaining cucumber and red pepper and finely chop the remaining red onion. Quarter the plum or vine tomatoes, discard the seeds and finely chop.

Taste the gazpacho and adjust the seasoning with salt, pepper, lemon juice and Tabasco. If you think the soup needs it – it makes it very creamy – whisk in the extra olive oil. Transfer to a chilled serving bowl (for super-smooth results, pass through a sieve, pressing down to extract all the juices) and decorate with a swirl of olive oil. Serve with the garnishes in small bowls, adding the remaining mint to the tomato.

CLASSIC TOMATO SALAD WITH TWO DRESSINGS
Serves 4

I don't usually follow a recipe when I make tomato salad. How I make it depends on the tomatoes, their shape and ripeness and what the salad is to accompany. If the tomatoes are knobbly, I usually cut them into wedges; if they are smooth and perfect, I slice them. My quick dressing for really ripe tomatoes is a dribble of balsamic vinegar and a splash of decent olive oil with a crumble of Maldon sea salt and a couple of twists of pepper. Sometimes I might add finely sliced spring onion or red onion with basil or flat-leaf parsley. Loads of chopped coriander goes well with tomatoes and so does mint or chives and new-season garlic.

4 large, ripe tomatoes

for the Italian dressing:
3 tbsp best olive oil
1 tbsp balsamic vinegar
salt and black pepper
basil leaves

for the cream dressing:
1 tbsp red wine vinegar
salt and pepper
150ml double cream
a few shakes of Tabasco (optional)
1 tbsp freshly snipped chives or a few finely sliced spring onions

Slice the tomatoes and lay out in a single layer on a large plate.

For the Italian dressing, dribble the olive oil into the balsamic vinegar while whisking continuously. Spoon the dressing over the tomatoes. Season with salt and pepper and snip the basil over the top.

For the cream dressing, whisk together the vinegar and seasoning, then pour in the cream, continuing to whisk until frothy and slightly thickened (the vinegar will naturally help this to happen anyway). Add the Tabasco and carefully spoon over the tomatoes. Sprinkle with the chives or spring onions and allow to sit for 20 minutes or so before serving.

SALADE ALGÉRIENNE
Serves 4

The closest I've ever been to Algeria was when I was in my early twenties, when I worked on an arts festival on the north-west coast of Tunisia at a place called Tabarka. The visit – I went three or four times and stayed for several weeks during the festival – was a real eye-opener as far as food was concerned. One of my most vivid memories is the taste of the wonky-looking tomatoes that we ate every day in the vibrantly flavoured salads that followed the *mechoui* (spit-roasted lamb) and barbecued fish.

There are very few references to Algerian, or, come to that, Tunisian, food in my vast collection of cookbooks. There is, however, a sizeable chapter on so-called *pied-noir* cuisine in David Burton's *French Colonial Cookery*, published by Faber. He calls *pied-noir* cooking, which features in Algeria and Tunisia, the lost cuisine of the European settlers in French North Africa and I definitely came across it in Tabarka. This salad reminds me of *salade niçoise* and Caesar salad but isn't faithful to either. I've added my own contribution of watercress, which, it seems to me, goes very well with ripe tomatoes, salty black olives and crunchy sweet red peppers and cucumber. This is the sort of salad that could be served as an accompaniment or as a complete meal. Try it next time you've got the griddle out or the barbecue going; it's excellent with mackerel, or chicken or lamb kebabs.

4 eggs
1 tbsp white wine vinegar
salt and pepper
3 tbsp extra virgin olive oil
1 small onion
½ cucumber
500g ripe tomatoes

3 red peppers
20 small black olives
50g trimmed and washed watercress (optional)
5 anchovy fillets (optional)

Cook the eggs in boiling water for 9 minutes. Drain, crack under cold running water and peel immediately. Add the vinegar to a salad bowl and stir in a generous pinch of salt until it disappears. Whisk in the olive oil to make a thick vinaigrette. Peel and finely chop the onion, then stir it into the vinaigrette. Peel the cucumber and split down the middle. Use a teaspoon to scoop out the seeds and their watery pulp. Slice the cucumber into chunky half-moons. Cut the core out of the tomatoes, then cut them in half through where the core used to be. Lay the tomatoes on their flat surface and slice quite thickly. Slice the peppers into thin strips, having discarded stalks, seeds and white filament. Smack the olives with something hard to loosen the stones, which can then be discarded. If including watercress and anchovies, pile them together with all the other salad ingredients into the bowl. Season with black pepper and mix well. Serve immediately.

LEBANESE TABBOULEH
Serves 4–6

In my early days as a restaurant critic I fell in love with Lebanese food. I learned to cook it at home thanks to Claudia Roden's *A Book of Middle-Eastern Food* and later through regular visits to The Phoenicia in Kensington. This was where I'd take Zach and Henry for a back-to-school treat or a birthday meal. I've also taken advantage of their home-delivery service and ordered a whole lamb stuffed with biryani-style rice for a party. With hummus and *moutabal*, salad and bread, the lamb will easily feed about 30 people, probably more. One essential dish, and one of my first accomplishments, is tabbouleh.

The main ingredient is flat-leaf parsley. It is chopped very finely into frilly strips and mixed with diced tomato, a little bulgur wheat and spring onion, the whole seasoned with lemon juice, olive oil and mint. It is refreshing and satisfying and goes with just about everything from grilled sardines to stuffed pitta bread. Traditionally tabbouleh is eaten scooped up in a curl of lettuce.

Bulgur is prepared cracked wheat which is ready to eat after a 30-minute soak in boiling water. It's a nuttier, more substantial alternative to couscous and prevalent in Lebanese cooking.

I often bulk up the quantity of bulgur wheat – the ingredients here can take up to 200g, although you might also wish to increase the quantity of onion – to make more of a meal of tabbouleh. If you do so, make up the quantity of liquid with water or stock so that it is just under double the weight of the bulgur.

> 6 ripe medium tomatoes, preferably plum
> 75g bulgur wheat (or up to 200g to make more of a meal of it)
> 2 spring onions
> salt and pepper
> 1 very large bunch of vigorous flat-leaf parsley
> small bunch of fresh mint
> 3 tbsp olive oil
> juice of ½ lemon
> curls of crisp lettuce

Cover the tomatoes with boiling water, count to 20 and drain. Core and peel the tomatoes, then quarter them lengthways. Place a sieve over a bowl. Scrape the seeds and juices into the sieve.

Finely chop the tomatoes and set aside the dice from one of them. Using the back of a spoon, press the seeds and their juices against the side of the sieve to extract maximum juice. Tip the main quantity of diced tomato, together with the juices, into a second bowl with the bulgur. Trim and finely chop (as opposed to slice) the spring onions. Stir the onion into the tomato mixture and season generously with salt and pepper. Leave to allow the tomato juices to rehydrate the bulgar.

Pick the leaves from the parsley and mint stalks. Chop very finely. When the bulgur is ready – it will remain slightly nutty but be tender – whisk the olive oil into the lemon juice and stir into the bulgur along with the parsley and mint. Stir well, taste and adjust the seasonings. Line a bowl with several layers of lettuce, spoon in the tabbouleh and tumble the remaining diced tomato over the top.

Onions, Leeks and Garlic

French Onion Soup
Cheat's *Pissaladière* with *Salade Niçoise*
Red-onion Marmalade
Pickled Onions
Roast Onions
Leeks Vinaigrette with Egg and Chives
Grilled Leeks with Parmesan and Deep-fried Tarragon
So Simple Leek and Potato Soup
Moroccan Leek and Tomato Soup
Vichyssoise with Caviar
Leek and Saffron Sauce
Minted Leeks with Bulgur
Leek Pithiviers
Leek and Almond Tart with Parmesan
Leek, Ham and Cheese *Gratin*
Wild Garlic Soup with *Croûtons*
Garlic with Balsamic Vinegar
Garlic Bread

An apple a day might keep the doctor away but herbalists believe an onion a day will prevent and cure coughs and colds. Despite being principally made of water, onions are a useful winter source of vitamins A, B and C as well as calcium, potassium and iron. Onions are reputedly good for the nervous system, help digestion, improve metabolism and promote healthy skin and blood cells. They are a natural antiseptic and antibiotic, and the equivalent of one small onion each day lowers cholesterol. They are also very good to eat and are a universal cooking ingredient and one of our oldest foods. Look out for firm, hard onions with dry, flaky skins and no green sprouts. Onions are made up of layers of fleshy skin, and their flavour becomes weaker the larger they grow. Properly stored, in a cool, dark place (not the fridge) that isn't damp, they will keep for months. Red onions have a milder flavour than brown-skinned ones; spring onions and white onions have a gentle flavour that resembles that of leeks.

Onions can be fried, boiled, cooked in the oven, steamed and bar-becued. They can be grated, chopped, sliced and cooked whole, with or without their skin. They are the starting-point of many savoury dishes. They can be used to thicken soups and stews. They work as a bridge to link and unite other ingredients, and they are a vegetable in their own right. They make wonderful pickles and relishes. In fact, where would we be without onions? For onions without tears, plunge shallots and small onions into boiling water for 1 minute before peeling. To slice a big onion, shove it in the freezer for 10 minutes or peel under water. Adding a splash of water when frying onions stops them drying out and burning. For soft, moist onions, heat the fat, onions and salt together. Add onions to hot oil if you want them browned. Adding acid – wine, vinegar or citrus juices – to onions before they've gone soft stops them softening and keeps them crunchy.

Leeks can sit happily at the bottom of the fridge for up to a week. They are the softie of the onion family and they go with everything. They are particularly delicious with eggs, with potatoes, mussels and white fish, with ham and bacon, and they can be made to look and taste so different.

They can be cooked whole, sliced into rounds, split then diced, or cut into *juliennes*. Single layers can be used as wrappers or draped over ramekins to encase delicate *mousselines*. They can be sautéed, gratinéed, baked, boiled, steamed and chargrilled. Finely sliced and deep-fried, they make a startling and surprisingly tasty garnish; and parboiled baby leeks are delicious tempura-style, dipped in batter and deep-fried. They can be whizzed into sauces to make more of poached eggs; stewed with mint to serve with lamb chops; and wrapped in ham or bacon, smothered with a cheese sauce, then grilled until the top is crusty.

Leeks are an exquisite addition to sauces and soups such as vichyssoise because, once cooked and liquidized, they turn into a thick, silky purée. They are good combined with tomatoes in cheese dishes, with pastry, or cooked with cream and with citrus juices.

One little tip for preparing leeks – even the elegantly long and slim, ready-trimmed kind of leek that supermarkets sell – is to soak them in cold water before cooking. This loosens the earth that gets lodged between the layers as the leeks grow. Home-grown leeks tend to be stumpy and fat and evenly divided between white and green. The green flags are coarser than the white and pale green part and are great for the stockpot.

Decent garlic can be difficult to buy in Cornwall. Look out for 'heads' that feel hard to the touch and aren't starting to sprout. In April and May and sometimes later into early summer, there is wild garlic to be had for free in hedgerows and woodland. There are two types. Jack-by-the-hedge, also known as hedge garlic and garlic mustard, has a strong garlicky smell but isn't related. It forms clusters of tiny white flowers from a single stem with an abundance of triangular leaves. Ramsoms is the real wild garlic. It has distinctive long thin stems and leaves, with ball-like clusters of dainty white flowers. Leaves from both plants are edible and give a delicate garlic flavour to salads and soups.

FRENCH ONION SOUP

Serves 6–8

I always make *soupe à l'oignon* with stock made from the Christmas turkey. There aren't many soups that rely on a good stock but this is one of them. It is a meal in itself and a real treat. It's thought to have originated in Lyon, the area of France famous for its onion dishes, although it's also claimed to have come from Les Halles in Paris, where it fortified the city's famous food-market porters.

2kg large onions
100g butter
½ tsp brown sugar
1 heaped tbsp flour
2 litres hot turkey, chicken or beef stock
1 wine glass, approx. 150ml, cider or dry white wine
3 tbsp brandy, Cognac or whisky
salt and pepper

for the croûtes:
1 small day-old baguette
1 garlic clove
50g melted butter
175g grated Gruyère cheese

Peel, halve and finely slice the onions. Melt 75g butter in a large, heavy-bottomed, lidded pan and stir in the onions. Cover and sweat very gently, stirring occasionally, for 15 minutes. Uncover, turn up the heat, sprinkle in the sugar and, when melted, reduce the heat and cook for at least 45 minutes, stirring regularly, until the onions are tender, a deep golden-brown and quite dry.

Meanwhile, make the *croûtes*. Pre-heat the oven to 425°F/220°C/gas mark 7. Rub the outside of the baguette with garlic until all used. Cut into approximately 16 slices and lay them close together on a buttered baking sheet. Drizzle over the melted butter, strew with most of the grated cheese, covering the slices evenly, and bake for about 15 minutes until all is a mass of golden bubbles. Leave to cool. When the cheese is hard and the bread crisp, separate the slices.

In a small pan, melt the remaining 25g butter, stir in the flour, add two ladles of the hot stock and whisk until thick. Stir it into the hot stock. When the onions are ready, add the cider or wine and allow to reduce and evaporate. Pour the thickened hot stock over the onions. Stirring constantly, bring to simmer and cook, uncovered, for 30 minutes. Stir in the brandy and correct the seasoning with plenty of salt and pepper. If possible, allow the soup to mature for 24 hours before serving.

To finish the soup, reheat the oven to its highest heat. Cover the surface of the soup, either the whole dish or decanted into individual heatproof bowls, with the *croûtes*, strew over the extra cheese and bake for a few minutes until the top is, once more, bubbling and blistered. Serve immediately.

CHEAT'S *PISSALADIÈRE* WITH *SALADE NIÇOISE*
Serves 6

Pissaladière is a Fish Store party piece, whipped up to serve with drinks or to turn into a meal with *salade niçoise*. It comes from the south of France, particularly in and around Nice, and it's a bit like onion pizza with an anchovy lattice dotted with black olives. To make it properly takes ages because the vast amount of onions required need to be cooked until soft and slippery. Thank heavens, then, for Eazy fried onions, which mean this delicious onion tart is ready to eat within minutes.

2 tbsp olive oil
2 tbsp flour
350g puff pastry
400g can Eazy fried onions
50g can anchovies
20 pitted black olives

for the salad:
500g small, new-season Cornish potatoes
250g French beans
1 small red onion
6 firm but ripe medium tomatoes

1 garlic clove
2 lettuce hearts
10 small black olives
1 tbsp red wine vinegar
3 tbsp olive oil
225g can of tuna
4 hard-boiled eggs
about 10 basil leaves

Pre-heat the oven to 400°F/200°C/gas mark 6. Generously smear a 24 x 34cm baking tin with half the olive oil. Dust a work surface with half the flour and roll the pastry thinly to fit the tin. Tease it to the edges, trimming any overhang and using it to fill gaps and mend tears. Use the tines of a fork to pierce the dough in several places to stop it rising. Spoon the onion over the dough, using a fork to smooth it evenly and going right up to the edges.

Split the anchovies lengthways in two or three pieces. Make a wide lattice with the anchovy over the onions. Place an olive in each gap. Dribble the tart with the remaining olive oil and cook in the oven for about 20 minutes until the pastry is cooked. If the pastry starts to billow, pierce it with a knife and encourage it back down flat. Serve the tart hot, warm or cold, from the tin, cutting it into slabs.

To make the salad, scrub then boil the potatoes. Drain. Top and tail the beans, cut in half and boil for 2 minutes. Peel, halve and thinly slice the onion. Quarter the tomatoes. Rub the salad bowl with the cut garlic. Add the lettuce, potatoes, beans, onion, tomatoes and olives. Whisk the vinegar and olive oil and dribble it over the salad. Add chunks of tuna and quartered hard-boiled egg and scatter with shredded basil leaves.

RED-ONION MARMALADE
Makes at least 1 x 450g jar

Here's a recipe that improves the quality of so much food. It goes with pâtés and terrines, with simply cooked chicken and liver; it turns ordinary sandwiches into feasts and it is the perfect base for all manner of bruschetta, from a floppy slice of Parma ham to roasted red peppers. It goes fabulously well with mozzarella, feta, Cheddar and Cornish Yarg – it transforms Welsh rarebit – and it is even good stirred into hot pasta.

Don't hurry the cooking of the onions, particularly before the wine is added. The whole point is to end up with silky, sweet–sour onions with a molten jam-like texture. The marmalade is served cold like a relish.

    4 large onions
    5 tbsp olive oil
    ½ tsp salt
    50g sultanas (optional)
    2 tbsp brown sugar
    black pepper
    2 glasses red wine, approx. 300ml
    4 tbsp red wine vinegar

Use a small knife to cut round the root and growing shoot of the onion in a small, pointed plug shape. Remove the skin, cut in half from root to shoot and slice very thinly across the halves. Heat the oil in a large frying pan or similarly wide-based pan (I usually use a wok) placed over a medium heat. Stir the onions into the hot oil, stirring frequently, until they begin to wilt and take on some colour. Reduce the heat after 5 or 6 minutes, season with ½ teaspoon salt and cook for a further 10 minutes, possibly longer, until the onions are floppy and juicy.

Add the sultanas and the sugar, season with black pepper and cook until the onions are sticky and slippery and the sultanas are beginning to plump up. Do not hurry any of this: the onions must be tender before the wine is added.

Transfer the onion mixture to a medium-sized, heavy-bottomed stainless-steel or cast-iron Le Creuset-style pan and add the wine and vinegar. Bring to the boil, stirring a couple of times, then reduce the heat so the stew simmers very, very gently. Partially cover the pan and leave to cook for at least an hour. The result you're after is thick, juicy and jam-like. Allow to cool slightly before decanting into a sterilized jar or jars. Cover, cool and then chill.

The marmalade will keep safely in the fridge for several weeks, but in my experience it will be in demand with everything. You'll probably end up eating it like jam.

PICKLED ONIONS

Fills 2 x 1 litre Kilner jars or equivalent

In an ideal world there will always be a big jar of home-made pickled onions at the Fish Store. Everyone loves them so much and they are one of the first things I learned to make from Betty. I used to have a copy of Betty's spice mix but now I buy ready-made sachets and use far more than recommended and bulk up the mixture with extra bay leaves and dried red chillies.

Home-made pickled onions are a labour of love, but over the years I've learned how to take the sting out of the process. They are still a messy, smelly job which is spread over two days, but I can't imagine not bothering because it's impossible to buy decent pickled onions. I've come to the conclusion that it is worth making a big batch and organizing yourself so that the work is as minimal and painless as possible.

It takes between 35 and 45 minutes to peel 1.8kg of small onions, slightly longer for shallots. So that's about 2 hours for the quantity specified here. Work in a well-ventilated room, preferably at a sink with a continual dribble from the cold tap. To make peeling easier, put a couple of pounds of onions at a time in the sink and cover them with boiling water. Leave for a couple of minutes, then drain and refresh in running cold water. This kills some of their tear-inducing smells and makes peeling easier. Use a small, very sharp, stainless-steel knife – which you will need to sharpen regularly as you work – and peel the onions from the top, leaving the root end till last. Peel into a plastic carrier-bag and tip the peelings on to the compost heap, or tie the bag and put it straight into the dustbin *outside*.

Have ready china gratin dishes or stainless-steel oven trays for the overnight salting process, or line ordinary metal oven trays with foil.

I sterilize Kilner and jam jars in the dishwasher.

We like our pickled onions to be crisp, brown all the way through and to pack a punch as well as being full of interesting flavours. They require at least 4 weeks maturing in a dark place, preferably much longer, and they get hotter the longer the pickles are left; superb, to my mind, after a year. I always put loads of the spice mix into the jars with the onions and pickling vinegar. You can moderate the mixture, or add very little to the jars, for a milder cure.

Onion-stained hands can be cleaned up with lemon juice.

    3.6kg small pickling onions or shallots
    225g coarse cooking or sea salt
    2 litres malt vinegar
    8 cartons/sachets pickling spices
    6 bay leaves
    about 10 dried red chillies

Peel the onions as described above. Lay out in glass or china dishes or roasting pans lined with tinfoil, generously sprinkling each layer with salt. Cover with foil and leave (preferably outside) for 24 hours. Meanwhile, bring the vinegar and spices to the boil, simmer for 5 minutes, cover and leave to cool – again, preferably outside, because the smells linger.

Rinse the salt off the onions, pat dry and pack into cold, sterilized jars. Cover with the vinegar, spoon in some of the spices, chillies and bay leaves, seal and store in the dark for at least 4 weeks before serving.

ROAST ONIONS
Allow at least 1 onion per person.

When you are roasting a chicken or a joint of meat, or cooking sausages in the oven, add a few unpeeled onions too. Smear them with a little olive oil – big onions can be cut in half through root and shoot and laid cut-side down – and stab them to avoid bursting. Allow 30–40 minutes, depending what else is in the oven. Scrape the silky, caramelized onion out of its skin: it will be sweet and luscious.

LEEKS VINAIGRETTE WITH EGG AND CHIVES
Serves 4

I sometimes prop the Chez Gourmet section of *The Prawn Cocktail Years* open to look at the photo (by Jason Lowe) of this recipe because it is so beautiful. The combination of silky young leeks and creamy Dijon-mustardy vinaigrette with grated hard-boiled eggs and a final sprinkling of chives is leeks vinaigrette perfection. This is a huge family favourite and a popular summer Fish Store starter. If it's a big party, it is often served as part of a cold spread with roast tomatoes or Piedmontese peppers.

> 16 leeks, about thumb thickness
> 2 tbsp smooth Dijon mustard
> 4 tbsp cold water
> 2 tbsp red wine vinegar
> salt and pepper
> 275–400ml peanut oil or other flavourless oil
> 2 hard-boiled eggs
> 1 tbsp snipped chives

Trim the leeks, leaving about 2.5cm green, and soak in cold water to remove dirt between the layers. Cook the leeks in fast-boiling, well-salted water for about 5 minutes until tender. Drain and allow to cool naturally. In a liquidizer, blend the mustard, water, vinegar and salt and pepper. With the motor running, pour in the oil in a thin stream until homogenized. If you think it is too thick, then thin with a little more water. The ideal consistency should be like thin salad cream.

Cook the eggs in boiling water for 9 minutes (once the water returns to boiling). Crack the shell all over, hold under cold water and remove the shell.

Slice the leeks lengthways, lay out on a platter or suitable dish, cut-side uppermost, drizzle with the (thick, creamy) dressing and grate over the hard-boiled eggs. Sprinkle with the chives and serve with good bread.

GRILLED LEEKS WITH PARMESAN AND DEEP-FRIED TARRAGON
Serves 6

A lovely starter with bruschetta but delicious, too, with grilled, smoked or soused pilchards.

12 leeks
olive oil
bunch of tarragon
4 tbsp vegetable oil
100g slab Parmesan

Trim the leeks and cut into 7.5cm lengths. Soak in cold water for a few minutes, agitating the water to remove any grit and drain. Steam over boiling water for about 6 minutes or until tender to the point of a knife. Heat a griddle pan for several minutes until very hot, brush both sides of the leeks with olive oil and place on the griddle, cooking in batches. Turn once through 45 degrees, to make a crosshatch of grill marks, and cook both sides until seared. Transfer to a platter or separate plates and dribble with olive oil.

Strip the tarragon off its stalk, heat the vegetable oil in a frying pan and, when hot, quickly deep-fry the leaves until crisp. Drain on absorbent kitchen paper. Use a potato peeler to shave Parmesan slices generously over the surface and sprinkle with the deep-fried tarragon.

SO SIMPLE LEEK AND POTATO SOUP
Serves 1–infinity

This is one of the easiest, quickest and most satisfying soups I know and it's as painless to make for one as it is for a crowd.

You need leeks, potatoes, water, salt and pepper and a knob of butter. If there's some thyme around, it lifts the soup slightly but is not essential to the success of the dish. All you do is boil everything up together until the leeks are tender and the potato has started to disintegrate and thicken the soup. Stir in the butter and it's done. If you happen to have a bunch of flat-leaf parsley to hand, chop the leaves and add them just before serving.

Allow one leek and one decent-sized old potato per person and follow this routine:

Trim the leeks and slice the white and pale-green part quite thickly and finely slice the inner part of the dark-green flags (the official name; don't ask me why). Soak in cold water for a few minutes, agitate to loosen any mud, rinse again and drain. Peel the potatoes, cut into chunks, rinse and place in a pan with the leeks. Season with salt and pepper, add a few sprigs of thyme if liked and cover generously with water. Boil for 10–15 minutes until the leeks are tender and potatoes are beginning to disintegrate. Add the butter, swirling it around as it melts. Taste and adjust the seasoning. If adding chopped flat-leaf parsley, do so now. Eat immediately. Lovely with well-buttered bread to dunk and slurp, but extra special with garlic bread.

MOROCCAN LEEK AND TOMATO SOUP

Serves 4

An interesting store-cupboard soup; perfect for the time when those leeks in the fridge are almost past it. Tomato fillets, incidentally, are interchangeable with whole or chopped canned tomatoes, but they are blessedly pip-free.

    1 red onion
    1 garlic clove
    2 tbsp olive oil
    600g leeks
    ½ tsp dried chilli flakes
    salt and pepper
    generous pinch saffron stamens
    1 tbsp honey
    4 tbsp couscous
    400g can tomato fillets
    1 litre chicken stock, or 1½ chicken stock cubes dissolved in 1 litre
        boiling water
    lemon juice to taste

Peel, halve and finely chop the onion and garlic. Heat the oil in a heavy-bottomed pan and stir in the onion and garlic. Cook, stirring occasionally and adjusting the heat, until the onions are soft and slippery. Meanwhile, trim the leeks, slice in half lengthways and then across into thin half-moons. Stir the leeks and chilli flakes into the onions, season with salt and pepper, cover the pan and sweat for 5 minutes. Soften the saffron in a little boiling water. Stir the saffron, honey, couscous and tomato fillets into the leeks. Add the stock, bring to the boil, reduce the heat, half-cover the pan and simmer for about 20 minutes until everything is cooked and flavours have merged. Taste and adjust the seasoning with salt, pepper and lemon juice.

VICHYSSOISE WITH CAVIAR
Serves 6

Vichyssoise is cold leek and potato soup – *crème Vichyssoise glacée* – invented and named by Louis Diat, French chef of New York's Ritz-Carlton, in the twenties. It's a refinement of *potage bonne femme*, the everyday fare, at the time, of thousands of households all over France. On the lookout for a new cold soup, Diat remembered his mother chilling theirs with milk. With a little tinkering – replacing the milk with cream, sieving the soup and adding a chive garnish – Vichyssoise was born. The name is taken from Vichy, the famous spa town near the Diat family home in Bourbonnais. A small dollop of salty, creamy caviar or *faux* caviar called onuga (actually naturally smoked and carbon-dyed herring) gives the soup a luxurious touch.

> 1kg white part of leeks
> 500ml light chicken stock or ½ chicken stock cube dissolved in 500ml boiling water
> 500g new potatoes
> 1 tsp salt
> 250ml milk
> 250ml whipping cream
> pepper
> small bunch of fresh chives, snipped
> 50g onuga or caviar

Slice the leeks and rinse in plenty of cold water to remove any grit and dirt, then simmer in the chicken stock for 15 minutes. Peel, chop and rinse the potatoes. Add the potatoes and salt to the pan and cook for a further 15 minutes with the milk until the potatoes are tender. Liquidize, then strain through a fine sieve. Allow to cool, stir in the cream and correct the seasoning. Chill the soup for at least 4 hours. Serve in shallow soup bowls sprinkled with chopped chives and onuga if you're pushing the boat out.

LEEK AND SAFFRON SAUCE
Serves 6

Leeks can be turned into a useful quick sauce. I love it with mashed potato and a poached egg with a chopped parsley or chive garnish. All you do is soften sliced leeks in butter, then liquidize the soft leeks with thick cream, salt and pepper. Flavours can be enhanced with mint or tarragon. Any of these combinations is lovely with grilled white fish.

Leek and saffron is one of those culinary marriages made in heaven which traditionally forms a *ménage à trois* with mussels. This sauce is good poured into *moules marinière* or as a coating sauce for steamed mussels, and goes very well with crusty pan-fried scallops or with seafood pasties.

  4 leeks
  75g butter
  salt and pepper
  glass of white wine, approx. 150ml
  1 scant tbsp flour
  275ml fish stock
  very generous pinch saffron stamens
  150ml thick cream
  lemon juice

Trim and finely chop, then wash the leeks. Drain in a colander. Melt half the butter in a spacious frying pan, stir in the leeks, season generously with salt and pepper, cover and cook for 10 minutes or until tender. Add the wine and boil vigorously, uncovered, until it has virtually evaporated. Add the remaining butter and, when melted, sift in the flour, stirring thoroughly to avoid lumps. Gradually incorporate the stock, stirring all the time, and bring to the boil. Soften the saffron in a little boiling water and add it together with the cream. Simmer gently for 5 minutes. Adjust the seasoning with salt, pepper and lemon juice.

MINTED LEEKS WITH BULGUR
Serves 6–8

Bulgur wheat is used in Lebanese dishes such as tabbouleh (see page 297) and needs to be soaked in boiling water for 30 minutes. In this recipe it's dressed with olive oil and lemon juice and mixed with lightly cooked leeks and mint. This is great standby food and is the sort of thing I used to make for post-school fridge-cruising. I love it with a soft-boiled or poached egg, with a slab of glistening feta cheese and a few roast tomatoes, or with hummus and lamb kebabs. It's great, too, for a change, with grilled fish.

> 225g bulgur
> 4 tbsp lemon juice
> salt and pepper
> 6 tbsp olive oil
> 6–8 leeks
> 4 tbsp finely chopped mint

Tip the bulgur into a sieve and hold under cold running water to wash it. Shake dry. Transfer to a bowl and pour on sufficient boiling water to a depth of 5cm above the wheat. Cover with a plate and leave for 30 minutes. Drain thoroughly if any water remains by tipping into a sieve.

Pour the lemon juice into a suitable serving bowl, season generously with salt and pepper, whisk in the olive oil and then stir in the bulgur.

Trim the leeks and slice the white and pale-green part into thick rings. Immerse in cold water, agitate the water to loosen any grit, drain and cook in vigorously boiling salted water for 5 minutes. Drain the leeks and stir into the bulgur with the mint, reserving a little to sprinkle on as a garnish. Check the seasoning and serve.

LEEK PITHIVIERS
Serves 4

An elegant leek pie which is quick and easy to make using ready-rolled puff pastry. Serve with a crisp green salad or roast tomatoes.

    1kg trimmed leeks
    75g butter plus a little extra
    3 tbsp thick cream
    2 x 375g round or oblong ready-rolled puff pastry
    1 egg
    salt and black pepper

Slice the leeks in 2cm thick rounds. Soak in cold water for a few minutes, then drain. Melt 75g butter in a wide frying pan, add the leeks, cover the pan and cook gently, stirring once during cooking, for about 20 minutes until the leeks are very soft. Stir in the cream, increase the heat and cook uncovered for a few more minutes until the leeks are creamy rather than wet. Spread them out on a plate to cool.

Pre-heat the oven to 425°F/220°C/gas mark 7. Place a baking sheet in the oven to get very hot – this ensures that the pastry base cooks thoroughly.

Butter a second baking sheet. Lay one piece of puff pastry on the buttered baking sheet. Beat the egg and use some of it to paint a 2.5cm border. Spoon the cooled leeks on to the pastry, going up to the border. Season with salt and pepper. Form a lid with the second piece of pastry. Press the edges together. Paint the pastry with beaten egg and then seal the edges with a fork. Make a couple of slashes in the middle of the pastry to allow steam to escape. The pie looks spectacular if you take the trouble to use the point of a knife to etch and decorate the pie.

Slide the second baking sheet on to the hot baking sheet and bake for 20–25 minutes or until the pie is puffed and golden. Serve in wedges like a cake.

Lavender Pears with White Wine

blackberry and apple pie

LEEK AND ALMOND TART WITH PARMESAN
Serves 6

Soft, sweet leeks and aromatic oregano are both popular in Greek cooking and go wonderfully well together. Here they are combined with toasted almond flakes and a thick, frangipane-style almond, egg and cream custard. A hint of Parmesan points up the flavours to arrive at a deliciously satisfying filling for a quick and easy yet very special tart. It makes a great make-ahead starter and goes down very well with vegetarians. Salad leaves or a baked potato and a few roast tomatoes make more of a meal of it. It keeps perfectly – covered, in the bottom of the fridge – for a couple of days and can be reheated or eaten cold. Ideal, then, for a picnic.

> 400g trimmed leeks
> 3 tbsp light olive oil
> 3 tsp dried oregano
> salt and freshly milled black pepper
> 25g butter
> 150g flaked almonds
> 2 eggs
> 100ml crème fraîche
> 4 tbsp freshly grated Parmesan
> flour for dusting
> 275g ready-rolled shortcrust pastry
> flour for dusting

Pre-heat the oven to 425°F/220°C/gas mark 7. Trim the leeks and slice into fine rings. Transfer to a colander, rinse with cold water and shake dry. Heat the oil in a spacious frying pan or similar wide-based pan over a medium heat and stir in the leeks. Sprinkle over the oregano and cook, stirring occasionally, for about 10 minutes until the leeks are soft and juicy but essentially dry. Season generously with salt and pepper and tip into a mixing bowl to cool. Melt half the butter in the pan and stir-fry the flaked almonds for a couple of minutes until golden. Stir the flakes into the leeks. Crack the eggs into a mixing bowl, add the crème fraîche, ground almonds and just over half the Parmesan. Mix thoroughly to make a smooth, thick paste. Rub a 23cm flan tin with a removable base with the rest of the butter. Dust with flour and shake out the excess. Line the flan tin with the pastry. Mix the warm leeks into the egg mixture and pour it into the pastry case. Smooth the top and sprinkle the remaining Parmesan over the top. Bake for 35 minutes until the filling has set and both the pastry and the top of the tart are golden. Remove the collar and serve hot, warm or cold.

LEEK, HAM AND CHEESE *GRATIN*
Serves 2

I am always fiddling about with this French bistro dish. It's usually made by wrapping cooked leeks (or chicory) in ham and hiding them under a cloak of Gruyère cheese sauce. I find it easier to eat if the leeks are cut into relatively short lengths; I've gone as far as to cut them into bite-sized pieces and parcel them up in Parma ham. For this thoroughly anglicized version, I've used assertively flavoured British ingredients: mature Cheddar and thick slices of strongly flavoured ham (as sold by the Mousehole shop). I've also cut the leeks lengthways so that the sauce gets a chance to mingle between the layers. The dish is liberally covered with a cheese and breadcrumb *gratin* topping and the skill of eating it is to achieve a combination of silky leek, chewy ham, creamy sauce and crisp cheesy topping in every mouthful. It's good alone but is the perfect companion to mashed potatoes and sprouts.

To make the dish for more people, just scale up the ingredients. The *gratin* could be made in advance, in which case reheat in a hot oven for about 20 minutes until cooked through with a crusty topping.

2 leeks
salt and black pepper
25g butter
1 tbsp flour
300ml milk
1 bay leaf
150g mature Cheddar
2 slices of decent British ham
1 thick slice of white bread

Trim the leeks and cut them in three to four pieces depending on their length. Agitate in cold water to remove any grit. Boil the leeks in salted water for 6–10 minutes until tender to the point of a sharp knife. Drain the leeks by standing them up in a colander but save about 4 tablespoons of cooking water. Split the leeks lengthways and lay out, cut-side up, in a gratin dish. Melt the butter in your favourite milk pan and stir in the flour. Mix thoroughly until smooth, then stir in the reserved water and milk. Add the bay leaf and a generous seasoning of salt and pepper. Stir vigorously while you slowly bring the liquid to the boil, then reduce the heat and simmer gently for 6 or 7 minutes. Grate the cheese and add half to the sauce. Stir while the cheese melts and turn off the heat. Discard the bay leaf. Tear the ham into pieces and stuff it between the leeks. You don't need to be neat about this; just bear in mind that you want most mouthfuls of leek to include some ham and you also want the cheese sauce to be able to leach between the layers of leek. Season with a little pepper, then pour the sauce over the top, shaking the dish so that it entirely covers the contents. Break the bread into pieces to blitz into crumbs. If doing this by hand, cut off the crusts and crumble the bread as best you can. Mix the crumbs with the remaining cheese and scatter it over the top of the gratin. Pre-heat the overhead grill (or oven to 425°F/220°C/gas mark 7) and cook until the cheese and crumbs are an appetizing golden carapace. Serve immediately.

WILD GARLIC SOUP WITH *CROÛTONS*
Serves 4

Gently garlicky and a terrific green soup from the hedgerow.

    3 medium potatoes
    1 small lemon
    salt and pepper
    1 litre chicken stock or 1½ chicken stock cubes dissolved in 1 litre
        boiling water
    2 medium onions
    a colander full of wild garlic leaves
    25g butter
    thick cream to garnish

for the croûtons:
3 slices stale bread
50g butter
1 tbsp vegetable oil

Peel, slice and rinse the potatoes. Remove a strip of zest from the lemon. Add potatoes, lemon zest, ½ teaspoon salt and a generous seasoning of pepper to a pan with the stock. Boil for 10 minutes or until the potatoes are tender. Meanwhile, peel, halve and finely slice the onions. Wash the wild garlic and shake dry. Melt the butter in another saucepan and gently soften the onion over a low heat. Turn up the heat, stir in the wild garlic and a generous squeeze of lemon and cook until it has wilted down considerably. Add to the potatoes and stock and simmer together for 5 minutes. Liquidize in batches. Taste and adjust the seasoning.

To make the *croûtons*, cut the bread into cubes, heat the butter and oil and fry the bread until crisp and golden.

Serve the soup with a scoop of cream and some of the *croûtons*.

GARLIC WITH BALSAMIC VINEGAR
Serves 4–6

I often add a few unpeeled cloves to roast potatoes during the last 15 minutes of cooking, to go with lamb, and the cloves soften like butter to smear over the meat. This is a deluxe version in which the garlic is enriched with olive oil and balsamic vinegar. Apart from lamb, the cooked garlic is also delicious with chicken or beef. The same treatment works with shallots or small onions.

24 garlic cloves
1 glass dry white wine, approx. 150ml
3 tbsp olive oil
3 tbsp balsamic vinegar

Peel the garlic cloves and place in a pan. Cover with water and bring to the boil. Discard the water and repeat. Return the garlic to the pan, pour over the wine and top up with cold water to cover. Bring to the boil and cook for about 6 minutes, until only just tender. Drain, reserving the liquid for another use. Heat the oil in a frying pan large enough to hold the garlic in a single layer. Add the garlic, stir-frying until golden all over. Pour on the balsamic vinegar, reduce the heat and let it sizzle and splutter and reduce away. The garlic will be a deep chestnut brown.

GARLIC BREAD
Serves 6–8

It's impossible to make too much garlic bread. It freezes perfectly in its tin wrapper and although it can be cooked from frozen, it only takes about 30 minutes to defrost.

> 6 big garlic cloves
> 50g bunch flat-leaf parsley
> 250g butter
> salt and pepper
> 3 baguettes or 4 ciabatta loaves
> you will also need tinfoil

Pre-heat the oven to 400°F/200°C/gas mark 6.

Peel and finely chop the garlic. Pick the leaves from the parsley and place in the bowl of a food processor. Blitz until finely chopped. Alternatively, chop by hand. Melt the butter in suitable pan, add the garlic and cook over a low heat for 45 seconds. Season with salt and pepper. Stir in the parsley.

Using a sharp knife, make diagonal incisions about 3cm to 5cm apart, as if you were slicing the loaf but without cutting right through. Take a sheet of foil large enough to parcel each loaf separately. Place a loaf in the middle of a piece of foil and spoon the garlic butter between the slices, encouraging it to soak into the bread. Pour leftovers over the top. Close up the parcels, tucking carefully to avoid leakage. Bake in the middle of the oven for 10 minutes. To achieve a crusted top, open the foil and bake for a further 5 minutes. Close the parcels again to keep the loaves warm.

Cucumbers and Courgettes

Greek Cucumber Salad
Iced Cucumber and Yoghurt Soup
Pickled Cucumber with Dill
Courgette and Mint Soup
Courgette and Pea Salad with Balsamic Vinaigrette
Courgette Pancakes with Parmesan
Courgette *Gratin*
Oven Ratatouille
Courgette and Pine Kernel *Spanokopitta*
Black Olive, Courgette and Parmesan Pie

I was brought up thinking that the only way to eat cucumber was in sandwiches or as part of an old-fashioned English salad, the sort that comes with salad cream and isn't complete without hard-boiled egg, tomatoes, beetroot and the heart of a floppy lettuce. I've since learned that it's an unexpectedly versatile ingredient and I'm not just talking about salads. Part of this versatility is the different way it can be prepared. Sometimes, but not always, the skin has to be removed. Other times – when, for example, you want to make half-moons or sturdy batons – it's necessary to scrape out the seeds and the watery pulp. Cucumber goes well with yoghurt to make soothing cold soups and fresh relishes like raita and tzatziki. But have you tried cooking it? Cucumber is lovely stewed in butter with peas and finished with cream and a little mint or tarragon. This is delicious hot or cold and goes well with grilled fish or poached chicken. Home-grown, so-called ridge cucumbers are so much more interesting than the uniform-length-and-shape cucumbers that the supermarkets sell. I like it when they refuse to grow straight and end up like a dark green kiss curl.

My dad used to grow marrows on his allotment and it was always exciting to check how much they'd grown overnight. Unfortunately, I never found them very exciting to eat. I hated their spongy, watery texture and lack of flavour, so when I first came across courgettes – in France while staying at a youth hostel –– I didn't expect to like them either. They are integral to ratatouille but there are few other occasions when they benefit from lengthy cooking. They make surprisingly delicate quick soups, particularly when matched with mint, and when thinly sliced, dusted with flour and fried they are a real treat. Another good idea is to slice them lengthways and cook them on the griddle before tossing them with thyme, lemon juice and olive oil.

In Mousehole, where courgettes turn into marrows overnight, most people with an allotment or kitchen garden grow them and occasionally they are sold at the village shop. Unless they are carefully cooked, courgettes will be as boring as their adult relative, the marrow. The general rule is to barely cook them, so that they retain their 'bite'.

GREEK CUCUMBER SALAD
Serves 4

Tzatziki is the real name of Greek cucumber salad and it's one of the many dips and relishes we regularly pile into our shopping basket for livening up just about everything from sandwiches to barbecues. Delicious and useful though most of them undoubtedly are, when you take the trouble to make your own they are always stunningly more interesting to eat. Store-bought, ready-made tzatziki is invariably made with grated cucumber and if the yoghurt is charged with fresh garlic and enriched with lemon juice and olive oil, it is rarely noticeable. When the tzatziki is made and eaten almost immediately, there is no need to worry about the wateriness of the cucumber. So, no bothering with removing the seeds and their pulp – the main culprit – or dredging with salt to draw out the liquid. The dish also becomes much more of a salad than a relish when the cucumber is cut in big chunky pieces. It takes a few moments to make and, like its shop-bought relative, goes wonderfully well with lamb kebabs or crusty lamb sausages.

1 garlic clove
salt and black pepper
1 tbsp fresh lemon juice
3 tbsp olive oil
500g pot of Greek yoghurt
1 medium cucumber
1 tbsp chopped dill, mint or coriander

Peel and chop the garlic. Sprinkle with a generous pinch of salt and work to a juicy paste with the flat of a knife. Transfer to a bowl that can accommodate the yoghurt. Add the lemon juice and olive oil. Beat in the yoghurt with a wooden spoon until all is thoroughly amalgamated. Trim the cucumber and halve lengthways, cut each half on the slant in chunky slices. Add cucumber and the chosen herb or a mixture of two or all three and stir the salad before serving.

ICED CUCUMBER AND YOGHURT SOUP
Serves 6

A favourite from *A Celebration of Soup* adapted by Simon Hopkinson from an old Cordon Bleu recipe.

    2 small cucumbers
    1 tsp salt
    300ml plain yoghurt
    300ml tomato juice
    1 small garlic clove
    900ml light chicken stock or
    1 chicken stock cube dissolved in 900ml boiling water
    a small bunch of mint
    300ml single cream
    8 drops Tabasco or chilli essence

Peel the cucumbers and split lengthways. Use a teaspoon to scrape away the seeds and chop the cucumbers. Sprinkle on the salt and leave to drain for 30 minutes. Liquidize the yoghurt, tomato juice, peeled and chopped garlic clove, chicken stock and mint (reserving a few leaves for garnish). Strain through a fine sieve. Rinse the cucumber and squeeze out excess moisture in a clean tea-towel. Stir into the strained soup along with the cream and Tabasco. Taste and adjust the seasoning. Chill until very cold, and garnish with the reserved mint finely chopped.

PICKLED CUCUMBER WITH DILL
Serves 4–6

One of the great things to have in the fridge ready to serve with almost anything. Particularly good with cold crab but try it with poached salmon or sea bass with mayonnaise. Good too as a barbecue add-on.

    1 cucumber
    salt
    ½ tsp sugar
    3 tbsp white wine vinegar
    1 tbsp chopped dill

Slice the cucumber wafer-thin, spread out in the sink, sprinkle with 2 teaspoons of salt, transfer to a colander and leave to drain for 30 minutes.

To finish the cucumber relish, squeeze the cucumber with your hands then wrap in a clean tea towel and squeeze dry. Dissolve the sugar in the vinegar, fold in the cucumber and dill, transfer to a bowl or Kilner jar and chill in the fridge.

COURGETTE AND MINT SOUP
Serves 6

A lovely soup. It's a very pretty pale green with darker green flecks.

> 1 small onion
> 1 shallot
> 50g butter
> 900g courgettes
> 1 cooked potato
> salt and pepper
> 1.75 litres chicken stock or 2 chicken stock cubes dissolved in
>   1.75ml boiling water
> 2 tbsp finely chopped mint
> 2 tbsp finely chopped flat-leaf parsley

Peel and finely chop the onion and shallot. Soften the butter and gently sweat the onion and shallot until transparent. Meanwhile, trim then grate the courgette on the large hole of the cheese grater. Dice the potato. Stir the courgettes and potato into the onion, season generously, cover and cook for 5 minutes, stirring a couple of times. Add the stock, bring to the boil, turn down the heat and simmer for 5 minutes. Liquidize in batches with the mint and parsley. Return to a clean pan, reheat, taste for seasoning and serve.

COURGETTE AND PEA SALAD WITH BALSAMIC VINAIGRETTE
Serves 4–6

Royden's vegetable patch has kick-started my Fish Store cooking on countless occasions and one summer we benefited from continual gluts of huge courgettes and giant marrows. Most courgettes that we buy are tender, delicate vegetables which haven't had the opportunity to develop seeds. If they have, and it's most likely that they will if you bought them at a Farmers' Market, you will get better results if you remove the seeds and their spongy surround. This is quickly done with a teaspoon, scraping out the soft centre as you might for cucumber.

Turning courgettes into a big, hearty salad was one of my glut ideas and it's a useful barbecue dish because it doubles as a vegetable and goes with everything from sausages to kebabs and fish. Just take care not to overcook the courgettes – they only need a quick dip into boiling water – so that they retain some bite.

> 4 medium courgettes
> salt and black pepper
> 500g frozen petits pois
> bunch of spring onions
> 2 firm, ripe tomatoes, approx. 250g in total
> 2 tbsp balsamic vinegar
> 4 tbsp extra virgin olive oil
> handful of flat-leaf parsley leaves

Trim the courgettes, halve lengthways and slice on the slant to make thick, chunky diagonal wedges. Bring a large pan of water to the boil, add 1 teaspoon of salt and the courgettes. Return to the boil and boil for 1 minute. Have ready a sinkful of cold water and scoop the courgettes out of the pan into the water to arrest cooking. Return the pan to the boil and add the peas. Cook for a couple of minutes according to packet instructions. Drain into a colander. Scoop the courgettes into the colander. Meanwhile, trim and finely slice the spring onions. Pour boiling water over the tomatoes. Count to 20, drain and remove the skin. Use a small, sharp knife to remove the core in a small cone shape. Chop the tomatoes. Whisk together the balsamic vinegar and olive oil in a salad bowl. Stir in the drained vegetables and tomatoes. Season lightly with salt and generously with pepper. Mix thoroughly. Coarsely chop the flat leaf parsley leaves, stir them into the salad and serve immediately or keep waiting until required.

COURGETTE PANCAKES WITH PARMESAN
Serves 4–6

A light and delicious alternative to potatoes with fish or chicken or as part of a vegetarian *meze*.

> 3 medium-sized courgettes
> 3 eggs
> 100g flour
> 60g melted butter
> bunch of chives
> salt and black pepper
> 150ml crème fraîche
> 50g grated Parmesan
> oil for frying
> 50g chunk of Parmesan

Trim, wash then grate the courgettes on the large hole of a cheese grater. Place the eggs in a bowl and whisk in the flour and melted butter until smooth. Stir in the courgettes. Snip 2 tablespoons of chives into the mixture. Season lightly with salt (Parmesan is very salty) and generously with pepper. Add a dollop of the crème fraîche and 50g grated Parmesan. If you need to keep the pancakes warm before serving, which you probably will, pre-heat the oven to a low temperature before you start cooking. Heat a non-stick frying pan over a medium heat and add spoonfuls of the mixture. Cook for a couple of minutes each side, turning when the pancakes are golden brown and slightly souffléd. Use a sharp knife or potato peeler to shave slivers from the chunk of Parmesan. Serve the pancakes with a scoop of crème fraîche, a scattering of Parmesan slivers and a generous garnish of chives.

COURGETTE *GRATIN*
Serves 4

This pleasingly plain, eggy *gratin* goes particularly well with cherry tomatoes which have been grilled until their skins pop and dressed with a splash of balsamic vinegar and olive oil. It is also a good accompaniment to boiled gammon or roast chicken.

500g small courgettes
25g butter
salt and pepper
2 eggs
150ml milk
100g mature Cheddar or other hard cheese
1 thick slice of bread

Pre-heat the oven to 350°F/180°C/gas mark 4. Wash, trim and slice the courgettes. Place them in a large frying pan or wide-based saucepan. Add 150ml water and most of the butter. Simmer uncovered for 3–4 minutes until they are just tender and the juices reduced. Season with salt and pepper. Use the remaining butter to smear a suitable *gratin* dish. Whisk the eggs and milk in a bowl. Grate three-quarters of the cheese directly into the mixture, season lightly with salt and pepper and mix thoroughly. Stir in the courgettes with about a tablespoon of the remaining cooking juices. Tip into the dish and shake to smooth the top. Blitz the bread to make crumbs. Grate the rest of the cheese and mix the two together. Sprinkle the cheesy crumbs over the top. Bake in the hot oven, testing after 20 minutes, until the custard has set and feels firm to the flat of the hand and the top is golden and crusted.

OVEN RATATOUILLE
Serves 6

Towards the end of my pregnancy with Zach I gave up work and immersed myself in Michel Guérard's seminal gourmet dieting book, *Cuisine Minceur*. To use the book successfully it is essential to surrender to the regime. One dish that really appealed to me was ratatouille with eggs poached in red wine. Intrigued by his pernickety approach, I decided to give it a go. Instead of simmering all the chopped vegetables in olive oil, M. Guérard fries each one separately and briefly in a little olive oil before mixing everything together in an oven dish and baking the ratatouille in the oven. The result is perfection every time, the vegetables keeping their shape and identity yet merging together almost like a vegetable terrine. There is none of the usual watery slop that so often spoils this dish, and when left overnight for the flavours to develop, it is extraordinarily good. In fact, I think I prefer ratatouille cold.

1 large onion
4 garlic cloves
1 large red pepper
1 medium aubergine
3 medium courgettes
8 ripe tomatoes
6 tablespoons olive oil
salt and pepper
1 bay leaf
3 sprigs of fresh thyme
12 basil leaves, torn
1 level tsp crushed coriander seeds

Pre-heat the oven to 400°F/200°C/gas mark 6.

Keeping separate piles, peel, quarter and thinly slice the onion. Peel and very finely chop the garlic. Quarter the red pepper lengthways, scrape away the seeds and white filament and finely slice. Quarter the aubergine lengthways and finely slice. Trim and finely slice the courgettes. Pour boiling water over the tomatoes, count to 20, drain, remove the skin and cut out the core. Cut each tomato into 8 pieces and discard seeds. Heat half the olive oil in a large frying pan and brown the onions, adding the garlic after a couple of minutes. Add the red pepper and allow to wilt slightly. Remove both from the pan to a large mixing bowl. Place the aubergine in a bowl and sprinkle over half the remaining olive oil. Use your hands to smear the slices thoroughly. Add to the pan, fry briefly until coloured, then transfer to the bowl along with the other vegetables. Using the last of the olive oil, repeat the smearing business with the courgettes and cook in the same way as the aubergines. Add to the other vegetables. Finally, give the tomatoes a quick fry so that they collapse slightly, and add to the mixing bowl. Season generously with salt and pepper and, using your hands, mix everything carefully together. Put the whole mixture into a shallow earthenware baking dish. Lay the bay leaf and thyme over the top and cover with a lid or foil. Bake for 40–45 minutes. Remove from the oven, stir in the basil and coriander seeds, cover and allow to stand for

15 minutes before serving. Alternatively, cool and serve chilled.

COURGETTE AND PINE NUT *SPANAKOPITTA*
Serves 6

Greek *spanakopitta* pie is usually made with spinach and looks like a golden filo pastry parcel, the top etched with portion control squares. This version is made with courgettes instead of spinach and it works perfectly with the egg custard flavoured in the usual way with feta cheese and flat-leaf parsley. The pie can be served hot, warm or cold but reheats perfectly to recapture a crisp filo finish.

> 750g courgettes (approx. 5 medium-sized ones)
> salt and black pepper
> 75g pine kernels
> 1 small onion or 4 spring onions
> 2 tbsp olive oil
> 2 garlic cloves
> generous handful basil leaves
> 3 tbsp finely chopped flat-leaf parsley
> ½ glass white wine, approx. 75ml
> 2 eggs
> 100g feta cheese
> 50g freshly grated Parmesan
> 200g filo pastry
> 75g melted butter or mixture butter and olive oil

Rinse and trim the courgettes. Grate them on the large hole of a cheese grater or food processor. Transfer to a colander, toss with ½ teaspoon salt and leave for 20 minutes to drain. Tip into a clean tea towel and squeeze dry. Meanwhile, heat a frying pan and dry-roast the pine kernels, tossing them constantly for 2–3 minutes until patched with gold.

Peel, halve and finely chop the onion or trim and finely slice the spring onions. Heat the oil in a large frying pan and cook the onion for a few minutes until soft but uncoloured. Add the courgette, season generously with salt and pepper and cook for 4 minutes, stirring occasionally.

Peel and finely chop the garlic. Finely chop the basil. Add the garlic, parsley, basil and white wine. Cover and cook for 3–4 minutes, then remove from the heat. Whisk the eggs in a bowl, crumble the feta over the top and grate the Parmesan into the bowl. Stir in the vegetables.

Pre-heat the oven to 400°F/200°C/gas mark 6. Brush an approximately 23 x 30 x 5cm oven dish with melted butter. Use half the filo to make layers in the dish, spreading each layer with melted butter and leaving an overhang. Sprinkle half the pine kernels between a couple of the layers. Tip the filling into the pastry case and smooth the top. Tuck the overhang in towards the middle and continue making buttered layers of filo, sprinkling a couple with chopped pine kernels as before. Finish with a good smear of butter. Use a sharp knife to cut portion-sized squares or diamonds, going through a couple of layers of filo. Bake in the oven for about 45 minutes until the pastry is golden and the filling set but still moist and juicy. Serve hot, warm or cold.

BLACK OLIVE, COURGETTE AND PARMESAN PIE
Serves 6–8

Cheesy, creamy, pastry smells will waft round the kitchen as this stupendous pie cooks and the result is a golden, crusty pie that gives on to a succulent, creamy and herby filling with bursts of salty, chewy black olives. It also reheats perfectly but is good cold and is perfect for a picnic. Delicious with a tomato salad.

200g flour plus extra for dusting
100g butter plus an extra knob
bunch of spring onions or 1 leek
3 tbsp olive oil
3 courgettes, approx. 450g
1 large garlic clove
10 flourishing basil leaves
handful of flat-leaf parsley leaves
250g ricotta
1 whole egg
2 egg yolks
50g Yarg or Cheddar cheese
3 tbsp grated Parmesan
salt and black pepper

14 black olives
splash of milk

Pre-heat the oven to 425°F/220°C/gas mark 7. Sift the flour and salt into a mixing bowl (or food processor). Cut the butter into small pieces and add to the flour. Quickly rub the butter into the flour until it resembles damp breadcrumbs or pulse the food processor. Stir or briefly pulse a couple of teaspoons of cold water into the mixture, continuing tentatively until the dough seems to want to cling together. Form into a ball; dust with more flour if it's too wet, adding a little extra water if it's too dry. To avoid shrinkage when the pastry is cooked, cover and leave for 30 minutes. Choose a flan tin with a removable base, approximately 22cm diameter. Grease it generously with a knob of butter, going up the sides as well as the base. Dust the tin with flour, roll it round in your hands and shake out any excess. This makes the tin non-stick. Divide the dough into two pieces, one much smaller for the lid. Roll out the large piece to fit the tin, leaving a good lip and working the leftovers into the lid dough.

Meanwhile, trim and slice the spring onions or quarter the leek lengthways and then cut across into small scraps. Heat the oil and gently soften the leek while you trim and grate the courgettes on the large hole of a cheese grater. Peel and chop the garlic. Shred the basil. Chop the flat-leaf parsley. Stir the courgette and garlic into the leek and cook, stirring often, for about 5 minutes until the courgette has softened slightly and is beginning to weep. Stir in the basil. Place the whole egg and one egg yolk in a mixing bowl. Add the ricotta, grated Yarg, 2 tablespoons of Parmesan, the chopped parsley, a pinch of salt and several grinds of black pepper. Tear the olives off their stones in big pieces and add them too. Beat the egg mixture together until amalgamated and then mix in the courgettes. Turn it into the prepared pie dish. Roll out and fit the lid, crimping the edges together and rolling them towards the centre to secure. Mix the remaining egg yolk with the milk, paint it over the lid and use to 'glue' the edge. Make a few air holes with a fork and scatter over the last of the Parmesan. Place in the oven, turn the heat down to 400°F/200°C/gas mark 6 and cook for 35–40 minutes until puffed and golden. Remove collar and serve.

Aubergines and Peppers

Grilled Pepper Salad
Piedmontese Peppers
Peperonata with Anchovy Bruschetta
Moutabal
Spiced Aubergine Salad with Cumin
Slipper Moussaka and Greek Salad

Glossy black aubergines and bright red, yellow and green peppers haven't made much of an impression on Cornwall. It's always been possible to buy them – at a price and as a speciality ingredient – from the redoubtable Tregenza's at the top of Market Jew Street in Penzance. These days they are also widely available in local supermarkets, imported from Holland, but they remain 'exotic'. Anyone who cares to grow either will have great success – they come from the same family as potatoes, tomatoes and chilli peppers – and can be planted in grow-bags or on a window ledge. Aubergines come in various shapes but it's unlikely you'll find a creamy-white egg-shaped one (hence the name eggplant) in Cornwall, or a tiny, thumb-sized baby like those I can buy at my Cypriot greengrocer in London.

Aubergines do take some understanding. Under the purply black skin, the manilla flesh turns soft and creamy when it is subjected to heat. It has a lusciousness that is hard to define and a subtle, almost smoky flavour. Bigger fruit, whatever their skin colour, are delicious sliced, rubbed with olive oil and cooked on a griddle. Aubergines are famously good at drinking up oil. One solution is to dredge prepared aubergine with salt and leave them for 20 minutes to break down the cells and make them less porous. Another is to dust it with flour.

Red peppers – sometimes called by their generic name of capsicums – are also known as pimientos, sweet or bell peppers. They are rich in vitamins A and C, carotenoids and a red colouring agent called capsanthin. Orange, yellow and green peppers are generally unripe red peppers. Peppers are transformed by roasting or grilling, turning their texture silky and slippery and intensifying their flavour.

GRILLED PEPPER SALAD
Serves 6

Roasted peppers are one of the most popular summer treats at the Fish Store. They look so beautiful laid out on a big platter and fill the place with the smell of hot Mediterranean sunshine.

- 6 red or 3 red and 3 yellow peppers
- 2 garlic cloves
- 1 tsp salt
- 4 tbsp red wine vinegar
- extra virgin olive oil

Preheat the overhead grill and cook the peppers on all sides until the skin is totally black. Put into a bowl, cover with clingfilm and leave to cool. Peel off the skin, remove seeds and stalks, and divide each pepper into quarters, following the shape of the fruit. Lay out, skin-side uppermost, on a platter.

Peel and chop the garlic, sprinkle with ½ teaspoon salt and crush to a juicy paste with the flat of a knife. Mix the garlic into the vinegar and add 5 times its volume with olive oil. Spoon the dressing over the peppers.

PIEDMONTESE PEPPERS
Serves 4–8

If ever a dish caught the public imagination it is this one, demonstrated by Delia in her television series *Summer Collection* and published in the book of the same name. It's become known as Delia's peppers but can be traced back to Elizabeth David's *Italian Food*, published in 1954. Franco Taruschio spotted it and put it on his menu when he opened The Walnut Tree in Abergavenny in 1963. That's where Simon Hopkinson first tasted it and included the simple but delicious dish on Bibendum's opening menu in 1987, where it was enjoyed repeatedly by Delia, amongst others, and Elizabeth David. Every so often the peppers pop up in a cookery feature, reinvented, as it were, with the addition of mozzarella or feta, black olives or capers, vegetable rice concoctions and other bits and bobs. The original is the simplest and the best.

Serve the peppers as a starter, as part of a *meze* meal or barbecue. They are great for picnics and parties. I usually make one or two trays of them when there's a glut of peppers.

    4 decent-sized red peppers
    salt and pepper
    4 garlic cloves, preferably new season or 'fresh'
    4 plum or similar-sized ripe tomatoes
    approx. 3 tbsp olive oil
    3 anchovy fillets

Pre-heat the oven to 425°F/220°C/gas mark 7. Halve the peppers, slicing evenly through the stalk. Remove any white filament and the seeds. Rinse the peppers and arrange, cut-side uppermost, on a heavy, shallow baking tray. Season inside the peppers with salt and pepper. Peel the garlic and slice in super-thin rounds. Lay the slices in the cavity. Pour boiling water over the tomatoes, count to 20, drain, cut out the cores in a pointed plug shape and peel. Halve the tomatoes lengthways and place, cut-side down, in the peppers covering the slices of garlic and nudged up closely together. Season again with salt and pepper and splash with olive oil. Place the tray in the oven and cook for 20 minutes then reduce the heat to 350°F/180°C/gas mark 4, and cook for a further 20 minutes. You want the edges slightly charred and the peppers tender. Remove from the oven. Slice the anchovies into 3 long strips. Decorate the peppers with an anchovy kiss and leave to cool in the dish. Use a fish slice to scoop them on to a serving dish – a white one is best for this – and spoon over the juices. If you need to keep the peppers hanging around, cover them generously with clingfilm and store in the fridge. They keep perfectly for about 4 days.

PEPERONATA WITH ANCHOVY BRUSCHETTA
Serves 4

Peperonata is a soft and gooey stew of red pepper, onion and tomato seasoned with garlic and a little wine vinegar. It makes a delicious vegetarian supper with anchovy bruschetta but is also very good with scrambled egg or a couple of soft-boiled eggs. It is excellent too with roast lamb or chicken and lovely with grilled red mullet. Because peperonata can be eaten hot or cold – it is at its finest, I think, luke-warm – it is the perfect thing to make to last over several days (covered, in the fridge) as the flavours improve and it goes with so many things. Great for a barbecue or party (because it can be made ahead).

1 large onion
2 cloves of garlic
5 tbsp olive oil
salt and black pepper
4 red peppers
900g large plum or other ripe tomatoes
1 tbsp red wine vinegar
1 tbsp honey or sugar

for the bruschetta:
1 ciabatta loaf or 4 thick slices sourdough or country-style bread
1 garlic clove
4 anchovy fillets in oil or 2 tsp anchovy paste
about 3 tbsp extra virgin olive oil

Peel, halve and finely chop the onion. Peel the garlic and slice in wafer-thin rounds. Chose a spacious heavy-bottomed pan and cook the onion in the olive oil with a little salt over a gentle heat, cooking until very soft. Allow about 15 minutes. Meanwhile, use a potato peeler to remove the skin from the peppers. Don't be too meticulous about this. Discard seeds and white membrane, then slice the peppers into strips. Add the garlic and peppers to the onions. Season lightly with salt and generously with pepper, reduce the heat slightly, cover the pan and cook for several minutes, giving the occasional stir. Place the tomatoes in a bowl and cover with boiling water. Count to 20, drain, remove the skin, cut the tomatoes lengthways into quarters and chop. Add the tomatoes and vinegar and leave to cook uncovered for about 45 min-utes or until the tomatoes and onions have cooked into a thick, creamy, jammy sauce and the strips of pepper are very soft but still distinctive. Check the seasoning, adding a smidgen of sugar or honey if you think it necessary. Allow to cool or serve immediately. If using ciabatta to make the bruschetta, split it lengthways and cut in half to make 4 pieces. Grill the bread lightly on both sides. Rub one side with the peeled garlic and smear with olive oil. Coarsely chop the anchovy fillets and mash them with a fork with a little of the oil in the tin to make a paste. Spread the anchovy paste over the bruschetta and serve with the peperonata.

MOUTABAL
Serves 6–8

Moutabal is one of many names for a creamy aubergine dip which is popular throughout the Arab world. Its special flavour comes from grilling or roasting the aubergines until the skin is scorched hard and the flesh inside is meltingly tender. It is then scraped off the skin and mashed with garlic, lemon juice and olive oil to make a thick, creamy and smoky mixture which is utterly addictive. The flavour can be softened by adding a little natural yoghurt and given a nutty back taste with tahini, the oily pounded sesame seed paste which is often also mixed into hummus. Traditionally, *moutabal* is made by hand, blended with a fork, and that gives it a pleasing undulating texture and makes it easier to control the balance of seasonings, but it can be made in a jiff with a food processor.

I make it all the time to serve with toasted pitta bread as a snack or with drinks but it is excellent with lamb as a sauce-cum-vegetable.

2 large aubergines, approx. 350g each
2 garlic cloves
salt and pepper
1 tsp ground cumin
1 small lemon
6–10 tbsp olive oil

Pre-heat the overhead grill and cook the aubergines, turning as the skin chars, wrinkles and hardens and the flesh insides begins to sag. Don't be timid about this, the aubergines need to be thoroughly cooked. Remove to a colander over the sink and use a sharp knife to slash the flesh from the stalk to its bulbous end so it can drain and cool. Meanwhile, peel and chop the garlic. Sprinkle it with ½ teaspoon of salt and crush to a paste with the flat of a knife. Transfer to a mixing bowl or the bowl of a food processor. Use the knife to scrape the flesh off the skin into the bowl. Add the cumin and a generous seasoning of black pepper. Add the juice of half a lemon and 4 tablespoons of olive oil. Use a fork to mash and stir. If using a food processor, pulse until just smooth. Taste the *moutabal* and adjust the flavours with more salt, extra lemon juice and olive oil.

SPICED AUBERGINE SALAD WITH CUMIN
Serves 6

This slippery, soft aubergine salad is a variation on the gooey Turkish salad dish called *imam bayeldi* and is succulent and sweet yet haunt-ingly spicy and very moreish. For anyone who has doubts about aubergine, this is a dish that will change your mind. It's almost a meal in itself but goes with everything from baked potatoes to lamb chops or roast chicken and is good, too, eaten *meze*-style. Try it, for example, next time you barbecue lamb kebabs, or are wondering what would be good with lamb steaks, or want something a bit different with a roast joint. The flavours, incidentally, will develop and get even more inter-esting after 24 hours. The exact origin of the dish is unknown in a way that's often the case with popular restaurant dishes as they pass between chefs and kitchens. I first ate it at Bibendum, and then Blueprint Café. I saw it on the menu at Fifth Floor in Henry Harris's day and at Chez Bruce in Wandsworth. The link here is that all these restau-rant chefs worked in Bibendum's kitchens at the same time as Nikki Barraclough. She picked it up from someone at the Carved Angel in Devon. Anyway, I do urge you to try it.

> 3 medium aubergines
> 1 tbsp salt
> 2 Spanish onions
> 8 plum tomatoes
> 3 garlic cloves, preferably new season
> 100ml olive oil
> 1 heaped tsp ground cumin
> 1 heaped tsp ground allspice
> ½ tsp cayenne

2 heaped tbsp currants

2 heaped tbsp chopped mint

2 heaped tbsp chopped coriander

Chop the aubergines into 1cm cubes. Pile into a colander and sprinkle with 1 tablespoon of salt. Leave for 20 minutes. Peel and finely chop the onions. Pour boiling water over the tomatoes. Count to 20, drain, peel and remove the cores. Coarsely chop the flesh. Peel and finely chop the garlic. Heat half the olive oil in a spacious pan, stir in the onions and gently sauté until tender and pale golden. This will take about 20 minutes. Mix in the tomatoes, spices and garlic. Stew gently for 10 minutes, stir in the currants and turn off the heat. Rinse the salt off the aubergines and pat dry with absorbent kitchen paper. In a wok or your largest frying pan, heat the remaining oil until smoking. Tip in the aubergines and stir-fry, adjusting the heat so nothing burns, until golden and cooked through. This takes about 15 minutes and you may need to do it in two batches. Mix both sets of ingredients together in a large bowl, stir in the fresh herbs and leave to cool. Taste for seasoning. You may need more salt.

SLIPPER MOUSSAKA AND GREEK SALAD
Serves 8–12

Perfect party food which can be made and cooked in advance *and* comes with in-built portion control.

6 medium aubergines, approx. 400g each

8 tbsp olive oil

salt and black pepper

2 onions, approx. 100g each

6 garlic cloves

1 tsp ground cinnamon

2 tbsp tomato purée

2 x 500g minced lamb

4 tsp dried oregano

2 large glasses red wine, approx. 400ml

6 tbsp chopped flat-leaf parsley

2 x 470g jar Dolmio white sauce for lasagne

2 large egg yolks
300g feta cheese

for the salad:
4 Cos lettuce hearts
1 large cucumber
2 medium red onions
12 ripe tomatoes or 200g cherry tomatoes
small bunch of coriander
20 pitted black olives
200g feta cheese
juice of 1 lemon
6 tbsp olive oil

Pre-heat the oven to 425°F/220°C/gas mark 7. Halve the aubergines lengthways cutting through the stalk. Cut a 2cm lattice in the flesh, slicing almost to the base without piercing the skin. Run the knife round the inside edge of each half. Smear the cut surface with a little olive oil and season with salt and pepper. Arrange on baking sheets and cook in the oven for 25–35 minutes until the flesh is completely soft and lightly browned.

Meanwhile, peel and chop the onion and garlic. Cook together, stirring occasionally, in the remaining olive oil in a large, wide-based pan until soft and lightly coloured. Stir in the cinnamon and then the tomato purée, cooking for a minute or so until the tomato looses its bright red colour. Add the lamb, breaking it up and stirring it into the onions with a wooden spoon. Cook for a few minutes until browned and then season with salt, pepper and the oregano before adding the red wine. Let the wine boil up and then simmer over a low heat for 25 minutes. When the meat is cooked and the wine absorbed, stir in the chopped parsley and tip the mixture into a sieve to drain. Spoon the meat on to the aubergine 'slippers', pushing it down lightly between the sagging lattice. Leave to cool. Finally, empty the white sauce into a bowl. Beat in the egg yolks. Crumble the feta into the sauce and stir. Spoon the sauce over the meat. Cook the slippers in the hot oven for 10–15 minutes until the top is blistered and golden. Leftover slippers reheat perfectly.

To make the salad, cut across the lettuce in 3cm wide strips, rinse and shake dry. Split the cucumber lengthways, scrape out the seeds with a teaspoon and slice chunkily into half-moons. Peel and halve the onions and slice wafer-thin. Quarter the tomatoes; halve cherry tomatoes. Chop the coriander. Place everything in a salad bowl. Add the olives. Slice chunks of feta over the top. When ready to serve, whisk the lemon juice with the olive oil together and pour over the salad. Toss and serve.

Puddings and Ice Cream

Pudding at the Fish Store is really just an excuse to eat more Jelbert's ice cream and their exceptional clotted cream. They sell both, these days, for eating later, in polystyrene cups. It is unusual if there isn't at least one ice cream tub in the freezer between Easter and the end of October – when the shop is open – and there is an unwritten rule which decrees that anyone who passes Jelbert's shop in Newlyn will buy for the freezer as well as themselves.

The best ice cream in the west

If the sun is shining in Newlyn on any day between the first of April and the end of October, the door of Jelbert's will be wide open and Jim Glover or one of his team will be filling cornets or stuffing tubs with ice cream. There is only one flavour – vanilla – and it comes with or without extra clotted cream. Whether to have a Cadbury's chocolate Flake to tuck into the ice cream or to go for a large as opposed to medium-sized cornet are the only decisions to be made. The small shop excites daily queues during a hot summer and it's not unusual to spot a suited businessman belted up inside his saloon or a builder and his mate parked up opposite risking a parking fine to enjoy their Jelbert's. Fisherman too, from nearby Newlyn Fish Market, aren't immune to the lure of the shop, queuing alongside schoolkids and holidaymakers. Anyone who knows anything knows that Jelbert's ice cream has no competitors. It is simply the best.

Jim is unclear exactly when the business originated but Jelbert is his mother's family name and he thinks the shop started early in the 1900s, although there is no real record before the end of the Second World War. Originally, the ice cream was allied to the family milk round, which goes back to his great-grandfather's day, when milk was delivered door to door in churns. Jim remembers as a small boy taking the milk to very steep places in a jug, and pouring out with a measuring cup directly into people's containers. There were no bottles. The business moved into the current location when milk rationing ended and ice-cream making started again. At that stage all the manufacturing was done in his grandmother's backyard, in the house where Jim was born. Every day the mix would be prepared by hand and the family would take it in turns to sit at the truncated barrel with its steel cylinder and internal steel paddles, winding the handle, turning it through tubs of salted ice until the churned milk got stiffer and stiffer and the job harder and harder.

Jim took over the business shortly after machines were installed in a tiny factory set up in a cottage used by Belgian evacuees during the war in the lower part of old Newlyn. These days the milk and cream are bought from a local dairy but the ice cream is made to the same formula daily, using fresh milk, butter and cream.

It must have been tempting at some stage or other to expand and open other shops. Fortunately Jim, like other Jelberts before him, appreciates that it is only by controlling the product and not expanding or diversifying that it's possible to maintain the standard.

So next time you have to queue for your Jelbert's, don't complain but remember to thank your lucky stars that it will taste exactly the same as it always has done.

Blackberries and Sloes

Bramble Jam
Blackberries with Apple Snow
Blackberry and Apple Cobbler
Blackberry and Blackcurrant Tart with Almond Custard
Blackberry Sauce with Vodka or Gin
Sloe Gin

Cornish hedgerows are dangerous for soft pampered hands like mine. Gorse, hawthorn, bramble, ever-present nettles and spiky blackthorn all thrive there. If there's been a sunny start to the summer, with plenty of rain to swell the fruit, the bramble bushes will be laden with plump, sweet blackberries by the middle of July. The sweetest, fattest berries grow on the south-facing walls and hedgerows of the fields and are the first to appear at the end of the stems. The bushes go on producing until mid-October. After that date, or so the legend goes, they become sour. That's because when Satan was kicked out of heaven he landed on a blackberry tree and cursed it.

There are hundreds of wild blackberry micro-species, all varying slightly in sweetness, flavour, nutritional value, size and time of ripening. Should you be lucky enough to find a bush with fruit you particularly like, keep quiet about it and go back each year. If picking for jam, it's a good tip to pick a few unripe red fruit. It will help set the jelly.

As a child, no summer walk or picnic was complete without gathering blackberries. My mother went into labour with me when she was blackberrying and in my dreams I owned a horse called Bramble, so it's always been normal for me to do the same in Mousehole. The best blackberries in Mousehole can be found in the fields above Raginnis, just before Pullen. That's where I was once chased by a bull, so I tend to take pot luck wherever I'm out walking. Betty, Ben's mother, was another keen blackberrier. She thought nothing of picking 2olbs at a time – with a little help from Ben and his tiny basket, which could fill up quickly – and all had to be prepared and cooked immediately. In my early days in Mousehole, when Ben and I used to drink at the Legion, I used to make blackberry pies in return for the fish which regularly turned up on the Fish Store doorstep.

Blackberries have a natural affinity with apples but are also good in fruit salad with pears, bananas and peaches, or other soft berries like raspberries and redcurrants. I often use them in summer-cum-autumn pudding. It's unusual to find blackberries in savoury dishes, but they make a lovely sauce to serve with game.

In the autumn, after the pretty white flowers have fallen from super-spiky blackthorn trees, small, blue–black fruits which look a bit like blueberries begin to appear. Sloes are the ancestor of all our plums but they are mouthpuckeringly sour. We collect them to make sloe gin.

BRAMBLE JAM
Fills 3–4 x 450g jam jars

Lovely with scones and clotted cream – Cornish cream tea – or with creamy rice pudding. Blackberries are low in the setting agent pectin, so adding a few unripe red berries and lemon juice helps in the setting process; but, try as you might, blackberry jam never sets hard.

> 1.3kg ripe blackberries plus a few red fruit to help the setting
> juice of 2 lemons
> 1.8kg sugar
> *no* water

Place the berries and lemon juice in a pan and simmer very gently until soft. Meanwhile, place the sugar in a ceramic mixing bowl and warm in the oven. Tip the warmed sugar into the soft fruit and stir until dissolved. Bring to the boil and boil for 5–8 minutes, or until setting point is reached. To check setting point, spoon a little jam on to a saucer. Tip to one side: it should be noticeably thick and wrinkle when pressed. Pot immediately in warmed jars. If liked, strain through a sieve to make bramble jelly.

BLACKBERRIES WITH APPLE SNOW
Serves 6

Blackberries are often cooked with apple because the apple absorbs some of the copious juices and complements the blackberries so deliciously. Any variety will do, but cooking apples are particularly good because they collapse into a fluffy mess which makes a lovely backdrop for blackberries. A bowl of this in the fridge will always go down well; try it with cornflakes or custard or over ice cream.

> 3 or 4 cooking apples
> squeeze of lemon juice

approx. 5 tbsp water
approx. 4 tbsp sugar
50g butter
approx. 350g ripe blackberries

Peel, quarter and chop the apples. Place in a pan with a squeeze of lemon juice and about 5 tablespoons of water, cover and boil hard. Check after 5 minutes; you want the apples fluffy as if puréed, so a little more water may be required and/or the heat reduced. Don't add too much extra water; you want it stiff. Stir in the butter and sugar, both of which thin the mixture. Taste and adjust sweetness. Stir the blackberries into the hot apple purée. The heat will soften the berries and the juices will stain the fruit. Stir again after a few minutes. Transfer to a bowl.

BLACKBERRY AND APPLE COBBLER
Serves 6

A cobbler, as in cobbled together, is a fruit (or savoury) pudding topped with scone mixture. It is a lovely alternative to a pie and is marginally quicker to make. As the scones rise, the blackberry juices bubble up round them, sending out wafts of mouthwatering smells. Definitely an occasion for clotted cream.

200g flour plus a little extra
pinch salt
2 heaped tsp baking powder
100g butter
100ml milk
4 Bramley cooking apples, approx. 900g
squeeze of lemon juice
approx. 5 tbsp water
approx. 4 tbsp sugar
300g blackberries
clotted cream to serve

Pre-heat the oven 450°F/230°C/gas mark 8. Sift the flour and salt into a mixing bowl, stir in the baking powder and add 75g of the butter cut into small chunks. Rub the butter into flour until no lumps remain.

Make an indentation in the middle and, using a knife or fork, stir in the milk quickly to make a sloppy, damp dough that clumps together. Form it into a ball with your hands. Leave to rest while you prepare the fruit.

Quarter, then peel the apples and cut out the cores. Cut the quarters into chunks and drop into a saucepan with the lemon juice and water. Cover the pan and boil hard for a few minutes until the apples begin to disintegrate. Remove from the heat and stir in a knob of butter and the sugar, which will thin the mixture. Taste and adjust sweetness before stirring in the blackberries.

Pile the fruit into a 1 litre capacity ceramic pie dish or similar. Leave to cool.

Sprinkle the extra flour on to a work surface and roll the soft and floppy dough into an approximately 15cm disc. Use a biscuit cutter or upturned wine glass and cut out 4–6 circles. Place them over the fruit and form a smaller disc with leftovers to sit in the middle. Sprinkle with a little sugar and dot with any remaining butter. Bake for 15 minutes, then reduce the heat to 350°F/180°C/gas mark 4 and cook for a further 10–15 minutes until the scones are golden and cooked through. Serve hot with clotted cream.

BLACKBERRY AND BLACKCURRANT TART WITH ALMOND CUSTARD
Serves 6

This tart-cum-pie is quite gorgeous, redolent of hot summer days in a make-believe world where everyone has a kitchen garden full of trees and bushes laden with soft fruit. Instead of blackberries and black-currants, this pie would be good with raspberries and redcurrants. Ground almonds stirred into 'fresh' custard give it an extra-special touch of luxury, but Jelbert's ice cream is ideal too.

> 500g blackberries
> 250g blackcurrants
> generous knob of butter
> flour for dusting
> 375g ready-rolled puff pastry
> 4 tbsp sugar

2 large eggs
splash of milk
150ml double cream
500ml carton fresh custard
4 tbsp ground almonds

Pre-heat the oven to 425°F/220°C/gas mark 7. Rinse the blackberries and blackcurrants and shake dry. Rub a quiche tin approximately 23cm diameter in size generously with butter and then dust all over with flour, moving the tin round in your hands so that the base and sides are covered. Empty out excess flour. This preparation makes the tin reliably non-stick. Roll the oblong piece of pastry lightly so that it can fit the round tin with a generous overhang that will be folded into the centre of the pie tin to semi-cover it. Trim the pointed corners. Once the pastry is positioned in the tin, pile in the blackberries and blackcurrants. Dust the fruit with 2 tablespoons of the sugar. Whisk the yolk of one of the eggs with the splash of milk and set aside. In a separate bowl, whisk together briefly, until just amalgamated, the whole egg, remaining egg white and the cream. Pour the egg and cream mixture over the fruit. Fold the pastry overlap in towards the centre of the tin, nipping and tucking to make a secure nest for fruit and custard. Paint the exposed pastry with the egg yolk and milk mixture, pouring any leftovers into the fruit mixture. Dredge the pastry with the remaining sugar, giving generous attention to the exposed fruit in the middle. Cook in the pre-heated oven for 30 minutes until the tart-cum-pie is puffed, crusty and golden. Serve it immediately or allow to cool slightly or completely.

Warm the custard, stir in the ground almonds – and *voila!*

BLACKBERRY SAUCE WITH VODKA OR GIN
Makes 150ml

A thin 'sauce' to serve over ice cream or fruit salads with banana or other soft fruit such as raspberries, strawberries and peaches. Also good added to salad dressings, in gravy or as a sauce with game.

225g ripe blackberries
squeeze of lemon juice
1 tbsp gin, vodka or kirsch
3 tbsp caster sugar

Place everything in a pan. Bring quickly to the boil, reduce the heat and cook for 2 minutes. Force through a sieve with the back of a spoon into a bowl, scraping under the sieve so that nothing is wasted. Taste and adjust the seasoning, depending on whether it's being served with a sweet or savoury dish.

SLOE GIN
Makes equivalent of 2 gin bottles

Sloe gin is a country tipple made by immersing sloes in gin with a massive amount of sugar. As the sugar dissolves and the colour bleeds out of the sloes, the gin turns a delicate burgundy pink, rather like a syrupy rosé wine. The sloes gives the gin a refreshing sour–sweet flavour. When the gin is finished, the sloes, which will have settled at the bottom of the bottle, can be stirred into plum crumble or used for martinis. Sloe gin makes a lovely gift. Wear sturdy gloves to pick sloes and sally forth in October after the first frosts, when the bloom on the fruit has faded and the little berries are starting to pucker.

500g sloes
250g sugar
75cl bottle of gin
various attractive empty bottles, preferably clear glass

Prick the sloes a couple of times with a pin. Put a handful in a bottle, top up with half their weight in sugar, pour on the gin and leave in a cool, dark place for at least two months. Shake the bottle occasionally to dissolve the sugar.

Apples and Pears

Crêpes with Caramelized Apples
Christmas Baked Apples with Rum Butter
Quick Apple Tart with Whipped Cream
Tarte Tatin
Apple Quiche with Nutmeg
Apple Pie
Apple Betty with Almond Crisp
Lavender Pears with White Wine

My favourite eating apples are Cox's, Russets and what I call scrumping apples because they have rosy cheeks and look as if they've come from an orchard. When it comes to big blowsy 'cookers', I'd chose Bramleys every time. Eating apples can, of course, be cooked and they are exactly what you need for a French apple tart or other dishes when you want the apple to keep its shape. Cookers, in contrast, explode into a fluffy purée when they are cooked. That's why they are so good baked and boiled up to make apple sauce.

It's the amount of malic acid and sugars in apples that determines their flavour. The more malic acid an apple variety contains the stronger its flavour and greater likelihood of the flavour being retained when the apple is cooked. Big, green cooking apples contain between two and five times as much malic acid as eating varieties and have a very low sugar content. Their pronounced appley flavour is fresh and clean, making them perfect for savoury as well as sweet dishes.

When it comes to pears, there is no such obvious distinction between eaters and cookers. All the varieties are slightly different in shape, skin colour, texture, acidity and juiciness. Firm pears with unblemished skins will ripen in a warm kitchen over a couple of days. The pearly white flesh of apples and pears quickly turns brown once peeled. To avoid this, sprinkle them with lemon juice or immerse them in acidulated water.

CRÊPES WITH CARAMELIZED APPLES
Serves 6

Frying peeled slices of apple in butter until they are soft and golden is a lovely extra to serve with pork sausages, pork chops or a pork roast. When the apple is then caramelized with sugar and finished with cream and a slug of something alcoholic, it makes a delicious quick pudding. I keep a pack of ready-made crêpes in the freezer specially for this dish.

   6 eating apples
   100g butter

6 crêpes or pancakes
sugar

Peel, quarter, core and slice the apple in chunky segments. Set aside about 25g of butter and use the rest to sauté the apples in batches in a large frying pan, tossing often, until soft and tender. Transfer to a plate as you go. Use half the butter to generously smear a suitable *gratin* dish, roll the apple in the crêpes and place, seam-side down, in the dish. Cut little scraps of the remaining butter directly on to the crêpes. Sprinkle with sugar. If necessary, the pudding can be kept waiting – covered with clingfilm in the fridge – like this for a couple of hours.

Pre-heat the oven to 450°F/230°C/gas mark 8. Cook in the oven for 10–15 minutes until the sugar caramelizes, the crêpes crisp slightly and the apple heats through. Serve with thick cream or ice cream.

CHRISTMAS BAKED APPLES WITH RUM BUTTER
Serves 8

Baked apples were one of my favourite puddings as a child because everyone had their own apple and everyone had their own way of eating it. I ate the skin first and then the fluffy, soft apple drenched with golden syrup and Bird's custard. Sometimes my mum would stuff them with sultanas, which would end up fat and juicy. Betty used to stuff hers with brown sugar and serve them with home-made custard. This version was dreamt up as an alternative to Christmas pudding.

8 cooking apples
50g butter
2 tbsp rum
8 tbsp mincemeat
8 tbsp maple or golden syrup
squeeze of lemon juice

for the rum butter:
3cm strip of lemon zest
75g butter
75g soft brown sugar

2 tbsp rum
squeeze lemon juice

carton of fresh custard to serve

Pre-heat the oven to 400°F/200°C/gas mark 6. Wash the apples. Use a corer or cut out the cores by slicing a 2cm square around the core and cutting right through the centre of the apple at both ends. Push the core through the apple to reveal an even hole. Cut the skin in a circle round the middle of the apples to avoid them bursting. This has the added effect of making the finished apples look very attractive because the soft flesh swells through the cut. Smear the apples lightly with butter and sit on a knob of butter on a suitable baking tray – I usually use a tart tin. Mix the rum into the mincemeat and fill the space left by the removal of the core. Dribble the maple syrup over the apples, add a squeeze of lemon juice and bake for about 35 minutes, basting occasionally, or until the apples are soft and the skin golden. While the apples are baking, make the rum butter. Finely chop the lemon zest until it resembles fine dust. Cream the butter thoroughly until it is light and fluffy. Beat in the sugar, a little at a time, adding a squeeze of lemon and the lemon zest. When thoroughly incorporated, add the rum. Taste. You may want more. Spoon the butter into a suitable dish, cover and chill. Serve the apples with extra maple syrup, custard and a spoonful of rum butter.

QUICK APPLE TART WITH WHIPPED CREAM
Serves 4

Every now and again there is a restaurant dish that is so quick and easy that it translates to the domestic kitchen with ease. One such dish is variously known as *tarte aux pommes minute*, *tarte fine* and, at fashionable Le Caprice, *tarte aux pommes chantilly*. Almost a play on words, this tart takes 10 minutes or so to cook, and is an individual Normandy-style apple tart on a wafer-thin, puff pastry base.

flour for dusting
250g puff pastry
1 tsp cooking oil

1 lemon

1 tbsp caster sugar

4 medium sized Cox's apples

2 tbsp icing sugar

knob of butter

150g whipping cream

2–3 tbsp whisky or Calvados (optional)

Pre-heat the oven to its highest setting: probably 475°F/240°C/gas mark 9. Dust a suitable flat surface with flour and roll out the puff pastry very, very thinly. Cut out 4 circles, using a saucer as a guide. Sprinkle a little water on an oiled baking sheet and lay out the circles of pastry. Lightly prick the pastry all over with the tines of a fork to stop it rising as it cooks and pushing off the apples. Squeeze the lemon juice into a mixing bowl and stir in the caster sugar. Peel, core and slice the apple into thin segments. As you work, place the slices in the sweetened lemon juice to stop them from discolouring. Cover the pastry with the slices in overlapping concentric circles. Then dredge each tart with icing sugar and dot with a little butter. Place the baking sheet in the hot oven and cook for 10 minutes or until the pastry is crisp and golden and the apples are tender and scorched in places. Serve hot, warm or cold with the cream, whipped, if you like, with whisky or Calvados.

TARTE TATIN
Serves 6–8

There are many excellent apple tarts but none so spectacular as *tarte Tatin* or upside-down apple tart. The tart gets its name from the Tatin sisters, who turned the snag of not having an oven to an advantage. Apples, butter and sugar went directly into the pan, with pastry tucked over the top. The pan was then covered with a cone-shaped metal dome, rather like a Moroccan tagine, called, apparently, a country oven. While the tart cooked, the sugar and butter caramelized, turning the chunks of apple a deep, dark golden brown. Then, when the pastry was done and the apples cooked through, they turned the whole thing out on to a dish, to show the rich brown syrupy apples. Apart from the dramatic look of *tarte Tatin*, it is the distinctive burnt flavour that is so addictive, and it goes particularly well with rich clotted cream. To make it successfully, you need a really heavy pan with straight or almost straight sides. A cast-iron frying pan is ideal but I have improvised with a flan tin and a heat diffuser. The other essential is Cox's apples – in France they use Reinettes – because they hold their shape and don't fall apart while cooking.

  1 lemon
  10 Cox's apples
  100g butter
  100g caster sugar
  flour for dusting
  200g puff pastry

Pre-heat the oven to 400°F/200°C/gas mark 6. Squeeze the lemon juice into a mixing bowl and add about half a cupful of water. Quarter, peel and core the apples, tossing them into the acidulated water as you go. This stops them browning (not that it matters on this occasion) and adds a hint of acidity to the buttery caramel. Thickly smear the lump of butter round the sides and over the bottom of the pan and dump the remains in the middle. Sprinkle the sugar on top. Place the pan over a moderate heat and keep stirring as it melts, froths and gradually turns through shades of amber to dark brown. This takes between 5 and 15 minutes depending on the pan. Remove the pan to a heatproof surface to cool slightly. Stir again to achieve a smooth, creamy liquid toffee. Don't worry if the sugar turns to crystals, which it sometimes does. Simply stir in a spoonful of runny honey or a squeeze of lemon juice. And don't worry if butter and sugar refuse to merge. They will when the mixture cools slightly and you give it a final stir. If it appears not to want to caramelize, keep going. It will eventually. Arrange the apples rounded-side down in the toffee, fitting them snugly in a single layer, with leftovers filling any gaps. Dust a work surface with flour and roll out the pastry to fit the pan. Lay it over the apples and tuck the edges down the inside of the pan. Cook in the oven for 30 minutes until the pastry is golden. Remove from the oven and run a knife round the inside edge of the pan. Cover the tart with a large plate and quickly invert the pan, taking care for the inevitable juices. Cut in wedges and serve hot, warm or cold.

APPLE QUICHE WITH NUTMEG
Serves 6

As someone brought up in Kent surrounded by apple orchards and a continual supply of apples, I sometimes feel oppressed by the inevitability of writing an apple cookbook. Sometimes I crave the smell of our attic, which every year would be filled with apples wrapped in newspaper laid out between the rafters. By the time I left home, I thought I'd be happy to never eat another apple pie, or apple crumble, or baked apple, or apple anything, because it felt as if I'd been eating apples every day of my childhood. Well, apples and me have never grown apart and I still love eating them and can still get excited by the smell of an apple pie or crumble cooking away in the oven. This tart is basically a quiche. Instead of the more usual savoury filling, it is flavoured with grated apple, sugar and nutmeg. The tart can be served hot, warm or cold, and, weather permitting, it would be a lovely dish to make for a picnic.

150g plain flour plus a little extra
a pinch of salt
75g butter cut into cubes
1–2 tbsp iced water
1 egg

for the filling:
3 medium or large egg yolks
3 tbsp caster sugar
2 large eggs
300ml thick cream
3 large eating apples
freshly grated nutmeg

Pre-heat the oven to 400°F/200°C/gas mark 6. Sift the flour and salt into a mixing bowl (or the bowl of your food processor). Cut the butter into small pieces and add to the flour. Either quickly rub the butter into the flour until it resembles damp breadcrumbs or pulse in the food processor. Stir the water into the egg yolk. Stir or briefly pulse the egg water into the mixture, continuing tentatively until the dough seems to want to cling together. Form into a ball; dust with extra flour if it seems too wet, adding a little extra water if it seems too dry. To avoid shrinkage when the pastry is cooked, cover and leave for 30 minutes before rolling. Dust a work surface with flour and roll out the pastry as thinly as possible and use it to line a greased 20cm x 4cm deep tart tin and bake blind. Do this by lining the uncooked pastry with a sheet of tinfoil and fill with, for example, dried beans or rice, to stop the pastry rising. Bake for 15 minutes, remove from the oven, and save foil and beans for further use. Brush the inside of the pastry case with beaten egg white (to seal any leaks) and return to the oven for 5 minutes. Turn down the oven to 325°F/170°C/gas mark 3. Whisk the egg yolks with the sugar and then add the whole eggs. Stir in the cream. Peel, quarter and then grate the apple directly into the cream and egg mixture. Season generously with nutmeg. Pour the custard into the case and cook for 30–40 minutes until set.

APPLE PIE
Serves 6

You can use any apple you like to make a delicious apple pie but the very best is made with cooking apples. They are cooked from raw and end up meltingly tender with their special clean apple taste. They need plenty of sugar and work best of all, in my view, in a buttery short pastry crust with a crisp egg white and sugar finish. Some people like to add ground ginger or cinnamon, a few cloves or a handful of sultanas. I love hot apple pie with ice cream and we keep cartons of Jelbert's in the freezer specially for autumn and winter puddings like this when Jelbert's is closed.

400g flour plus extra for dusting
pinch of salt
200g butter or half butter and half lard
3–6 tbsp cold water
juice of 1 lemon
750g cooking apples
50g butter
4–5 tbsp caster sugar
1 egg white
clotted cream or ice cream to serve

Sift the flour and salt into a mixing bowl (or the bowl of your food processor). Cut the butter into small pieces and add to the flour. Either quickly rub the butter into the flour until it resembles damp breadcrumbs or pulse in the food processor. Stir or briefly pulse a couple of tablespoons of cold water into the mixture, continuing tentatively until the dough seems to want to cling together. Form into a ball; dust with extra flour if it seems too wet, or add a little extra water if it seems too dry. To avoid shrinkage when the pastry is cooked, cover and leave for 30 minutes before rolling. Set aside just over one-third of the pastry. Lavishly butter a suitable metal pie dish, dust with flour and shake out the excess. Dust a work surface with flour, roll out the large piece of pastry and line the pie dish, leaving a generous overhang.

Pre-heat the oven to 375°F/190°C/gas mark 5. Squeeze the lemon juice into a large bowl of water. Peel, quarter and core the apples. Cut into chunks directly into the bowl of water. When all the apple is prepared, drain it and pile the fruit into the pastry case. Cut scraps of butter over the top and dredge with most of the sugar. Roll out a lid, place in position, trim the edges neatly, smear with a little water and crimp the edges together with a fork or your thumbnail. Lightly whisk the egg white and paint it over the pie. Cut out decorative shapes with any pastry leftovers. Sprinkle with sugar. Slash the pastry in a couple of places to allow the steam to escape. Cook in the oven for about 40 minutes or until the pastry is golden and cooked through.

APPLE BETTY WITH ALMOND CRISP
Serves 4–6

Stale bread and cooking apples are what you need for this lovely pudding, which ends up extraordinarily succulent, soft, fluffy and light with an ability to assume some of the flavour of the last-minute topping of butter-tossed flaked almonds. It is wonderful eaten while the apple still seethes in the dish but it is also very good lukewarm or cold. Serve it with thick cream or home-made custard. It is also delicious with Jelbert's ice cream.

juice of 1 lemon

100g butter

3 large cooking apples

4 tbsp demerara sugar

1 tsp cinnamon

125g fine fresh white breadcrumbs

3 heaped tbsp flaked almonds

thick cream and icing sugar to serve

Pre-heat the oven to 350°F/180°C/gas mark 4. Set aside 50g of the butter and use a knob of the remaining 50g to smear the base and sides of an approximately 25 x 18cm dish that is at least 5cm deep. Squeeze the lemon juice into a bowl that can hold all the apple when it has been cut into slices and pour on about 300ml water. Quarter, core and peel the apples. Slice them thinly into the acidulated water as you go. This has the double effect of stopping the apple discolouring, which happens almost instantly with Bramleys, and adds a slight lemon tang to the flavours. Tip the apples into a colander and shake vigorously to drain. Scoop half the apples into the dish, spreading them flat. Sprinkle with 1½ tbsp demerara sugar and half the cinnamon. Cut scraps from one-third of the remaining butter over the top. Cover with half the breadcrumbs. Make a second layer of apple, this time pressing down evenly. Sprinkle over another 1½ tbsp demerara, remaining cinnamon and half the remaining butter. Top with the last breadcrumbs and last of the butter. Place a sheet of foil over the top and cook for 35 minutes. Remove the foil and turn the oven up to 400°F/200°C/gas mark 6. Meanwhile, melt the reserved 50g butter in a small pan and stir in the almonds. Spoon this mixture evenly over the top of the dish, sprinkle with the remaining demerara and cook for a further 15 minutes or until the top is caramelized and crusty and the apple is bubbling up round the side. Cold, it looks pretty dusted with icing sugar.

LAVENDER PEARS WITH WHITE WINE
Serves 6

Lavender and lemon zest with honey and white wine make a lovely poaching liquid for peeled, whole pears. They are best eaten cold and look very pretty, almost translucent.

> 6 lavender flower heads with small amount of stalk
>
> approx. 600ml white wine
>
> 1 tbsp runny honey
>
> 1 unwaxed lemon
>
> 6 even-sized firm but ripe pears
>
> thick cream to serve

Place the lavender flower heads and a small amount of stalk in a pan that can hold the pears comfortably in a single layer. Add the wine and honey. Remove 2 paper-thin strips of zest from the lemon. Add them to the pan. Place the pan over a medium-low heat and gently bring to the boil, swirling the pan a few times while the honey melts. Boil the liquid hard for a couple of minutes to burn off the alcohol. Meanwhile, carefully peel the pears, removing all the skin but leaving the stalk intact. Use a small, sharp knife to remove the core in a small cone shape. Place the pears in the pan, reduce the heat, cover the pan and cook for about 20 minutes, turning the pears once halfway through cooking, until cooked through. Remove the pears to a serving dish, standing them up and leave to cool. Remove the lavender and lemon zest from the pan and cook the liquid at a steady simmer until reduced to a quarter of the original quantity. It will be slightly syrupy. Pour the liquid over the pears, so they glisten. Serve with cream immediately, or wait until the liquid is cold.

Strawberries, Gooseberries and Rhubarb

Balsamic Strawberries with Clotted Cream Rice Pudding
Eton Mess with Clotted Cream
Strawberry Galette with Clotted Cream
Rose Hilton's Strawberry Cheesecake Birthday Tart
Strawberry Jam
Custard Gooseberry Fool
Gooseberry Frangipane Tart
Baked Rhubarb with Orange Semolina Pudding
Rhubarb or Gooseberry Pie

Some of the sweetest and most intensely flavoured strawberries I've ever eaten have been grown in this part of Cornwall. When the conditions are right, the plants are extra prolific down here and it's common to come across impromptu road-side stalls selling gluts of succulent little strawberries at bargain prices. They are, of course, the perfect foil for clotted cream. Together they appear in milk shakes, fools, rice pudding, cream teas and summer pudding.

Gooseberries and rhubarb don't have the general appeal of strawberries and other soft fruit, yet they make the most sublime desserts of summer. What would an English summer be without stewed gooseberries and custard, gooseberry pie (with ice cream) or gooseberry fool? On chilly summer days, it is hard to beat gooseberry crumble. The tart, fresh flavour, redolent, as Elizabeth David noted, of sorrel, has savoury applications too. A tart purée of gooseberries, perhaps whipped with creamed horseradish, goes well with mackerel, goose and duck, complementing and counterbalancing the oily quality of the flesh.

Rhubarb comes originally from northern Asia, where it was prized for it's medicinal use. It has the ability to give the digestive tract a good spring clean, with the added advantage of being packed with vitamins and minerals. It was the Victorians who discovered that the hardy, fast-growing, early spring shoots were delicious in cooking. It's weird name, incidentally, is derived from the Latin 'Rha' (the ancient name for the Volga, the route by which rhubarb came to the West via Siberia) and 'barbarus', which means barbarian. Rhubarb has a high water content and collapses easily when cooked. To keep it firm, cover the cut stems in a minimum amount of liquid and cook gently. It can be stewed, baked or poached and is particularly good in pies and crumbles, steamed puddings and fools. Rhubarb is classified as a vegetable and although commonly used as a fruit, like gooseberries, it makes a lovely tart sauce to serve with pork or duck and it can be delicious with lamb. Its huge ornamental leaves are poisonous.

Which brings me neatly to the only joke I have ever been able to remember:

What's green and hairy and goes up and down?
A gooseberry in a lift shaft.

Sorry about that.

BALSAMIC STRAWBERRIES WITH CLOTTED CREAM RICE PUDDING
Serves 6

A classy way to ring the changes with strawberries. Lovely on their own but superb with this quick, really creamy rice pudding.

750g ripe strawberries
1 tbsp caster sugar
1 tbsp aged balsamic vinegar

for the rice pudding:
1 vanilla pod
900ml milk
150g pudding rice
50g sugar
150ml clotted cream

First make the rice pudding. Place the vanilla pod in a pan with the milk and bring to boiling point. Reduce the heat and simmer gently for 5 minutes. Give the vanilla pod a good bash with a wooden spoon to release the seeds. Add the rice. Simmer very gently, stirring occasionally, for about 20 minutes or until the rice is tender and most of the liquid absorbed. Stir in the sugar. Add half the cream and cook for a couple of minutes until thick but sloppy. Leave to cool (and thicken) in the pan. When tepid, remove the vanilla pod (it can be wiped and reused) and stir in the rest of the cream. Transfer to a serving bowl.

Rinse the strawberries and remove their stalks. Halve or quarter large strawberries lengthways into a mixing bowl. Sprinkle with the sugar and leave for a few minutes to get juicy. Add the balsamic vinegar. Toss thoroughly and leave for at least 10 minutes before serving.

ETON MESS WITH CLOTTED CREAM
Serves 6

Mushy strawberries with cream and chunks of meringue.

> 800g very ripe English strawberries
> 2 tbsp caster sugar
> 400g clotted cream
> 12 mini meringues (optional)

Quickly rinse the strawberries under cold running water and shake dry. Remove the stalks – the neatest way to do this is with a small, sharp knife, cutting at an angle around and under the stalk, to remove a small cone, turning the strawberry rather than the knife. Leave small strawberries whole, halve medium ones and quarter large fruit. Place the fruit in a bowl, sprinkle over the sugar and leave to melt and turn the strawberries juicy. Toss and leave for at least 10 minutes, then give a quick stir, crushing them slightly as you do so. Add scoops of the cream to the strawberries, then gently fold and stir. If using meringues, break them into quarters and loosely fold into the fool. If you prefer, hold back half the strawberries, then pass them through a sieve directly into the fool, stirring to get swirls of seed-free strawberry purée.

STRAWBERRY GALETTE WITH CLOTTED CREAM
Serves 6

My mother was friendly enough with our local baker, a fierce lady called Tessa Battle (no prizes for guessing her nickname), that she occasionally gave us slightly bashed-up pastries and cakes unfit for sale in her quaint little bakery-cum-tearoom. My favourite was strawberry *mille-feuille* and this super-simple tart is distantly related, giving the same sublime combination of light, crisp pastry and strawberries muddled up with lashings of cream. It can be made to whatever size or shape you like and is a usefully hassle-free dessert for a summer party.

> icing sugar
> knob of butter
> 250g puff pastry
> 750g small ripe strawberries

250ml clotted cream

25g toasted almonds

Pre-heat the oven to 400°F/200°C/gas mark 6. Dust a work surface with icing sugar and roll the pastry thinly to fit an oblong approximately 25 x 30cm. Liberally butter a baking sheet and lay out the pastry. Prick all over with the tines of a fork, dust with icing sugar and cover loosely with a double fold of greaseproof paper. Bake for 10 minutes until the surface is brown and semi-risen. Remove the paper, cook for a further 5 minutes, then use an egg slice to flip the pastry. Press down to flatten and return to the oven for a further 5 minutes until flaky and golden. Flatten the now thoroughly cooked pastry again if necessary. Slip on to a cake rack to cool completely.

Meanwhile, rinse the strawberries, shake dry and remove the stalks, cutting them out with a small, sharp knife, cutting at an angle around and under the stalk, to remove a small cone, turning the strawberry rather than the knife.

Spread the cream thickly over the cold, crisp pastry, going right up to the edges. 'Plant' the strawberries on top. Sprinkle with the almonds and dust with icing sugar. Serve in chunky slabs.

NB: This tart can be assembled up to an hour in advance but to avoid the almonds going soft, add them until just before serving.

ROSE HILTON'S STRAWBERRY CHEESECAKE BIRTHDAY TART
Serves 8

The artist Rose Hilton's birthday falls in the middle of August and every year she holds a big lunch party, usually in the garden, to celebrate. It's a lovely wild kind of garden, with ancient but comfortable chairs, where children can safely roam into meadows beyond, which lead, eventually, to the dramatically severe Bottallack coastline. It's quite normal for guests to bring something towards lunch and one year I made two cheesecake tarts and decorated one with an *R* made of peach against a strawberry background and another with an *H* made of black grapes against a 'palatte' of green ones. They looked beautiful and tasted so good that the recipe has joined the Fish Store pudding repertoire.

200g flour

salt

50g lard

100g butter plus an extra knob

2 tbsp sugar

2 x 125g packets Philadelphia cream cheese

1 tsp vanilla essence

2 heaped tbsp thick cream

500g English strawberries

2 tbsp redcurrant jelly or similar

Pre-heat the oven to 400°F/200°C/gas mark 6. Sift the flour and a generous pinch of salt into the bowl of a food processor or mixing bowl. Dice the lard and 50g butter directly into the flour and, if using a machine, pulse briefly until formed into a ball. Alternatively, rub the fat into the flour with your hands and form it into a ball. Rest the dough for at least 15 minutes, preferably 30 minutes. This allows the gluten to stretch and thus avoids the pastry shrinking as it cooks. Chose a flan tin with a removable base with an approximately 22cm diameter. Grease it generously with a knob of butter, going over the sides as well as the base. Dust with flour, rolling the tin round in your hands, and shake out any excess. This makes the tin non-stick. Roll out the pastry to fit the tin, coming up the sides and rolling the edges to make a good lip. Cover loosely with foil, add pastry weights or rice to stop the pastry rising and bake for 10 minutes. Remove the foil and bake for a further 10 minutes until the pastry is a light golden colour and cooked through. Set aside to cool. Meanwhile, place the remaining 50g butter in a mixing bowl and add the sugar. Use a wooden spoon to cream the two together, continuing for several minutes until the mixture is light, fluffy and pale and the sugar hardly distinguishable. Pass the Philadelphia through a sieve directly into the creamed butter; this will make the mixture lighter and creamier. Now add the vanilla essence and cream. Beat all the ingredients together until smooth and light. Rinse and hull the strawberries. If you are going for looks as well as flavour, arrange the strawberries on a dinner plate with the biggest one in the middle and ending up with the smallest strawberries at the edge. Smooth the

Philadelphia mixture into the cooled pastry case and transfer the straw-berries. Melt the redcurrant jelly in a small pan and use a pastry brush to paint the strawberries to give them a glossy professional finish. Stand the tart on a can or similar to remove the collar and stand back for 'Oohs' and 'Ahs'.

STRAWBERRY JAM
Fills 3–4 x 450g jam jars

Strawberries make intensely flavoured jam but are notoriously poor setters. That's where the redcurrants come in. Lovely with scones for a Cornish cream tea or on toast spread with clotted cream instead of but-ter. Excellent, too, with rice pudding and in tarts.

> 800g sugar
> 1kg firm but ripe strawberries
> 250g redcurrants
> knob of butter

Warm the sugar and place in a suitable pan with the hulled strawber-ries. Leave overnight.

The next day, wash the redcurrants and place, stalks and all, in a pan with just enough water to cover. Bring to the boil, mash with a wooden spoon and simmer for 15 minutes.

Bring the strawberries and sugar very slowly to the boil, then boil rapidly for 8 minutes. Pour the redcurrants through a sieve, pressing down to extract maximum juice, directly into the strawberries. Stir and boil for 2 minutes. Remove from the heat, stir in the butter, stir for 5 minutes, then pot into jars.

CUSTARD GOOSEBERRY FOOL
Serves 6–8

It isn't traditional to include custard in gooseberry fool but it gives it a pleasing nursery-food quality, turning this lovely dessert into deluxe stewed gooseberries and custard. Don't be tempted to add extra sugar – the whole point of the dish is the contrast of the sour, soft berries and very sweet custard and cream.

500g green cooking gooseberries

50g caster sugar

1 tbsp cold water

300ml fresh (carton) custard

150ml clotted cream

Top and tail the gooseberries, rinse and shake dry. Put sugar, water and gooseberries in a pan and place over a low heat. Shake the pan as the sugar melts and the juices from the gooseberries begin to run. As soon as the gooseberries have paled in colour, turn off the heat, cover the pan and leave for 10 minutes so the fruit finishes softening in the steam. Remove the lid and let the fruit cool.

If the gooseberries have produced a lot of juice – very likely – drain some of it away and use a potato mashed to squash and break up the fruit. Pour the cold custard into a serving bowl, stir in the crushed gooseberries and add spoonfuls of cream. Mix in a haphazard kind of way and tip the whole thing into a pretty bowl or glass dish. Chill before serving.

GOOSEBERRY FRANGIPANE TART
Serves 8

Frangipane is made by mixing ground almonds with egg, sugar and butter to make a thick and gluey paste which billows as it cooks and ends up as a glorious, dense almond sponge. In this tart, the frangipane swells over and around blanched gooseberries and is ready when the surface has risen to the edge of the pastry and turned an attractive pale golden colour.

This recipe can be adapted for use with plums, cherries, apricots and raspberries.

200g plain flour

pinch salt

100g butter

2 tbsp natural yoghurt or water

400g gooseberries

2 tbsp sugar

100g ground almonds

50g caster sugar

2 eggs

Pre-heat the oven to 375°F/190°C/gas mark 5. Sift the flour and salt into a mixing bowl (or the bowl of your food processor). Cut the butter into small pieces and add to the flour. Either quickly rub the butter into the flour until it resembles damp breadcrumbs or pulse in the food processor. Stir or briefly pulse the yoghurt into the mixture, until the dough seems to want to cling together. Form into a ball; dust with extra flour if it seems too wet, adding a little extra yoghurt or water if it seems too dry. To avoid shrinkage when the pastry is cooked, cover and leave for 30 minutes before rolling. Butter a 20cm loose-bottomed flan tin and roll out the pastry to fit. Cover with tinfoil and weight it with rice. Bake for 10 minutes, remove the foil and bake for a further 10 minutes.

Meanwhile, top and tail the gooseberries and place in a saucepan with the 2 tablespoons of sugar and not quite enough water to cover. Bring to the boil, reduce the heat immediately and cook for 1 minute. Drain the gooseberries and leave to cool. Blitz the ground almonds, butter and caster sugar in a food processor for 1 minute. Add the eggs and pulse briefly until blended. Arrange the gooseberries in the pre-baked pastry case, pour over the frangipane and bake until the top is firm, risen and golden, checking after 20 minutes. Allow to cool slightly before removing the collar. Serve in wedges.

BAKED RHUBARB WITH ORANGE SEMOLINA PUDDING
Serves 4–6

When I was growing up, in fifties post-post-war Britain, hardly a week went by without a milk pudding making an appearance on the supper table. Rice pudding, tapioca, custard, a sweet white sauce made with cornflower, and semolina. What all these traditional British puddings share is the ability to be absolutely ghastly, and semolina is possibly the worst culprit. However, when made with care – it has a nasty habit of forming into lumps – the milk well seasoned and a couple of eggs added, it is sublime.

I've divided the cooking into three distinct stages which make it fool-proof and result in a creamy, hauntingly flavoured, soufflé-like pudding with a pleasingly crusted surface. The rhubarb is cooked at the same time in the oven and the gentle, slow cooking ensures the chunks don't float apart into silky strands. Both semolina and rhubarb are delicious on their own (try passion fruit over the rhubarb) but go together in one of those culinary marriages made in heaven, specially when eaten with a dusting of extra sugar and a dollop of clotted cream. Like all milk puddings, this is best served warm. Semolina, incidentally, is ground from durum wheat, used to make pasta.

    2 medium oranges
    750ml milk
    1 vanilla pod
    4 tbsp demerara sugar
    50g semolina
    pinch of salt
    2 large eggs
    freshly grated nutmeg
    knob of butter
    500g rhubarb
    caster sugar

Use a potato peeler to remove the wafer-thin zest from one orange. Place 4 strips in a saucepan with 600ml of the milk and the vanilla pod. Bring slowly to the boil, allowing about 10 minutes for this, giving the vanilla pod a good bash to release its tiny black seeds. Remove from the heat, stir in 2 tablespoons of the demerara, cover the pan and set aside. Meanwhile, place the remaining milk, semolina and pinch of salt in a small pan. Place over a low flame and stir constantly while it thickens. It will quickly stiffen up. Remove from the heat and allow to cool slightly. Meanwhile, separate the eggs and use a wooden spoon to stir the yolks into the semolina, thus slackening the mixture. Season generously with nutmeg. Pour the flavoured milk through a sieve into the mixture, first a cupful, stirring until smooth, and then continue with the rest. You shouldn't have any lumps, but if you do, give the mixture a good beating with a wire whisk. Meanwhile, whisk the egg whites into firm peaks. Fold the whites into the mixture and pour the semolina into a buttered earthenware or ceramic *gratin* dish.

Cut the rhubarb into chunks, discarding root and silky strands that present themselves. Rinse and lay out in a gratin dish. Tuck the remaining orange zest between the layers, squeeze over the juice of the oranges and sprinkle over the remaining demerara. Cover with foil. Turn the oven to 325°F/170°C/gas mark 3, place the rhubarb near the bottom and when the temperature comes up put the pudding on a middle shelf. Cook for 30 minutes or until the pudding has a golden surface and is just-set and the rhubarb tender.

RHUBARB OR GOOSEBERRY PIE
Serves 4–6

Simply the best. Lovely buttery, crumbly, sugary pastry and slightly tart fruit with lashings of clotted cream and maybe some ice cream too.

> 400g flour plus extra for dusting
> pinch of salt
> 200g butter or half butter and half lard
> 3–6 tbsp cold water
> 750g rhubarb or gooseberries
> 50g butter
> 4–5 tbsp caster sugar
> 1 egg white
> clotted cream or ice cream to serve

Sift the flour and salt into a mixing bowl (or the bowl of your food processor). Cut the butter into small pieces and add to the flour. Either quickly rub the butter into the flour until it resembles damp breadcrumbs or pulse in the food processor. Stir or briefly pulse a couple of tablespoons of cold water into the mixture, continuing tentatively until the dough seems to want to cling together. Form into a ball; dust with extra flour if it seems too wet, adding a little extra water if it seems too dry. To avoid shrinkage when the pastry is cooked, cover and leave for 30 minutes before rolling. Set aside just over one-third of the pastry. Lavishly butter a suitable metal pie dish, dust with flour and shake out the excess. Dust a work surface with flour, roll out the large piece of pastry and line the pie dish leaving a generous overhang.

Pre-heat the oven to 375°F/190°C/gas mark 5. Trim the rhubarb and cut into 5cm lengths. Top and tail the gooseberries. Pile the fruit into the pastry case, cut scraps of butter over the top and dredge with most of the sugar. Roll out a lid, place in position, trim the edges neatly, smear with a little water and crimp the edges together with a fork or your thumbnail. Lightly whisk the egg white and paint it over the pie. Cut out decorative shapes with any pastry leftovers. Sprinkle with sugar. Slash the pastry in a couple of places to allow the steam to escape. Cook in the oven for about 40 minutes or until the pastry is cooked.

Plums and Peaches

Red Plums with Port
Sherry Trifle with Plums
Plum Pie with Almond Cream
Plum and Almond Crumble
Duck with Plum Sauce
Summer Fruit Amaretti Crumble
Roast Peaches with Amaretti

Silk, satin, cotton, rags
Rich man, poor man, beggar man, thief
This year, next year, some time, never
Coach, carriage, wheel barrow, dung cart

When Ben was growing up during the war in Cornwall, it wasn't always easy to get fresh fruit. He remembers oranges, crates of oranges, floating in on the tide, bobbing about in the harbour like rare jewels. He didn't see his first banana until he was in long trousers. In those days and until relatively recently, pudding was an integral part of the main meal of the day. Betty, like other housewives throughout the country, relied on dried fruit, particularly prunes, which were soaked overnight, then stewed until soft. Ben used to have them with custard: '. . . and I always had to have five, so I could count good fortune'. In these abundant times, fresh plums have taken over from prunes and they too are delicious stewed in their own juices with sugar. They are good with custard, yoghurt or ice cream, or over cornflakes, but can be turned into a lovely purée to serve with sliced fresh bananas, or to dribble over vanilla ice cream. They are good in trifles with soft Amaretti macaroons, whipped cream and toasted almonds and can be used to make some quintessential English summer puddings, such as plum fool, plum summer pudding and plum sorbets.

I'm always trying out new ways of flavouring stewed plums. Any spice, from cloves and cinnamon, to cardamom and ginger, goes wonderfully well, as do star anise and vanilla. Different sugars also change the flavour in a subtle but noticeable way. Icing sugar and caster sugar sweeten without adding anything extra, but muscovado and other golden and brown sugars, now available in a wide range of organic and unrefined, insinuate their distinctive flavour with great charm. Wine is another good partner to plums. I've had great success with fruity sweet wines such as Muscat de Beaume de Venise, but my all-time favourite is ruby red port. Sometimes I cook the plums whole, very slowly, in a covered dish in the oven. They look very pretty if they are halved round their plumpness but the stones can be a fiddle to remove.

Greengages are a very special plum with a short season. There is no mistaking their pretty pale green colour and if you are unfamiliar with their sweet greenish-yellow flesh, you are in for a delicious surprise. Their size and texture and loose stone always remind me of apricots and they can be treated in much the same way. Try them halved round their middles and briefly cooked in a light sugar syrup. Serve them lukewarm with cream. They are delicious puréed with a hint of vanilla and set with gelatine to make jellies. Greengages love almonds. Combine them in a tart or use ground almonds to make greengage crumble.

I have yet to come across peaches growing in Mousehole but they are always abundant in the shops throughout the summer. I particularly include them because Ben has made a speciality out of stuffing them with almond ratafias.

RED PLUMS WITH PORT
Serves 4–6

A blessedly easy dessert to make, so delicious, and it goes with so many things. To appreciate their full flavour, serve the plums lukewarm or cold.

> 750g red plums
> 6 tbsp light muscovado sugar
> 4 tbsp port
> 4 tbsp water

Slice the flesh off the plums in large chunks, probably about 5 pieces per plum, and place in a suitable saucepan. Add the sugar, port and water. Place the pan over a medium-low heat and swirl the pan as the sugar melts and the liquid comes up to the boil. Reduce the heat, cover the pan and simmer briskly for 5 minutes until the pieces of plum are just-tender to the point of a sharp knife. Turn off the heat and leave the pan covered for at least 10 minutes, preferably until lukewarm or cold. There will be plenty of juice and the plums will be meltingly tender. Serve with custard and cream or ice cream.

SHERRY TRIFLE WITH PLUMS
Serves 8–10

It is necessary to start this lovely old-fashioned trifle well in advance because both plums and the finished dish need to be chilled. The top is finished in the traditional way with a thick layer of cream and decorated with silver balls and angelica. It is important, however, that the trifle is thoroughly chilled before it's decorated, otherwise the silver from the balls begins to melt into the cream. If necessary, the trifle could be made up to 24 hours in advance. However long it is left to set, this trifle will always retain a soft and gooey texture on account of shop-bought, ready-made custard having a pouring consistency. Were you to make it with home made custard or Bird's custard powder, you would get a firmer finish redolent of the rock-hard jelly trifles of my childhood.

> 750g plums
> 1 vanilla pod
> 3 tbsp sugar
> 4 tbsp water
> 200g soft macaroons
> 2–3 tbsp sherry
> 300g whipping cream
> 500g carton M&S fresh egg custard
> 30g angelica
> 1 tbsp silver cake decorating balls

Slice the flesh off the plum stones in several big chunks. Place the vanilla pod, sugar and water in a saucepan large enough to hold the plums too. Heat gently, swirling the pan until the sugar melts. Add the plums, cover the pan, increase the heat and cook for about 10 minutes until the plums are tender. Tip into a bowl and leave to cool. If you're in a hurry, I find that popping the pan into the freezer does the job in about 15 minutes. Cut the macaroons into quarters and place in a suitable bowl, preferably a glass one so that you can see the layers of trifle. Pour the sherry over the top, tipping the bowl so it is absorbed into the macaroons. Whip the cream until it forms soft peaks, stopping before it turns hard and grainy. Spoon half the plums over the macaroons, cover with a layer of cold custard and another of cream. Spoon the rest of the plums over the top and repeat the layers, ensuring there is a luxuriously thick layer of cream on top. Smooth the top and use a fork to make a few swirls round the edges. Cover with cling-film and chill for as long as possible and at least 30 minutes.

Slice the angelica thinly and decorate the top of the trifle with silver balls and angelica. Finish with a few swirls of the thick, plum juices that will remain in the pan.

PLUM PIE WITH ALMOND CREAM
Serves 6

All plums, be they small, black damsons, golden-green greengages or burgundy-red Victorias, are delicious in pies.

The quickest and easiest way to achieve that heavenly combination of buttery pastry with sugary yet still sour plums is with ready-made puff pastry. Roll out an oblong slab and make slits across one side at regular intervals. Lay stoned and chopped plums on the uncut side, sprinkle with sugar then paint a border with water before folding over the slatted side and crimp to seal. Paint the top with beaten egg, dredge with sugar and bake for 20 minutes to be greeted with a mouth watering, golden pastry oozing with plum juice. If you want to personalize your tart, add chopped almonds, walnuts or pistachios, with a hint of cinnamon or ground allspice.

This pie takes slightly longer to make and three times as long to cook but it really is the Rolls-Royce of plum pies. Ground almonds are mixed with melted butter, sugar and egg to make a soft almond cream, which provides a deliciously sweet, buttery and grainy background for the juicy, soft plums. With the noticeably tender, golden pastry, which is made with yoghurt instead of water, you end up with mouthfuls of pudding heaven.

250g flour plus extra for dusting
300g butter plus an extra knob
3 tbsp natural yoghurt
100g ground almonds
100g sugar plus 1 tbsp

2 eggs
500g Victoria plums
splash of milk

Pre-heat the oven to 425°F/220°C/gas mark 7. Sift the flour into the bowl of a food processor or mixing bowl. Dice 200g butter directly into the flour and, if using a machine, pulse briefly to mix. Alternatively, rub the butter into the flour with your hands. Mix in the yoghurt and let it form into a clump, kneading the dough a little to form it into a ball. Rest the dough for at least 15 minutes, preferably 30, to avoid shrinking as it cooks.

Chose a flan tin of about 22cm diameter. Grease it generously with a knob of butter, going over the sides as well as the base. Dust with flour, shaking away the excess. Set aside about one-third of the pastry to make a lid, then roll out the rest on a floured surface to fit the tin, coming up the sides and leaving a generous overhang. Melt the remaining butter in a small pan, then remove from the heat and stir in the ground almonds, 100g sugar and one beaten egg. Spoon the thick but sloppy mixture into the dough-lined tin. Coarsely chop the plums and discard the stones. Pile the plums over the almond cream. Roll out the lid to fit the overhang. Dampen the overhang with water and position the lid, press the edges and then roll towards the middle to make a secure binding. Mix the remaining egg with a splash of milk and paint the surface of the pie generously, taking special care to 'glue' the edges. Dredge with sugar. Bake for 10 minutes then reduce the heat to 400°F/200°C/gas mark 6 for a further 40 minutes. If the top is browning too quickly, cover loosely with tin foil. Serve hot with clotted cream.

PLUM AND ALMOND CRUMBLE
Serves 4

It's so light, everyone always says, when they slide a spoon through the golden lumpy mess that looks, to all intents and purposes, like any other crumble. This one, though, is made with equal quantities of ground almonds and the usual flour, butter and sugar and it's the nuts that keep the crumble deliciously light and crumbly. I first came across the idea of adding nuts to the crumble mixture via a friend, the novelist Paul Bailey, and he'd found the recipe in Jane Grigson's seminal *Fruit Book*. She matched this light, elegant crumble with apricots and it suits similar stone fruits such as peaches and nectarines but is lovely too with raspberries or a mixture of raspberries and peaches. The ratio of crumble to fruit in this recipe is, to my mind, perfect but if you prefer more crumble to fruit, then increase the quantities by a third. Another tip I got from Paul is to cook the crumble before the main course so that it is sitting on the side while you eat and will be at the optimum, warm rather than mouth-burning hot, temperature when you are ready for it. Serve it with hot or cold custard, thick cream or vanilla ice cream.

> 600g Victoria plums
> 100g caster sugar plus 1 tbsp
> 100g flour
> 100g ground almonds
> 100g butter

Pre-heat the oven to 400°F/200°C/gas mark 6. Quarter the plums lengthways and discard the stones. Tip the plums into a gratin-style ceramic dish with a 2-litre capacity and sprinkle the tablespoon of sugar over the top. Mix together 75g sugar, flour and almonds in a mixing bowl. Cut the butter into small pieces directly over the top and use your fingers to rub it into the mixture. Tip the crumble mixture over the plums, spreading it out evenly. Cook in the oven for 25 minutes until the crumble is a pale golden colour and the juices from the plums are starting to bubble up round the edges. If you think the crumble is colouring to quickly, cover it loosely with tinfoil. Allow the crumble to cool slightly before eating.

SUMMER FRUIT AMARETTI CRUMBLE
Serves 4

I'm a bit of a purist when it comes to summer soft fruit. Nothing, I reckon, can beat a bowl of plump, ripe raspberries with a scoop of vanilla ice cream. Or small, super-sweet British strawberries with clotted cream. And the joy of a ripe peach is a private affair. There are times, through, when it's good to mix this luscious munificence in a fruit salad or a crumble. This crumble is made with crushed macaroons and their sweet almond crunch goes wonderfully well with the fruit. The icing on the cake is a purée of strawberries. Serve the crumble at room temperature.

> 3 ripe nectarines or peaches
> 170g raspberries
> 125g redcurrants
> 2 tbsp sugar
> 100g Amaretti macaroons
> 25g butter
> 200g strawberries
> clotted cream or ice cream to serve

Pre-heat the oven to 400°F/200°C/gas mark 6. Remove the skin from the nectarines or peaches. If the skin doesn't come away easily, place the fruit in a bowl and cover with boiling water. Count to 20, drain and splash with cold water before removing the skin. Cut into small chunks or dice. Rinse the raspberries and redcurrants. Shake dry. Strip the redcurrants from the stalks directly into a gratin-style china dish that can hold the fruit comfortably in a thick layer with enough room for the topping. Add raspberries and peaches or nectarines. Mix the fruit together in the bowl and then sprinkle with 1 tablespoon of sugar. Tip the macaroons into a dish and use the end of a rolling pin to crush into coarse lumps. Melt the butter in a frying pan and, off the heat, add the macaroons and stir thoroughly so all the pieces are coated with butter. Spoon the crumbs over the fruit. Cook in the oven for 15 minutes. Meanwhile, remove the stalks from the strawberries and cut them into quarters. Place in a bowl and sprinkle over the remaining sugar. Stir well and leave for a couple of minutes before stirring again to encourage the sugar to dissolve. When all the sugar has disappeared and the strawberries are juicy, tip them into a sieve placed over a bowl. Use the back of spoon to force the strawberries through the sieve. Stir, collecting all the pulp under the sieve, to make a thick coulis. Serve the crumble with a dollop of cream or ice cream and a share of the coulis.

ROAST PEACHES WITH AMARETTI
Serves 6

This is Ben's *pièce de résistance*.

>   6 ripe peaches
>   1 vanilla pod or ½ tsp vanilla essence
>   large wine glass Amaretto
>   4 Amaretti macaroons
>   thick cream to serve

Run a sharp knife round the middle of the peaches, twist apart and discard the stones. Split the vanilla pod, scrape out the seeds and stir into the Amaretto. Grill the peaches or roast in a hot oven (pre-heated to 400°F/200°C/gas mark 6) until tender. Spoon the Amaretto and vanilla into the cavities and leave the peaches to cool. When cold, crumble the macaroons into the cavities. Serve with cream.

Bread and Egg Puddings

It's easy to buy good bread in Mousehole and even easier in nearby Newlyn. Ironically, with the exception of the brioche required for a rather special bread and butter pudding, any old white bread is ideal for these recipes. All of them are made over and over again at the Fish Store. Needless to say, they all go fantastically well with clotted cream and ice cream.

SUMMER PUDDING
Serves 6–8

I remember clearly my first encounter with summer pudding. It was at a garden party on one of those cloudless summer days, with the smell of mown grass and the occasional puff of breeze fluttering the roses. The table was set in the shade of a huge tree and when it was time for pudding, this gorgeous apparition arrived. Two purple-pink puddings glistened with magenta-coloured juice puddled around them. As the serving spoon slid into the soft pudding, a tumble of red summer fruit spilled on to the plate. As I slipped my first mouthful on to my tongue it felt like angel food but with a sharp freshness which saved it from blandness. This heavenly combination of lightly cooked fruit and bread – as I later discovered it to be – soaked with juices is utter perfection with clotted cream.

Summer pudding was far from my mind when, years later, I spent a morning in the kitchens of the Connaught with Michel Bourdin, then its celebrated *chef de cuisine*. By chance I picked up one or two summer pudding tricks that day and I can now claim summer pudding perfection.

Quantities given are approximate and fruits interchangeable, but what you're after is a mixture of sweet and sharp summer soft fruits. Redcurrants or blackcurrants are verging on crucial and so too, I think, are raspberries. The leaf gelatine – a Bourdin tip – isn't essential but holds the fruit in a very soft juicy jelly and stops the pudding collapsing when it is cut. A tumble of redcurrants and a few halved strawberries on the top of the pudding – and a few more round it – look stunning.

6 slices thin-cut white bread
150g redcurrants or blackcurrants
125g blackberries
200g strawberries, preferably small ones
125g blueberries
400g raspberries
100g sugar
½ leaf gelatine
squeeze of lemon
a few extra fruit for decoration
thick cream to serve

Cut the crusts from the bread. Line a 1 litre capacity pudding bowl with bread, making a round base and then laying overlapping pieces round the sides – these help prevent the pudding collapsing and make a pretty pattern. Cut a lid. Bring 200ml water to the boil. Keeping separate piles, rinse all the fruit. Strip the currants from their stalks. Hull the strawberries, cutting large fruit into quarters, medium fruit in half and leaving small fruit whole. Drop the fruit into the boiling water, one type at a time, and use a perforated spoon to quickly scoop it out of the water and into a colander placed over a bowl. When it comes to the raspberries, only blanch half of them. Scatter 50g sugar over the hot fruit. Stir the gelatine into the liquid drained from the fruit. Continue stirring until dissolved. Tip the fruit into this syrup, stir once with a wooden spoon or spatula and use a perforated spoon to lift the fruit directly into the bread-lined basin. Gently pour the syrup between bowl and bread, taking care not to disturb. Place the disc of bread on top. Pour syrup on top disc. Add the reserved raspberries and remaining sugar to the cooking liquid. Add a squeeze of lemon juice and boil for 1 minute. Pass through a sieve into a jug, press down on the raspberries and under the sieve. Top up the pudding so that the bread is drenched and spilling over. Lay a saucer on top and cover with clingfilm. Chill overnight. Turn out and drench with the reserved raspberry juice. Decorate with extra juice and serve with clotted cream.

TREACLE TART

Serves 6–8

No record of favourite food at the Fish Store would be complete without treacle tart. It isn't made with treacle but with golden syrup from the green and gold tin with its lion and bee logo. To achieve the required slightly gooey yet firm texture for the filling, the breadcrumbs must be loosely but generously loaded into the pastry case – and the case should be hot from the oven to help settle the golden syrup. A tang of acidity from the lemon provides the perfect counterbalance to all this sweetness.

Hot treacle tart cries out for vanilla ice cream – Jelbert's ice cream. Leftover tart should be warmed slightly in the oven before serving because it hardens as it cools.

> 7–8 tbsp golden syrup
> 200g plain flour
> pinch salt
> 100g cold butter, cut into pieces
> 2–3 tbsp cold water
> 175g fresh white breadcrumbs
> juice of ½ lemon
> vanilla ice cream to serve

Pre-heat the oven to 400°F/200°C/gas mark 6. Stand the tin of golden syrup in a pan of boiling water (this just makes it easier to pour).

Sift the flour into a large mixing bowl with the salt. Add the butter and quickly rub it into the flour until the mixture resembles heavy breadcrumbs. Add the water, a little at a time, and use a knife to stir it up into a clump. Knead a couple of times, pat the pastry into a ball, cover and set aside for 30 minutes.

Flour a work surface and roll the pastry until you can cut a circle to fit a 25.5cm tart tin. Wrap the dough around the rolling pin and loosely drape it over the tin, lifting the edge of the dough with one hand and pressing it into the base and up the side of the dish with the other hand – this prevents shrinkage. Trim off the excess dough and use scraps to plug any tears or cracks. Loosely cover with a large sheet of foil and fill with pastry beans (or rice). Cook in the middle of the oven for 10 minutes. Remove the foil, lower the oven temperature to 350°F/180°C/gas mark 4 and return the tart to a lower shelf and cook for a further 5 minutes.

Tip the breadcrumbs into the hot tart case – they should come almost right up to the edge of the pastry – and spoon or pour over the golden syrup, working from the outside in. Allow the syrup to sink down and saturate the bread – you don't want any pools of syrup remaining but, equally, you don't want blond patches – and then squeeze over the lemon juice. Cook in the middle of the oven for 25–30 minutes until the filling has set and turned a light toffee colour. Allow to cool for 5 minutes before serving.

QUEEN OF PUDDINGS WITH FRESH PLUM JAM
Serves 6–8

The English are very good at bread puddings. Summer pudding, obviously, and bread and butter pudding, but others, with glorious names such as Satisfaction Pudding and Paradise Pudding, are in danger of being forgotten. The aptly named Queen of Puddings is one of the most elegant of the lot and manages to be most things that we want from a pudding. It is light to eat yet surprisingly satisfying, it looks impressive but is simple to make, it uses up ingredients that rarely need to be specially shopped for, and it is an excellent vehicle, as it were, for using up stale bread.

Queen of Puddings is made by boiling milk with very finely chopped lemon zest, stirring in a big knob of butter and mixing it into fresh breadcrumbs sweetened with a little sugar. It is left to settle for a few minutes so the milk is absorbed into the bread before several egg yolks are added. When the mixture has been thoroughly beaten, it is poured into a buttered dish and baked in the oven until the bread custard has set. When the custard is just-set, it is carefully spread with raspberry jam – in this case with puréed plums – then covered with a bouffant of egg white. It is ready when the meringue is crisp and golden.

> 2 unwaxed lemons
> 570ml milk
> 40g butter

7–8 slices brown or white bread

4 tbsp caster sugar

3 large eggs

400g plums

1 vanilla pod, optional

4 tbsp sugar

clotted cream to serve

Pre-heat the oven to 350°F/180°C/gas mark 4. Remove the zest from the lemons in paper-thin sheets. Chop it very finely, almost to dust. Place the chopped zest in a small saucepan and pour on the milk. Bring quickly to the boil, turn off the heat and stir in half the butter. Meanwhile, cut the crusts off the bread. You need approximately 150g weight of bread. Tear into pieces and blitz in the food processor until you have fine crumbs. Tip the crumbs into a bowl. Sprinkle with 1 heaped tablespoon of sugar. Stir the buttery lemon milk into the bread-crumbs, scraping any lingering bits of lemon out of the pan into the bowl. Meanwhile, use the remaining butter to smear the inside of a ceramic, glass or earthenware gratin-style dish that can hold 1 ½ litres. Separate the eggs and add the yolks to the milky breadcrumbs, stirring thoroughly so everything is well mixed. Pour into the buttered dish and place it in the middle of the pre-heated oven. Cook for 20–25 minutes until the custard is set, preferably with a slight wobble in the middle. While the custard is cooking cut the flesh off the plums and place in a pan with 200ml water, the vanilla pod and 4 tablespoons of sugar. Swirl the pan to dissolve the sugar as you bring the liquid to the boil. Cover and boil for about 5 minutes until very soft. Remove the vanilla pod and press the plums and some of their juice through a sieve to make a thick coulis. Carefully and generously spread some of the coulis over the top of the custard. Whisk the egg whites until firm, add 2 tablespoons of sugar and continue beating for 1–2 minutes until the whites are glossy. Add another tablespoon of sugar and beat for a further 1–2 minutes until stiff and shiny. Spoon the meringue on to the pudding and use a fork to spread it in swirls. Return to the oven for a further 10–15 minutes until the meringue is slightly browned and crisp. Serve immediately with clotted cream and leftover plum purée in a bowl.

BRIOCHE BREAD AND BUTTER PUDDING WITH LIME MARMALADE

Serves 4–6

A little bottle of Angostura bitters always sits alongside the Tabasco and other essential seasonings on the kitchen shelf at the Fish Store. It gets splashed over ice cream or barbecued bananas (cooked in the skin and served with a chunk of dark chocolate with ice cream) and sometimes finds its way into gin (for pink gin). It is a secret ingredient in this deluxe bread and butter pudding for grown-ups.

Angostura, incidentally, is made with 40 per cent proof rum.

> 50g sultanas
> 2½ tbsp Angostura
> 400ml milk
> 1 vanilla pod
> 2 tbsp caster sugar
> 50g butter
> 300g brioche loaf (or stale white loaf)
> 200ml thick cream
> 3 large eggs, beaten
> nutmeg
> 6 tbsp sieved lime marmalade mixed with 2 tbsp boiling water
> clotted cream to serve

Pre-heat the oven to 400°F/200°C/gas mark 6. Bring the sultanas, 2 tablespoons of Angostura and 1 tablespoon of water quickly to the boil. Leave to soak. Simmer the milk and vanilla pod together for 5 minutes, giving the vanilla pod a good bashing with a wooden spoon to release the seeds. Stir in the sugar, cover the pan and leave to infuse for 10 minutes. Use a little of the butter to smear the inside of a 1 litre capacity gratin-style ceramic or glass dish. Slice the bread medium thickness. Butter one side of each slice. Lay half the slices, buttered side down, in the dish. Sprinkle with the soaked sultanas and make a sandwich with a second slice with the buttered side in the middle in the normal way. Mix the cream into the eggs. Strain the milk into the mixture and stir. Pour the milk and egg mixture over the sandwiches. Stir the remaining Angostura into the sieved marmalade. Spoon a little of the marmalade over each sandwich and top with a scrap of the remaining butter. Place the dish on a shelf in the middle of the oven. Turn the heat down immediately to 350°F/180°C/gas mark 4 and cook for 35 minutes until puffed and golden. Spoon the rest of the marmalade over the top. Serve hot, tepid or cold with clotted cream.

CRÈME CARAMEL
Serves 6

Puddings without portion control are what we like best at the Fish Store but crème caramel is a favourite from Ben's childhood which everyone always loves. Made properly with decent milk and fresh, quality eggs, this darling of the international dessert trolley lives up to its reputation as a delicate, set custard sauced with dark, caramelized sugar.

> 500ml full-fat milk
> 1 vanilla pod
> 225g caster sugar
> 2 whole eggs
> 4 egg yolks

Pre-heat the oven to 300°F/150°C/gas mark 2. Place the milk and vanilla pod in a pan and bring slowly to the boil. Cover the pan and leave to infuse for 30 minutes before removing the lid and allowing the milk to cool. Meanwhile, place 125g sugar and 75ml water in a small pan and boil, swirling the pan a couple of times as the sugar melts, until the liquid turns a dark golden colour. Pour the caramel into 6 dariole moulds, ramekins or small cups. Place the remaining sugar, whole eggs and eggs yolks in a bowl and whisk to mix. Rest for 10 minutes or so and then whisk again to ensure that the sugar has melted into the eggs. Strain the milk into the eggs and whisk lightly to incorporate. Rest for 15 minutes, then whisk again. Skim the surface to remove excess bubbles, then strain the custard over the caramel. Place the little dishes in a deep oven dish and pour in sufficient boiling water to come two-thirds of the way up the dishes. Cook in the oven for 1 hour. Remove the *bain marie* from the oven and leave the dishes *in situ* for 30 minutes to finish setting. Cool, then chill overnight. Invert the dishes on to plates just before serving.

EGG CUSTARD FOR POURING
Serves 4

    300ml full-fat milk
    300ml clotted or thick cream
    1 vanilla pod
    4 large egg yolks
    4 tbsp sugar

Bring the milk, cream and vanilla pod to the boil in a non-stick saucepan. Give the vanilla pod a good bashing to release the seeds. Remove from the heat, cover the pan and leave for a few minutes. Remove the vanilla pod. Beat the egg yolks with the sugar in a bowl until smooth, then pour on the milk, whisking as you pour. Return the custard to the saucepan and cook over a low heat, stirring constantly, for about 10 minutes until the mixture is thick enough to coat the back of a spoon. Do not allow the custard to boil.

Local Shops and Suppliers

Seafood

W. Harvey and Sons
The Combe
Newlyn
Penzance
TR18 5HF
Tel. 01736 362734
Open 8 a.m.–12.45 p.m. and 2 p.m.–4.45 p.m. Mon–Fri, 8 a.m.–11.45 p.m. Sat.

The place for crab. Freshly boiled crab, laid out each day with hens on one side and cocks on the other. Sold by weight. Also sell freshly picked crab meat divided into white and brown and dressed crab.

W. Harvey and Sons Shellfish Tanks
South Pier
Newlyn
Penzance
TR18 5JZ
Tel. 01736 367536

On the water's edge a large industrial building full of large, shallow concrete tanks full of live crabs, spider crabs, crayfish and lobster. You choose and Harveys will scoop it out of the tank. Available all year round.

J. H. Turner & Son
The Coombe
Newlyn
Penzance
TR18 5HF
Tel. 01736 363726

One of the best places to buy fresh fish from the market. Whatever is in season is laid out on an iced display counter but they can get anything to order. There's always a box of carcasses and small, damaged fish for free; just help yourself. Perfect for fish stock and soup.

Trelawney Fish
78 The Strand
Newlyn
Penzance
TR18 5HW
Tel. 01736 361793 and Freephone 0800 5877984

Trawler owners offering freshly caught fish from their distinctive fishy-mural harbourside shop. 'Shore to door' service; order before noon Mon–Fri for delivery by 11.30 a.m. the next day.

The Newlyn Fish Company
Unit 15
Stable Hobba Industrial Estate
Newlyn
Penzance
TR20 8TL
Tel. 01736 369814, Fax 01736 350916

One of many EU-approved wholesalers on this unprepossessing industrial estate but one of our favourite suppliers when someone wants to take fish back to London. Place your order and they chill-pack for the journey.

Seafayre Cuisine
Unit E
St Erth Industrial Estate
Rose-An-Grouse
Hayle
TR27 6LP
Tel. 01736 755961
www.seafayrecuisine.co.uk

Daily fresh, locally caught fish. Same-day collections/deliveries must be made before 10 a.m. Prices fluctuate daily on their website according to Newlyn market prices, so always ring to check or leave order on overnight message service and they will come back to you with prices or alternatives. Orders, individually packaged and gel-packed, despatched within 24 hours and sent by Amtrak at £15 per order; £25 on Sat.

Cornish Fish Direct
Tel 01736 332112
dee@cornishfish.co.uk and www.cornishfish.co.uk

Sadly, as we went to press, the only working traditional salt-fish-processing factory (aka fish store) run as a 'working museum' in Newlyn closed. Until October 2005 it was possible to see, amongst other things, seventy-year-old screw presses used to pack the fish in wooden boxes for export to Italy, where they had been sent since 1905, and Britain's oldest pilchard-net-making machine. It is still possible to buy traditional Cornish salt pilchards, cured and canned or bottled, from the shop. Ring for nationwide stockists. Also mail-order fresh Cornish fish.

Local Fisherman
Jake Freethy/*Go for It*, based at Newlyn Harbour.
Tel. 07977 027351
Fresh fish in season. Advance notice required.

Andy's Fresh Fish Door to Door Deliveries
Tel. 01736 731396 or 07714 439847
Market-fresh and smoked fish delivered daily, plus shellfish to order.

Meat and Poultry

Vivian Olds
2 Chapel Road
St Just
Penzance
TR19 7HS
Tel. 01736 788520
www.vivianolds.co.uk

Local meat including game, home made sausages, home cured bacon, organic eggs etc.

Lentern Family Butchers
1 Chapel Street
Penzance
TR18 4AJ
Tel. 01736 363061

Local meat only, from farms where animal welfare is a priority. Hog's pudding, a Cornish version of black pudding, is a speciality.
    Mail order.

Ice Cream and Clotted Cream

S. Jelbert
9 New Road
Newlyn
Penzance
TR18 5PZ
Tel. 01736 66634

Open between 1 April and end October. Totally dairy ice cream made daily with clotted cream. Sold in cornets or polystyrene tubs for the freezer. Also clotted cream, which can be ordered for delivery by mail order.

Fruit and Vegetables

Cusgarne Organics
Cusgarne Wollas
Near Truro
TR4 8RL
Tel. 01872 865922
cusgarne@freenet.co.uk

Buy direct from the farm or enrol for their vegetable box scheme of organic, home-grown produce.

Bosavern Farm
Bosavern
St Just
Penzance
TR19 7RD
Tel. 01736 786739
joandguy@bosavern.fsnet.co.uk

Everything sold is home-grown or home-reared, including grass-fed Hereford beef, free-range pork and organic, free-range eggs. Also organic vegetables. Farm shop.

Keigwin Natural Growers
Keigwin Farmhouse
Morvah
Pendeen
Penzance
TR19 7TS
Tel. 01736 786425
g.wyatt–smith@virgin.net

Organic salads, herbs and vegetables.

Penzance Country Market
St John's Hall
Every Thursday

Penzance Farmers' Market
Wharfside
Every Saturday

Useful food websites
www.foodtrails.co.uk
www.foodfromcornwall.co.uk
www.organicssouthwest.org
www.country-markets.co.uk

Bibliography

Lindsey Bareham, *A Celebration of Soup* (Michael Joseph, 1993, reprinted by Penguin Books, 2001)

Lindsey Bareham, *In Praise of the Potato* (Michael Joseph, 1989)

Paul Bertolli with Alice Walters, *Chez Panisse Cooking* (Random House, New York, 1994)

David Burton, *French Colonial Cookery: A Cook's Tour of the French-speaking World* (Faber and Faber, 2000)

Sam and Sam Clark, *Moro Cookbook* (Ebury Press, 2001)

Caroline Conran and Susan Campbell, *Poor Cook* (Macmillan, 1971)

Elizabeth David, *A Book of Mediterranean Food* (Penguin, 1955)

Elizabeth David, *Italian Food* (Macdonald, 1954, reprinted by Penguin Books, 1993, 1998)

Rose Gray and Ruth Rogers, *River Café Cook Book Easy* (Ebury Press, 2003)

Jane Grigson, *Fruit Book* (Penguin, 1983)

Michel Guérard, *Cuisine Minceur* (Macmillan, 1979)

Ermine Herscher and Agnes Carbonell, *Dining with Picasso* (Pavilion, 1995)

Simon Hopkinson and Lindsey Bareham, *The Prawn Cocktail Years* (1997, reprinted by Michael Joseph, 2006)

Simon Hopkinson with Lindsey Bareham, *Roast Chicken and Other Stories* (1995, reprinted by Ebury Press, 1999)

Rowley Leigh, *No Place Like Home* (Fourth Estate, 2000)

Joyce Molyneux with Sophie Grigson, *The Carved Angel Cookery Book* (Collins, 1990)

Claudia Roden, *A Book of Middle Eastern Food* (Thomas Nelson, 1968, reprinted by Penguin, 1970)

Claudia Roden, *A New Book of Middle Eastern Food* (Penguin Books, 1986)

Richard Stein, *English Seafood Cookery* (Penguin, 1988)

Index

PICTURE CREDITS

Photographs of seven-year-old Ben in Mousehole harbour in 1942 and Betty outside the Fish Store in 1940 courtesy of Ben John.

The harbour in 1927 and Mousehole in 1927 copyright © The Frith Collection.

All other photographs are by Chris Terry.

Line drawings on pages i, 36, 132, 166, 174, 192, 210 and 342 are by Henry John.

ACKNOWLEDGEMENTS

This book has been simmering away quietly for years but it was my friend Tessa de Mestre who saw its potential and goaded me into writing a synopsis. Luckily for me, Camilla Stoddart, who commissioned *Just One Pot* and was newly arrived at Penguin, loved the idea. When I married into the John family, I inherited a legacy of Fish Store recipes from Betty John, my mother-in-law. I learned to cook like Betty, often from Ben's memory of childhood dishes, and, like her, it was frequently in response to gifts of fish and vegetables from Ben's childhood friends in Mousehole. Many of the anecdotes and stories of life in the village come from these same people and I particularly want to thank Royden Paynter and Jake Freethy, Barry Cornish, Leon Pezzack, Lionel Wallis, Adam and Cyril Torrie, Merrick Torrie, Peno Barnes, Robbie Capes and Judy O'Shea of the Cornish Range. Special thanks, too, to Rose Hilton, Nick Howell, Jim Glover and Eia von der Flur. This book wouldn't have been possible without Ben John, but it was our children, Zach and Henry John, who made me want to write it. Special thanks to Henry for his delightfully evocative drawings, which pepper the book, and to Rick Stein for giving me such a generous quote to put on the jacket. Thank you also for the support of Janet Joyce and Bob Osborne.